A Better World Is Coming Soon
Don't Miss It

Kit R. Olsen

World Bible Society
Costa Mesa, California

A Better World Is Coming Soon
Don't Miss It

Copyright 2011, 2013 © by Kit R. Olsen
Written for: Friends of Yeshua Ministries

Published by the World Bible Society

Expanded Edition
Third Printing

ISBN9780578113982

This heartfelt book is dedicated by Friends of Yeshua Ministries to sharing the prophetic Word of God with both Jews and Gentiles; strongly supporting Israel's right to exist as a nation in their God-given land.

Almighty God's Promise to Israel

"So the LORD gave to Israel all the land of which He had sworn to give to their fathers, and they took possession of it and dwelt in it" (Joshua 21:43).

Contents

Chapter Four

Chapter Five

Chapter Six

Chapter Seven

Chapter Eight

Preface

Vast numbers of people do not understand that the entire Bible is a Jewish book and that Christianity has Jewish roots. God used all Jewish men to pen the Bible from beginning to end, both Old and New Testaments. The first Christians were all Jews. Jews brought the gospel to the Gentiles. And contrary to popular thinking, no one is *born* a Christian. The true meaning of what or who a Christian is has been often sorely distorted and misrepresented. Scripture teaches that each person must decide to accept or reject the truths of Christ.

God has given us free will to choose and He holds each one of us personally accountable for our acceptance or rejection of Him. Many historical and current portrayals of Christianity have nothing to do with an authentic born-again personal relationship with Jesus the Christ—which constitutes genuine Christianity as intended in the true biblical sense. For example, historically, the crusades have most often been called the "Christian Crusades." Overall, the men involved in the crusades had little or nothing to do with Christ—the Spirit of the indwelt Savior or His teachings.

The purpose of this publication is to give an overview of what is coming soon, to sound an alarm, to alert others to what is in store for this generation—a glimpse and overview of what is yet to come. This is a message of hope and encouragement, while also exposing the dangers we face in an out of control world of uncertainty. Also, a number of popular, challenging doctrinal teachings as well as spiritual growth and awareness issues are discussed. Topics pertaining to believers of Messiah Jesus are presented in order to be better equipped when discerning spiritual matters. These are important concerns to consider as we seek to gain a solid-biblical foundation for everyday life and also for achieving and maintaining biblical integrity.

As believers, we have been exposed to the published works and public media displays of many other believers. Some merit exceptional praise. Others run contrary to the Holy Scriptures. We are very concerned about the growing apostasy. We have found through our interactions with many good people that they show some interest in knowing more about God, but are skeptical because they have had negative interactions with some Christians. Because of those unpleasant experiences they have become closed to learning more about the Lord and His inherent Word. We address some of those dynamics in this book, and hope to help "bridge" that gap. Through the information presented in this book our heart's desire is to assist others in forming a strong basis of

7

faith in Christ Jesus, and to become well-grounded in the Word of God, in order to identify and discern true biblical teachings; especially the prophetic Word in relation to today's current events.

You will find a number of website links throughout this book. We suggest simply reading through the entire text first, then going online and exploring the links that are of interest to you. Please keep in mind although we have done our best to generally vet all the recommended resource material, we cannot be in full-agreement with every point of view taken by some individuals. Not every detail found in the presented resource material reflects our views. We would like to include many more excellent websites and resources, but due to space constraints we have done the best we can to offer a good variety of information. Seriously and steadfastly studying primarily the Bible itself is our strongest recommendation. We urge all readers to thoroughly study the Word of God with the guidance of the Holy Spirit (1 Corinthians 2:10).

Countless attractive media resources can be found in the world today promoting a broad-spectrum of opinions often contrary to careful and accurate Bible interpretation, resulting in confusion for the seeker. However, we offer enough information in this text to use as a reliable guide. We of course look to the infallible, inherent Word of God—the Bible, as the final authority on all matters. The primary goal of Friends of Yeshua Ministries is to distribute the messages in this book to as many people as possible, especially to those who are searching for answers as to what is really happening in this corrupt, fragmented world. We have many important subtitles in each chapter that are cannot fit on the Contents pages addressing pertinent issues such as: *Jihad Training of Muslim Children Using Television and Schools* in chapter eight.

We seek no notoriety and the author of this work does not wish to get caught-up in any type of personal self-promotions. We work to glorify the Lord, not ourselves. We simply want to share this book and do the work of evangelists (2 Timothy 4:5). The better world prophesied in the Scriptures *is* coming soon. Please don't miss it. We ask you to use the expanded edition of this text as a guidebook to your final destination. We pray that you (including believers) read this book with an open heart and mind setting aside any previous opinions you may have regarding the Scriptures and the many topics discussed on the following pages—at least until after carefully reading and studying the information presented.

—Friends of Yeshua Ministries

A Special Invitation

People write books to encourage and edify others and to inform them of things that are important, things that touch their hearts. Solomon wrote about this when he said: "As iron sharpens iron; so a man sharpens the countenance of his friend" (Proverbs 27:17). I have been sharpened by many dear friends with one of them being Dr. Kenton Beshore. He has also been sharpened by great men of God and has in turn sharpened other men of God such as Dr. Timothy LaHaye—while attending Bob Jones University together and then while taking Bible classes taught by the late Dr. David L. Cooper of the Biblical Research Society.

Dr. Beshore was instrumental in steadily mentoring Dr. LaHaye during their college days and many years thereafter, long before the popular *Left Behind* novels and later he was also very involved in helping Tim La Haye become the pastor of several churches located in South Carolina, Minnesota and the Scott Memorial Baptist Church in San Diego, California (eventually changed to Shadow Mountain Community Church currently pastored by Dr. David Jeremiah). Dr. Beshore had already pastored his first church at age 18 and was ordained at age 19 at Bellevue Baptist Church in Memphis, Tennessee by his pastor, the late Dr. Robert G. Lee. He has spent a lifetime studying, preaching and teaching mostly Bible prophecy.

I am very honored and delighted that Dr. Beshore, "Doc," as he is affectionately known has written the Foreword to my book. His outstanding biblical scholarship is second to none with writings that have been translated into more than sixty languages. I invite you to become part of God's family, if you are not already. Our prayer is that all those who read this book will walk away encouraged with a better understanding of the dynamics in this life and be joyfully ready to step into eternity when God calls us home. Once we understand the awesome Deity of Jesus Christ it becomes clear that it is He and He alone who holds the key to a glorious eternal destiny. —Kit Olsen

John 1:12

"But as many as received Him, to them He gave the right to become children of God, even to those who believe in His name."

The Deity of Jesus Christ—The Eternal Word

"IN the beginning was the Word, and the Word was with God, and the Word was God. He was in the beginning with God.

All things were made through Him, and without Him nothing was made that was made. In Him was life, and the life was the light of men.

And the light shines in the darkness, and the darkness did not comprehend it. That was the true Light, which gives light to every man coming into the world.

He was in the world and the world was made through Him. He came to His own, and His own did not receive Him.

But as many as received Him, to them He gave the right to become children of God, to those who believe in His name: who was born not of blood, nor the will of the flesh, nor the will of man, but of God.

And the Word became flesh and dwelt among us, as we beheld His glory, the glory as of the only begotten of the Father, full of grace and truth.

And of His fullness we have all received, and grace for grace. For the law was given through Moses; *but* grace and truth came through Jesus Christ."

—John 1:1-5, 9-14, 16-17

Foreword

I have been a student of the Bible and involved in ministry for a very long time, and have met many people throughout my academic career. I have mentored and worked with the brightest and most sought after scholars, authors and Bible teachers—all highly esteemed individuals. I am especially impressed with Kit's intelligence and ability to grasp biblical truth.

Our editor here at the World Bible Society has worked with many writers and finds her excellent writing skills and her ability to bring together important points in a straightforward, intelligent down to earth, easy to follow style—exceptional. Her multiple talents are extraordinary. I am very pleased with the expanded edition of this book. I think of it as an important eschatological anthology, a very relevant reference book.

When I first spoke with Kit she had written an article on Psalm 83—the imprecatory prayer. I was very impressed with her excellent article and how she had so accurately captured the psalm's meaning. As her article was about to be published, she came across my work on the topic and asked if she could quote from some of it to further support her position. I was glad to assist her with such an important matter. I consider her to be very perceptive and discerning. I can see it is her tremendous heart for the Lord, her love for Israel and the Jewish people that motivate her. Her rich background stemming from her European heritage—parents who were both highly educated professionals in the fields of chemistry, medicine and languages gave her a strong foundation to explore a multitude of her own interests.

Kit has had a far-reaching classical education primarily in media communications and business experiences in music—composing and recording; also trained in stage and camera work by the renowned late Lee Strasberg and Stella Adler as part of her college education. She has written and published a number of secular books used for her media communications work; wrote and produced documentary slide shows for the State of New York. Her first professional writing job (ad copy) was at Meredith Enterprises on Madison Avenue, NYC during her senior year in college. She is experienced in audiovisual production, media photography, varied forms of copywriting; editing, design and layout of advertising material, media graphics, marketing, and currently specializes in Christian book editing and ghostwriting including pre-production pagination of manuscripts. Kit has worked in front of and

11

behind the camera, and in the medical field editing statistical oncology studies for the National Institutes of Health in Bethesda, Maryland. She was co-owner of a very successful office equipment business. These are only some highlights of her extensive background. She is a member of the Screen Actors Guild, although she no longer has any interest in working in that field. Kit walked away from the entertainment world at a time when she had tremendous opportunities to excel as a secular writer and entertainer. She could not reconcile her commitment to Christ and live a lifestyle that daily invited many compromises to her faith and Christian values.

These vast experiences, coupled with Kit's strong studies in Bible prophecy have given her a unique understanding of our current state of affairs. She has traveled to, lived and worked in London, Japan, Italy, and many other destinations. Her continued study and exposition of the Bible has given her exceptional understanding of these last days in which we live. Her love for writing, although English is her third language, has always been part of her life. I understand she had to work very hard to learn the English language when she was a young child, causing her to become interested in writing.

Kit is one of the most charming, interesting people I have ever met. She has a striking, lovely appearance with a warm, caring, giving personality. She has been involved in Jewish evangelism since 1995 as a researcher, writer, and publisher. Her magazine—*Southern Nevada Christian Review*—a witnessing venture was her first Christian publication. Its intent was to share the salvation message and was produced in a very inviting style. It was a very well packaged magazine with the emphasis on prophecy in relation to these last days. It was distributed to Christian bookstores throughout Nevada and California in 1995 and 1996. Even secular retailers eagerly displayed and offered it to their customers. It was a strong witnessing piece, and was very well received.

From that point on Kit has worked as researcher, writer, editor, and also as media representative for a Hebrew-Christian television ministry. She is now primarily involved with her own evangelistic ministry, Friends of Yeshua Ministries and has written this outstanding book with the intent to distribute it to as many people as possible. Her brother Rick first encouraged the project, as well as some of her closest friends and especially her ministry partner for this project, Terry Nasca. What was intended to be a small four-page brochure has turned into this extraordinary witnessing book with extensive research, a wealth of information on topics relating to these last days; Kit's heart is totally devoted to sharing the Word of God, and especially with the Jewish people. She is on fire for Israel and very excited about the soon return of the Lord.

This is an excellent treatise. In this expanded edition additional significant points are included as we move closer to the climax of world history, as we know it. Every seeker of spiritual integrity should read it and give it to as many people as possible. I have once again shared her manuscript with a number of respected individuals and they have unanimously commented that this is one of the best witnessing pieces they have ever read. Some of the points Kit makes on important topics are very detailed making this book a much needed educational tool.

What I didn't know about Kit at first is that she had a very rough start in life. As an infant she nearly died from food poisoning. When she was seventeen years old a group of medical experts told her and her parents that she would be a "partial invalid at best," and to forget any aspirations whatsoever she had as far as having a family or *any* type of career. Most people would have given up. She was a very determined young lady and with the help of God and her parents she totally overcame her illnesses, primarily by eating a careful, very healthy diet and living a healthy lifestyle. It is evident the Lord had some important plans for her life.

When Kit isn't sharing the Word of God and working on one of her many projects she loves taking care of her young son, preparing delicious meals and spending time with her family.

Dr.F.Kenton Beshore
(D.D., Litt.D.,D.Sac.Th.,Ph.D.,Th.D.)
President and Executive Director, World Bible Society

The Incomparable Messiah

The Holy One of Israel

"The earth is full of the goodness of the LORD. By the word of the LORD the heavens were made and the host of them by the breath of His mouth. Let all the inhabitants of the world stand in awe of Him. For He spoke, and it was done; He commanded, and it stood fast" (Psalm 33:5b-6, 8b-9).

"The heavens declare the glory of God; and the firmament shows His handiwork" (Psalm 19:1).

"Who has ascended into heaven, or descended? Who has gathered the wind in His fists? Who has bound the waters in a garment? Who has established all the ends of the earth? What is His name, and what is His Son's name, if you know?" (Proverbs 30:4).

"O LORD, You have searched me and known me. You know my sitting down and rising up; You understand my thought afar off. You comprehend my path and my lying down, and are acquainted with all my ways. You formed my inward parts; you covered me in my mother's womb" (Psalm 139:1-3, 13).

"I will praise You, for I am fearfully *and* wonderfully made; marvelous are Your works, and *that* my soul knows very well. My frame was not hidden from You when I was made in secret, *and* skillfully wrought in the lowest parts of the earth.

Your eyes saw my substance being yet formed. And in Your book they were all written, the days fashioned for me, when *as yet there were* none of them" (Psalm 139:14-16).

"Thus says the LORD, the Holy One of Israel, and His Maker; I have made the earth and created man on it. I—My hands—stretched out the heavens, and all their host I have commanded" (Isaiah 45:11a-12).

Introduction

"Greater love has no one than this, than to lay down one's life for his friends. 'He [Jesus] said, it is finished!' And bowing His head, He gave up His spirit." —John 15:13; 30b

If you have ever longed for a real friend, one you can truly count on no matter what, a friend who will stand with you in the midst of your deepest heartaches and greatest disappointments and love you just as you are—then it is here where you will read about such a friend; a friend who longs to call you His own.

The one you will read about in this book is the one and only Person in the entire universe who you or I can ever really consistently count on—forever. The incomparable greatness of the Creator of the universe, His incomprehensible love for us is a concept we can barely begin to fully-grasp. But we must listen and hear the messages He has left behind for us. His love is incomprehensible because it is so far beyond what we with our limited, finite capabilities could ever begin to understand. When the God of the universe stepped out of eternity and came into this world, He came as the ransom for every living person on this planet. Here, in this book you will learn about the spiritual war that has been going full-force ever since the powers of darkness set out to overthrow Almighty God.

The forces of darkness try to use mankind as pawns to do their dirty work, to hurt God. They want to destroy Him. They want to destroy you and me. If you are seeking a friend who will never forsake you, one who promises a glorious future in a place so incredible, a place so awe-inspiring, a place only the living God can create, then open your heart and prepare to receive the most awesome love and life possible. A better world *is* coming soon, and it looks very, very much like it will be within *our* lifetime, but we must be ready for it.

You may already have heard some things about God, the one who loves us unconditionally. The One who died for you, and for me. He took the darkness of the entire world upon Himself. He gave Himself up as the ultimate payment for a fallen world—for all our sins. Sins the rebellious Lucifer (the devil) introduced into the world. God came in the flesh in the Person of Jesus Christ to repair the damage—the corruption of sin introduced and unleashed by the devil into what had been a perfect world (1 John 1:8). Jesus Christ came to destroy the devil's evil work, to rescue us from falling into Satan's eternal grip. He freed us from the forces of darkness with his blood sacrifice on the cross. Yet he was scorned and ridiculed. His identity was ferociously challenged and denied. He was savagely condemned, by hate-filled enemies. They yelled out, "Crucify him! Crucify him!" (Luke 23:1). But He *came* to die—that was His mission—so *we* can be eternally free. The Savior—the Messiah Jesus, is indisputably the ultimate freedom fighter.

Have you ever been falsely accused of something you did not say or do? How did you feel? Didn't you just want to shout out to the entire world: "No, that's not true, they are wrong!" Yet the one, who died for you, and for me, *knew* He would be hated and falsely accused. He knew He would be spit on. He knew He would be betrayed, scourged, mercilessly beaten, tortured and put to an agonizing death—His flesh torn apart, ripped, brutalized and disfigured beyond recognition (Isaiah 52:14; 53). He knew His suffering would be horrific, mercilessly cheered and mocked by those who would despise Him. Yet He came forward and took all of humanity's misdeeds upon Himself. So everyone who would believe in Him and receive Him as Lord and Savior would be set eternally free. Free from a frightening, unimaginable horrific eternal destiny, free from a terrifying place where the most sinister forces are trying to lead us.

And today, within our own generation we hear the naysayers, the mockery, the lies and the deceit hurled at Him—at the one who gave us the greatest gift that ever was, is or ever will be. Because of His death sacrifice we can live forever free of the evil forces that would love nothing more than to see us all suffer from now and throughout eternity. Attempts to reduce the God of the universe to nonexistence, is the foremost agenda of those who do the devil's bidding. The devil, the Bible tells us, is: "the prince of the power of the air, of the spirit that is now working in the sons of disobedience" (Ephesians 2:2b). He roams the earth like a roaring lion seeking whom he can devour (1 Peter 5:8).

I ask you to come along on a journey which I pray with all my heart will take you right into the heart of the true and living eternal God, Yeshua Ha Mashiach, Jesus the Christ. He is waiting for you. He is the very best friend you could ever hope for. But first you must know who He is. Leave behind any preconceived thoughts you might have. Even if you are skeptical please come along and continue reading because you are loved more than you can possibly imagine.

Jesus Is the Word Made Flesh

And the Word [Jesus] was made flesh and dwelt among us, and we beheld his glory as of the only begotten of the Father, full of grace and truth" (John 1:14)

The Son of God appeared for this purpose, to destroy the works of the devil" (1 John 3:8b).

"Then Jesus [Yeshua] spoke to them [disciples] again saying 'I am the light of the world. He who follows Me shall not walk in darkness, but have the light of life. I am the one who bears witness of Myself, and the Father who sent me bears witness of Me. I and the Father are one'" (John 8:12, 18; 10:30).

The Lord promises He will dramatically beautify and regenerate the earth bringing real and lasting peace to the world after He returns at the end of the prophesied seven-year Tribulation. The literal millennial reign of Christ on the newly rejuvenated earth will last one thousand years (see pages 157-167).

The Glorious New Creation

"For behold, I create new heavens and a new earth; and the former things shall not be remembered or come to mind. But be glad and rejoice forever in what I create. For behold, I create Jerusalem *for* rejoicing; and her people *for* gladness. I will also rejoice in Jerusalem, and be glad in My people; and there will no longer be heard in her the voice of weeping and the sound of crying" (Isaiah 65:17-19).

"The wolf also shall dwell with the lamb, the leopard shall lie down with the young goat, the calf and the young lion and the fatling together; and a little child shall lead them" (Isaiah 11:6).

"Thy Kingdom come, Thy will be done, **on earth** as it is in heaven" (Matthew 6:10).

"And they lived and reigned with Christ for a thousand years" (Revelation 20:4b).

17

The Lord Is Our Strength

The information in this book will help the reader become more strongly equipped for the better world Jesus Christ promises to all those who are committed to Him by faith—for all those who accept His plea for salvation. When you make Christ your Savior you will not miss the glorious future intended for all those who belong to Him. Be sure you are among those who will spend eternity with the Lord.

"There is no neutral ground in the universe. Every square inch and every split second is claimed [owned] by God and countered [challenged] by Satan." —C.S. Lewis

Isaiah 40:31

"But they that wait upon the LORD shall renew their strength; they shall mount up with wings as eagles; they shall run, and not be weary; and they shall walk and not faint."

Chapter One

What Is Really Going On?

Do you ever wonder if God *really* exits and who God really is? There are so many enticements and distractions surrounding us today; television programs, computers, smartphones, electronic gadgets, social events, hobbies, entertainment sports, work, careers—all situations that rarely promote the importance of having a meaningful and personal relationship with God, the heavenly, "Everlasting Father" (Isaiah 9:6). It seems the Creator of this universe has been pushed aside and forgotten.

Doesn't it look, feel and sound like there are just too many unsettling, negative and strange things happening all at the same time, and with a never before intensity? No one likes to talk about evil, but it obviously exists. There are various ways this evil is described by different people. There is also great beauty and synchronicity that challenges these dark forces. We can find it in our everyday lives.

The following pages present a view I once rejected for at least a decade. I rejected it because I did not understand it. Instead, I chose to listen to those involved in the New Spirituality—New Age concepts. I read infinite numbers of books on various "spiritual" practices. I "meditated" in ashrams and for years, frequently meditated at a Buddhist Zen Center. I did countless hours and years of yoga. I experienced shaktipat. I investigated various traditional religions. I considered myself "spiritual" and experienced great joy at times.

I was soaring high with what I perceived to be the "oneness" of the "universe." I would ask the "universe" for something or for a particular situation, and very often that something or situation would simply present itself. I felt I had tapped into some sort of magical-celestial genie, evolving as a human being and believing there are many roads that lead to the same place. If anyone suggested otherwise I would dismiss that "narrow-minded" opinion as unimportant, intolerant, unsophisticated, and definitely unenlightened.

There was a time when I consulted with a psychic who helped me locate my misplaced diamond marquis necklace. She told me where to look for it, and there it was. Amazing! She was one of the nicest people I ever talked to in my life. So what is the problem? The problem is this: None of these "spiritual" practices or people who adhere to them deal with the positive, beautiful side of life, even though it very much looks and sounds like they are. They can be so nice, but in truth, they are being used by the most seductive, dark forces imaginable. These maligning forces have power and can trick people into believing they are good and kind by helping to solve problems. Their ultimate goal is to keep you and me from God by pretending to be messengers of God. It wasn't until the Holy Spirit, *Ruach Ha Kodesh* in Hebrew, rescued me in a popular New Age bookshop in Virginia that I *began* to understand the tremendous spiritual battle we are ALL involved in whether we want to be or not. Without a doubt, we *are* living in a spiritual battlefield.

One day I was standing in that familiar spot where I would investigate the latest self-help, "spiritual" books. Suddenly, a strong, urgent voice coming from deep within me said: "Get out, get out." I can almost feel it and hear it to this day. I could not ignore that urgent push to leave the bookshop. I knew something important was happening and that my life would never be the same again. I walked out, got into my Porsche and drove down the hill. Without a second thought I drove to the closest bookstore where Bibles were sold. As it turned out, I had driven to the most popular Christian bookstore in town. Imagine that! A girl, who had laughed at Christians for being so hung up on that "one way" to heaven, was now standing in amazement marveling at the vast selection of Christian "stuff."

Inside the bookstore I found a huge variety of Christian books. After I looked over the Bible section, my eyes caught a display sign: "Bible Prophecy." Since I already knew plenty about New Age psychics and prophets, I was especially intrigued. One book in particular helped confirm my suspicions about the disingenuous New Age teachings: *The Sunshine Road*, an autobiography by David and Juneau Chagall.

Traveling throughout Europe and the US, the Chagall's search for spiritual meaning and gravitate toward the tantalizing and blossoming New Age movement. In their book, they express absolute outrage as they discover the satanic lies behind the alluring New Age practices. It was the perfect book for me to start with since I too, had been fooled by deceptive New Age ploys. I bought at least three armloads of Bibles and Christian books that day. I then began my journey of untangling the web of New Age lies that had become such a strong part of my life.

In their exposé, David and Juneau mentioned the name of their Agoura Hills church. I eagerly telephoned the church hoping to track them down. I spoke to a very nice lady. She said she would give the Chagall's my contact number. The very next day, they called. Although we were generations apart in age, I explained how I could very much relate to some of their testimony. We became instant friends. I distinctly remember the love and concern in their voices. They became my spiritual "aunt" and "uncle." I thank God to this day, for placing them in my life.

David and Juneau's loving guidance helped me understand the treacherous New Age road I had traveled and fled. I was in an agonizing state of mild-shock, realizing I had dedicated myself to a very dangerous and destructive "spiritual" lifestyle that had affected every aspect of my life. But an extraordinary event transpired. I finally understood that the living Christ, Yeshua Ha Mashiach, *is* the truth, and the answer to all of life's problems. Every decision I made from that point on would be tied to my sincere devotion to the Lord. Although it took a number of years of studying my Bible, reading scores of Christian books, and much fervent prayer before I gained strong footing as a believer.

As I recovered from a near-miss collision with my true eternal destiny, the Lord never left me floundering. He was always a prayer away and the Chagall's were kindly "waiting in the wings," ready to hold my hand whenever I needed support. Many, many years have passed since the Lord intervened in my life that day in Virginia. I look back now and still fall to my knees in reverence, in complete awe of Almighty God for loving me enough to go out of His way to rescue me: a once-rebellious, albeit a sincerely confused seeker, naïvely stumbling through life.

The only explanation for my intervention is that the Lord listened to and answered my prayers. I had been sincerely asking that the truth would be revealed to me. For quite some time, I had become very wary and suspicious of much of the impersonal idolatry and far-out teachings within New Age circles. Something was wrong. I really wanted to know God, the real God. Those involved in New Age teachings and false religions worship gods of their own design. For example, they often consider the "universe" a god, a supreme power. I had appealed to that god myself.

In the Bible, that "genie" I mentioned earlier is called a "familiar spirit"—in other words, a demonic entity, backed up by the devil. Interestingly, even in the false religion of Islam, evil genies are said to "lead humans astray." In Arabic, Satan is known as Iblis, the iconic "genie." No doubt, I had been deceived and led astray by "familiar spirits." They are so devious. There is *real* power behind New Age spiritual practices heavily steeped in the occult. But that power is demonic. So many souls are being deceived and believe they are interacting with friendly forces, unaware of the tremendous spiritual danger they are in. It is amazing how these demons can make us feel so empowered, as if the entire universe is ours.

But with each passing day they are leading us into everlasting darkness. I know; I have experienced this first hand. These demonic entities, through the physical world try to appeal to our vanity, our prideful egos—pushing us to pursue godless lifestyles filled with self-importance and self-righteousness, luring us away from our greatest ally—the very God who created us, the One who holds together the entire universe and provides every breath we take. Satan, the god of this world has power and uses it strategically to try to destroy us, but God has all power and uses it to save us.

The Lord taught that we should not build our lives based upon our own self-importance, that we should esteem others as greater than ourselves—that we should be Christ-centered, not self-centered.

"Do nothing from selfishness or empty conceit, but with humility of mind regard one another as more important than yourselves; do not merely look out for your own personal interests, but also for the interests of others" (Philippians 2:3-4).

"For where envy and self-seeking *exist,* confusion and every evil thing *are* there" (James 3:16).

But of course the world and especially New Age precepts teach the opposite—that life is about self-empowerment, all about: "Me, me" and more "me." But it's okay to once in a while do something nice (charities and fundraising) for the less fortunate—to look good socially if for no other reason; so even *that* becomes a "me" thing. The need for celebrity and self-significance (VIP, more "me") in our culture has become a fiercely sought after preoccupation and obsession. I believe this is one way the devil harasses people—through the world's lies—that more is better. You might have thoughts like this about yourself:

You really aren't good enough, but if you become a very important, successful person or better yet—a celebrity, everyone will think you are really special and that will prove you are good enough. So go ahead, break some rules. Do whatever it takes to become very rich and even famous.

In this media-dictated society we are bombarded non-stop with messages at every turn that say we should strive to "have it all" and becoming number one should be our top priority. Social elitism (social snobbery) is encouraged and with it its condescending attitude of, "I'm better than you"—is rewarded. Young girls are constantly compared to the perfect child model, never feeling "good enough." Young boys are pushed to the point of exhaustion so they will become the next sports superstars. It is important to do our best in our chosen fields of interest and earn a good living, but when our priorities are unbalanced, primarily self-centered with little regard for others we are setting ourselves up for great disappointments. Our heart motives must be kind and loving with genuine concern for others.

Preoccupation with one's "look" in the entertainment field is a constant way of life. There is no getting around it. The pressure to look "perfect" is enormous. So is the intense pressure to outdo and succeed beyond one's peers. Of course this struggle for perfection, significance and success trickles down to the rest of the world. Notice how many rich and famous celebrities die much too young or become alcoholics and drug addicts. Even with all their fame and money, without being truly surrendered to Christ they lack inner-peace and are riding waves of emotional and spiritual recklessness. At Whitney Houston's funeral, Kevin Costner—obviously grief stricken, talked about how even as extraordinarily beautiful and gifted she was Whitney Houston always worried—if she was "good enough." Her tragic death, accelerated by years of substance abuse is symbolic of the immense pressure even a celebrity of her status is under to look physically perfect and deliver flawless dynamic performances on stage and in real life.

What is really going on with these "celebrated" people? I believe they are casualties of the spiritual battle that we are all subjected to in one way or another. Immense wealth coupled with preoccupation with one-self has a way of destroying good sensibilities. Too much self-absorption only leads to feelings of anxiety and even depression while making others feel like they don't matter. If you want to reap the Lord's blessings and feel good about yourself go do something nice for someone else. And don't make a big public display about it. Keep your good deeds private. If we really examine our lives, usually there are many things we can be grateful for. Doing things with an attitude of gratitude (as the old saying goes), is very therapeutic and also helps keep things in their proper prospective. Jesus said, "But when you do a charitable deed, do not let you right hand know what your left hand is doing, that your deed maybe in secret; and your father who sees in secret will reward you openly" (Matthew 6:4).

Share generously your heart, your finances and your time with those who are in need of a caring friend. Even if you don't have a lot of material wealth, share the little you do have. Giving of our time and showing a sincere interest in someone else is something that many people need. Even a small act of kindness can go a long way. When believers are busy "serving" God with various projects but willfully neglect those who are reaching out to them, they miss the point of Jesus' teachings, to: "Bear one another's burdens, and so fulfill the law of Christ" (Galatians 6:2).

Money is a great tool. We all need it to function in this complex world. It is the ruthless fixation to have large sums of it, to be stingy and selfishly hang onto it (miserly greed) that causes problems. Sadly, greed is a chronic problem with many people, both Christians and non-Christians alike. The Lord loves a cheerful giver, yet few give chivalrously when they are in a position to do so (2 Corinthians 9:7). Many take their wealth and hoard it or spend it frivolously on themselves when they could easily help further God's work or improve the day-to-day lives of struggling families. The worst offense is when an avowed Christian *has* the means to do something beneficial for fellow believers during tough times, but refuses to do so—exposing a blatant disregard for the needs of others. Where is the Christian love and concern?

As long as we are in this fallen, corrupt world we will always have challenges. Negative messages of inadequacy will always be directed at us. Advertisers get very rich using this strategy in order to get consumers to purchase their products. If you buy what they are selling, surely you will feel better about your self—that is the overriding message in nearly every ad campaign. Only in Christ are we made whole. Only in Christ do we have genuine significance, freedom and peace. We are totally sufficient in Christ through His redemptive grace. When we are truly surrendered to Christ we are released from the social and cultural pressures of the world. Without Christ we are lost and have no chance of ever being whole.

No amount of money or material possessions can fill the God-vacuum within our souls. Some people may appear to be happy on the outside but without a genuine personal relationship with the living Christ, inner-turmoil is sure to exist on some level. At some point in everyone's life, we are faced with something that will reveal our spiritual stability or instability. If our emotions are unstable, it is a reflection of our spiritual condition.

One of the most popular songs of all-time promoting the concept of selfishness made wildly popular by the old-timer—the late Frank Sinatra is titled: *My Way*. Even after forty-years other artists are still singing it all over the world. This socially accepted jargon of striving for self-importance, for self-adulation—me, me and more me, has had a shattering, bulldozing-effect upon relationships, families, businesses—all aspects of society. That old song pretty much says, go ahead and do it all *your* way with no regard to others or the negative consequences it brings. And even if you make a mistake, at least you can say you did it *your way*. What arrogance! This concept of prideful-control is nothing new. It goes way back to when Lucifer, the devil, first rebelled against God.

Earlier in my life, before I started college I made a commitment to Christ and received Him as my Lord and Savior. Shortly before I started my junior year of college I made a decision to walk away from all of it. I walked away from unanswered questions, inept Bible teachers, and social "Christians" who talked about the Lord but were living lifestyles that did not match their professed faith. I felt emotionally abandoned and spiritually shattered from the spiritual shallowness I had encountered. Instead of focusing on Jesus and the Scriptures, I only saw the weak commitments of many who were Christians in name only. I was too young emotionally and spiritually to realize that people will always let us down and God's Word is the truth no matter how people behave.

I had also simultaneously moved into New York City from my cozy little upstate town to complete my college education. Very quickly I found myself surrounded by seemingly endless seductive New Age mantra—everywhere. I enrolled in a popular yoga class for exercise but metaphysical meditation techniques were also cleverly incorporated into the classes. It was not long before I was seeking-out more pagan-based rituals and teachings that steadily chiseled away at my weak foundation in Christ—causing me to seriously question the true God of the Bible.

Recovering from disappointments with my Christian experience, I found myself functioning like the walking wounded. I was so ready to hear anything but the insincere fake Christian rhetoric I had left behind. The devil had me just where he wanted me. Signed, sealed and nearly delivered into hell. I was totally vulnerable to false teachings because I did not have a strong foundation of faith in Christ. I did not know and understand the Word of God. Although deep in my heart I knew the Lord was really important, but I felt lost. I kind of put God in my back pocket and went on a long journey, on a very strange and bumpy road.

Even though I took a long-detour from Him and searched the world for "truth," He never let me go. He answered my call when I cried out for the truth at the height of my spiritual frustration. He reached out His invisible loving hand to me that day in Virginia, long after my college years. It was then I began to understand that I had been deceived by the New Age lies. I never set foot inside that New Age bookshop again. How could I after the Lord had been so faithful to me?

Later, when I realized it was the God of the Bible whom I had been seeking all along, I recommitted my life to Him. It was the Holy Spirit who intervened on my behalf in that New Age bookshop and carried me straight back into the arms of Jesus. I do remember a number of kind souls I met along the way who tried to tell me there is a "beautiful side to evil" but I would not listen. Foolishly, I thought I was more spiritually advanced than they. I can only wonder how different my life would have been, had I not bought into the New Age lies that so strongly influenced my life. I thank God every day for saving me from the clutches of darkness. I also learned that God makes all things right: "And we know that all things work together for good to those who love God, to those who are called according to His purpose" (Romans 8:28).

Now please don't stop reading here. The terminology and the messages are going to get more intense. But what I am going to say on the following pages has credibility and is backed up historically and prophetically. The New Age teachings and false religion systems I've investigated have shown themselves to be nothing less than harbingers of spiritual fraud and portals to the abyss. **Hundreds of Bible prophecies have already come true. It stands to reason all other future prophecies will also come true.**

As you read on now, remember my testimony. I once had a very different point of view. For a long time, I rejected traditional Judeo-Christian beliefs although even then I felt an unexplainable closeness to Israel. If you care about yourself and your future, and if you love your family and friends, I plead with you to go along with me with an open mind and continue reading. Surely on some level you must recognize things are not quite what they seem; things are not quite "right." It's as if an invisible puppet master is methodically pulling the strings behind the scenes. Please listen and read very carefully. Then, after listening and reading, please investigate what I am saying. Seriously examine the information throughout this text and in the resource sections in the back pages of this book. Later, as we get to the "Spiritual Deception" section, there will be much more said about the truths and lies of "spiritual" identities and practices. Don't assume what you have been taught or what you have heard about spirituality, God, the Bible, and other "holy" books is truth *regardless* of the source. No matter how much you like or respect someone, it is important to search the Scriptures yourself, and that includes Bible believing Christians.

Countless people are involved in some sort of "spirituality." But a large majority of them form their religious beliefs without ever having studied the Bible in its proper context, in its entirety. Many excellent resources are available today that make Bible study easier than ever. Nevertheless, there are plenty of so-called religious experts who have not yet grasped the basic fundamentals of Scripture. These same people are telling one tale after another, leading themselves and those who will listen to them into a cataclysmic-web of spiritual confusion.

"These were more fair-minded than those in Thessalonica, in that they received the word with all readiness, and searched the Scriptures daily to find out whether these things were so" (Acts 17:11).

Many years ago, respected Bible teacher, John F. MacArthur Jr., wrote a great book titled, *Reckless Faith—When the Church Loses its Will to Discern* on the subject of spiritual deception as it relates to Christians. The message is still very relevant today (excerpt, pg. 56).

In a society that is hostile to anyone who declares absolutes; that tolerates faith in any form, that values emotion over reason and trendiness over conviction, it's no surprise that many American churches have lost their ability to discern between biblical truth and doctrinal error. Such emotional reckless "faith" inevitably leads to spiritual disaster, taking its followers on a dangerous journey that leaves them defenseless against false teaching.

27

Knowing the Truth—Rejecting the Lies

1 John 5:19-20

"We [believers] know that we are of God, and the whole world lies under the sway of the wicked one [the devil]. And we know that the Son of God has come and has given us an understanding, that we may know Him who is true; and we are in Him who is true, in His Son Jesus Christ. This is the true God and eternal life."

The Fight for Our Souls

Satan. Yes, that is his name and he *is* the god of this world (2 Corinthians 4:4). He is the ultimate deceiver—the father of lies (John 8:44). His number one weapon against the truth, against the Word of God is promoting false philosophies and religions. He is working day and night trying to convince you and me and everyone else that the true God of the Bible does not exist—or that if He does exist, He is just one of many gods. But please don't fall for that deadly trap like I almost did. The devil wants you to think that as long as you are a nice person and do nice deeds, your eternity will be just fine. He would even like you to go to church on Sunday as long as you don't take that "Jesus" who sacrificed Himself on the cross—too seriously.

"There is a principle which cannot fail to keep man from everlasting ignorance. That principle is condemnation before investigation."

Those wise words written by the late Edmund Spenser have been passed down generation after generation. He was an English poet highly recognized in his day (1552-1559) as the leading craftsman of modern English. Apparently, he also had an understanding of a common error many people make—dismissing the truth about a topic or situation *before* truly understanding it, without genuinely researching the matter. What a tragic state of affairs: individuals saying "yes" or "no" to something without really knowing what they are saying "yes" or "no" to!

Almighty God wants us to recognize Him for who He truly is. He says we have to accept His Son as our Savior and Lord before we can get into heaven. He wants a true commitment. Suppose you are a devoted, loving parent. You sacrifice and work so your child can have the best of everything. How would you like your child to refuse to acknowledge you as his or her parent, instead running off to find someone else to call "Mom" or "Dad"?

Imagine chasing after your child, saying, "But I have done everything for you"—"I am your mom" or "I am your dad," and your child looks you straight in the eye and says, "No you're not." Then you say, "Here look, I am listed on your birth certificate as your parent. It proves you are my child." Your child says, "I don't believe what that birth certificate says. In fact I don't believe in you, either." God loves you. He is the heavenly Father. Scripture teaches all those who place their trust in the Lord automatically become His children.

"But as many as received Him, to them He gave the right to become children of God, to those who believe in His name: who were born, not of blood, nor the will of the flesh, nor the will of man, but of God" (John 1:12-13).

You are part of God's creation. You are very special to Him, regardless of your past. He is the God of forgiveness. Even if you lead a good and virtuous life, we all have shortcomings and still need God's forgiving grace. In this fallen world we all have the propensity to easily fall into sin—that is precisely why we need the Savior (Romans 5:12). He wants us to recognize Him for *who* He really is.

He left the Bible behind for that very reason. Please give the Lord a chance to reveal Himself to you. The God of the Bible is very much alive. Through Christ we find our true home in a very lost, corrupt, morally and spiritually bankrupt world. This homecoming is what we all long for but we are too often blindsided by the anti-God teachings that so strongly influence us from the day we are born. We are deceived into thinking a relationship with God is only a recreational pastime or a delusional crutch and that humanity as a whole has the answers to life and that we do not need God.

Millions of people try to fill the disconnection from their Maker by seeking love and acceptance from those who cannot fulfill the need for unconditional love and acceptance—from those who are slaves to the ways of this world and are lost (separated from God), although they might appear to be very "successful" by the world's standards.

If worldly success is enough, why are so many people not satisfied with their riches alone? Why do so many people continuously seek more thrills and material possessions, yet are never fully satisfied? Why are so many individuals on prescription drugs for depression even when they have plenty of money in the bank? And why is substance abuse so prevalent everywhere, regardless of one's social status? Because of the God disconnect, the God-void—the separation from the One who created us, the One, who longs to restore that broken relationship. Instead of recognizing the need for reconciling with our Creator to fill the inner-void, lifestyle choices are made that take a person farther away from God and closer to the forces of darkness.

It is evident that an age-old battle for our souls has been raging and it is getting more and out of control, affecting the lives of millions of people. This spiritual war-zone in which we live is about ready to explode. We must recognize the spiritual dynamics of this battle or we will be caught off guard and destroyed. Physical manifestations of this spiritual war are increasing all around the world. Violence is increasing; weather patterns are going berserk, including a dangerous and devastating drought looming across America. An obvious calculated push toward forming a one-world government is intensifying under the veil of creating *forced* social and economic programs that would inevitably undermine our freedoms. Our First Amendment religious and free speech rights are being challenged. Numerous other biblical prophecies are being played out every day, especially in the Middle East.

We are not going to quietly tiptoe around here about this all-encompassing spiritual conflict because our eternal lives are at stake. The Bible is an SOS cry from the Lord imploring us to listen to His salvation message. He invites us to respond to His call, to engage in a personal never-ending relationship with Him. He wants to rescue us from harm, just like any good parent.

> "Jesus said to him, 'I am the way, the truth, and the life. No one comes to the Father, except through Me.' And there is salvation in no one else; for there is no other name under heaven that has been given among men, by which we must be saved" (John 14:6; Acts 4:12).

If you are thinking you can wait until after you die to make a decision for Christ, think again. Scripture makes it very clear you must receive Christ *before* you die in order to be saved. The Scripture above says:

> "No one comes to the Father, except through Me."

You cannot enter heaven and the holy presence of God without receiving Jesus' atonement for your sins.

> [Jesus said,] "Therefore I said to you that you will die in your sins; for if you do not believe that I am He, you will die in your sins" (John 8:24).

In the Old Testament, the prophet Isaiah wrote of the one and only true God, the God of the Bible:

> "And there is no other God beside Me, a just God and a Savior; there is none besides Me. Look to Me and be saved, all you ends of the earth! For I am God, and there is no other" (Isaiah 45:21b-22).

31

In the following verses—Jesus, who is also called, Yeshua, in Hebrew—cautions us about Satan, the devil:

"He [the devil] was a murderer from the beginning and does not stand in the truth, because there is no truth in him. Whenever he speaks a lie, he speaks from his own nature; for he is a liar and the father of lies" (John 8:44b).

"For we wrestle not against flesh and blood, but against principalities, against powers, against the rulers of the darkness of this world, against spiritual wickedness in high places" (Ephesians 6:12).

Evil and Satan are complex topics. The devil is not just some type of fictitious evil concept, or a figment of one's imagination. Satan, whose original name was Lucifer, was a marvelously beautiful angel who held a very high position. He was not created to be evil, but he became so through his own corruption. His own pride, greed and self-importance caused him to try to replace and overthrow his own Creator—Almighty God. In the following verse you will see how Satan tried to usurp God's authority, resulting in his eviction from heaven:

"How you are fallen from heaven, O Lucifer, son of the morning! *How* you are cut down to the ground, you who weakened the nations! For you have said in your heart, 'I will ascend to heaven; I will exalt my throne above the stars of God; I will sit on the mount of the congregation on the farthest sides of the north; I will ascend above the heights of the clouds; I will be like the Most High'" (Isaiah 14:12-14).

You can also see from the previous Scripture that Satan broke the first of Almighty God's Ten Commandments: "You shall have no other gods before Me" (Exodus 20:3). Although Satan was thrown out of heaven—his first rebellion (Luke 10:18), he still has access to the heavenly domains and also roams around on earth prowling about like a roaring lion (1 Peter 1:8). But halfway through the Tribulation he will be ousted from the heavenly realms permanently (Revelation 12:7-12).

"Now there was a day when the sons of God came to present themselves before the LORD, and Satan also came among them. And the LORD said to Satan, "From where do you come?" So Satan answered the LORD and said, "From going to and fro on the earth, and from walking back and forth on it" (Job 1:6-7).

Satan tried to overthrow God's throne. He became his own god, worshipping himself rather than the true God of the universe. God's response was to cast him from heaven down to earth. Ever since that time there has been an enormous struggle going on between good and evil, between God and Satan. Arrogance, pride and brazen self-aggrandizing are all traits that took Satan out of God's good graces. Satan took advantage of the power God initially gave him and used it against Him. Since then the devil has stopped at nothing to try to usurp the King of the universe. He wants to destroy God's creations and cause havoc and heartache any way he can.

The same human inclination for self-importance and power later enticed Adam and Eve into sinning when Satan lied to Eve and said: "You will be like God" (Genesis 3:5). Because of the fall of Man into sin all of mankind is separated from the God of creation, the Holy God of Israel. Mankind inherited this separated sin condition from Adam and Eve. The inclination to sin is in our spiritual DNA and only through Christ can we be freed from that deadly affliction (the Adamic nature we are all born under).

"Wherefore, as by one man sin entered into the world, and death by sin; and so death passed upon all men, for that all have sinned" (Romans 5:12).

God's way of reconciling humanity to Himself is through Christ's death sacrifice on the cross, which paid the penalty for all of mankind's sins. Reconciliation with God and the gift of eternal life is based upon the confession of Jesus of Nazareth, accepting the only begotten Son of God, as Savior.

"But God demonstrates His own love toward us, in that while we were still sinners, Christ died for us. Much more then, having now been justified by His blood, we shall be saved from wrath through Him. For if when we were enemies we were reconciled to God through the death of His Son, much more, having been reconciled, we shall be saved by His life. And not only *that,* but we also rejoice in God through our Lord Jesus Christ, through whom we have now received the reconciliation" (Romans 5:8-11).

I think we can fairly assess that Satan will stop at nothing to try to defeat Almighty God. He is the consummate definition of evil, shrewdly plotting to get his own way. He thrives on creating agony and total destruction. Where there is unspeakable calamity, we can find the signature of Satan. We need only tune into local and world news reports each day to learn about dark and disturbing events. These matters cannot be explained except for the undeniable presence of evil, orchestrating one tragedy after another. Evil has infiltrated the hearts and minds of inordinate numbers of people. But in Christ we have hope and the assurance of spiritual victory. It is up to each one of us individually to accept His free gift of salvation. Don't let Satan steal away your life.

"I am the door. If anyone enters by Me, he will be saved, and will go in and out and find pasture. The thief does not come except to steal, and to kill, and to destroy. I have come that they may have life and that they may have *it* more abundantly" (John 10:9-10).

PLEASE believe in Christ and accept Him as your Lord and Savior; by doing so you become a true child of God, as Scripture teaches. Recognize this dying world for what it is and the living risen Christ for Who He is. He *is* the way, the truth and the life. Only through Him can any of us escape the wrath that will be poured out during the soon coming prophesied seven-year Tribulation. Only through Him can we be saved from an eternity of suffering. Please let go of preconceived ideas that separate you from the living Christ and the abundant life that He wants so very much to share with you.

The devil, through the enticements of this world is trying to cleverly persuade everyone into thinking there is no need for the Savior. The devil only wants to hurt us, to rob us of our chance to have eternal freedom and life in Christ. He is playing a deadly game with a loaded gun aimed directly at each man, woman and child—never hesitating to pull the trigger. Unless we are reconciled with Christ we are all in full firing-range of the devil and his loaded gun. When we choose salvation in Christ the devil is disarmed and we are made permanently victorious—our eternal destiny is shielded from any bullets he fires.

"You are of God little children, and have overcome them [the devil and his influences] because greater is He who is in you than he who is in the world" (1 John 4:4).

Jesus the Faithful Messiah

"And the Lord, He is the One who goes before you. He will be with you, He will not leave you nor forsake you; do not fear nor be dismayed. —Deuteronomy 31:6

Only the Lord can make a way where there seems to be no way. Nothing is impossible with God (Luke 1:37). He will never forsake you or leave you. I can attest to that from personal experience many times over. God intervened in my life even after I ran away from Him, when I tried to demote Him from the God of the universe to just one god of many. Yet He drew me back to Him. My faithful heavenly Father never took His eyes off me even when I questioned the truth of who He is, even after so many years of floundering in the demonic strongholds of New Age teachings.

Those false teachings appealed to me because I did not want to believe so many nice people who are convinced (deceived) that there are many roads to heaven—could be *all* wrong. I also did not understand the devil's intense subterfuge to keep humanity bound in sin. But Scripture explicitly reveals why we need Christ's saving grace in this fallen world and exposes the devil for the liar and stalker that he is.

"And we have seen and testify that the Father has sent the Son *as* Savior of the world. Whoever confesses that Jesus is the Son of God, God abides in him, and he in God" (1 John 4:14-15).

Near the end of this book in Appendix E, I have included excerpts from an article by Dr. Thomas Ice titled: "Satan's War Against God." It has some additional good insights about the tremendous spiritual war in which we are ensnarled. For now, I will give you the first paragraph:

In order to make sense out of End Times Bible prophecy one must first understand what happened at the beginning in order to know where we are headed and why. Although mankind is intricately involved in history one cannot understand the purpose and goal of history without God's revelation of the angelic dimensions. The starting point begins with Satan's declaration of independence from God shortly after the creation.

A World Drowning in Moral Depravity

2 Timothy 3:1-4

"But know this, that in the last days perilous times will come: For men will be lovers of themselves, lovers of money, boasters, proud, blasphemers, disobedient to parents, unthankful, unholy, unloving, unforgiving, slanderers, without self-control, brutal, despisers of good, traitors, headstrong, haughty, lovers of pleasure rather than lovers of God."

What Time Is It?

It appears as if everyday life is crumbling into unrecognizable fragments, with little hope of being reassembled into a familiar silhouette anytime soon. Wars and rumors of wars are everyday news. Economic hardships are not rebounding as well as they have in the past. The landscape of America is changing. Ghost towns where life once thrived are now part of the ransacked American dream. Shopping malls that buzzed with happy shoppers are eerily splattered with empty storefronts unable to survive the economic meltdown.

Paychecks are shrinking, 401K plans are in free-fall, yet the cost of living soars. The economy is in chaos and no one is quite sure if there will be rampant inflation or deflation. Government debt is recklessly soaring with no end in sight. American streets are lined with foreclosed homes. American jobs have been methodically hijacked and outsourced by greedy, heartless men who line their own pockets with profits earned from slave labor. Society in general is perverse and moral leadership is lacking. There is more uncertainty about the future than ever before. Jesus said it would be like this.

Signs and Times of the End of the Age

The disciples asked Jesus:

"And what will be the sign of Your coming, and the end of the age?" And Jesus answered and said to them: "Take heed that no one deceives you. For many will come in My name, saying, 'I am the Christ,' and will deceive many. And you will hear of wars and rumors of wars.

See that you are not troubled; for all these things must come to pass, but the end is not yet. For nation will rise against nation and kingdom against kingdom. And there will be famines, pestilences, and earthquakes in various places. All these things *are* the beginning of sorrows. And because lawlessness will abound, the love of many will grow cold" (Matthew 24:3b-8, 12).

We have entered a time in our history that will end in everlasting joy for some and in perpetual devastation for others. I told you this is going to get intense, so stay with me. God cares deeply about you and sometimes the truth really hurts. Some call it tough love. But rejoice, because you, too, can become one of those who will have the everlasting joy. There is tremendous hope for the future if you belong to the Lord.

Ancient, numerous biblical prophecies in Scripture speak about ever-increasing global chaos in the last days, a time of unparalleled misinformation and fraud. Prophetically, we are just about where we are supposed to be. "Perilous times" have surely come and will intensify. A careful study of these prophetic Scriptures gives us the information we need so we can stay grounded during these turbulent times. Nevertheless, Scripture shows that there will be doubters and those who will deny the signs of the times:

"Knowing this first: that scoffers will come in the last days, walking according to their own lusts, and saying, "Where is the promise of His coming? For since the fathers fell asleep, all things continue as they were from the beginning of creation." The Lord is not slack concerning His promise, as some count slackness, but is longsuffering toward us, not willing that any should perish but that all should come to repentance" (2 Peter 3:3, 9).

Thousands of years ago the Jewish Rabbi, Jesus the Christ, Yeshua Ha Mashiach—the true Messiah, promised to return to clean-up an increasingly desperate, degenerate world, to literally rule and reign over this earth.

"Nathanael answered and said to Him [Yeshua], 'Rabbi, You are the Son of God! You are the King of Israel'" (John 1:49).

The time for Christ's return at the Second Coming is fast approaching. Before that time many prophecies are yet to be fulfilled, but all within a relatively short time. My prayer for every reader is that you will embrace the love and heart of the living Christ—the Savior of mankind and realize we are living at a time in our history that very much appears to be destined to witness His soon return. In the following chapters you will read much more regarding the intense misinformation and spiritual deception we are faced with every day—all intentional life draining schemes directed by the enemies of God. Guard your heart, soul, spirit and mind. The forces of darkness know their time is short and want to take as many souls with them into their eternal abyss as possible. And if you are saved, they will work vigorously to make your life here on earth miserable—if you are not spiritually armed (Ephesians 6:13-18). Deception and mayhem are the devil's middle names. He knows how to push our buttons in order to draw us away from the truth of Christ. But he is no match for God Almighty who has an undying love for His creation.

Some of the things you read in this book might sound strange at first, but New Age/occult books commonly refer to all kinds of unorthodox things such as, UFOs, trances and messages from aliens. So if you think some teachings in the Bible are way out, think again! And be of good cheer, God *has* overcome the world! As long as a person is alive it is still possible to become part of His kingdom, forever and for eternity. He died so we can live. He broke the powers of darkness on the cross so we can be free of a frightening eternity bound in the trenches of eternal damnation (see pages 223-226).

> "These things I have spoken to you, that in Me [Jesus] you may have peace. In the world you will have tribulation; but be of good cheer, I have overcome the world" (John 16:33).

> "He has delivered us from the power of darkness and conveyed us into the kingdom of the Son of His love, in whom we have redemption through His blood, the forgiveness of sins" (Colossians 1:13-14).

I used to naïvely think hell is a place Christians talk about to try to scare people into believing in God. In time, when I finally actually studied the topic I discovered Christians talk about hell because it is a real place and without Christ's intervention—His death sacrifice on the cross, we would all end up first in hell and then in the lake of fire for eternity with no chance of escape (Revelation 20:15). I also used to think that the Bible was an important book of historical value, but filled with plenty of nice mythological allegories. I did not think everything in it is the truth. I could not have been more wrong about anything in my life (2 Timothy 3:16). The Word of God is all truth, and I am eternally grateful that God took pity on my ignorance and saved me.

> "For the Son of man is come to seek and save that which was lost" (Luke 19:10).

"The Voice of One Crying in the Wilderness:

Prepare the way of the LORD; make straight in the desert a highway for our God. Every valley shall be exalted and every mountain and hill brought low; the crooked places shall be made straight and the rough places smooth; the glory of the LORD shall be revealed."

—Isaiah 40:2-5a

Chapter Two

Middle East Turmoil—Preview of Armageddon and What Is the Big Deal about Israel?

"Pray for the peace of Jerusalem:
May they prosper who love you." —Psalm 122:6

"I will make you [Israel] a great nation; I will bless you and make your name great; and you shall be a blessing. I will bless those who bless you, and I will curse him who curses you; and in you all the families of the earth shall be blessed." —Genesis 12:2-3

Without question it is apparent that we have an inordinate number of misinformed critics throughout the world who boisterously condemn Israel, yet have never fully studied the *true* histories affecting the current status of the so-called Palestinians, the Persians (Iranians) or the Jewish people. Biased critics even make the absurd statement that if Israel can have nuclear weapons, Iran should be able to as well. Apparently these critics fail to recognize that Israel is the *only* true democratic nation in the Middle East where women are treated with equality and dignity, where all religions are accepted and can worship freely, where minorities *including* Arabs are given full civil rights.

On March 23, 2012, I read in the *Toronto Sun* newspaper that a local bookstore in Toronto completely sold-out of a book titled: *A Gift for Muslim Couple,* advising men on how to best beat their wives, written by Maulavi Ashraf Ali Thanvi—who is considered to be a prominent Islamic scholar. If you are a Muslim woman you don't have to live in the Middle East to feel the wrath of Allah through his devotees. You can experience it at home—by the hand of your husband—anywhere in the world!

In the trenches of the extremist hellhole nations, those who convert to Christianity from Islam are severely persecuted. Only the Muslim religion is tolerated. Children are used to help destroy what is perceived to be the enemy for the cause of Allah—pure insanity and evil. Iran and her allied nations' lists of inhumane acts are long and frightening. In Iran as well as within its proxy nations and affiliates terrorist acts reign. For example, the Shiite Muslim political group Hezbollah—Iran's proxy, ruthlessly fires rockets from Gaza into Israel. Yet the same critics who think Iran should have the right to have nuclear weapons are naïve to believe Iran wants them for scientific purposes (energy, medicine). How blind are these critics? Blind enough not to recognize that the bully in the neighborhood has a sinister agenda and would have no hesitation exterminating anyone including them. The majority of the Western world also does not understand the Islamic principles of takiya (taqiyya) and tawriya, described on page 44.

The worst offenders against Israel in the West are those who actually openly speak the name of the Lord, "Yahweh" (the God of the Bible in Hebrew—**the Holy One of Israel**). And yet in their next breath condemn Israel with great disdain and hatred. What's worse, some of these people believe they are well-informed because they unreasonably buy into the lies, the distortions, the intentional anti-Israel propaganda fabricated and underwritten by Israel's sworn enemies, "news" that finds its way into the mainstream media all over the world.

Though Adolf Hitler tried to destroy the Jews, God providentially used the world's guilt at that terrible fact to cause the creation of the nation of Israel. In 1948, May 15 at midnight, Israel took its place on the stage of world history. My friends, the clock started ticking. The prophetic countdown to Armageddon had begun. In my book, *Armageddon*, **I show that Ezekiel literally prophesied May 15, 1948 to the day. It literally works out to May 15, 1948.** Israel's rebirth was not an accident of politics or history. It is the plan of God and the clock has started ticking. —Grant Jeffrey (emphasis added)

"Now learn the parable of the fig tree [Israel]: when its branch has already become tender, and puts forth its leaves, you know that summer is near; even so you too, when you see all these things, recognize that He is near, right at the door. Truly I say to you, this generation will not pass away until all these things take place" (Matthew 24:32-34).

Recognition of modern-day Israel in 1948 began the "prophetic countdown to Armageddon" and the final years of history, as we know it. The rebirth of Israel is a major fulfilled prophetic sign showing that we are living very close to Christ's promised return. Does it make a bit of sense that this tiny nation is continuously being badgered, by the much larger countries surrounding her? Trying to force Israel to surrender pieces of land in order to appease her enemies for an unattainable "peace" is essentially picking a fight with God. What other nation on earth is hounded like this? Israel is the center of spiritual warfare because it is God's Holy Land. He has entrusted it to the Jewish people. It is not up for sale. It is God who ultimately holds the title deed. Jesus Christ took on a Jewish identity when He came to die for all of humanity, to be the sacrificial "lamb" for all our sins. Israel was His earthly home, and it is still "the apple of His eye."

> "For thus says the LORD of hosts; He sent Me after glory, to the nations which plunder you; for he who touches you touches the apple of His eye" (Zechariah 2:8).

> "For you are a holy people to the Lord your God; the Lord your God has chosen you to be a people for Himself, a special treasure above all the peoples on the face of the earth" (Deuteronomy 7:6).

If you reread the previous Scripture, notice: "in you [Israel] all the families of the earth shall be blessed." In other words, the blessings for all nations and people, "the families of the earth," are contingent on how Israel is treated. This includes, of course, the United States. Never before has Israel—the only democracy in the Middle East—received as much pressure and derogatory interference from the "Washington elite" as now. No one has the right to tell the people of Israel to give up land, stop building homes, or stop breathing air in their God-given land. The United States has always been Israel's greatest ally until very recently. That long-term friendship is on very shaky ground, thanks to the increased nefarious, busybody posturing of the current US administration. It is foolhardy to conspire against Israel. Israeli Prime Minister, Benjamin Netanyahu made the following statements in his speech before members of the American Israel Public Affairs Committee (AIPAC) on March 23, 2010 in Washington D.C.:

> The connection between the Jewish people and the Land of Israel cannot be denied. The connection between the Jewish people and Jerusalem cannot be denied. The Jewish people were building Jerusalem three thousand years ago, and the Jewish people are building Jerusalem today. Jerusalem is not a settlement. It is our capital!

The Western nations seem to be utterly blind to the life-and-death cultural differences between Islamic nations and the West. In his book, *Planet Earth—2000 A.D: Will Mankind Survive*, Hal Lindsey discusses a principle called "takiya":

[Takiya is] the right within Islam to fake peace when you're weak, so you can wait for better timing to conquer your enemy. There is a famous Arab saying: "When your enemy is strong, kiss his hand and pray that it will be broken one day." Hudayblya is a small oasis between Mecca and Medina where Muhammad fought a battle in the early years of Islam. When he saw he was losing the struggle, Muhammad signed a 10-year peace agreement with the people of Mecca. Two years later, when his forces were stronger and the Meccans were living securely and off their guard, Muhammad marched into the city and captured it (pp.256-257. Reference is made to Isaac Cohen: Chicago Tribune, September 23, 1993).

Moreover there is yet another Muslim technique called: Tawriya ("Creative Lying") advocated by Muslims. A doctrine that allows lying in just about any circumstance:

The authoritative *Hans Wehr Arabic-English Dictionary* defines *tawriya as,* "hiding, concealment; dissemblance, dissimulation, hypocrisy; equivocation, ambiguity, double-entendre, allusion." Conjugates of the trilateral root of the word, *w-r-y*, appear in the Quran in the context of hiding or concealing something (e.g., 5:31, 7:26). As Sheikh al-Munajid puts it: "Tawriya is permissible if it is necessary or serves a Sharia interest." Consider the countless "sharia interests" that can run directly counter to Western law and civilization; from empowering Islam, to subjugating infidels. To realize these Sharia interests, Muslims, through tawriya, are given a blank check to lie, which undoubtedly comes in handy—whether at high-level diplomatic meetings or the signing of peace-treaties. [1]

Endnotes
[1] http://www.raymondibrahim.com/11325/muslim-apologetic-tawriya

Land for Peace?

Previous American administrations, besides the current one have also strongly suggested sovereign Israel should forsake land with the naïve notion that the result would be "peace." The "peace process" cannot succeed because it is based on an unreasonable and totally fraudulent proposal, incomprehensively suggesting that by giving away land, there will be an assurance of peace. In 2005, Israel relinquished Gaza to the Palestinians. Soon after, the terrorist group Hamas was actually voted in by the same Palestinians who reside there. So they can blame no one but themselves for their continued demise.

It has been nothing but hell for the Palestinians who live there, and the Israelis have been constantly under attack from the terrorists in that region ever since. Where is the peace? And now Israel is required to hand over more land because some foreign political thugs say so? The Palestinians have Gaza, and Israel surrendered it for nothing but misery and heartache. But I can tell you this tragic situation, was specifically prophesied long ago by the Old Testament prophet, Zephaniah:

> "For Gaza shall be forsaken, and Ashkelon desolate; they shall drive out Ashdod at noonday. And Ekron shall be uprooted" (Zephaniah 2:4).

According to God's Word, trying to force Israel to give up land is definitely bad "policy." Those who oppose Israel should tread very carefully. Author Bill Koenig, has written a provocative book titled: *Eye to Eye - Facing the Consequences of Dividing Israel*, available in both English and Hebrew. He makes a strong case for how "land-for-peace" efforts have simultaneously resulted in negative, sometimes deadly, circumstances for those attempting to force Israel into an impossible situation. The following information is a brief synopsis well worth contemplating (from the contents of his book) as posted on Bill Koenig's website at: watch.org.

What do these [the following] major-record setting events have in common?

1. Nine of the ten costliest insurance events in U.S. history.
2. Six of the seven costliest hurricanes in U.S. history.
3. Three of the four largest tornado outbreaks in U.S. history.

45

4. Nine of the top ten natural disasters in U.S. history, ranked by FEMA relief costs.

5. The two largest terrorism events in U.S. history.

All of these major catastrophes and many others occurred or began on the very same day or within 24-hours of US presidents Bush, Clinton and Bush applying pressure on Israel to trade her land for promises of peace and security, sponsoring major land for peace meetings, making major public statements pertaining to Israel's covenant land and /or calling for a Palestinian state.

America is now experiencing the consequences of Middle East policies, which have been opposed to God's Word and to the preservation of His covenant land. Ever since the Madrid Conference of October 1991, the United States participation in Israel's destiny has been flawed when put in context of Holy Scripture. The event of September 11, 2001, was a national wake-up call.

In *Eye to Eye - Facing the Consequences of Dividing Israel*, the book documents what happens the same day or within 24 hours of Israel being pressured to divide her land. Here are a few examples:

There were 29 record-setting catastrophes or major events during President George H.W. Bush and [also] President Bill Clinton's presidencies.

There were 27 record-setting catastrophes or major events during President George W. Bush's first 45 months in office. There were eight periods of disruption in the United States following the 9/11 terror events from October 1, 2001 to January 9, 2004 when President George W. Bush attempted to divide Israel's land.

Europe began experiencing its hottest summer in 500 years and record-setting weather the week the Quartet's Road Map was delivered in 2003.

There were 31 major suicide bombings in Israel from December 1, 2001 to November 10, 2004, that occurred at the same time President George W. Bush or one of his top-level staff and/or one of Israel's top officials were working with the U.S. on either a cease-fire agreement, a peace deal, publicly stating Israel's approval of a Palestinian state, or Israel was about to evacuate property.

The book also documents what happened to previous American presidents (beginning with the presidency of Richard Nixon to the present) and Middle East leaders who were actively involved in the Middle East peace process during their time in office and/or afterwards.

After reading the previous information—just a small part of the events Bill Koenig reports in his book—it would be difficult to think every incident listed is just some sort of "coincidence." On April 19, 2010 Israel celebrated its independence. The *same* day, on April 19th the current U.S. administration announced that the United States would no longer automatically support Israel in the United Nations Security Council. Never before has there been such a strong abandonment of Israel by the United States. It is the first time—ever that the United States will no longer defend and stand with Israel in the UN Security Council. The very next day, on April the 20th the Deepwater Horizon oil rig exploded, causing the worst environmental disaster in United States history. Some might call this a coincidence. Or is it the insignia and judgment of God?

Another excellent book on this topic is titled: *God's Final Warning to America* by John McTernan. Although it was published in 1998, the author documents very important information everyone should be aware of. Here is a brief excerpt:

[October 30, 1991]: President George Bush opens the Madrid Conference with an initiative for a Middle East peace plan involving Israel's land. On the same day, an extremely rare storm forms off the coast of Nova Scotia. (It was eventually tagged "The Perfect Storm," and a book and movie were made about it.) Record-setting 100-foot waves form at sea and pound the New England Coast, even causing heavy damage to President Bush's home in Kennebunkport, Maine.

Jesus the Messiah and Israel Are Inseparable
Intricately Entwined Forever

Anyone who attacks or threatens Israel is in essence attacking the God of Abraham, Isaac and Jacob—God Almighty Himself.

47

Israel's Faithful Messiah

From God's Covenant with David
1 Chronicles 17:22-24

"And who *is* like Your people Israel, the one nation on the earth whom God went to redeem for Himself *as* a people—to make for Yourself a name by great and awesome deeds, by driving out nations from before Your people whom You redeemed from Egypt?

For You have made Your people Israel Your very own people forever; and You, LORD, have become their God.

And now, O LORD, the word which You have spoken concerning Your servant and concerning his house, *let it* be established forever, and do as You have said.

So let it be established, that Your name may be magnified forever, saying, 'The LORD of hosts, the God of Israel, *is* Israel's God.' And let the house of Your servant David be established before You."

Jeremiah 24:6-8

"For I will set My eyes on them for good, and will bring them back to this land; I will build them and not pull *them* down, and I will plant them and not pluck *them* up.

Then I will give them a heart to know Me, that I *am* the LORD; and they shall be My people, and I will be their God, for they shall return to Me with their whole heart."

Satan's Crusade Against Israel and God

Israel as a whole has totally rejected Christ. Israel generally does not recognize Him for who He is. But Israel *will* repent. The Lord tells us through Old Testament Scripture that Israel must repent and cry out to Him. That is what God says must be done before there can be a Second Coming.

> "And it shall come to pass in all the land," says the LORD, "*That* two-thirds in it shall be cut off *and* die. But one-third shall be left in it: I will bring the one-third through the fire, will refine them as silver is refined, and test them as gold is tested. They will call on My name, and I will answer them. I will say, 'This is My people'; and each one will say, 'The Lord is My God'" (Zechariah 13:8-9).

The majority of Jews have rejected their Messiah for thousands of years. Israel must (and will) recognize and acknowledge Jesus the Christ, their true Messiah before He will return. Israel must urgently cry out to Him. God's archenemy—the devil is obsessed with eradicating the Jews. If the Jews can be eliminated, they will not be able to send that pleading, prophesied, necessary and urgent call to the Lord, begging for His return.

Satan would then have complete control of this planet. He knows Scripture states Messiah Jesus will not come back until Israel gets it together, recognizes, and accepts the identity of their true Messiah, and repents. So: No Jews, no Messiah. That is Satan's goal. What a dream come true that would be for the devil and his wicked aspirations. It would mean certain unrestrained terror would be unleashed on the entire human race. Of course that will not happen. The devil will not be able to highjack Messiah's plan of redemption for Israel. God will prevail and win this intense and complex war between good and evil. And Satan knows it.

> "He was in the world, and the world was made by Him, and the world knew Him not. He came to His own, and those who were His own [the Jews] did not receive Him" (John 1:10-11).

Jesus the Messiah Wept over Jerusalem

Christ Is the Image of the Invisible God

Colossians 1:15-17

"He [Christ] is the image of the invisible God, the firstborn over all creation.

For by Him all things were created that are in heaven and that are in earth, visible and invisible, whether thrones or dominions or principalities or powers.

All things were created through Him and for Him. And He is before all things, and in Him all things consist [are held together]."

"Now as He drew near, He saw the city and wept over it" (Luke 19:41).

Israel Will Accept Messiah Jesus and Repent

In the following verses we read that Israel *will* seek their Savior, Yeshua Ha Mashiach, wholeheartedly repent and finally accept Him as their Messiah:

"I will go away and return to My place until they acknowledge their guilt and seek My face; in their affliction they will earnestly seek me" (Hosea 5:15).

For two days at the very end of the Tribulation the Jews will be praying and pleading for the Lord's return, then on the third day He will come and save repentant Israel.

"Come and let us return to the LORD; For He has torn, but He will heal us; He has stricken, but He will bind us up. After two days He will revive us; on the third day He will rise us up, that we may live in His sight. Let us know, let us pursue the knowledge of the LORD. His going forth is established as the morning; He will come to us like the rain, like the latter and former rain to the earth" (Hosea 6:1-3).

"And I will pour out on the house of David and on the inhabitants of Jerusalem, the Spirit of grace and of supplication; so that they will look unto Me whom they have pierced; and they will mourn for Him, as one mourns for an only son, and they will weep bitterly over Him, like the bitter weeping over a first-born" (Zechariah 12:10).

Evil, vicious, satanic forces are behind the ongoing attacks against Israel. God intends to put an end to it. The hate campaign and the verbal and physical assaults that threaten to totally demolish Israel will ultimately bring on Armageddon. Tragically, the prophet Zechariah forewarned that two-thirds of the Jewish population would be already wiped out *before* that final battle at Armageddon.

Armageddon is really more of an event than it is an actual battle. As a location, Armageddon relates to the northern part of Israel, in the hill country surrounding the Plain of Megiddo and the nearby Plain of Esdraelon. It is there that all the nations led by Antichrist will be gathered to challenge and assault Jesus Christ when He returns at the very end of the seven-year Tribulation. That will be the final battle. And make no mistake about it: The Lord Himself will draw His enemies and the enemies of Israel to that last climactic battle. It might look like Antichrist and his yes-men are in control, but ultimately it will be the Messiah of Israel who will gather them to their final place of expulsion:

"I will also gather all nations, and bring them down to the Valley of Jehoshaphat; and I will enter into judgment with them there on account of My people, My heritage Israel, whom they have scattered among the nations; they have also divided up My land" (Joel 3:2).

Armageddon will be a long, drawn-out series of incursions beginning around the mid-point of the coming seven-year Tribulation. This series of battles will culminate in one conclusive short war at the end of the Tribulation (Revelation 16). The actual final war—the War of the Great Day of God the Almighty will take place around Jerusalem (Zechariah 12:2-3). Current events undeniably point to that final war and the soon return of Messiah Jesus. Conditions in Israel will severely deteriorate during the Great Tribulation, to the point that Israel will be beaten down dramatically.

Jerusalem will most definitely fall to the prophesied one-world ruler, Antichrist—after very intense fighting. A small number of Jews will survive and stay in Jerusalem but under Antichrist's diabolic, oppressive rule. Scripture reveals some will have already escaped from Israel to Southern Jordan to hide from Antichrist and his armies. In the book of Daniel, part of the Old Testament, we learn that Jordan will be the one country that does not fall under Antichrist's vicious, tyrannical control during the Tribulation years (Daniel 11:41): Moab (Central Jordanians), Ammon (Northern Jordanians) and Edom (Southern Jordanians).

These surviving Jews will be at their wits' end. Finally, after Israel's long history of rejecting Jesus of Nazareth—their Messiah, they will finally cry out to Him for forgiveness and beg Him to rescue them from the horrors they face. They will recognize and confess the sins of their forefathers who rejected Yeshua, Jesus and will ask for deliverance. As I said before, their plea to the Lord will last two days, and then on the third day He will answer their cries (Hosea 6:2).

We have already established that Old Testament Scripture tells us the Lord will not return until Israel recognizes her Messiah—repents, and with tremendous grief, asks Him to return to rescue them, to restore their covenant land and nation mercilessly ravaged by war. In reference to this, Jesus said: "For I say to you, from now on you shall not see Me until you say, 'BLESSED IS HE WHO COMES IN THE NAME OF THE LORD'" (Matthew 23:39).

Romans 11:25-27

"For I do not desire, brethren, that you should be ignorant of this mystery, lest you should be wise in your own opinion, that blindness in part has happened to Israel until the fullness of the Gentiles has come in. And so all Israel will be saved, as it is written:

The Deliverer [Messiah Jesus] will come out of Zion, and He will turn away ungodliness from Jacob; for this is My covenant with them, when I take away their sins."

How Much Longer until the Second Coming?

In the Old Testament, Psalm 80 is a prayer for Israel's restoration and Isaiah 64 is a prayer for mercy and help. These are good examples of the type of heartrending call Israel will dispatch to Messiah Jesus. Considering the intensification of prophetic signs we have observed since Israel became a nation in 1948, it is apparent that all signs point toward this generation as the generation that will see Messiah's return; the Second Coming of Christ.

The majority of scholars agree that those who were born around the time modern Israel was reestablished can expect to see all prophecy, including the return of Messiah Jesus come to pass. The soon return of the Lord is directly tied to the return of the Jews to the land of Israel and the rebirth of the nation of Israel. Israel's problems will escalate, but Messiah Jesus will faithfully intervene at the end of the seven-year Tribulation, defeating Antichrist and his armies, and restoring Israel forever.

"The days of our lives are seventy years; and if by reason of strength they are eighty years" (Psalm 90:10a).

A generation, according to Psalm 90 is seventy years—or eighty for those who are exceptionally able-bodied. The rebirth of Israel as a nation came about in 1948. We are now well into the year 2012. Those who were born around 1948 fall into this life-span category. If you do the math based on this Scripture, you will see there isn't much time left before the Lord returns. Earlier on page 42, I quoted Matthew 24:32-34 when Jesus said: "this generation will not pass away until all these things take place." "This generation" is in reference to those who will witness the things Jesus described relating to the end of the age in Matthew 24, including the restoration of the nation of Israel in *one* day (May 14, 1948).

An Awesome Fulfillment of Prophecy

"Before she travailed, she brought forth; before her pain came, she gave birth to a boy. Who has heard of such a thing? Who has seen such things? **Can a land be born in one day?** Can a nation be brought forth all at once?" (Isaiah 66:7-8a).

54

The previous Scripture shows that the prophet Isaiah foretold the rebirth of Israel, which came about "in one day" (on May 14, 1948). We are living in the generation pictured by the Jewish boy in Isaiah 66:7-8a. The Jewish boy portrays how Israel will grow-up as a nation, and by the time he is eighty (2028), the Millennium could very well begin. I think this is an interesting and a probable analysis, but the bottom line is that no one can say for sure when the Lord will return. The Lord's return may happen sooner or even sometime past the eighty-year mark. Scripture is not exactly precise on where within or around these life-span years (70-80) the Rapture and Tribulation will take place. Although if we watch for the foreshadowing signs we can have a general idea when these critical prophetic events will come to fulfillment, and when the millennial reign of Messiah Jesus will begin. The important thing is to stay vigilant and share the gospel at every opportunity while there is still time.

On the following pages is an excerpt from the late Grant Jeffrey from his book, *Triumphant Return - The Coming Kingdom of God*, wherein we learn more about the Fig Tree—the symbol of Israel.

Ancient Evidence that the Fig Tree Is a Symbol of Israel
Apocalypse of Peter (Ethiopic Edition)

The Apocalypse of Peter is a non-canonical manuscript from approximately A.D. 120 that is an early Christian commentary on Jesus' famous prophecy given to His disciples on the Mount of Olives regarding the signs to His return in the last days. This remarkable manuscript documents the understanding of the early post-apostolic church that Jesus' famous prophetic parable about the budding of the fig-tree was understood by the Jewish Christians to be a clear prophecy of the rebirth of the nation Israel in the last days prior to Christ's return.

1. And when he was seated on the Mount of Olives, his own came unto him, and we entreated and implored him severally and besought him, saying unto him:

"Make known unto us what are the signs of thy Parousia and of the end of the world, that we may perceive and mark the time of thy Parousia and instruct those who come after us, to whom we preach the word of thy gospel and whom we install in thy church, in order that they, when they hear it, may take heed to themselves that they mark the time of thy coming."

And our Lord answered and said unto us, "Take heed that men deceive you not and that ye do not become doubters and serve other gods. Many will come in my name saying 'I am Christ.' Believe them not and draw not near unto them.

For the coming of the Son of God will not be manifest, but like the lightning which shineth from the east to the west, so shall I come on the clouds of heaven with a great host in my glory, with my cross going before my face will I come in my glory, shining seven times as bright as the sun will I come in my glory, with all my saints, my angels, when my Father will place a crown upon my head, that I may judge the living and the dead and recompense every man according to his work."

2. And ye, receive ye the parable of the fig-tree thereon: as soon as its shoots have gone forth and its boughs have sprouted, the end of the world will come. And I, Peter, answered and said unto him, "Explain to me concerning the fig-tree, [and] how we shall perceive it, for throughout all its days does the fig-tree sprout and every year it brings forth its fruit [and] for its master.

What (then) meaneth the parable of the fig-tree? We know it not." And the Master answered and said unto me, "Dost thou not understand that the fig-tree is the house of Israel? Even as a man hath planted a fig tree in his garden and it brought forth no fruit, and he sought its fruit for many years.

When he found it not, he said to the keeper of his garden, "Uproot the fig-tree that our land may not be unfruitful for us." And the gardener said to God, 'We thy servants (?) wish to clear it (of weeds) and to dig' the ground around it and to water it.

If it does not then bear fruit, we will immediately remove its roots from the garden and plant another one in its place.' Hast thou not grasped that the fig-tree is the house of Israel?

Verily, I say to you that when its boughs have sprouted at the end, then shall deceiving Christs come, and awaken hope (with the words): 'I am the Christ, who am (now) come into the world.'

And when they shall see the wickedness of their deeds (even of the false christs) they shall turn away after them and deny him to whom our fathers gave praise (?), the first Christ whom they crucified and thereby sinned exceedingly.

But this deceiver is not the Christ. And when they reject him, he will kill with the sword (dagger) and there shall be many martyrs.

Then shall the boughs of the fig tree, i.e. the house of Israel, sprout, and there shall be many martyrs by his hand: they shall be killed and become martyrs.

Enoch and Elias will be sent to instruct them that this is the deceiver who must come into the world and do signs and wonders in order to deceive.

And therefore shall they that are slain by his hand be martyrs and shall be reckoned among the good and righteous martyrs who have pleased God in their life.

What Will God Do
When Israel Is Attacked?

"This is what will happen in that day: When Gog attacks the land of Israel, my hot anger will be aroused, declares the Sovereign LORD.

In my zeal and fiery wrath I declare that at that time there shall be a great earthquake in the land of Israel.

The fish of the sea, the birds of the air, the beasts of the field, every creature that moves along the ground, and all the people on the face of the earth will tremble at my presence.

The mountains will be overturned, the cliffs will crumble and every wall will fall to the ground.

I will summon a sword against Gog on all my mountains, declares the Sovereign LORD. Every man's sword will be against his brother.

I will execute judgment upon him with plague and bloodshed; I will pour down torrents of rain, hailstones and burning sulfur on him and on his troops and on the many nations with him."

—Ezekiel 38:18-22

Battle of Ezekiel 38 and 39—The Gog-Magog War

Another important prophesied war is on the near horizon. Of course, Israel will be the target. In the Bible, the battle of Ezekiel 38 and 39 (Gog-Magog war) is given the most *detailed* description of any prophesied future war. It is going to happen soon and the entire world will be affected by it. This war will bring about great devastation, but during and at the end of the Tribulation there will be utter destruction.

Russia will lead a coalition of mostly Islamic nations against Israel. This war will occur before the Tribulation. It could begin as early as three and one-half years *before* the Tribulation. It will take seven years to clean up the damage, and seven-months to bury the dead (Ezekiel 39:9,12). The Lord Himself will supernaturally intervene, and the majority of the caustic aggressors will be obliterated. These warriors will turn against each other. God will shake the earth with tremendous power and the invaders will wish they had never even had a bad thought about Israel. Scripture tells us this war will spread:

> "And **I** [God] **will send fire** on Magog [Russia] and those who live in security in the coastlands. Then they shall know that I *am* the LORD.
>
> So I will make My holy name known in the midst of My people Israel, and I will not *let them* profane My holy name anymore.
>
> **Then the nations shall know that I *am* the LORD, the Holy One in Israel**" (Ezekiel 39:6-7).

No one but God Himself will help rescue Israel when she is attacked. Without God's intervention, Israel will have no chance to survive this invasion. God *will* preserve His chosen nation. He will not be doing this for Israel's sake, but for His own sake, to make a powerful statement that He is in control, and that He is Almighty God and can no longer be ignored. God will actually bring these nations against Israel who has rejected Him—for His glory. It is a major wake-up call to the entire world, and primarily for Israel, that the God of Abraham, Isaac, and Jacob lives forever and is King.

Everyone should realize that without Him, they are condemned. Followers of Allah will be left scrambling trying to figure out how they can possibly continue claiming that Allah is God. Allah will be nowhere to be found when these heavily numbered, primarily Muslim forces march against Israel.

The "coastlands" referred to in the previous Scripture are also destined to experience the wrath of God for participating in the offense against Israel, indicating that the Muslim population will significantly decrease. The coastlands are maritime regions in the Middle East with heavy Muslim populations. These are homelands to those who will assist Russia against Israel with their fleets and troops. The "coastlands" extend to what would actually encompass global Islam, reaching all around the world, including Indonesia.

One of the results of this war will very likely be the removal of a significant portion of Islamic domination. It is also very likely that Mecca, the al-Aqsa Mosque and the Dome of the Rock will to be severely damaged or destroyed by the tremendous earthquake cited in Ezekiel 38:19. It will not be possible for a one-world government, a one-world church and a one-world economic system to take hold unless the influence of Islam is tremendously reduced or removed.

It is apparent to me that it would be nearly impossible for the prophesied one-world government, a world economic system, and a world church to be established while Islam is standing in the front wings of world dominance. From studying Scripture, it is my point of view that an ecumenical, apostate one-world church is much more likely than an Islamic religious take-over. Although at the moment, it certainly does appear that Islam, because of its enormous population and wealth could rule the entire world. But as we see from Scripture, there is a point when God will no longer sit quietly on the sidelines and allow His holy name to be desecrated.

Israel is the "apple of God's eye." Jerusalem *is* the capital of Israel. The Dome of the Rock is located in Jerusalem on the Temple Mount, along with the al-Aqsa Mosque. These Muslim representations are an insult and disgrace to the God of Abraham, Isaac and Jacob. The irreverent Islamic inscriptions on the Dome of the Rock of course deny that Jesus is the Son of God, and attempt to reduce His identity to a mere messenger and a servant to the god they refer to as: Allah. Another one of their inscriptions denies the blessed Trinity.

On the following page is a sample of an Islamic inscription (translated) etched at the Dome of the Rock on the Inner Face of the Octagonal Arcade, blaspheming Almighty God:

"The unity of God and prophecy of Muhammad are true. The Sonship of Jesus and the Trinity are false."

—*Biblical Archaeology Review*, July 2006

In the Bible we learn the truth about the Trinity: 1 John 5:7, "and these three are one." Also, in the same verse, Jesus the Messiah is addressed as the "Word." When the apostle John described the Second Coming of Christ in Revelation 19:13, another reference again is made to Jesus as: "The Word of God." Jesus *is* the Word of God.

"For there are three that bear witness in heaven; the Father, the Word [Jesus], and the Holy Spirit; **and these three are one"** (1 John 5:7).

"And *He is* clothed with a robe dipped in blood; and **His name** [Jesus] **is called The Word of God**" (Revelation 19:13).

Scripture is clear that the God of Abraham, Isaac and Jacob will cause the world to know He is in control. The battle of Ezekiel 38 and 39 will also open the door for the continuing fulfillment of key prophetic Scriptures that will lead to the Tribulation and the final battle of Armageddon.

"I will set My glory among the nations; all the nations shall see My judgment which I have executed, and My hand which I have laid on them. So the house of Israel shall know that I am the LORD their God from that day forward" (Ezekiel 39:21-22).

"Therefore behold, the days are coming, says the LORD, that it shall no more be said, 'The LORD lives who brought up the children of Israel from the land of Egypt, but the LORD lives who brought up the children of Israel from the land of the north and from all the lands where He had driven them.' For I will bring them back into their land which I gave to their fathers" (Jeremiah 16:14-15).

God and God alone should get all the credit for saving Israel from the determined invaders. His indisputable presence *will* be revealed. It will be obvious to the entire world that He subverted the advancing armies and that the Israelis could not have survived the assaults without His supernatural hand reaching out to save them. The nations will know that God interjected His awesome might into that precise time in history. No longer will He be identified as the God who saved the Old Testament Jews from Egyptian enslavement. But because the Lord's overwhelming miracles during the battle of Ezekiel 38 and 39 will override even those of the Exodus He will be known as the God "who brought up the children of Israel from the land of the north" (Jeremiah, 16:14-15, 23:8).

"You will come up against My people Israel like a cloud, to cover the land. It will be in the latter days that I will bring you against My land, so that the nations may know Me, when I am hallowed in you, O Gog, before their eyes" (Ezekiel 38:16).

"And I will bring him to judgment with pestilence and bloodshed; I will rain down on him, on his troops, and on the many peoples who *are* with him, flooding rain, great hailstones, fire, and brimstone.

Thus I will magnify Myself and sanctify Myself, and I will be known in the eyes of many nations. Then they shall know that I *am* the LORD" (Ezekiel 38:22-23).

Notice the verse says the Lord will intervene and execute His judgment on the invading troops with "pestilence and bloodshed" and by using extremely intense weather patterns and natural elements: Flooding rain, great hailstones, fire, and brimstone. **Because of this intervention by God Almighty, no one will be able to deny that it was He, who saved Israel from the descending armies.** Some students of Bible prophecy suggest that there will be a nuclear exchange during this battle and even attempt to derive a nuclear holocaust from the passages in Ezekiel 39:11-16; pure speculation which cannot be substantiated.

We dare not allow any commentators to take away from God the great victory of this battle. Scripture tells us in no uncertain terms that it is He who will be magnified. Scripture tells us that it is distinctly God who will obliterate the enemy. Radioactive material from the nuclear weapons would affect not only the invading troops, but the Israelis as well. Even if nuclear weapons could be used successfully *only* against the enemy, then those who would deliver them would receive the credit, and not the Lord.

The book of Exodus is filled with examples of how God took complete control over the elements when He unleashed plagues and judgments upon Egypt. God has a history of exerting absolute control utilizing matter: "nature" to bring about his judgments and miraculous interventions. When He executed judgment on Sodom and Gomorrah, He rained down fire and brimstone (Genesis 19:24). It makes no sense that the same living God would suddenly rely on human technology to bring about His signature, sovereign judgment.

God is the same yesterday, today and forever. When God tells us in Scripture that He is going to showcase His enormous overpowering miracles displaying His authenticity to the world, we should believe Him. He does not need to employ understudies using man-made super weapons to assist Him with the job.

"For I *am* the LORD, I do not change" (Malachi 3:6a).

Now let's read the definition of "brimstone"—one of the natural elements that God will use against the invading troops during this prophesied attack against Israel. We will also read about the Lord's history of using natural materials when delivering judgment onto a people or situation:

Brimstone - gaphrith, related to gopher wood, and so expressing any inflammable substance, as sulphur, which burns with a suffocating smell. It is a mineral found in quantities on the shores of the Dead Sea. It was the instrument used in destroying Sodom and Gomorrah, the adjoining cities of the plain (Genesis 19:24), for divine miracle does not supersede the use of God's existing natural agents, but moves in connection with them. An image of every visitation of God's vengeance on the ungodly, especially of the final one (Deuteronomy 29:23; Job 18:15; Psalm 11:6; Isaiah 34:9; Ezekiel 38:22; Revelation 19:20; Revelation 20:10; Revelation 21:8).

Because of the awe-inspiring miracles performed by the Lord during the battle of Ezekiel 38 and 39, Israel and the Jews as a whole will experience a huge resurgence in their quest for God—for their Messiah. The entire world will have a chance to see God in action, as the true protector of Israel and many will come to salvation around that time.

Scripture indicates the astonishing battle of Ezekiel 38 and 39 will take place before the prophesied Tribulation opening up tremendous opportunities to share the Word of God. After this battle a large segment of Israel will be saved (converted) and the nation of Israel will turn back to Jehovah God after having rejected Him for over 2,000 years. The Holy Spirit will be poured out on them bringing about a revival in Israel fulfilling the prophecies of Joel 2:28b-29, double referenced in (Acts 2:17-18), when the Jews will prophesy, dream dreams and see visions. In verse 29 Joel wrote: "And also upon the servants and upon handmaids in those days will I pour out My Spirit."

Joel is speaking about the Millennium in verses 21-28a, and then halfway through verse 28 he switches to the time prior to the Rapture and the Tribulation. The Joel 2:28b-29 prophecies are directed to the nation of Israel—to the Jews. It should be noted, earlier in verse 23; Joel's prophecies are specifically to the nation of Israel, to the "children of Zion.

In verses 28-29 he is still making reference to the "children of Zion." These prophecies are about God pouring out His Spirit upon Jews. In the New Testament Peter takes an application of these passages in Acts 2:17-18. As mentioned earlier, nations throughout the entire world will witness and realize the miraculous intervention by God Himself (Ezekiel 38:23; 39:7, 21).

Furthermore, in Joel 2:30-32, Joel distinctly presents a case for the Pre-Tribulation Rapture. He describes *when* this outpouring of the Spirit upon the Jews will happen: Prior to the Rapture and the Tribulation. All believers, including the new converts will "escape" the Tribulation by way of the Rapture *before* the Tribulation begins. In the next chapter, the Rapture—the snatching away by God of all true believers is discussed extensively.

Joel 2:30-32

"And I will show wonders in the heavens and in the earth: The sun shall be turned into darkness and the moon into blood, **before the great and awesome day of the LORD.** And it shall come to pass, that whosoever shall call on the name of Jehovah shall be delivered for in mount Zion and in Jerusalem **there shall be those that escape** as Jehovah hath said, and among the remnant those whom Jehovah doth call."

Footnote
Dr. Arnold Fruchtenbaum also supports the view that the Gog-Magog invasion will take place prior to the Tribulation, *Footsteps of the Messiah*, page121, (The Pre -Tribulation View).

Escalating Middle East Strife

Before the Tribulation begins, there will be great devastation in Egypt as shown in the following passages. Considering what we currently hear and read in the daily news headlines, this prophecy (tied in with the battle of Ezekiel 38 and 39) is nearing its time of fulfillment. Egypt is plagued with problems, protests and extreme political upheaval.

"The word of Jehovah came again unto me, saying, 'Son of man, prophesy,' and say, thus saith the Lord Jehovah: Wail ye, Alas for the day! **For the day is near, even the day of Jehovah is near**; it shall be a day of clouds, a time of nations, and a sword shall come upon Egypt, and anguish shall be in Ethiopia, when the slain shall fall in Egypt; and they shall take away her multitude, and her foundations shall be broken down, Ethiopia, and Put [Libya], and Lud and all the mingled people, and Cub, and the children of the land that is in league, shall fall with them by the sword. Thus saith Jehovah: They also that uphold Egypt shall fall; and the pride of her power shall come down" (Ezekiel 30:1-8).

We know that a number of intense Middle East wars have already taken place in our lifetime. To some degree, war is constantly going on around Israel. Russia is a staunch ally of Iran, and if there is a war involving Iran, it could be a precursor to bring about or hasten the battle of Ezekiel 38 and 39. After all, Russia is prophesied to lead the Muslim alliances against Israel (Ezekiel 38:18). In the book of Isaiah, there is a prophecy that has not yet been fulfilled:

"The burden against Damascus. Behold, Damascus will cease from *being* a city. And it will be a ruinous heap" (Isaiah 17:1).

Syria's involvement in the ongoing aggression to eliminate Israel will bring catastrophe to that nation. Additionally, current news reports point to extreme political and civil devastation growing within Syria. In 2007, Israeli intelligence discovered that in the desolate Syrian Desert, a facility was in the process of manufacturing nuclear weapons. It was being aided by North Korea. Of course, Israel did what she had to do and sent a few jets overhead to take care of the problem. The Israelis were able to unscramble the radar so the visit was a complete surprise to the Syrians and everyone else involved, including Iran. It is often said that

Syria is just Iran's proxy. Russia also, is a great ally and defender of Syria arming the anti-Israel neighbor with missiles and other weapons.

Damascus is a major hub for terrorists. There is a very strong possibility that the future destruction of this ancient city will be somehow tied into the war of Ezekiel 38 and 39 when the Russians, along with the group of primarily Islamic nations attempt to destroy Israel. As previously stated, that attack will end in defeat for that perverse coalition because of God's supernatural intervention. The destruction of Damascus could very well jumpstart that attack against Israel.

On page 91, I have included a letter written by, Amir Tsarfati, a native Israeli, regarding Syria. Amir is a Jewish believer, a Hebrew Christian from the tribe of Judah. He accepted Messiah Jesus as his Savior as a young teen-ager in Israel. He is a former deputy governor of Jericho, and was also a captain in the Israeli army. While Amir was deputy governor, the Israeli government entrusted him with what are now known as the famous Oslo Accords documents. This was long before his Israeli counterparts and the rest of the world knew anything about these important declarations regarding the Israeli-Palestinian conflicts. Today Amir resides in Jerusalem.

When he is not traveling and teaching the Word of God, he is a licensed tour guide in Israel—and as I understand, he is a very good one. He is an excellent and charming speaker who frequently travels to the US and other countries to share the gospel and prophetically relevant news from Israel. In 2007, he told audiences at some Calvary Chapel churches in America that Israeli newspaper headlines stated: "Will Syria Be Next?" Certainly, the situation with Syria is becoming very intense, and has most definitely not improved since 2007. There is a very strong possibility that the biblical prophecy regarding the destruction of Damascus is not far off in the future.

In February of 2011, Western Intelligence agencies discovered another nuclear plant in Syria—in a Damascus suburb. In addition, a German newspaper, the *Süddeutsche Zeitung (SZ)*, reported that it received photos of the site, but will not publish them because inferences can be made as to when they were taken, and thus to who leaked them. In addition, Washington's Institute for Science and International Security (ISIS) published photos on February 23, 2011 of one of three more sites that are believed to be connected to the Al-Kibar facility destroyed in 2007, as reported in *Arutz Sheva, Israel National News* on February 24, 2011.

An incident involving the destruction of Iran's nuclear facilities is very possible in the near future. As difficult and challenging as it may seem strategically, Israel may find a way to take out the areas that house Iran's nuclear weapons programs such as the Fordo site located deep in the mountains of Iran, near the city of Qom (see page 68). Or perhaps the Israeli's have some other clever clandestine strategies in mind to put an end to Iran's potential nuclear holocaust. I would not underestimate the Israeli's when it comes to protecting their homeland and their very existence.

Intense uprisings in the Middle East countries are quickly escalating. Iran is gaining more control of the entire region while its leaders are continuing to loudly threaten Israel and all Jews with comments like: "The Zionist regime will be wiped soon" (see pages 101-103). Radicals are gaining strength, while traditional moderate Arab leaderships are weakening. Egypt has fallen apart and is in total chaos—a dangerous situation most likely leading to an Iranian type extremist hard-line government—leading to its complete demise. In July of 2012 Egypt's Muslim Brotherhood President-Elect Morsi, vowed to free the blind Sheikh the mastermind of the 1993 World Trade Center bombing, exposing himself for the radical Islamist that he is. His newly elected regime has also promised to impose Sharia Law upon Egypt despite the ongoing protests.

Lebanon, Israel's neighbor to the north has essentially been taken over by Iran gaining much closer proximity to Israel. Iraq is on the verge of being taken over by pro-Iran Shiite factions. It is only a matter of time until all the prophesied Middle East wars will take place. It is very possible that Israel will defend herself against Iranian nuclear threats, even *before* the battle of Ezekiel 38 and 39 takes place. We certainly are living in very perilous times in these last days.

It is impossible to keep up with the fast-moving events involving the Middle East. The following headlines and brief excerpts are just a tiny glimpse into the intense uprisings, turmoil and power plays that have dominated the world news headlines year after year, progressively increasing to the point of bringing some major biblical prophecies into the forefront of everyday discussions. No doubt some of these situations are being methodically manipulated; by those who have diabolical, hidden agendas and want to bring about "change." Change, that is not in the best interest of freedom-loving people. But God cannot be outwitted. He has the final say regardless of what any government or group of elitists try to do.

Iran builds New Eastern Front in Iraq against Israel, Jordan
DEBKAfile Exclusive Report January 6, 2011
Iraq's neighbors, Jordan and Saudi Arabia, could only shudder at the sight of the two black-turbaned Shiite extremists taking charge of Iraq on behalf of Revolutionary Iran against no opposition. This pair and Maliki have taken out of the hands of Washington and Baghdad the decision on whether a reduced US force stays on in Iraq after the main force departs in 11 months' time. Moqtada Sadr has vowed to remove every last American from Iraqi soil and no one shows any sign of stopping him. US troops will be replaced by Shiite-dominated Iraqi forces, the Shiite militias commanded and funded by the Iranian Revolutionary Guards Al Qods Brigades and Hizballah militia detachments transferred from Lebanon.Iran will in the coming months consolidate the Shiite takeover over Iraq.

Hizballah will win a place in the sun and strategic depth after being squeezed between Syria, Israel and the sea. After U.S. troops exit Iraq, the Iranians will be able to deploy their missiles and Hizballah's rockets in the bases the Americans leave behind in Iraq and point them at Israel, Jordan and Saudi Arabia.

Iran plans one-kiloton underground nuclear test in 2012
DEBKAfile Special Report January 10, 2012
According to debkafile's Iranian sources, Tehran is preparing an underground test of a one-kiloton nuclear device during 2012, much like the test carried out by North Korea in 2006.Underground facilities are under construction in great secrecy behind the noise and fury raised by the start of advanced uranium enrichment at Iran's fortified, subterranean Fordo site near Qom. All the sanctions imposed so far for halting Iran's progress toward a nuclear weapon have had the reverse effect, stimulating rather than cooling its eagerness to acquire a bomb.

Russia Suspected of Sending Ammo to Assad
By Chana Ya'ar First Publish: 1/15/2012
Israel National News - Russia last week managed to out smart the EU sanctions against Syria and slipped a ship filled with bullets through to the port of Tartus.

Russia: Attack on Tehran Is Attack on Moscow
By Tzvi Ben Gedalyahu First Publish: 1/15/2012,
Israel National News - Russia has given Iran its bear hug and warns Israel and the West that an attack on Tehran would be considered an attack on Moscow.

Some 200,000 missiles aimed consistently at Israel, Top IDF Says
Haaretz.com Published Friday, February 3, 2012
By Amos Harel
Head of military intelligence Aviv Kochavi reiterates army estimates that Iran could further enrich that uranium it already has to create 4 atomic bombs. About 200,000 missiles are aimed at Israel at any given time, a top Israel Defense Forces officer said on Thursday, adding that Iran's ability to obtain nuclear weapons was solely dependent on the will of Iranian Supreme Leader Ayatollah Ali Khamenei.

Analyst: Israel could destroy Iran nuke capacity with selective strikes - Geostrategy-Direct.com March 5, 2012
LONDON - A former senior German defense official says that the Israel Air Force is capable of destroying Iran's key nuclear facilities within hours. Hans Ruhle, planning director of the German Defense Ministry from 1982 to 1988, said Israel could torpedo Iranian nuclear weapons development for years by bombing only six of up to 30 Iranian sites. "Israel has enough aircraft with suitable weapons to destroy Iran's sustainable nuclear program," Ruhle said.

Iran threatens Northern Israel with bombardment from Lebanon
DEBKAfile Exclusive Report March 14, 2012
Tehran has begun capitalizing on its allies" two perceived victories: Bashar Assad's success in seizing Idlib from rebel hands and the Palestinian Jihad Islami's triumphal missile assault from Gaza. The Iranians are now moving forward with plans to match the Palestinian assault on southern Israel with an offensive on the north from Lebanon. This is reported by debkafile's exclusive sources in the wake of a visit paid by high-ranking Iranian and Hizballah officials Wednesday morning, March 14, to the Lebanese-Israeli border region opposite Metulah, Israel's northernmost town at the tip of the Galilee Panhandle. The Iranian group, led by Ali Akbar Javanfekr, President Mahmoud Ahmadinejad's spokesman, arrived in a heavily guarded

convoy at the Fatma outpost opposite Metulah for its rendezvous with Hizballah military intelligence officers. Once there, they kept moving around near the Lebanese-Israeli border fence. At times, they came up close and examined the Israel Defense Forces' ongoing work for fortifying the border fence and upgrading it from a boundary marker to a military barrier able to withstand terrorist incursions into the Galilee panhandle. The Iranian visitor, Javanfekr, commented in the hearing of our sources: **"The Zionists can build any wall they like, whether of concrete, iron or plastic, but we and Hizballah will knock it down, like Israel itself."** He pitched his voice loudly enough to carry across the border (emphasis added).

Iran threatens Hormuz and world oil supply after trade links cutoff DEBKAfile Exclusive Report March 18, 2012
Former Intelligence Minister Ali Falahian, Iran's senior spokesman on sanctions, said Sunday, March 18, that if the US and Europe think they can ignore international law to promote their interests, they should know that Iran will respond in kind everywhere it can. "I suggest that the West take seriously our threat to close the Strait of Hormuz," he said in Tehran's first response to the SWIFT decision to sever ties with Iranian banks to enforce European sanctions on its nuclear program.

A large fleet of 4 U.S. and French nuclear aircraft carriers and a dozen or more minesweepers and mine-hunting helicopters have piled up on both sides of the Strait of Hormuz, through which 17 percent of the world's daily oil supply passes, and Israeli naval vessels have deployed in the Red Sea. Debkafile's military and intelligence sources estimate Tehran may make good on its threats by trying to drop sea mines in the strategic strait and/or the approaches to the huge Saudi Ras Tanura oil export terminal. A small explosion by an unknown hand hit a major Saudi pipeline between Awamiya and Safwa on March 1. The damage was not great because the saboteurs used a small quantity of explosive but it appeared to be the work of professionals.

Syria WMD report: Country is a Chemical Powder Keg Ready to Explode – www.worldtribune.com - March 22, 2012

WASHINGTON - President Bashar Assad could order weapons of mass destruction attacks to save his regime, a report said. The James Martin Center for Nonproliferation Studies asserted that Assad could employ Syria's massive WMD arsenal against any rising Sunni revolt. In a report, the center warned that the Damascus regime could also fire biological or chemical weapons to stop any foreign military intervention to save the rebels. Damascus, which hasn't signed the Chemical Weapons Convention, possesses chemical weapons, surface-to-surface missiles and Korean No-Dong/Scud-D missiles. "Indeed, in this fluid environment and uncharted territory, everything is possible," the report, "Assad's Toxic Assets," said. The report said none of the scenarios could be ignored. The center recommended that the United States and its allies offer immunity to Syrian troops who protect WMD sites. "The country is a chemical powder keg ready to explode."

Iranian Mouthpiece Media Calls on Syria to Attack Israel
Israel National News - By Tzvi Ben Gedalyahu
First Publish: 7/24/2012, 12:53 PM

Syrian President Bashar Assad should attack Israel says an Iranian newspaper considered the mouthpiece of the Supreme Leader.

Syrian President Bashar Assad should attack Israel, says an Iranian newspaper considered the mouthpiece of the Supreme Leader. Iran is concerned that the fall of Assad's regime will cost the Islamic Republic its closest ally and could ignite anti-Syrian elements in Lebanon, base of the Iranian-funded Hizbullah terrorist organization and political party.

The Kayhan newspaper, which operates directly under the supervision of the Islamic Supreme Leader of Iran, wrote last week that Assad has every reason to strike Israel because of Israel's alleged responsibility for the bombing in Damascus, which killed several of Assad's' top military officers. The suicide blast has been widely attributed to Al Qaeda or other terrorists, if not the Syrian rebels themselves, and no journalist has even implied that Israel was involved.

The newspaper's call for war cannot be taken lightly. Kayhan "offers insight into the most extreme views of Iran's leaders and into the mind-set and plans of those who are at the center of power," according to New York Times correspondent Michael Slackman.

The daily charged that Israel's military deployment along the Syrian border prior to the bombing was further evidence of its responsibility for it, even though the IDF has posted troops there ever since the Six-Day War in 1967.

To read entire article visit:
http://www.israelnationalnews.com/News/News.aspx/158200

The previous excerpts from the various worldwide news clips relate to the very serious ongoing problems escalating in Iran, Syria, Egypt, Lebanon, and all throughout the Middle East—all affecting Israel. It easy to surmise that seeing the current troubles in those areas imply further fulfillment of biblical prophecies in the very near future. Prophetically significant situations in the Middle East are moving forward at an astounding rate.

The Importance of Psalm 83

In the Bible, Psalm 83 is important in relation to end-times events and has been recognized as such by scholars throughout the years. Psalm 83 has been especially near and dear to my heart for a long time because it is a plea to save Israel—a prayer asking God to tear down her enemies. Psalm 83 is an imprecatory prayer to bring down judgment against the enemies of Israel, to protect Israel and bring about the fulfillment of the battle of Ezekiel 38 and 39. The straightforward correlation between Psalm 83 and the coming battle of Ezekiel 38 and 39 is evident upon studying the Scriptures. The passages that tie together the imprecatory prayer of Psalm 83 to the verses describing the battle of Ezekiel 38 and 39 are good examples of the Lord's intricate message system woven throughout the Bible.

Some of the nations mentioned in Psalm 83 are not specifically mentioned with those in Ezekiel 38 and 39, but this is not unusual. Throughout Scripture there are instances when only *some* nations are listed when making reference to a war. This can be found when studying the final war of Armageddon. For example, Joel 3:1-18 is relating to

72

when God judges the nations during the battle of Armageddon. Some of the primary nations that will participate in that war are not mentioned in those passages. Psalm 83 is not a war, it is an imprecatory prayer calling down judgment upon Israel's enemies and the answer to that prayer is when God destroys Israel's enemies in the battle of Ezekiel 38 and 39.

At some point in the near future, Russia will gather its Muslim allies and go after Israel. Israel does not need to have expanded borders to place her in a position of living more securely (see pages 85-91) or have more wealth so her enemies can take a greater "spoil" in order for this war to occur. What the Jew-hating coalition will be going after are the *people* of Israel (Ezekiel 38:16). However, after the Lord returns at the end of the Tribulation, Israel *will* have much greater boundaries because she will be a major part of the coming millennial kingdom (Isaiah 62:1-4; Daniel 7:27).

Another matter to keep in mind when reading and interpreting the imprecatory prayer of Psalm 83 is to keep the psalm in its *proper* context. An imprecatory prayer is a prayer for God to bring down judgment against one's enemies. By attempting to turn the passages within the imprecatory psalm into something entirely different is disregarding the *core premise* of the psalm—turning the inspired infallible Word of God from an imprecatory prayer into something it is not (taking away from the Word and adding to it). Psalm 83 is Israel's prayer to God for *protection* from an impending war, not a war in and of itself.

This basic fact cannot be ignored and it is as basic as English Comprehension 101. The psalmist is pleading with the Lord for help from those who are *conspiring* (ganging up) against Israel, *preparing* to destroy Israel, "O my God, make them like the whirling dust, like chaff before the wind, like fire that burns the forest and like a flame that sets the mountains on fire" (Psalm 83:13). And we see the answer to that prayer in the battle of Ezekiel 38 and 39 and ultimately again at the final battle at Armageddon.

"You shall not add to the word which I command you, nor take from it, that you may keep the commandments of the Lord your God which I command you" (Deuteronomy 4:2).

This imprecatory prayer should be given the full-respect it deserves and not be disparagingly dismissed as *just a prayer*. Scripture teaches that prayer is a powerful spiritual tool. The Word of God is more

73

powerful than a two-edged sword (Hebrews 4:12). Prayer *is how* Almighty God asks us to *communicate* with Him. Psalm 83 is an intense *imprecatory prayer* for God Himself to bring about the demise of Israel's enemies in an impossible situation—when surrounded by enemies on every front. Psalm 83 is an imprecatory *prayer* for protection from Israel's enemies, for God Himself to intervene. No matter how you spin it, Psalm 83 is not a war. It is an imprecatory prayer for God to come to the aid of Israel and save her from impending doom, which some well-meaning critics sadly fail to understand and without careful contextual reading and thinking, assumptively disregard.

All proposed hypothetical statements and equations become null and void regardless of how many suppositions are presented in an attempt to turn this imprecatory psalm into a war—**when it is explicitly a prayer for the enemies of Israel to be destroyed by God Himself**. Philosophical conjecture cannot transcend the correct laws of scholarly biblical hermeneutics (the Golden Rule of Interpretation as cited in chapter five of this book). If one needs an analogy, imagine driving a car but then suddenly deciding the car is an airplane. No matter how many ways one tries to turn the car into a plane, the car will not fly and will always be a car and not an airplane. Psalm 83 is the imprecatory prayer that points to the events of Ezekiel 38-39:16—for the destruction of the invaders to take place; for the Lord to intervene because of the insurmountable situation Israel faces as she is surrounded by enemies. The participants in the battle of Ezekiel 38 and 39 are many of the same nations emphatically expressing their hatred against Israel today.

The Lord implores us to "rightly divide the word of truth" (2 Timothy 2:15) which includes detecting seriously questionable teaching regardless of who is delivering the message and not blindly accepting a postulation simply because it is popular, regardless of how many books or articles are written supporting a widely accepted hypothetical premise. Two wars are actually prophesied in Ezekiel. The first is the battle of Ezekiel 38 and 39 which takes place before the Tribulation begins (Ezekiel 38-39:16) and then in verse 39:17 by the law of double reference (Revelation 19:20-21) Ezekiel shifts to describing the final battle of Armageddon.

It will become very evident after the coming battle of Ezekiel 38 and 39 when the Russian-led army falls "upon the mountains of Israel" (Ezekiel 39:2), that Psalm 83 is indeed an imprecatory prayer for God to bring down judgment against Israel's enemies and *not* a separate newly invented event: a Psalm 83 "war." Some Bible commentators use the passages from Ezekiel 38:8 from the New International Version (NIV) of the Bible to try to support this hypothetical "war."

The New International Version's translation for Ezekiel 38:8 is a simplified, modernized translation. Some of the verses translated in the New International Version of the Bible are good, I use some of them occasionally but in this case it is problematic and can be misleading. In Ezekiel 38:8, Ezekiel describes how the Jews are re-gathered into their land in the latter days (since 1948). In Psalm 83, the Psalmist describes Israel's cries to the Lord for help as countless enemies conspire against her, which ultimately results in the coming battle of Ezekiel 38 and 39. Yet some commentators try instead to use the New International Version of the Bible to make a case for a large regional war apart from and prior to the battle of Ezekiel 38 and 39. The NIV translation states, "In future years you will invade a land that has recovered from war" instead of "brought back from the sword" or "restored from the sword." The more accurate translations are as follows; King James Version:

"After many days thou shalt be visited: **in the latter years thou shalt come into the land that is brought back from the sword**, and is gathered out of many people, against the mountains of Israel, which have been always waste: but it is brought forth out of the nations, and they shall dwell safely all of them."

New American Standard Version:

"After many days you will be summoned; **in the latter years you will come into the land that is restored from the sword**, whose inhabitants have been gathered from many nations to the mountains of Israel which had been a continual waste; but its people were brought out from the nations, and they are living securely, all of them."

The 1901 American Standard Version of the Bible, translated out of the original tongues:

"After many days thou shalt be visited: **in the latter years thou shalt come into the land that is brought back from the sword**, that is gathered out of many peoples, upon the mountains of Israel, which has been a continual waste; but it is brought forth out of the peoples, and they shall dwell securely, all of them."

Israel has *already* been ("brought back from the sword"). Additionally, another obvious and important fact—simple fourth grade math and common sense show—that population growth disproves the possibility of a large regional Israeli conquest (war) against the Arab nations. Israel has about 7.8 million people including women and children (75.3% are Jews). The total population of the Arab countries encircling Israel is over 372.3 million! The Jewish population is dramatically outnumbered and could not *control* those nations.   The overall tone emanating from the Israeli people is that they simply want to live in peace in their God-given land. They are not ravenous wolves scheming to lead a Genghis Khan type, conquering-binge to expand their borders. To think that there must be some sort of large regional war prior to the Gog-Magog event to expand Israel's borders and supposedly create a stronger sense of peace and security is pure conjecture and makes no sense.

However, I would say that we could very well be closer to the eruption of the battle of Ezekiel 38 and 39 than some might think. Since the Six Day War of 1967, Israel has regained her "mountains" (Judea and Samaria, also known as the West Bank) leaving no further land acquisitions necessary for the prophetic battle of Ezekiel 38 and 39 to be fulfilled.

I am including an article I wrote for a popular website in 2009 because it contains some additional, detailed points relevant to what you have just read. You will recognize some information I have already touched on. You will also see how the prophetic Word of God is very precise and how Scripture is intricately interwoven. When you read the article, you will see how some aspects of the prophetic *imprecatory prayer* have *already* been fulfilled (the formation of the Arab League) and the constant verbal threats to destroy Israel— Israel's enemies conspiring together *are being fulfilled* today, *leading up* to the fulfillment of the battle of Ezekiel 38 and 39.

Psalm 83
God Is Implored to Confound His Enemies
A Song—a Psalm of Asaph

"O God, do not remain quiet; do not be silent and, O God, do not be still. For behold, Your enemies make an uproar, and those who hate You have exalted themselves. They make shrewd plans against Your people, and conspire together against your treasured ones. They have said, "Come, and let us wipe them out as a nation, that the name of Israel be remembered no more. For they have conspired together with one mind; against You they make a covenant.

The tents of Edom and the Ishmaelites, Moab and the Hagrites; Gebal and Ammon and Amalek, Philistia with the inhabitants of Tyre; Assyria also has joined with them; they have become a help to the children of Lot. Selah.

Deal with them as with Midian, As with Sisera *and* Jabin at the torrent of Kishon, who were destroyed at En-dor, who became as dung for the ground. Make their nobles like Oreb and Zeeb and all their princes like Zebah and Zalmunna, who said, "Let us possess for ourselves the pastures of God.

O my God, make them like the whirling dust, like chaff before the wind. Like fire that burns the forest and like a flame that sets the mountains on fire. So pursue them with Your tempest and terrify them with Your storm. Fill their faces with dishonor, that they may seek Your name, O LORD.

Let them be ashamed and dismayed forever, and let them be humiliated and perish, that they may know that You alone, whose name is the LORD, are the Most High over all the earth."

Psalm 83 and the Battle of Ezekiel 38 and 39

Psalm 83 is an imprecatory prayer, an imprecatory psalm, it seems very obvious to me.

"But know this first of all, that no prophecy of Scripture is *a matter* of one's own interpretation." —2 Peter 1:20

Some popular theories regarding the meaning of Psalm 83 are circulating claiming the psalm is an unfulfilled prophecy, describing a major separate war that will take place before the battle of Ezekiel 38 and 39. Accompanying that particular interpretation is a belief that the Israeli Defense Forces (IDF) will successfully defeat Arab enemies, therefore getting all the credit for defeating the Arab nations that surround Israel.

It is true that in Ezekiel 37:10, an "exceedingly great army" is mentioned, but the verse does not say that a great army will be responsible for the destruction of Israel's enemies. I would also say it is much more likely that a war we *will* see *before* the battle of Ezekiel 38 and 39 will be the fulfillment of Isaiah 17:1, which could very possibly take place shortly before the battle of Ezekiel 38 and 39 or even be tied into it. The Arab states mentioned in Psalm 83 are the modern Arab states who are members of the Arab League. Their agenda is to reduce Israel to nothing. In reference to Psalm 83, verse 5, the word "confederacy," berith, in Hebrew can be translated into the word "league" from Hebrew to English. Also, according to The New Strong's Exhaustive Concordance of the Bible, the Hebrew word berith is translated "covenant" in the English Bible. The concordance also states the word berith appears 227 times in the Old Testament, and means "confederacy, league or covenant."

Psalm 83 is a fulfilled prophecy, a prophecy that continues to be fulfilled, and a prophecy that will be fulfilled when the battle of Ezekiel 38 and 39 takes place; and completely fulfilled when Jesus the Messiah returns at Armageddon and personally destroys the nations that come against Him and Israel. The battle of Ezekiel 38 and 39 will most likely be the next major prophetic war in the Middle East.

By carefully comparing Psalm 83 with Ezekiel 38 and 39, Psalm 83 appears very much to be an imprecatory prayer *for Israel*, and certainly relates to current events. Both Christians and Jews have been praying for God's intervention—to stop Israel's enemies from the continuous barrage of threats and assaults from those who also happen to be members of the Arab League.

This fervent appeal can be witnessed today. Every time Israel is threatened, prayers go before the throne of God on Israel's behalf. An imprecatory prayer is pleading with God to bring down judgment upon a dangerous enemy. To imprecate means to call God's judgment down upon a people. The following verses sound like what the enemies of Israel are saying today, including those who are members of the Arab League:

"They have taken crafty counsel against Your people, and consulted together against Your sheltered ones. They have said, Come and let us cut them off from being a nation, that the name of Israel may be remembered no more. For they have consulted together with one consent, they form a confederacy against You" (Psalm 83:3-5).

Psalm 83 speaks about a "confederacy" and some of the nations listed in that psalm are part of the Arab League, whose members are frequently calling for Israel's demise. The political leader of Iran, Mahamoud Ahmadinejad, is well known for spewing his hatred for Israel and calling for its total destruction.

Psalm 83 is a *prayer* to circumvent the conspiracy against Israel. I would further say that Psalm 83 describes and correlates what will happen during of the battle of Ezekiel 38 and 39, when the nations of the world will know God and God alone will save Israel from the Russian-led invasion. To imply that the Israeli Defense Forces will liberate Israel from Islamic threats cannot be confirmed or supported by any Scripture found in Psalm 83, or Ezekiel 38 and 39. If the IDF is given the credit for winning that war, then God will not be known for saving Israel.

Where does it say in Psalm 83 that man-made military forces will save Israel? Where does it say in Ezekiel 38 and 39 that an army will save Israel? Only God will save Israel during the judgments *described* in Psalm 83 and Ezekiel 38 and 39. There will be no mistaking His supernatural intervention when He rescues Israel. This event will be a monumental, defining moment in history. The entire world will see God in a new light, in a different way because of His undeniable, supernatural miraculous intervention. Weapons of war will of course exist but God will somehow make them inoperable or skew them away from the Israelis sending the enemy into frenzied confusion. The invaders will turn against each other (Ezekiel 38:21).

Psalm 83 is not a war, but an imprecatory prayer calling for Ezekiel 38 and 39 to be fulfilled. The circumstances of the battle of Ezekiel 38 and 39 will surpass even the historic miracles of the Exodus. The Exodus will take a back seat in comparison to what God will do at the battle of Ezekiel 38 and 39. God's new historic identity will be, "The Lord who brought up the children of Israel from the land of the north," based on Jeremiah 16:14:

"Therefore behold, the days are coming," says the LORD, that it shall no more be said, 'The LORD lives who brought up the children of Israel from the land of Egypt,' but, 'The LORD lives who brought up the children of Israel from the land of the north and from all the lands where He had driven them.' For I will bring them back into their land which I gave to their fathers" (Jeremiah 16:14-15).

Approximately one million Jews have already immigrated to Israel from Russia (the north). The Islamic population will be tremendously decreased because of that war. Russia will be destroyed:

"And I will send fire on Magog [Russia] **and on those who live in security in the coastlands**. Then they shall know that I *am* the LORD" (Ezekiel 39:6).

According to Ezekiel 38:13, Saudi Arabia (ancient Sheba and Dedan) will not participate in the Ezekiel 38 and 39 invasion of Israel. Even now the Saudi's are leading the central banking group into pressuring Israel into a land-for-peace deal, and most probably will keep pushing for that deal, rather than joining the future Russian-led Islamic forces when Israel is attacked.

The Saudi's appear to be leaning in the direction of those who form the Mediterranean Union, pressuring Israel to make land-for-peace concessions. The prospect of a nuclear-armed Iran is of great concern to the leaders of Saudi Arabia. Saudi Arabia has never been very cozy with Iran or Russia, although the Saudis did recently purchase some weapons from Russia. In my opinion, the attempt to subvert Israel will continue to be done in a more "civilized" way, by pressuring them to make land-for-peace agreements.

Amir Tsarfati is a popular sought-after Israeli speaker and a very knowledgeable Bible teacher. He lives in Jerusalem. During a number of speaking engagements at Calvary Chapel churches, he has stated that he believes the battle of Ezekiel 38 and 39 is coming soon. He also stated that he disagrees with the argument by some prophecy teachers regarding Ezekiel 38, teaching that Israel has to be living peacefully before that battle can take place. He believes all the physical conditions for the battle of Ezekiel 38 and 39 are already in place today.

Amir is a strong Hebrew Christian, carefully following prophetic events. Living in Israel (Jerusalem) gives him an advantage when discussing and discerning the meaning of the relevant prophetic passage: Ezekiel 38:11. "Dwelling safely'' does not mean the Israelis dwell peacefully, but that the conditions that exist are considered "safe," to a degree. Some walls to protect the Israeli population from Palestinian missile attacks do exist. However, there are no extensive walls surrounding *all* of Israel. Each village or community in Israel does not have "bars" or "gates." The common situation for cities or villages during the time of Ezekiel was one where rock walls and gates were very prevalent. In my opinion, these are the types of walls, fences and barriers Ezekiel was referring to in verse 11. These rock barriers no longer exist. In general, the people of modern Israel move about freely and have secure borders, and the current border circumstances qualify for the fulfillment of Ezekiel 38 and 39.

Another point to consider is the fact that Israel as a whole is quite rebellious against God and is not engaged in a genuine spiritual relationship with the Lord. Generally speaking, Israel is secular to the core, and government leaders have a history of settling for false peace agreements by giving away chunks of land, land that was given to them by God Himself. Therefore, we could say that Israel has no spiritual walls, fences or barriers. Israel at the moment is lacking spiritual walls or hedges of protection from the Lord. In general, they are living carelessly, without a genuine relationship with the Lord, and this is a contributing reason why they are opening themselves up to being pounced on by many enemies.

In order for the battle of Ezekiel 38 and 39 to occur, there will be plenty of enemies who will eagerly march against Israel. To imply that the Israelis will ever be living peacefully before the Gog-Magog battle simply cannot be. Clearly those who participate in the Gog-Magog war will be great enemies of Israel. I don't believe for a minute that Israel will let down her guard until the son of perdition, the Antichrist, deceives them into thinking he is their savior. This argument is also in keeping with the conditions necessary for the Pre-Tribulation Rapture of the church.

"You will say, I will go up against a land of unwalled villages; I will go to a peaceful people, who dwell safely, all of them dwelling without walls, and having neither bars nor gates" (Ezekiel 38:11).

The passage says the people of Israel are a "peaceful people"—not that they are living in "peace." The verses from Psalm 83:17 and 18 correlate with what will transpire when the Lord almighty supernaturally intervenes during the battle of Ezekiel 38 and 39. As a student of Bible prophecy, it is my opinion that a portion of Psalm 83 is speaking of a partially fulfilled prophecy—the Arab League, and their despotic verbal rumblings. I have already addressed the prayer aspect of the psalm. Next, it also speaks of events that will take place as described in Ezekiel 38 and 39 and, when the Lord confounds the enemies of Israel and shows His indignation, halting the onslaught against His nation, Israel. If you carefully read through all the passages in Ezekiel 38 and 39, and Psalm 83, their unmistakable interdependence and similarities cannot be denied.

"O my God, make them like a whirling dust like the chaff before the wind! As the fire burns the woods and as the flame sets the mountains on fire, so pursue them with Your tempest, and frighten them with Your storm.

Fill their faces with shame, that they may seek Your name O LORD. Let them be confounded and dismayed forever; Yes, let them be put to shame and perish. That they may know that You, whose name alone is the LORD, and the most high over all the earth" (Psalm 83: 13-18).

The previous verses are very similar to the verses of Ezekiel 39 and 2, 3, and verse 7. They appear to be speaking about the same event as you can see here:

"And I will turn you around and lead you on, bringing you up from the mountains far north, and bring you against the mountains of Israel. Then I will knock the bow out of your left hand and cause the arrows to fall out of your right hand.

So I will make My holy name known in the midst of My people Israel, and I will not *let them* profane my holy name anymore. Then the nations shall know I am the LORD, the Holy One of Israel" (Ezekiel 39:2, 3, 7).

In both Psalm 83 and Ezekiel 39, the Lord is describing what will happen when the Russian-led, predominately Muslim army marches down from the north to decimate Israel. It is the Lord Himself who will give the Russians the idea to invade Israel (Ezekiel 38:4, 11) so He can be glorified, and reveal Himself to the nations. He will not be defending Israel for Israel's sake, but for His Name's sake, so the nations of the world will see He is in control—Almighty God that He is. No dangling carrot is necessary for this invasion to take place. Israel does not have to be bigger or richer for this battle to ensue. It is God's battle to fight, and He intends to make Himself known.

God Almighty has a plan to personally foil the wicked plans of the enemy. He will use the enemy's extreme hatred for Israel to bring His redemptive plans for His chosen nation and the world to fruition. Both Psalm 83 and Ezekiel 39 make it perfectly clear that it is the Lord Himself who will intervene in such a mighty way that no one will be able to deny His awesome power.

The nations will realize God defended Israel, and destroyed the enemy. The Israeli Defense Forces—as great as they—are will not be responsible for Israel's victory. To say that they will save Israel from the enemy is an assault upon the promises of God and His Holy Word. Psalm 83 and Ezekiel 39 both state God and God alone will be the One to deliver Israel during this prophesied battle. Psalm 83 and Ezekiel 38 each reveal that God's awesome presence will be undeniable.

"These were more fair-minded than those in Thessalonica, in that they received the word with all readiness and searched the Scriptures daily to find out whether theses things were so" (Acts 17:11).

Ezekiel 35

Speculation that there will be a separate major Arab-Israeli war prior to the Gog-Magog war (battle of Ezekiel 38 and 39) is built upon on a weak foundation. Both Psalm 83 and Ezekiel 35 are cited to support this hypothesis. As already discussed in great length Psalm 83 cannot be a war because it is an imprecatory prayer. Furthermore, Ezekiel 35 is a parallel passage of Isaiah 63:1-6 that firmly states when Yeshua returns at the Second Coming He will personally slaughter His enemies who are hiding in the ancient territory of Edom. He will then wipe out the wicked—those who have mobilized their armies on the Plain of Megiddo before He touches down on the Mount of Olives. Ezekiel 35 refers to the destruction of Edom (the territory of Southern Jordan east of the Dead Sea) at the Second Coming and cannot be used to support an earlier war.

Jerusalem, Israel: Gateway

Jerusalem: Gateway

When Israel Is Living Securely

Some naïvely and illogically propose that an Israeli conquest resulting in larger borders would give Israel *more* security, subduing Islam and bringing hundreds of millions of Allah worshippers under docile control. In fact, the *opposite* would be true. Expanded borders would ultimately endanger Israel *even more* because her enemies would know full-well that an army the size of the Israeli Defense Forces (IDF) could not handle the massive number of enemies that would need to be controlled within greatly expanded borders. Israelis would be even *more on guard* and *less secure* than they are today. It is during the Gog-Magog invasion that Islam will take a serious hit, by God Himself. This will happen when Israel has a security agreement(s) as she has now. In the future, just prior to the beginning of the seven-year Tribulation period, Scripture tells us that Israel *will* sign a *peace* (shalom) covenant with the Antichrist (Daniel 9:27).

> "After many days you will be summoned; in the latter years you will come into the land that is restored from the sword, whose inhabitants have been gathered from many nations to the mountains of Israel which had been a continual waste; but its people were brought out from the nations, and they are living **securely,** all of them.
>
> And you will say, 'I will go up against the land of unwalled villages. I will go against those who are at rest, that live **securely**, all of them living without walls and having no bars or gates, therefore prophesy, son of man, and say to Gog, 'Thus says the Lord GOD, "On that day when My people Israel are living securely, will you not know it?" (Ezekiel 38:8, 11, 14)

What does "living securely," mean in reference to Israel and the battle of Ezekiel 38 and 39? We see in the previous passages that the Lord says Israel will be living "securely" when attacked. In verse 14, He states even more specifically, **"My people Israel are living securely."** The word for secure or safe when translated into Hebrew is "batach." The word batach does not imply peace or absolute peace, but rather "to trust in," "to be secure," "be careless." The word for safe (as some translations have it) or secure, as used in the three verses above (NASB) is not the Hebrew word "shalom" (peace). Dr. Fruchtenbaum agrees that Israel is dwelling securely, as you will read next:

They dwell securely (38:11, 14). This has often been misconstrued as meaning a state of peace, but this is not the meaning of the Hebrew root *batach*. The nominal form of this root means "security." This is not the security due to a state of peace, but a security due to confidence in their, own strength. This, too, is a good description of Israel today. The Israeli army has fought four major wars since its founding and won them swiftly each time. Today Israel is secure, confident that her army can repel any invasion from the Arab states. Hence, Israel is dwelling securely. Israel is dwelling in unwalled villages (38:11). This is very descriptive of the present-day *kibbutzim* in Israel. (Arnold G. Fruchtenbaum, *Footprints of the Messiah*, pages 121-122.)

The Israelis will not be living peacefully when they are attacked. But they will be living under a *sense* of "security" or "securely" with generally secure borders as would be implied by already having a number of security agreements, for example going back to the Camp David Accords. In 1978 at Camp David a treaty between Israel and Egypt was negotiated known as the Camp David Accords, setting the groundwork for a final agreement between Egypt and Israel. On September 17, 1978 Egyptian President Anwar Sadat of Egypt and Israeli Premier Menachem Begin signed the pact at the White House in Washington D.C, and again on March 26, 1979 they signed the final official, document reflective of the Camp David Accords, formally ending the state of war between Egypt and Israel.

Unfortunately, it also included a provision for Israel to withdraw from the Sinai-Peninsula—which she did in stages—in exchange for the promise of more "secure" borders. The news cameras broadcasted and witnessed these historic events to the entire world. And there have been other treaties since. Although the treaties with Israel often contain the word "peace," all the so-called peacemakers seem to really want is for Israel to give up more land for the hollow promise of more peace. Peace is not really part of the equation. Land grabbing is, however. Israel is a tiny nation about the size of New Jersey surrounded by enemies who have large parcels of land. **Israel could fit into the state of Florida 8 times**!

We read in Ezekiel 38:14: "On that day when My people Israel are living securely, **will you not know it**?" In essence this prophetic verse has been fulfilled. Security agreements have been signed and we "know it." The Camp David Accords were not peace (shalom) treaties, but rather *security* agreements. Secure borders were established. Even the security fences that have been constructed throughout parts of Israel over the years denote a feeling of *security*, despite the endless and frequent missile attacks launched by the Palestinians. Having protective fences as Israel has now in some areas does not create an isolated existence, as would be the case when an entire nation or "village" is living behind "bars or gates." The Israeli Defense Forces (IDF) also provides a sense of confident security. Certainly the Jews in Israel are more secure than they have been in the past considering prior to their regathering in 1948 they were dispersed throughout the world seeking a safe-haven. Nowhere were the Jews in more danger than in Europe when they were hunted down, brutally tortured and murdered by Hitler and his bloodthirsty, satanically driven henchmen.

Since that time, the Iranian hierarchy and its proxy nations and allies have been the most vocal enemies in their intention to totally destroy Israel and murder Jews. At the time of this writing, Israel is encircled with enemies and the anti-Israel rhetoric is sharply ramping up. The Muslim Brotherhood and other Islamists now dominate the Egyptian parliament. *The Global Muslim Brotherhood Daily Report* carried this statement on March 12, 2012: "Revolutionary Egypt will never be a friend, partner or ally of the Zionist entity, which we consider to be the number one enemy of Egypt and the Arab nation." This mean-spirited statement was made after the Egyptian parliament unanimously voted to expel Israel's ambassador and to halt gas exports to Israel. A few months later (June 24, 2012) the elected leader of the Muslim Brotherhood's Freedom and Justice Party, Mohammed Morsi, was sworn in as Egypt's first Islamist president, encouraged and strongly supported by the Obama administration. Prophetically, this is all very significant, a real switch in cast and script since the original security treaty with Egypt.

On August 24, 2012 the *World Tribune* reported that Egypt deployed US-made surface-to-air missiles (SAMS) and tanks near the border with Israel, in breach of the 1979 peace (security) treaty—not exactly a "symbolic" action, adding a new—acute dimension—to Israel's plight. Reliable sources in Egypt report the radical Islamists have now totally taken over Egypt (mid-August 2012). The implementation of national Sharia law is anticipated. As recently as September 2012 US intelligence identified a secret meeting with Egypt's intelligence chief and a senior Iranian spy causing concern that Egypt's new government is complicit in covertly supporting global terrorism. On July 27, 2012 the US President signed a politically motivated bill to strengthen SECURITY cooperation with Israel: H.R. 4133, the United States Enhanced Security Cooperation Act of 2012. Once again the word "security" is the dominating word.

The Old Testament Hebrew Lexicon

Strong's Number: 982	encodedOriginalWord

Original Word	Word Origin
בטח	a primitive root

Transliterated Word	Phonetic Spelling
batach	baw-takh'

Parts of Speech	TWOT
Verb	233

Definition

1. to trust
    a. (Qal)
        1. to trust, trust in
        2. to have confidence, be confident
        3. to be bold
        4. to be secure
    b. (Hiphil)
        1. to cause to trust, make secure
        2. to feel safe, be careless

Translated Words

KJV (120) - bold, 1; careless, 1; confidence, 4; confident, 2; hope, 1; hoped, 1; ones, 1; secure, 4; sure, 1; trust, 103; women, 1;

NAS (120) - bold, 1; careless, 1; complacent, 3; confident, 2; fall down, 1; felt secure, 1; have, 2; have confidence, 1; put my trust, 3; put their trust, 2; put your trust, 1; relied, 1; rely, 8; secure, 5; trust, 51; trusted, 15; trusting, 3; trusts, 19;

Unwalled Villages

Before modern Israel was reestablished nearly everyone in ancient Israel lived in walled villages. Jerusalem was surrounded by walls until 1860 when Sir Moses Montefiore built the first dwellings outside its walls. Throughout Israel today most all of the population lives in unwalled towns and cities. In Ezekiel's time villages were surrounded by walls built from heavy rocks for protection to fend off her enemies.

More recently when the Jews began to return to Israel they established new Jewish settlements. In order to protect against Arab attacks, watchtowers and stockade fences were built, especially used at night. These settlements were essentially small villages based on agriculture but were primarily established for defense and were surrounded by a wall or fence. The first kibbutzim (plural of "kibbutz") were founded some forty years before the establishment of the modern State of Israel (1948). Degania (from the Hebrew "dagan," meaning grain), located south of Lake Kinneret, was established in 1909 by a group of pioneers on land acquired by the Jewish National Fund.

In contrast, modern Israel is a nation consisting of unwalled settlements (villages) and cities. This is true despite the security checkpoints that control entry into some of the settlements, and also true regardless of the wall(s) that Israel has between certain Jewish and Palestinian-controlled areas. Walls, bars and gates still exist, *but they do not* play the same first line of defense position that they did in ancient times or in the recent history of Israel when the Jews began to return to their land. Additionally, to a great extent modern weapons have made the protection provided by walls, bars and gates of little effect. They do not provide protection from rockets, mortars or missiles. So when Ezekiel wrote that Israel would be living in "unwalled villages" when attacked, it is correct to say they once did live in "walled villages" but they no longer do. Today they live in "unwalled villages," secure borders as Ezekiel described when he said that at the time of the Gog-Magog invasion the nation of Israel would be living "securely" and in "unwalled villages" and "without bars and gates."

The following comments are quoted from the late Grant Jeffrey's book, *Prince of Darkness – Antichrist and the New World Order*, (pp.193-194), wherein he gave some intelligent insights relating to the timing of the battle of Ezekiel 38 and 39 (Gog-Magog war) as well as his thoughts regarding Israel's position relating to "dwelling safely" when attacked.

A final question concerns the timing of this future war of Gog and Magog. Some writers conclude that the battle will occur during the seven-year treaty period leading up to the battle of Armageddon. However, there is no mention of the Antichrist or his seven-year treaty to protect Israel. If this battle takes place within the seven-year treaty period leading to Armageddon you would expect the prophet to refer to either (1) the Antichrist defending Israel against this attack or, (2) to his betrayal of Israel by refusing to protect them as agreed in his treaty.

Ezekiel's prophecy about the war of Magog is silent about the Antichrist or the Messiah although they are central figures in the period leading to the battle of Armageddon. This silence convinces me that the war of Gog and Magog will occur at some point in time prior to the Antichrist arising to conclude his fateful seven-year treaty with the Jews. Some have suggested that the prophet's description found in Ezekiel 38:8 (that Israel will "dwell safely") can only occur after the Antichrist signs his treaty to guarantee their security. Ezekiel declared: "After many days you will be visited. In the latter years you will come into the land of those brought back from the sword and gathered safely" from many people on the mountains of Israel, which had long been desolate; they were brought out of the nations, and now all of them dwell safely.

Does the phrase "dwell safely mean that Israel has found true lasting peace with her neighbors? In the light of the grim history of the Middle East during the century it is unlikely that Israel will disarm to any degree before the Messiah returns. Israel will remain an armed camp surrounded by enemies committed to her destruction until God changes the hearts of mankind. The phrase "dwell safely" may simply indicate that Israel will be living in an expectation that they will not be attacked at that time, perhaps because of the recent peace agreement with the PLO [Palestine Liberation Organization].

The True and Complete Story of the Syrian Incident

By Amir Tsarfati
Behold Israel - Wednesday, 13 October 2007

My last commentary from September 10, 2007 regarding the Syria incident involving 8 Israeli fighter jets ended up with the statement below:

"There is much more to be said about this incident - however this is not the right time and the right place to do so...."

In the meantime the world media are releasing more and more details, so I guess it is safe on my behalf to comment on it and not to be regarded as "the first" to leak the info: It was a nuclear facility that the Russian anti-aircraft system was there to protect.

Iran I guess inspired Syria. North Korea was there to supply the material, Russia was there to supply the defense and Iran was there to pay the bill to both. This is the axis of evil that will cause the domino effect in the Middle East, very soon....

The story begins in the month of July, this year. A mysterious explosion is rocking the Syrian city of Haleb on July 26th while Iranian engineers and Syrian officers were trying to get a warhead loaded with mustard gas on a new scud missile. The explosion killed 15 Syrian military men and dozens of Iranian engineers

North Korea has announced to the whole world its decision to suspend its nuclear program in return for billions of dollars. The only thing North Korea forgot to report is what its intentions are in regards to its already existing storage of weapon-graded enriched Uranium.

The North-Koreans were approached by both Iran and Syria during last summer and in the most top secret levels there was the understanding that Uranium should be exported as an innocent cement cargo to the Syrian Port of Tartous and from there by trucks to the Syrian desert where dozens of North Korean engineers, Iranian officials and Syrian military men were all around.

Russia was part of this whole scheme as it was the one to supply the air defense system around this newborn nuclear facility. Let me make it very clear – this was NOT a nuclear reactor. It was more dangerous than that. It was ready-to-go uranium already enriched. Just put it into a bomb or a missile and there you go.

The night between June 10 and June 11 was a very exciting night for Israeli scientists as well as the intelligence community as the world's most advanced satellite "Ofek 7" was launched. The pictures were great to the degree of the size of a mosquito. There is no doubt that we are in the major-league now!

The moment the photos of the Syrian Desert arrived to the desk of the Israeli intelligence analysts it was clear as the sun that something is terribly wrong. We knew the North Korean connection for several years but there was yet no physical proof to the matter.

President George Bush was informed immediately but was afraid that any exposure of this whole thing might disrupt the talks with North Korea.

The decision was to try to get the right proof and even then to do everything to avoid the exposure of this whole thing to the world-media.

A TOP-SECRET operation was launched in the middle of August. The Israeli commando wearing Syrian uniforms managed to get to the Syrian Desert and get a hold of a sample of the suspected material.

Lab-checks proved beyond any shadow of doubts that the worse of Israel nightmares is right at our doorstep. **ISRAEL IS ABOUT TO MISS DISTANT IRAN. NOW SYRIA IS ALREADY A NUCLEAR THREAT!**

Time was running out and the drums of war started sounding their sound, in the Middle East. In order to calm the Syrians and to let them think we were not at all aware of their vicious plan – Israel started passing in the right channels calming messages that we have no intention to attack and that we are even willing to talk about the Golan Heights. After a green light from the White House, Israel decided that the operation would take place after midnight to minimize casualties and to minimize exposure of cameras and civilians. The rest I guess is history. Syria was terribly embarrassed and the Israeli silence (which is a thing I must commend) added to this whole drama.

Syria was in a great dilemma – on one hand they can't expose the target and its content. On the other hand if they say nothing, then they will admit that there was something about it and by that will also open the door for other Israeli pin pointed attacks. The interesting thing is that the first to denounce the "Israeli Aggression" was North Korea! Syria was busted. The world knows it. Syria is now with its back to the wall. Any wrongdoing and Damascus will be destroyed, Buckle your seat belts. As I stated before: The next biblical event I can see that will be fulfilled is the Scripture below:

> "The burden against Damascus. Behold,
> Damascus will cease from *being* a city,
> And it will be a ruinous heap." —Isaiah 17:1

Syria will be dealt with first to cause the others to be exposed and then act in reaction with aggression! The escalation will most likely not happen before the coming US presidential-elections. America must first elect a president that will cause America to withdraw its troops from Iraq and then the mice will come out of their holes. Then I believe Ezekiel's prophecy of Gog and Magog will be fully fulfilled!

Blessings in the name of Yeshua who will soon show His power and remove us from this evil world!

In Him,

Amir

As an important note of interest: On March 19, 2012, Russia sent troops into Syria to assist the tyrannical Assad regime with its bloodbath against anti-government protesters (9,000 dead mostly civilians and steadily increasing to over 60,000 plus by Jan.3, 2013 according to the U.N.'s Syria death toll). Russia has also been strongly backing, Iran. Syria is about ready to explode and Damascus, its capital city, is in acute danger of being totally annihilated as violence increases. Although on or around March 27, 2012 UN envoy Kofi Annan made a deal with Syrian President Bashar Al-Assad which may or may not prove to be anything more than window dressing to appease the rest of the world. I would say it is all a rouse—the savage dictator has anything but peace in mind for the people of Syria.

The day after the UN cease-fire deal was made fighting continued in several cities, raising concerns that Assad is buying regime time. Remember the Islamic principles of takiya and tawriya. I would say that is exactly what Assad is doing. Nothing good will come out of this situation and the violence and bloodshed will continue to escalate.

Nevertheless, the fulfillment of Isaiah's prophecy (Isaiah 17:1) appears to be getting closer by the moment. And the prophecy of Ezekiel 38 and 39 is very close to being fulfilled, especially considering that Russia is getting more blatantly involved with defending Israel's most aggressive enemies.

Russia Sends Warships to Mediterranean: On July 11, 2012, The Journal of Turkish Weekly reported: Although for the last year Russia has tried to project an image of neutrality in the increasingly bloody conflict in Syria, it may be sending a signal of support to its longtime ally, President Bashas Al-Assad, by sending warships to the Mediterranean where Russia maintains a bas at Tartus, Syria. But with Russian navy ships from three Russian fleets now steaming toward Syria's coast, the Kremlin seems to be sending a clear signal that it will stand by Assad.

More Demands on Israel

Every day we continue to hear through world news reports about the ongoing "peace process" which essentially translates into, "Israel, give up some more of your land so we can place you into an indefensible position." Surely ye jest ye ladies and gentleman, ye powerbrokers of the world! The Israelis are not fools and should not be treated as if they are.

Let's go back about a year to May 19, 2011 when President Obama unreasonably and some would say diabolically made a public plea to Israel that she should return to her 1967 borders relinquishing her precious land; which would leave her utterly vulnerable in the face of her many enemies. Media reports stated that the White House was pressuring Israeli Prime Minister Benjamin Netanyahu to publicly adopt the American president's view that Israel's pre-1967 border should be the basis for future peace talks.

I would like to ask all those who think that this is a good idea which part of their *own* personal property they would like to hand over to the neighborhood bullies who keep firing rockets at their house and backyard? It would be to keep "peace" in their neighborhood..... I don't see any hands raised.

The request by the White House in the spring of 2011 for Israel to surrender her land to their enemies actually goes beyond the pre-1967 borders, as reported by Jennifer Rubin in the *Washington Post* on June 12, 2011 in the following article:

Obama Bullies Israel; So Much for His Promises at AIPAC

"Is the [U.S.] administration now asking Israel to sit down with Abbas absent a commitment by Hamas or a break-up of the unity government? By gosh, that should be an easy answer ("No!"), yet the administration won't say. This is a very, very big deal. Former deputy national security adviser Elliott Abrams explained to me [Jennifer Rubin] Friday evening:

The Palestinian 'concession' if these negotiations start would be to pull the plug on seeking U.N. membership." Moreover, it is a "concession" with very little meaning. Abrams told me that the Palestinians "can't get U.N. membership if the US vetoes it, so this looks like a desperate White House effort to avoid having to veto. It would leave Israel negotiating with Abbas in the mornings while he is negotiating with Hamas in the afternoons. Then when he gets the Hamas deal the negotiations will collapse, just like they did last year." He cracked, "The only thing left of that effort is the memory of Mubarak's purple-black dyed hair in the East Room." And like clockwork, Obama's position now becomes the Palestinians' latest precondition. It's almost like they are on the same team.

Although it was a Friday evening, Capitol Hill was already rumbling. A GOP adviser told me, "If the administration really wanted to, it could pressure the Quartet to formally oppose the Palestinians' unilateral move at the U.N. and nip the whole issue in the bud in a long weekend. Clearly, they would rather use this situation to box Prime Minister Netanyahu into a false choice between unilateral statehood and '67 borders. The Congress will reject this false choice and so should the PM." Moreover, Democrats who have been spinning the president's conflicting statements as best they can may now feel burned.

A longtime Middle East insider put it this way: "If there are preconditions [for Israel], then that is a change in policy. Just like the mistake we made over settlements, as Abbas said, leading him up a tree. And this time, not only creating a new Palestinian precondition to talks, but in essence giving the P.A. an excuse to pursue the U.N. track, if this latest gambit to wrest pre-negotiations concessions from the Israelis—and nothing from the Palestinians—ends in failure."

Now what about the 1967 borders? Democratic defenders of the president have insisted that "1967 borders with land swaps" is nothing new. But it appears it certainly is. As the insider noted, "Yes, they are pressing for '67 with swaps, not exactly '67.But that's not really the point—they've already adopted what was a Palestinian 'goal' as US policy." And it is actually worse than that.

On Saturday I asked a State Department official authorized only to speak on background: Does "1967 borders with land swaps" mean "1967 and then we discuss swaps" or does it mean "1967 borders plus the swaps that the parties previously agreed to in negotiations including the Jerusalem suburbs"? The latter, I pointed out is consistent with the 2004 Bush-Sharon letters, but the former is not. In fact, if it is 1967 and then they discuss land swaps, that is the same as starting with the 1967 borders. Period.

And sure enough the State Department official told me, "It means swaps that the parties will agree on in the course of direct negotiations." To be clear, Israel is being pressured to give up prior understandings that the Western Wall and the Jerusalem suburbs, for example, would never be part of a Palestinian state. A veteran negotiator explains, "This administration believes that every single deviation from 'the 1967 borders' must be paid for by Israel in a one to one swap. That has never before been the US government's demand, and it weakens Israel's bargaining position.

In other words, there is zero difference in the Obama scheme between "1967 borders" and "1967 border with land swaps." In both, the starting point is borders Israel has deemed indefensible.

Congressional friends of Israel are likely to be enraged. A spokesman for Sen. Orrin Hatch (R-Utah) conveyed the senator's view: "The president's insistence last month that Israel return to the pre-1967 borders represented a significant departure from past U.S. policy and has been roundly repudiated by members of both parties. Given this lack of support, even from his own party, it is inconceivable why the President would continue to undermine the position of our democratic ally, Israel in its negotiations with a hostile neighbor."

I spoke to Rep. Peter King (R-N.Y.), who plainly was angry over the continued effort to bully Israel. He said in a phone interview, "President Obama never learns. His real instinct is to weaken Israel. You don't treat an ally this way." He said he has never seen this sort of behavior from any US president. After the apparent "rapprochement" following the Arab Spring speech, King says the current posture is "shameful." Given the strong support in the Congress for Israel, will there be resolutions or a cutoff of funding for the Palestinians? He said firmly that it is time to start "fighting fire with fire." In other words, as much as Obama seeks to pressure Israel while whispering vague promises to the American Jewish community, the Congress may very well try to recalibrate the balance. We should at least have one branch of government in our ally's corner, right?

The (Middle East) Quartet mentioned in the article you just read is a forum to follow-up on the so-called Israeli-Palestinian peace process made up of representatives from the United States, European Union, United Nations, and Russia.

On September 23, 2011, the Palestinians submitted a formal request for statehood to the United Nations. Mahmoud Abbas, president of the Palestinian Authority made the bid. He asked for a Palestinian state with Jerusalem as its capital. Their outlandish request is now on hold. The US and the EU are halting that bid for the time being and urging the Palestinians to resume negotiations with Israel. However, as already discussed, the US and the EU have both publicly stated that the Palestinians *should* be given a state based on pre-1967 borders. This is nothing less than a stab in Israel's back.

Scripture indicates that further negotiations will only lead to more war, and there will be no true peace until Messiah Jesus intervenes at end of the Tribulation. Considering the intense threats of war in the heart of the Middle East, the battle of Ezekiel 38 and 39 could happen in the immediate future. Iran is potentially one of the greatest nuclear threats to the Western world, especially to Israel.

In December 2011 and January 2012, Iran threatened to block Gulf oil from going through the Strait of Hormuz if international sanctions against it proceed. Soon, the enemies of Israel including Iran will march against her with great expectations of destroying her—once and for all. But as already noted the predominately Islamic army will be met by the vengeance of God Himself—the Holy One of Israel—who will execute His mighty powers against the hate-filled invaders—fulfilling more key prophetic Scriptures; thrusting us forward into the very final years of world history as we know it.

On May 10, 2012 the US President, met with a group of staunch anti-Israel critics, leftist hardliners who are not friends of Israel in the slightest way. Please read the report by Adam Kredo written for the *Washington Free Beacon,* on May 11, 2012:

President Obama sat down yesterday with a cadre of far-left foreign policy writers, several of whom regularly lambast the state of Israel, to get advice on a range of critical foreign policy issues, among them Afghanistan, Israel, and NATO, according to press accounts.

The group of nine included several writers who promulgate fringe views about the state of Israel, advocate in favor of divestment from Israel, and describe the Jewish State as an "apartheid" state—views that are also endorsed by the most extreme anti-Israel advocates.

Liberal author, Peter Beinart—who has compared Israel to the segregated South and advocates boycotting areas of the country that he deems "non-democratic"—is reported to have joined forces with several other Israel bashers, such as the New Yorker's David Remnick and *Time* magazine's Joe Klein, for a powwow with the president. Left-wing activist Jane Mayer of the New Yorker also attended the meeting.

"The group is also notable for the inclusion of writers with radically different views on the Israel debate," observed Politico's Dylan Byers. Remnick has described Israel as undemocratic and akin to Syria and Egypt, while Klein is known for penning a series of misleading articles chastising the Jewish state. He also has expressed sympathy for Iran, a country run by Holocaust-denying anti-Semites who are intent on developing a nuclear weapon.

Bienart, however, might be the most surprising name on the list given his outspoken and vociferous criticism of Israeli policies. Those viewpoints place him far outside the mainstream of Jewish public opinion. The former TNR editor recently advocated divestment from Israel at a J Street event, a technique employed by activists who aim to destroy Israel's economy and thereby the tiny state. The meeting also raises questions about how Obama might approach the issue of Israel in a more flexible second term.

"If President Obama believes Peter Beinart's opinions are credible or anywhere near mainstream thought, then that is a five-alarm fire for Israel supporters all across the world," said one senior GOP adviser.

"It's completely irresponsible to have the president meet with a radioactive writer and anti-Israel activist who has been shunned, alienated, and isolated by even the most left wing factions of the organized pro-Israel community."

"Even so come Lord Jesus" (Revelation 20:21).

The Old City—The Heart of Jerusalem

"Redeem Israel, O God, out of their troubles."
—Psalm 25:22

Iran's Leader's and Muslim Clerics—Not Friends of Israel

President Mahmoud Ahmadinejad of Iran

December 2006 Conference on Holocaust

Main article: "International Conference to Review the Global Vision of the Holocaust."

On December 11, 2006, at the International Conference to Review the Global Vision of the Holocaust in Tehran, Ahmadinejad said:

The Zionist regime will be wiped out soon the same way the Soviet Union was, and humanity will achieve freedom", and elections should be held among "Jews, Christians and Muslims so the population of Palestine can select their government and destiny for themselves in a democratic manner.

2008 Statements on Israel's 60th Birthday

On Israel's 60th birthday, Ahmadinejad said:

Those who think they can revive the stinking corpse of the usurping and fake Israeli regime by throwing a birthday party are seriously mistaken. Today the reason for the Zionist regime's existence is questioned, and this regime is on its way to annihilation.

Ahmadinejad also stated that Israel, "has reached the end like a dead rat after being slapped by the Lebanese." Later, he said: "The Zionist regime is dying," and "The criminals imagine that by holding celebrations (...) they can save the Zionist regime from death." Ahmadinejad also stated that, "They should know that regional nations hate this fake and criminal regime and if the smallest and briefest chance is given to regional nations they will destroy (it)."

2011 Comparison of Current Zionist Regime to Cancer

In May 2011, after a protest in which 12 Palestinians were killed, Ahmadinejad said on television "... like a cancer cell that spreads through the body, this regime infects any region. It must be removed from the body;" according to a report from Agence France Presse. [1]

IRAN SAYS: DEATH TO ISRAEL AND JEWS

February 5, 2012 Iran's Ayatollah Khamenei Calls for Destruction of Israel, Jews

Ayatollah: KILL All Jews, Annihilate Israel
By Reza Hahlil World Net Daily Exclusive

Iran lays out legal case for genocidal attack against 'cancerous tumor.' The Iranian government, through a website proxy, has laid out the legal and religious justification for the destruction of Israel and the slaughter of its people. The doctrine includes wiping out Israeli assets and Jewish people worldwide. [2]

Top Commander Reiterates Iran's Commitment to Full Annihilation of Israel

TEHRAN Fars News Agency (FNA) May 20, 2012 - Chief of Staff of the Iranian Armed Forces Major General Hassan Firouzabadi said threats and pressures cannot deter Iran from its revolutionary causes and ideals, and stressed that the **Iranian** nation will remain committed to the full annihilation of the Zionist regime of Israel to the end. [3]

Endnotes
[1] http://en.wikipedia.org/wiki/Mahmoud_Ahmadinejad_and_Israel
[2] http://www.wnd.com/2012/02/ayatollah-kill-all-jews-annihilate-israel/
[3] http://english.farsnews.com/newstext.php?nn=9102112759

Egypt's Highest-Ranking Moslem Cleric Wants All Jews Removed from Jerusalem

By Jimmy DeYoung - June 6, 2012 www.prophecytoday.com

Ahmed a-Taib, the highest ranking cleric in Egypt and one of the most important clerics in the entire Sunni Arab world, has called on all Moslems who value their religion, to join him in his effort to stop the Judaization of Jerusalem. Ahmed a-Taib has set up a special committee to prevent the progress of the Zionist plan to Judaize Jerusalem and the Islamic cleric has called on all Moslem leaders to commit to using whatever sources that they have at their disposal to defend al Aksa Mosque on the Temple Mount in Jerusalem.

The call by an Egyptian Moslem cleric to liberate the city of Jerusalem is a call to arms in the Islamic world but it is also a page out of Bible prophecy for the last days. The highest-ranking Moslem cleric in Egypt and perhaps the entire Sunni Arab world has set in motion a plan to remove all Jews from the city of Jerusalem. Underneath the banner of a campaign to stop the Judaization of Jerusalem, Ahmed a-Taib has called on all Moslems everywhere to join his efforts to remove Jews from Jerusalem and to use every source at their disposal to achieve their goal. A meeting between Ahmed a-Taib and the leaders of the Islamic terror group Hamas brought a strategy together for achieving their goal of a Jew free Jerusalem. This report is tangible evidence of how the prophetic scenario found in Bible prophecy is quickly approaching the fulfillment on each of the prophecies related to the city of Jerusalem.

Zechariah 12:2 says that in the last days Jerusalem will be the center of controversy. The Davidic Covenant found in 2 Samuel 7 reveals that the Lord will place the Jews in Jerusalem forever and there He will protect them from all of their enemies. Jesus Christ said that He would return to Jerusalem (Zechariah 14:4) and there build a temple where He will rule and reign forever (Zechariah 6:12-13). Jerusalem is the place where the Lord said that He would dwell among His people, the Jewish people—forever (Psalm 132:13-14). No Moslem cleric or anyone else for that matter can stop Bible prophecy from being fulfilled.

In Defense of Israel

Excerpts from Israeli Prime Minister Benjamin Netanyahu's 2012 AIPAC Speech

Delivered at the AIPAC Conference in Washington D.C. 2012

March 5, 2012

Ladies and Gentlemen, tonight, I'd like to talk to you about a subject that no one has been talking about recently: Iran. Every day, I open the newspapers and read about these redlines and these timelines. I read about what Israel has supposedly decided to do, or what Israel might do.

Well, I'm not going to talk to you about what Israel will do or will not do. I never talk about that. But I do want to talk to you about the dangers of a nuclear-armed Iran. I want to explain why Iran must never be allowed to develop nuclear weapons.

We [Israel] are determined to prevent Iran from developing nuclear weapons; we leave all options on the table; and containment is definitely not an option. The Jewish state will not allow those who seek our destruction to possess the means to achieve that goal. A nuclear-armed Iran must be stopped.

Amazingly, some people refuse to acknowledge that Iran's goal is to develop nuclear weapons. You see Iran claims to do everything it's doing, that it's enriching uranium to develop medical isotopes. Yeah, that's right.

A country that builds underground nuclear facilities, develops intercontinental-ballistic missiles, manufactures thousands of centrifuges and that absorbs crippling sanctions is doing all that in order to advance…medical research?

So you see, when that Iranian ICBM is flying through the air to a location near you, you've got nothing to worry about—it's only carrying medical isotopes.

Ladies and Gentlemen, if it looks like a duck, walks like a duck, and quacks like a duck, then what is it? That's right, it's a duck.

But this duck is a nuclear duck. And it's time the world started calling a duck a duck. Fortunately, President Obama and most world leaders understand that the claim that Iran's goal is not to develop nuclear weapons is simply ridiculous.

Yet incredibly, some are prepared to accept an idea only slightly less preposterous: that we should accept a world in which the Ayatollahs have atomic bombs. Sure, they say, Iran is cruel, but it's not crazy. It's detestable, but it's deterrable.

My friends, responsible leaders should not bet the security of their countries on the belief that the world's most dangerous regimes won't use the world's most dangerous weapons. And I promise you that as Prime Minister, I will never gamble with the security of the State of Israel.

From the beginning, the Ayatollah regime has broken every international rule and flouted every norm. It has seized embassies, targeted diplomats. It sends its own children through mine fields; it hangs gays and stones women; it supports Assad's brutal slaughter of the Syrian people; it is the world's foremost sponsor of terrorism: It sponsors Hezbollah in Lebanon, Hamas in Gaza and terrorists throughout the Middle East, Africa, even South America.

Iran's proxies have dispatched hundreds of suicide bombers, planted thousands of roadside bombs, and they fired over twenty thousand missiles at civilians. Through terror from the skies and terror on the ground, Iran is responsible for the murder of hundreds, if not thousands, of Americans.

In 1983, Iran's proxy Hezbollah blew up the Marine barracks in Lebanon, killing 240 U.S. Marines. In the last decade, it's been responsible for murdering and maiming American soldiers in Afghanistan and in Iraq.

Just a few months ago, it tried to assassinate the Saudi Ambassador to the U.S. in a restaurant just a few blocks from here. The assassins didn't care that several Senators and members of Congress would have been murdered in the process.

Iran calls for Israel's destruction, and they work for its destruction each day, every day. This is how Iran behaves today, without nuclear weapons. Think of how they will behave tomorrow, with nuclear weapons. Iran will be even more reckless and a lot more dangerous.

There's been plenty of talk recently about the costs of stopping Iran. I think it's time we started talking about the costs of not stopping Iran. A nuclear-armed Iran would dramatically increase terrorism by giving terrorists a nuclear umbrella.

Let me try to explain what that means, a nuclear umbrella. It means that Iran's terror proxies like Hezbollah, Hamas will be emboldened to attack the United States, Israel, and other countries because they will be backed by a power that has atomic weapons. So the terrorism could grow tenfold.

A nuclear-armed Iran could choke off the world's oil supply and make real its threat to close the Straits of Hormouz. If you're worried about the price of oil today, imagine how high oil prices could get once a nuclear-armed Iran starts blackmailing the world.

If Iran gets nuclear weapons, it would set off a mad dash by Saudi Arabia, Turkey, and others to acquire nuclear weapons of their own. The world's most volatile region would become a nuclear tinderbox waiting to go off.

And here's the worst nightmare of all, with nuclear weapons, Iran could threaten all of us with nuclear terrorism. It could put a nuclear device in a ship heading to any port or in a truck parked in any city, anywhere in the world.

I want you to think about what it would mean to have nuclear weapons in the hands of those who lead millions of radicals who chant: "Death to America" and "Death to Israel."

When you think about that you'll reach a simple conclusion: for the sake of our prosperity, for the sake of our security, for the sake of our children, Iran must *not* be allowed to acquire nuclear weapons!

Of course, the best outcome would be if Iran decided to abandon its nuclear weapons program peacefully. No one would be happier than me and the people of Israel if Iran dismantled its program. But so far, that hasn't happened. For fifteen years, I've been warning that a nuclear-armed Iran is a grave danger to my country and to the peace and security of the entire world. For the last decade, the international community has tried diplomacy. It hasn't worked.

For six years, the international community has applied sanctions. That hasn't worked either. I appreciate President Obama's recent efforts to impose even tougher sanctions against Iran. These sanctions are hurting Iran's economy, but unfortunately, Iran's nuclear program continues to march forward.

Israel has waited patiently for the international community to resolve this issue. We've waited for diplomacy to work. We've waited for sanctions to work. None of us can afford to wait much longer. As Prime Minister of Israel, I will never let my people live in the shadow of annihilation.

Ladies and Gentlemen, some commentators would have you believe that stopping Iran from getting the bomb is more dangerous than letting Iran have the bomb. They say that a military confrontation with Iran would undermine the efforts already underway; that it would be ineffective; and that it would provoke an even more vindictive response by Iran.

I've heard these arguments before. In fact, I've read them before. In my desk I have copies of an exchange of letters between the World Jewish Congress and the United States War Department. Here are the letters:

The year was 1944. The World Jewish Congress implored the American government to bomb Auschwitz. The reply came five days later. I want to read it to you. Such an operation could be executed only by diverting considerable air support essential to the success of our forces elsewhere…and in any case it would be of such doubtful efficacy that it would not warrant the use of our resources. And, my friends, here's the most remarkable sentence of all, and I quote:

"Such an effort might provoke even more vindictive action by the Germans."

Think about that — "even more vindictive action" — than the Holocaust.

My Friends, 2012 is not 1944. The American government today is different. You heard it in President Obama's speech yesterday. But here's my point: The Jewish people are also different. Today we have a state of our own. And the purpose of the Jewish state is to defend Jewish lives and to secure the Jewish future. Never again will we not be masters of the fate of our very survival. Never again.

That is why Israel must always have the ability to defend itself, by itself, against any threat. We deeply appreciate the great alliance between our two countries. But when it comes to Israel's survival, we must always remain the masters of our fate.

Ladies and Gentlemen, Israel's fate is to continue to be the forward position of freedom in the Middle East. The only place in the Middle East where minorities enjoy full civil rights; the only place in the Middle East where Arabs enjoy full civil rights; the only place in the Middle East where Christians are free to practice their faith; the only place in the Middle East where real judges protect the rule of law.

And as Prime Minister of Israel, I will always protect Israel's democracy—always. I will never allow anything to threaten Israel's democratic way of life. And most especially, I will never tolerate any discrimination against women.

Ladies and Gentlemen, This week, we will read how one woman changed Jewish history. In Synagogues throughout the world, the Jewish people will celebrate the festival of Purim. We will read how some 2,500 years ago, a Persian anti-Semite tried to annihilate the Jewish people. And we will read how that plot was foiled by one courageous woman—Esther. In every generation, there are those who wish to destroy the Jewish people. In this generation, we are blessed to live in an age when there is a Jewish state capable of defending the Jewish people.

And we are doubly blessed to have so many friends like you, Jews and non-Jews alike, who love the State of Israel and support its right to defend itself. So as I leave you tonight I thank you for your friendship. Thank you for your courage. Thank you for standing up for the one and only Jewish state.

Below are some excerpts from a good article by Hal Lindsey. He makes some strong points regarding the extreme and brutal conditions in Syria and throughout the Middle East. He also shares some important information in reference to the speech given by Prime Minister Benjamin Netanyahu, which you have just read.

Excerpts from the Hal Lindsey Report March 9, 2012

One can make a strong argument that we've never seen the American mainstream media so "in the tank" for a sitting Administration as we're seeing today. But then the Left argues that Fox News is the PR department for the Republican Party! The reality is that almost every news organization operating today has some sort of "slant."

Truth be told, to get just a middle-of-the-road presentation of the news, you probably need to go online and read everything you can from both sides, then filter it through your lens of common sense, historical knowledge, and intuition. But who has time to do that? So what does this mean? It means that we all need to keep in mind that the slant and intent of almost everything we see and hear and read from the mainstream media is decided in advance in corporate boardrooms and political backrooms. It's based on what works best for the corporation or party making the decision. If they decide that you shouldn't hear certain news reports, then you won't. Welcome to the brave new world.

Just as the media turned a blind eye to the deaths of innocents in Afghanistan and focused on American insensitivity to the Koran, the United Nations followed suit. While Syrian security forces continue to murder Syrian citizens in astonishing numbers (nearly 5,500 so far); even after a UN commission reported "widespread and systematic violations" of women's rights by Syrian forces, including sexual violence, rape, and torture, the UN Commission on the Status of Women chose to pass a resolution condemning... Israel.

According to the Commission, the major obstacle to the advancement of Palestinian women is Israel's occupation of the disputed territory. In fact, the UN Commission condemned the "systematic violation of their human rights resulting from the severe impact of ongoing illegal Israeli practices." Never mind the rape, murder, and torture of women going on in Syria; never mind the oppression of women in Iran or Saudi Arabia; don't worry about the slave trade in Sudan and Darfur, this cruel Israeli scheme to suppress the self-reliance and advancement of Palestinian women has got to stop!

Do you remember what the apostle Paul said about those who do not love the truth in the last days? He said that God would send a "deluding influence" upon them "so that they will believe what is false, in order that all may be judged who did not believe the truth, but took pleasure in wickedness." I believe that's precisely what we're witnessing in the earth today.

Finally, Israeli Prime Minister Benjamin Netanyahu visited the White House last Monday. The Prime Minister chose the occasion of the Feast of Purim to emphasize to the President that Israel finds itself once again under mortal threat from Persia, or modern-day Iran. President Obama continued to insist that there is still time to try further negotiations and tougher sanctions against Iran. Netanyahu persisted in affirming Israel's sovereign right to defend itself, by itself, if needed.

Then emerged a story that may prove the fallacy of President Obama's assertions: Apparently German and Japanese intelligence sources last week confirmed stories that have appeared in Der Spiegel and Welt am Sonntag that western intelligence has known for 11 months that North Korea carried out covert nuclear tests on an Iranian radioactive bomb or nuclear warhead.

And they did it in 2010! A Debkafile report concluded that, "The disclosure invalidates the main point the US President made... that there was still time for diplomatic pressure and sanctions to bring Iran's leaders to a decision to halt their nuclear momentum before military action was called for, whether by the US or Israel."

I think it may be wise to remember Paul's words in Romans 13:11: "...knowing the time, that now it is high time to awake out of sleep; for now our salvation is nearer than when we first believed."

Make sure you're ready for the moment when Jesus calls, "Come up here" [the Rapture]. And use this time and the drama of these events to make certain that those near you have heard the "good news" that Jesus Christ died to purchase a pardon for all their sins so that when it comes time for the believers to leave this earth, they, too, will hear His call. [2]

Endnotes
[1] http://www.algemeiner.com/2012/03/05/full-text-of-netanyahu-speech-to-aipac-2012/
[2] http://www.hallindsey.com/the-hal-lindsey-report-392012/

Almighty God—Protector of Israel

A fact that many people are unaware of is that well-over a decade ago on July 17, 1998, *The Jerusalem Post* on its editorial page posted an article citing that Henry Siegman (a secular Jew), "a senior fellow at the Council of Foreign Relations (CFR) in New York threatened Israel with *extinction* if she doesn't do as the American (CFR) wishes and dictates." This draconian, blatant anti-Israel sentiment and stance against God's chosen nation—including the push to take away Israel, again land and reduce her to nothing—is not only an ongoing agenda of Muslim hierarchies, but also that of the global elitists here in the U.S. and abroad—regardless of their cultural heritage. Enemies of Israel are enemies of the God of the Bible. Scripture seems to indicate that when Israel is attacked in the coming battle of Ezekiel 38 and 39, not even the US will help protect her except by possibly making a mild-verbal protest (Ezekiel 38:13). But God *will* protect Israel—His chosen nation—to the amazement of all her avowed enemies.

A Better World with Messiah Jesus

John 14:1-3

"Let not your heart be troubled; you believe in God, believe also in Me. In My Father's house are many mansions; if it were not so, I would have told you. I go to prepare a place for you. And if I go and prepare a place for you, I will come again and receive you to Myself; that where I am, there you may be also."

Our Great God and Savior Jesus Christ

"Looking for the blessed hope and glorious appearing of our great God and Savior Jesus Christ. Now to Him who is able to keep you from stumbling, and to make you stand in the presence of His glory blameless with great joy, to the only God our Savior, through Jesus Christ our Lord, *be* glory, majesty, dominion and authority, before all time and now and forever. Amen" (Titus 2:13; Jude 1:24-25)

Chapter Three

Messiah, Beam Me Up!

Scripture teaches there will be no shortage of false teachers and false prophets in these last days attempting to discredit the truths of the Bible. The most confusing and dangerous are those who knowingly (or unknowingly) extract passages from the Bible and turn them into their own warped renditions of what they extol as "truth."

Media sensationalism regarding false Rapture predictions serves the enemies of God very well. Whenever someone sets a date for the Rapture and shouts it from the rooftops the media does not hesitate to make cannon fodder out of the prognosticator as well as the message—casting serious doubts on the true Rapture position distinctly taught in the Scriptures. Surely by now much of the world has heard of the Rapture but in a negative way—dismissing it as some sort of contrived, delusional teaching. But the good news is this: They are wrong. The Rapture is the blessed hope for all true believers.

A seven-year Tribulation period is coming as prophesied with great specificity throughout the Bible. It is a time when you will not want to be here. We have already touched on this a bit earlier. Those years will be filled with everything that evil can possibly conjure up. It is also when God will send His long overdue judgments, His "wrath" upon a world that has rejected His moral laws and Him. Before that frightening time, God promises to physically remove all true, born-again believers in the Rapture, the great snatching away—Messiah's "heavenly airlift."

"For God has not destined us for wrath, but for obtaining salvation through our Lord Jesus Christ, who died for us, that whether we are awake or asleep, we may live together with Him. Therefore, encourage one another, and build up one another, just as you also are doing" (1 Thessalonians 5:9-11).

"And to wait for His Son from heaven, whom He raised from the dead, *that is* Jesus who died for us, **delivers us from the wrath to come**" (1 Thessalonians 1:1).

When Jesus returns to remove all born-again believers from the coming wrath He will come in the same manner in which He ascended

113

into heaven. When He returns at the end of the Tribulation, at the Second Coming, He returns with His heavenly army. At the Rapture He does not have the armies of heaven with Him, as you can see in the following verse recorded by Luke in the book of Acts. The Rapture and the Second Coming are two separate events.

"They also said, 'Men of Galilee, why do you stand looking into the sky? This Jesus, who has been taken up from you into heaven, **will come in just the same way as you have watched Him go** into heaven'" (Acts 11:1).

Are you thinking the Rapture, also referred to as the "harpazo" sounds like some sort of science fiction fantasy, an event that could not possibly happen? Please read the Bible verses again; they are very clear. The Creator of the universe, in the span of a few moments will remove all those who have placed their faith in Him. The Greek word "harpazo" is translated as "caught up." Remember, we are talking about the God of the universe. If He can *create* an extremely intricate universe, lifting out some of His creation to the safety of heaven will be just another minor mission for Him. Scripture, the inerrant Word of God declares this will happen, and God does not lie. He is the dependable friend you always wished you had.

"Behold, I tell you a mystery: We shall not all sleep [die], but we shall all be changed—in a moment, in the twinkling of an eye, at the last trumpet, For the trumpet will sound, and the dead will be raised incorruptible, and we shall be changed" (1 Corinthians 15:51-52).

"For the Lord Himself will descend from heaven with a shout, with the voice of an archangel, and with the trumpet of God. And the dead in Christ will rise first.

Then we who are alive *and* remain shall be caught up together with them in the clouds to meet the Lord in the air. And thus we shall always be with the Lord. Therefore comfort one another with these words" (1 Thessalonians 4:16-18).

The Rapture, this very intriguing prophesied miracle, this biblical phenomenon, will change the face of the world like no other event in history. It will especially and most radically change the dynamics in

United States because of the large number Christians living here. Millions of people will be gone, without a trace. Can you even begin to imagine the chaos and panic that will follow? I pray that whoever you are reading this, that you will never experience the post-Rapture days, the Tribulation. I pray that you will take this information to heart and realize that all those who place their trust in the Lord are on the brink of being ushered into His holy presence. I would say that is about as exciting a future as one could ever imagine.

Most good Bible teachers agree on the Pre-Tribulation Rapture, but differ in their opinions on the *timing* of the event. Through Scripture, the Lord has given us plenty of signs to discern that we are most likely that prophesied final generation. The word "final" in this instance really means "beginning" for those who are true believers. The Lord is our blessed hope. He is about to break into a world that is teetering, dying and gasping for its last breaths. No amount of fame or fortune in this world can begin to compare with the phenomenal future He has in store for His children.

Don't let the temporary accolades and trophies of this world fool you into thinking there isn't yet a much more exciting future with the ultimate "head coach" Himself, Jesus the Messiah. Some time ago, I heard a guest on "Coast To Coast AM," the late-night radio show, respond to a caller's question about the Rapture. He stated that the Rapture is not biblical and answered the question with some sort of very vague nonsensical point about the 1800s. It was obvious that he was uneducated on the topic, as are many others—including millions who attend church regularly.

The Rapture and the Day of the Lord

"Prove all things; hold fast that which is good" —1 Thessalonians 5:21a

> "Make your ear attentive to wisdom, incline your heart to understanding; for if you cry for discernment, lift your voice for understanding; if you seek her as silver, and search for her as hidden treasures; then you will discern the fear of the LORD, and discover the knowledge of God" (Proverbs 2:2-3).

The late J. Vernon McGee, a popular respected Bible teacher (Thru the Bible radio programs) taught the Tribulation (Day of the Lord) would begin *immediately* after the Rapture:

The one event of the Rapture will end the day of grace and begin the Day of the Lord. It closes one day and opens another." (J. Vernon McGee, *Thru the Bible, Volume Five,* p. 400)

On the same page of the same book, J. Vernon McGee also discusses how the world will be expecting to enter a new era of peace, but instead will be "plunged" unexpectedly into the Tribulation, indicating that there will be a false peace just *prior* to the beginning of the Tribulation.

> "While they are saying, "Peace and safety!" **then destruction will come upon them suddenly** like birth pangs upon a woman with child; and they [unbelievers] shall not escape" (1 Thessalonians 5:3).

Does it look like we are in the midst of "peace and safety" or about to *start* an era of peace and safety? Are there signs that a very charismatic leader is just about to sign a covenant with Israel? It certainly does not appear that way at the moment, but we do see foreshadows of these coming prophesied events, which could come to pass very quickly. Dave Hunt, a noted prophecy teacher who has written several books on eschatology has stated clearly that the Rapture takes place during a time of peace while the Second Coming takes place during a time of war:

"The Rapture comes in the midst of peace (1 Thessalonians 5:3), the Second Coming in a time of war (Revelation 19:11-21)." (*How Close Are We?* page 204)

The late Dr. John Walvoord made the following statement:

> "When the day of grace ends with the translation of the church, the Day of the Lord [the Tribulation] begins at once."
> —*The Rapture Question,* page.162

We should watch for specific prophetic signs to take place before the Tribulation so we will know the return of the Lord is getting closer, and that the Rapture is near.

A false peace as already stated on the previous page (1 Thessalonians 5:3) is a foreshadowing sign. I would also say that the prophetic fulfillment of the battle of Ezekiel 38 and 39 to be a strong indicator that we are getting very close to the Tribulation. And if there is no interval between the Tribulation and the Rapture, we know then that the Rapture cannot happen at *any moment.*

"Watch therefore, for you do not know what hour your Lord is coming" (Matthew 24:42).

"**But ye brethren** [believers], **are not in darkness**, that the day should overtake you like a thief; for you are all sons of light and sons of day. We are not of night nor of darkness; so then let us not sleep as others do, but let us be alert and sober" (1 Thessalonians 5:4-6).

Those who have truly received Messiah Jesus: as Savior will be spared from the Tribulation. Through Scripture we learn that when Jesus takes out all true believers in the Rapture, it will happen in a span of several moments, not in an instant. I will quote the passage again:

"For the Lord Himself will descend from heaven with a shout, with the voice of an archangel, and with the trumpet of God ["at the **last trumpet**"]. Then we who are alive *and* remain shall be caught up together with them in the clouds to meet the Lord in the air" (1 Thessalonians 4:16-18).

The Rapture takes place after the forewarning signs of Joel 2:30-31 and Luke 21:25-26 (see page 148). Then, as I quoted earlier from 1 Corinthians 15:52, the mortal bodies of believers at the "last trumpet" will actually be changed into immortal bodies in the "twinkling of an eye."

This does not necessarily mean that the *entire* Rapture phenomenon will take place instantaneously or in the "twinkling of an eye." In 1 Corinthians 15 the apostle Paul wrote: "but we shall all be **changed** in a moment, in the twinkling of an eye."

It is the conversion from mortal to immortal beings (new, glorified bodies) that happens "in a moment, in the twinkling of an eye," not the entire Rapture. Scripture does not indicate how long the blowing of the trumpets will last. It could well be longer than most Bible expositors teach. I have read that on Rosh Hashanah one hundred trumpet blasts are made all day long, but we really cannot be sure how long it will take. The important thing is to be ready, to be truly born-again, saved and covered by the blood atoning sacrifice of Jesus.

When Messiah Jesus returns at Armageddon along with "the armies in heaven," "every eye shall see Him." The Second Advent or the Second Coming of Messiah Jesus is a distinctly different event from the Rapture.

The last trump referred to here, at the Rapture is *not* the same trumpet or "seventh angel sounded" spoken of in Revelation 11:15.

"Behold, He is coming with clouds, and every eye shall see Him, even they who pierced Him. And all the tribes of the earth mourn because of Him. Even so, Amen" (Revelation 1:7).

James and the Patient Husbandman

When we use Scripture to support an argument, it is important to keep the use of the verses in context with each other. A popular Scripture that is used for an "imminent" Rapture is James 5:8:

"Be ye also patient; establish your hearts: for the coming of the Lord is at hand."

The key phrase from that verse, used by those who teach the Rapture can happen at any moment is: "the Lord is at hand." But we must first read verse 7 to understand the entire and intended meaning of verse 8:

"Be ye patient therefore, brethren, until the coming of the Lord. Behold the husbandman waiteth for the precious fruits of the earth, being patient over it, until it receive the early and latter rain" (James 5: 7).

Together the verses read:

"**Be ye patient**; establish your hearts: for the coming of the Lord is at hand. **Be ye also patient** therefore, brethren, **until the coming of the Lord. Behold the husbandman waiteth** for the precious fruits of the earth, **being patient over it, until it receive the early and latter rain**" (James 5:7-8).

Understanding the following illustration is of paramount importance and essential to understanding the intended meaning of James: 7-8 and the timing of the Rapture.

"Behold the husbandman [the farmer] **waiteth** for the precious fruits of the earth, **being patient over it, until it receive the early and latter rain**" (James 7b).

118

The previous Scripture references the farmer (husbandman) who plants seeds, and knows the harvest is **certain**. Then he waits for the crops to come in until the spring and fall rains bring forth the "fruits of the earth." We see that the harvest is "at hand" (eggus in Greek). This illustration shows that the end result of the planted seeds can only mean "certain" without any regard to time, except for the "early and latter rains" and things that have to precede the harvest. The farmer does not expect the harvest to come in at any moment, and there are events before the farmer sees the spring and fall crops come in. There is a process of germination for the seeds, the rains must come, and time must pass. So the farmer waits patiently for his bounty after the coming spring and fall rains.

Now having given that illustration, so as a farmer waits for his crop we in like manner wait patiently for the coming of the Lord with signs of the times ("the latter rain"), without any regard for time. The farmer does not expect the harvest to happen at any moment; there are events that need to take place before he sees the spring and fall rains, and before the crops come in. James was speaking to believers to wait for the coming of the Lord, to be patient, just as the farmer is patient, and waits, **"be ye also patient therefore, brethren, until the coming of the Lord."** As a farmer waits for his crops, **we wait for the Lord's return**; there is an order to His return. It is not simply a happenstance that can occur at any given moment. Using James 5:8 without giving careful thought to the previous verse, results in faulty interpretation of the intended meaning of the passages.

Imminence or Certainty?

No specific passages in the Bible teach the doctrine of "imminence" and there are a number of passages that do not support the concept, as just shown with James 5:7-8. Some Old Testament passages use terms that at first glance could suggest immediacy are: Isaiah 13:6; Ezekiel 30:3; Joel 1:15; 2:1; Obadiah 15 and Haggai 2:6. But the words "near" and "at hand" and in "a little while" in these passages cannot mean that the "Day of the Lord" was near in regard to time. These passages were written from seven hundred to five hundred years *before* the First Coming of the Messiah. How could the "Day of the Lord" be near when the First Coming of the Messiah had not taken place?

Scripture distinctly shows that there are two comings of the Messiah. In one coming Messiah dies for mankind (Psalm 22:6-8, 11-18; Isaiah 53:1-12) and the Second Advent He judges mankind and then reigns on earth (Isaiah 52:13-15; 63:1-6; 66:15-17; Habakkuk 3:3-6; Zechariah 14:1-4, 9; Matthew 25:31-46; 2 Thessalonians 1:7-10; Revelation 19:11-21).

Messiah Jesus had to come the first time to die and the second time He comes to judge and reign on earth. The "Day of the Lord" which starts with the Tribulation could not be "near" or "at hand" or "a little while" until the Messiah had come the first time to die for man. We know the Messiah could not return to judge the world until the fourth kingdom of Daniel's prophecy (Rome) was established (Daniel 2:31-45; 7:2-28). When these prophets wrote, the third kingdom (Greece) had not yet risen.

If the words in the Old Testament, "near" and "about" and "a little while," have nothing to do with the timing of the Rapture and the Second Coming, neither do similar words that are used in the New Testament. We know this because it has been over 1900 years since the New Testament was written and Christ has not returned.

Instead of having to do with "nearness" in time, these phrases have to do with the "certainty" of those events. We now understand that certain things had to take place *before* the Rapture could occur such as Israel becoming a nation; and we await the fulfillment of other forewarning signs such as those indicated in Joel 2:30-31 and Luke 17:26-30.

I came to the very same conclusion regarding the doctrine of imminence as Dave Hunt, in his book: *How Close Are We*? His argument makes perfect sense. On the next page, follow the paragraphs quoted from page 115:

One cannot escape the fact that Christ and His apostles gave definite signs to watch for that herald the nearness of His return. Why give these signs if some generation at some time in the future was not expected to recognize them and know that His Second Coming was as He Himself said, "near, even at the doors?"

Yes, but if the Rapture occurs seven years prior to the Second Coming, then those signs are not for us. So it would seem. Yet Christ commanded His own to watch for His coming and warned against being caught by surprise at His return—and surprise could only apply to the Rapture. Are we faced again with a contradiction, and this time one that cannot be resolved?

We may be certain that the answers are to be found if we desire to know them and diligently search His Word. Jesus also said, "And when these things begin to come to pass, then look up, and lift up your heads; for your redemption draweth nigh" (Luke 21:28).

When these things begin...look up. The commencement of the signs cannot be herald the Second Coming, for that event cannot occur until the signs are all complete Therefore, with this statement, Christ can only be referring to the Rapture.

When Jesus, in response to His disciples' request for signs of His return, enumerated a long list of events (wars, rumors of wars, pestilence, earthquakes, famines, etc.), He also used that same word, *begin*.

He made this very interesting comment: "All these things are the *beginning* of sorrows" (Matthew 24:8). The Greek word Jesus used for "sorrow" is most interesting as well. It referred especially to a woman's birth pangs.

Jesus is apparently revealing that these signs will *begin* to occur substantially ahead of the Second Coming. They will increase in frequency and intensity like birth pangs. Moreover, it would seem that these signs *begin* prior to the Rapture. Then how could the Rapture be a surprise?

An interesting book, *When:When Will the Rapture Take Place?*, authored by Dr. F. Kenton Beshore, the very popularly accepted doctrine of imminence is discussed pointing out that imminence is not an essential "doctrine" for a Pre-Tribulation Rapture, contrary to the opinion of some well-meaning individuals. In the first chapter, Isaiah 61:1-11 is sighted as the **key** to Pre-Millennial and Pre-Tribulation eschatology (study of end times, the "last things").

Staggering insights on some confusing positions on imminence taken by a number of prominent Bible teachers are included in the book. The following excerpts are taken from chapters ten, eleven, and twelve, followed by Isaiah 61:1-11 quoted from chapter one:

The Days of Noah and Lot

Jesus taught the Rapture and the start of the Tribulation take place on the same 24-hour day:

"And as it came to pass in the days of Noah, even so shall it be also in the days of the Son of man. They ate, they drank, they married, they were given in marriage, until the day that Noah entered into the ark, and the flood came, and destroyed them all. Likewise even as it came to pass in the days of Lot; they ate, they drank, they bought, they sold, they planted, they builded; but in the day that Lot went out from Sodom it rained fire and brimstone from heaven, and destroyed them all: after the same manner shall it be in the day that the Son of man is revealed. In that day, he that shall be on the housetop, and his goods in the house, let him not go down to take them away: and let him that is in the field likewise not return back. Remember Lot's wife. Whosoever shall seek to gain his life shall lose it: but whosoever shall lose his life shall preserve it" (Luke 17:26-33).

The flood began on the same 24-hour day that Noah entered the ark:

"**In the selfsame day** entered Noah, and Shem, and Ham, and Japheth, the sons of Noah, and Noah's wife, and the three wives of his sons with them, into the ark; and the flood was forty days upon the earth; and the waters increased, and bare up the ark, and it was lifted up above the earth" (Genesis 7:13, 17)

Jesus said that on the day that the Rapture takes place the Tribulation will start. On the day that Lot departed Sodom, God brought judgment upon it:

"And when the **morning arose**, then the angels hastened Lot, saying, Arise, take thy wife, and thy two daughters that are here, lest thou be consumed in the iniquity of the city. But he lingered; and the men laid hold upon his hand, and upon the hand of his wife, and upon the hand of his two daughters, Jehovah being merciful unto him; and they brought him forth, and set him without the city" (Genesis 19:15-1).

"The **sun was risen upon the earth** when Lot came unto Zoar. Then Jehovah rained upon Sodom and upon Gomorrah brimstone and fire from Jehovah out of heaven; and he overthrew those cities, and all the Plain, and all the inhabitants of the cities, and that which grew upon the ground" (Genesis 19:23-25).

The flood began on the very 24-hour day Noah and his family entered the ark. Sodom was destroyed on the same 24-hour day that Lot departed. Therefore, the Rapture should occur on the 24-hour day that the Tribulation starts. A "day" must be a normal 24-hour day or the statement about not going down from the rooftop or back to the house makes no sense (Luke 17:31).

Conclusion

Jesus said that on the very "day that Noah entered into the ark, and the flood came, and destroyed them all" (Luke 17:27), and "in the day that Lot went out from Sodom it rained fire and brimstone from heaven, and destroyed them all" (Luke 17.29). He then said, "After the same manner shall it be in the day that the Son of man is revealed" (Luke 17.30).

This is the first revealing at the Rapture. If there is no *gap* between the Rapture and the Tribulation, all the prophecies that must be fulfilled before the Tribulation starts will be fulfilled before the Rapture. Therefore, the Rapture should not take place until all those prophecies (*warning signs*) have been fulfilled.

Dr. John Walvoord, who was an ardent Pre-Tribulationist, admitted that imminence is a doctrine that is not stated in the Bible: "Pretribulationalism is an induction rather than an explicit statement of the Bible." (*The Rapture Question: Revised,* 11th printing, 1973, p. 181)

If the doctrine of the Pre-Tribulation Rapture "is an induction rather than an explicit statement of the Bible," then the doctrine of imminence is also "an induction rather than an explicit statement." I disagree with Walvoord that imminence "is an essential doctrine of pretribulationalism."

There is no need for it to defend the Pre-Tribulation doctrine as will be shown in the following chapter. The arguments for imminence are not based on Scripture. Most who teach it say there are signs of the approaching Tribulation and the Glorious Appearing of Jesus Christ. Those signs are also signs of the Rapture. The Rapture is either an imminent event with no warning signs, or it is not imminent and signs precede it.

Some prophecy teachers think the Rapture became an imminent event that could have taken place any moment since the destruction of Jerusalem in 70 A.D. One argument says the command by Jesus to "look up" when the things spoken of in the Olivet Discourse begin to come to pass (Luke 21:28), referred to the destruction of the Temple (Luke 21:21-24).

When the Temple was destroyed "that fulfilled every and any prophecy that had to be fulfilled before the Rapture." That event "rendered the Rapture of the church imminent." (Fruchtenbaum, Arnold, *Footsteps of the Messiah*, 1993, pp. 636-637)

This quasi-Preterist thinking ignores some very important facts. According to this hypothesis the Rapture could have taken place before the book of Revelation was written about 25 years after the destruction of the Temple.

It also rejects the fact that Israel had to return to Palestine and become a functioning nation so it could fulfill the prophecy that says she will make a covenant with the Antichrist (Isaiah 28:15-18; Daniel 9:27).

The only way to get around this prophecy that had to be fulfilled as we saw in 1948 is to argue there could be a gap between the Rapture and the start of the Tribulation. That gap could have been over 1900 years according to this hypothesis!

We know this hypothesis is not valid because we are still here, the book of Revelation was written, Israel became a nation and many other pretribulational prophecies have been fulfilled. We also know it is not biblical because the Bible teaches there is no gap between the Rapture and the Tribulation as explained in the previous chapter.

This hypothesis also ignores verses 25 through 27 of Luke 21, which says that just prior to the Rapture there will be signs in the sun, moon and stars, and dismay among nations. The oceans will be roaring and people will be fainting from fear of what is about to happen.

It is after this prophecy of cosmic warning signs that Jesus commanded all Christians to "look up, and lift up your heads; because your redemption draweth nigh." According to the Bible the Rapture cannot take place until those cosmic warning signs come to pass.

Fruchtenbaum also believes the seven churches in the book of Revelation (chapters 2-3), are symbolic of seven periods in the Church Age. The promise of being kept from the "hour of trial," which he interprets as a promise of the Pre-Tribulation Rapture, was made to the church of Philadelphia (Revelation 3:10). He believes the period of the Philadelphia church ran from 1648-1900 (Ibid, pp. 48-50).

His beliefs that the Rapture became an *imminent* event that can take place at *any moment*, and that the Philadelphia church was promised to escape the "hour of trial" (Tribulation) are contradictory. If the Rapture has been *imminent* since 70 A.D. the Philadelphia church could not be symbolic of the church from 1648-1900.

If the Philadelphia church is symbolic of the church from 1648-1900 the Rapture could not have been imminent since 70 A.D. as he says. Therefore the Rapture could not have become imminent until after 1648.

Another mistake that Fruchtenbaum and others make who believe the seven churches are symbolic of seven periods of church history is that the Philadelphia church period is over, and the Rapture has not taken place. Since, according to Fruchtenbaum, the Philadelphia church period ended in 1900 the promise of being raptured was not to that church. Instead the apostate Laodecian church will be spared the "hour of trial" (Tribulation) because it began in 1900.

We believe the Philadelphia church period began in 1792 when William Carey sailed to India and opened the door of foreign missions. It will continue until the Rapture, thus receiving the promise of being kept from the "hour of trial" (Revelation 3.10). This is the answer to the disciples' prayer "lead us not into temptation"

(Matthew 6:13). The Greek word that is translated "trial" and "temptation" is peirasmos.

Millions of Christians have lived holy lives without believing in imminence. Belief in that doctrine does not edify one to live a holy life. Jesus does not have to return at any moment to "catch one by surprise doing those things that no Christian should" do. He knew everything everyone would do before He created the universe.

Some pastors believe the Holy Spirit deliberately wanted Christians throughout the Church Age to believe Christ could return at any moment. We must always keep in mind that the Holy Spirit is omniscient, and He knew that Christ was not scheduled to return for over 1900 years when He inspired Paul, James, Peter and John to write their letters.

The Holy Spirit did not deceive the disciples into thinking Christ could return in their lifetime, and in no way did He seek to have millions of Christians misled into believing Christ could return at any moment with no warning signs preceding His return!

To say the Holy Spirit deliberately deceived the apostles, and that He has deceived Christians for the last 1900 years into believing Christ could return at any moment would be accusing Him of Jesuit casuistry (the end justifies the means). "What shall we say then? Shall we continue in sin, that grace may abound? God forbid" (Romans 6:1-2).

The doctrine of *imminence* is based on a few passages, which do not teach it directly while some passages teach the opposite.

Passages That Seem to Allude to Imminence

The defenders of the doctrine of imminence argue that the key phrases "at hand" and "draweth nigh" prove the Rapture has been an imminent event since Pentecost. These phrases can be found in (Luke 21:28, James 5:8; 1 Peter 4:7; Romans 13:12; Philippians 4:5; Revelation 1:3).

The Greek adverb eggus, means "to bring near, to draw nigh, be at hand" (Liddell & Scott, Greek Lexicon, p. 189). Greek language expert Dr. Joseph Thayer says that when it is used in reference to time it is "concerning things imminent and soon to come to pass." (Greek-English Lexicon, p.164).

The passages noted above do not teach that the return of Jesus was "at hand" in the first century. Instead, they say that the return of Christ is certain. The passages do not refer to time as will be shown.

The Holy Spirit knew that Christ was not scheduled to return for over 1900 years when He inspired Paul, James, Peter and John to write their letters.

The Holy Spirit did not deceive the disciples into thinking Christ could return in their lifetime, and in no way did He seek to have millions of Christians misled into believing Christ could return at *any moment* with no *warning signs* preceding His return! Evidence that this is correct is the fact that Jesus told His disciples directly that He would not return while they were alive:

"And He said unto the disciples, "The days will come, when you will desire to see one of the days of the Son of man, and you will not see it" (Luke 17:22).

This statement is clear that the disciples would not be alive when Jesus returns. They understood this. That is why none of them taught that Christ could return at any moment and it proves that the above passages have nothing to do with the timing of the Rapture.

ISAIAH 61

The key to Pre-Millennial and Pre-Tribulation eschatology is found in the 61st chapter of the book of Isaiah:

"The Spirit of the Lord Jehovah is upon me; because Jehovah hath anointed me to preach good tidings unto the meek; he hath sent me to bind up the broken-hearted, to proclaim liberty to the captives, and the opening of the prison to them that are bound; to proclaim the year of Jehovah's favor, and the day of vengeance of our God; to comfort all that mourn; to appoint unto them that mourn in Zion, to give unto them a garland for ashes, the oil of joy for mourning, the garment of praise for the spirit of heaviness; that they may be called trees of righteousness, the planting of Jehovah, that he may be glorified.

And they shall build the old wastes, they shall raise up the former desolations, and they shall repair the waste cities, the desolations of many generations. And strangers shall stand and feed your flocks, and foreigners shall be your plowmen and your vine-dressers.

But ye shall be named the priests of Jehovah; men shall call you the ministers of our God: ye shall eat the wealth of the nations, and in their glory shall ye boast yourselves. Instead of your shame ye shall have double; and instead of dishonor they shall rejoice in their portion: therefore in their land they shall possess double; everlasting joy shall be unto them

For I, Jehovah, love justice, I hate robbery with iniquity; and I will give them their recompense in truth, and I will make an everlasting covenant with them. And their seed shall be known among the nations, and their offspring among the peoples; all that see them shall acknowledge them, that they are the seed which Jehovah hath blessed.

I will greatly rejoice in Jehovah, my soul shall be joyful in my God; for he hath clothed me with the garments of salvation, he hath covered me with the robe of righteousness, as a bridegroom decketh himself with a garland, and as a bride adorneth herself with her jewels. For as the earth bringeth forth its bud, and as the garden causeth the things that are sown in it to spring forth; so the Lord

Jehovah will cause righteousness and praise to spring forth before all the nations" (Isaiah 61:1-11).

This prophecy shows the Messiah will usher in three different periods of time:

1. A long time likened to a year.
2. A short period of time likened to a day.
3. A time of comfort to all that mourn in Zion.

These three periods of time are:

1. The Christian dispensation.
2. The seven-year Tribulation.
3. The millennial kingdom.

Jesus began his ministry by bringing in the first period of time — the Christian dispensation (Luke 4:18-19). On the day that He raptures the church, He will usher in the second period – the Tribulation. Then at the end of the Tribulation with His glorious appearing, He will bring in the third period of time – the millennial kingdom.

The length of the Tribulation in relation to the Christian dispensation is like one day is to a year. The Tribulation will be seven years in length, so the Christian dispensation will be about 360 times as long, or approximately 2520 years. Remember, it is not an exact relationship, but an approximate one.

It has been a tradition for more than 2000 years for Jews in every congregation to read the same passage on the Sabbath. On the Sabbath Jesus went to the synagogue and read the passage in Isaiah 61, that same passage was read in every synagogue in the world. Jesus stopped reading after the phrase, "to proclaim the year of Jehovah's favor." He rolled up the scroll, gave it back to the attendant and then said, "Today hath this scripture been fulfilled in your ears" (Luke 4:21).

He did not read on and say, "And the day of vengeance of our God" (the Tribulation) and "to comfort all that mourn; to appoint unto them that mourn in Zion" (millennial kingdom), because those prophecies would not be fulfilled for nearly 2000 years.

This is the foundational passage for the doctrine of Pre-Millennialism, which teaches that the Second Coming of Jesus will take place before the millennial kingdom.

The Olivet Discourse follows the same pattern. The First Coming of Christ and the Church Age are described in Matthew 24:4-8, and the Tribulation and Second Coming are covered in verses 9-31. The beginning of the millennial kingdom is then described in Matthew 25:31-34. Chapters 1-3 of Revelation describe the First Coming of Christ and the church dispensation. Chapters 4-5 give the scene in heaven after the Rapture ("Come up hither," 4:1), and chapters 6-19 describe the Tribulation and the Second Coming. Chapters 20-22 describe the millennial and eternal kingdoms.

Conclusion

The apostles and early church fathers may not have guessed how long the Church Age would be, but we know that it will be almost 2000 years. Thusly, the interpretation given in this book that there is a long period of time of approximately 2000 years between the First and Second Comings of Christ is therefore absolutely correct.

Make Christ the Foundation of Your Life

Avoid Worldly Wisdom

1 Corinthians 3:18-20

"Let no man deceive himself. If any man among you thinks that he is wise in this age, he must become foolish, so that he may become wise. For the wisdom of this world is foolishness before God. For it is written, "*He is* THE ONE WHO CATCHES THE WISE IN THEIR CRAFTINESS"; and again, "THE LORD KNOWS THE REASONINGS of the wise, THAT THEY ARE USELESS."

"And do not be conformed to this world, but be transformed by the renewing of your mind, that you may prove what *is* that good and acceptable and perfect will of God. So then each of us shall give account of himself to God. So then each of us shall give account of himself to God" (Romans 12:2; 14:12).

The Judgment Seat of Jesus the Messiah

All believers after they are taken in the Rapture will stand before the Lord in what is often termed as the Bema seat of Christ or the judgment seat of Christ:

> "For we must all appear before the judgment seat of Christ, that each one may be recompensed for his deeds in the body, according to what he has done, whether good or bad" (2 Corinthians 5:10).

The Scripture above is referring to believers, not the unsaved. Unbelievers who die in their sins without accepting Christ's free gift of salvation will face the Great White Throne judgment after the one-thousand-year millennial reign of Christ. The judgment seat of Christ takes place after the Rapture, and involves believers giving an account of their lives face to face with Messiah Jesus. The judgment seat of Christ does not determine our salvation. We know that was resolved forever by His sacrifice on the cross on our behalf (1 John 2:2 and John 3:16). All born-again believers' sins are forgiven, and they will never be condemned or judged for them (Romans 8:1).

Also, at the judgment seat of Christ rewards will be given to believers based on how steadfastly and faithfully we serve Him (1 Corinthians 9:4-27) and (2 Timothy 2:5). The motives for everything a believer does for the Lord will be judged. Some will lose their rewards because their motives for serving the Lord are insincere and self-serving (1 Corinthians 3:10-15). Or those who may think they are serving the Lord will find out that they have been stubborn and headstrong, unwilling to seriously search the Scriptures and admit errors in teaching and repent. Accountability for our faithfulness to the Lord and His Scriptures, not the approval of our core group of friends will determine our rewards or loss of them.

> "For no other foundation can anyone lay than that which is laid, which is Jesus Christ. Now if anyone builds on this foundation *with* gold, silver, precious stones, wood, hay, straw, each one's work will become clear; for the Day will declare it, because it will be revealed by fire; and that fire will test each one's work, of what sort it is.
> If anyone's work which he has built on *it* endures, he will receive a reward. If anyone's work is burned, he will suffer loss; but he himself will be saved, yet so as through fire" (1 Corinthians 3:11-15)

Crowns will be given for different reasons based on how faithfully the Lord was served. The crowns are described in 2 Timothy 4:8; 2 Timothy 2:5; James 1:12; 1 Peter 5:4; Revelation 2:10.

The Tribulation—Seven Years of Hell on Earth Marked by Unprecedented Deception

Before the final battle, which the Scriptures refer to as: "the battle of that great day of God Almighty" (Revelation 16:14) a devastating seven-year Tribulation period is foretold. This final battle, the gathering of Antichrist and his demonic soldiers against Jesus Christ, will conclude the Tribulation years.

"For then there will be great tribulation, such as has not been since the beginning of the world until this time, no, nor, ever shall be" (Matthew 24:21).

In the Book of Malachi, the last book of the Old Testament, Scripture tells us that the prophet Elijah who faithfully and unabashedly stood-up against the pagan strongholds of his day in defense of the Holy God of Israel, will reappear shortly *before* the "great and dreadful day of the Lord" (the Tribulation). According to Scripture, he will be one of the "two witnesses" to fulfill the prophecy of Revelation 11:3-12.

"Behold I will send you Elijah the prophet **before the coming of the great and dreadful day of the LORD.** And he will turn the hearts of the fathers to the children, and the hearts of the children to their fathers, lest I come and strike the earth with a curse" (Malachi 4:5).

The Tribulation is the seven-year period when God will unleash His judgments against those who reject Him. It will be during those seven catastrophic years that the Lord will complete His plan of salvation for the nation of Israel, as prophesied by the prophet Daniel (Daniel 9:24-27).

The prophesied 144,000 Jews are part of this redemptive plan as noted in (Revelation 14:4). Israel's redemption was prophesied in Zechariah 12:10 and also in Romans 11:25-27. The 144,000 will go forth throughout the world to evangelize the unsaved, those who are not taken up in the Rapture. Because of the efforts of the 144,000 Revelation 7:9

133

indicates that "a great multitude which no one could count, from every nation, and *all* tribes, and peoples and tongues" will accept Messiah Jesus as Lord and Savior.

The Falling Away—The Apostasy

Scripture gives us more information on what we can expect prior to the Tribulation. The Day of the Lord is in reference to the Tribulation years.

"Now we request you, brethren, with regard to the coming of our Lord Jesus Christ, and our gathering together to Him, that you may not be quickly shaken from your composure or be disturbed either by spirit or a message or a letter as if from us, to the effect that the day of the Lord has come, Let no one deceive you, for it will not come **unless the apostasy comes first, and the man of lawlessness is revealed**, the son of destruction [the Antichrist]" (2 Thessalonians 2:1-3).

The previous passages are concerned with signs to look for to help identify the time of the Rapture, the Tribulation and the return of Messiah Jesus. Some individuals try to translate the Greek word "apostasia" to mean "departure" in an attempt to turn the meaning of the word into a reference for the Rapture. The Greek word "apostasia" stems from "aphistemi" which means to stand away from a body of truth.

The Scriptures tell us that the Tribulation *will not come* until the apostasy (the falling away from biblical truth) and "the man of lawlessness is revealed" (Antichrist). Notice that Scripture tells us the Antichrist will be "revealed" *before* the Tribulation (the Day of the Lord). His identity will be recognizable, but his *true character* will not be known until the mid-point of the Tribulation. But as soon as the Antichrist confirms the covenant with Israel his identity will revealed (Daniel 9:27).

The Greek definition of the word "apostasy" means "a defection; a renunciation." *Webster's Dictionary*, the 1928 Edition provides a solid definition, "An abandonment of what one has professed; a total desertion, or departure from one's faith or religion." Not a spatial, physical departure up into the air as in the Rapture.

The *Liddell and Scott Greek Lexicon*, 7th edition defines "apostasia" as, "**the late form** of apostasis, defection." Apostasia, as defined by Liddell and Scott makes no reference to "physical departure" or

134

"disappearance." They also offer no secondary definition. They do offer definitions for the Greek word *apostasis*, of which *apostasia* **is a later form** (emphasis added):

Apostasis (aphistami) *a standing away from*, and so,
1. Defection, revolt *apo timos* or *tinos Herodotu,* Thucydides*; pros tins* Thucy.
2. Departure, *Biou* Euripides
3. Distance, interval, Plato.

Note the word "departure" is given a secondary meaning in the lexicon, and to the later form of the Greek word *apostasies.* Therefore it is not the primary dominant meaning and certainly not a core, root meaning. In the *Holman Illustrated Bible Dictionary,* the first definition for "apostasy" is:

Act of rebelling against, forsaking, abandoning, or falling away from what one has believed. The English word "apostasy" is derived form a Greek word (apostasia) that means, "to stand away from."

Also, in that same dictionary under the New Testament category for the word "apostasy" we find the following notations:

In 2 Thessalonians 2:3 Paul addressed those who had been deceived into believing that the day of the Lord had already come. He taught that an apostasy would precede the day of the Lord. The Spirit had explicitly revealed this falling away from the faith (1Timothy 4:1). Such apostasy in the latter times will involve doctrinal deception, moral insensitivity, and ethical departures from God's truth.

Associated NT (New Testament) concepts include the parable of the soils, in which Jesus spoke of those who believe for a while but "fall away" in time of temptation (Luke 8:13). At the judgment those who work iniquity will be told to depart" (Luke 13:27). Paul "withdrew" from the synagogue in Ephesus (Acts 19:9) because of the opposition he found there, and he counseled Timothy to "withdraw" from those who advocate a different doctrine (1Timothy 6:3-5). Hebrews speaks of falling away from the living God because of "an evil heart of unbelief" (3:12).

Furthermore, according to Greek New Testament language experts D.A. Carson and J.P. Louw *form* does not determine *meaning*. The meaning of a word is determined by usage, or *semantically*. The meaning is not derived because it does or does not agree with the presumptive root meanings or constituent parts. It is not possible to move from *form* to *meaning* to determine the meaning of a word accurately. Also, if one was to assign the meaning of a word based *completely on etymology*, by the root or roots of a word, that method of interpretation is not a reliable guideline.

J.P. Louw writes:

> It is a basic principle of modern semantic theory that we cannot progress from the form of a word to its meaning. Form and meaning are not directly correlated. Just as we cannot explain the English term 'understand' as meaning 'under'+'stand,' so we cannot explain diaxeirzo in Acts 5:30 as 'to lay hand upon vehemently.' The word only means 'to kill.' How it was done is a matter of context, not lexicography. (*Semantics of New Testament Greek*, page 29.)

D.A. Carson states:

> One of the most enduring errors, the root fallacy presupposes that every word actually has a meaning bound up with its shape or components. In this view, meaning is determined by etymology; that is by the root or roots of a word. Normally we observe that any individual word has a certain limited semantic range, and the context may therefore modify or shape the meaning of a word only within certain boundaries. The total semantic range is not permanently fixed, of course; with time and novel usage, it may shift considerably.
>
> Even so, I am not suggesting that words are infinitely plastic. I am simply saying that the meaning of a word cannot be reliably determined by etymology, or that a root once it is discovered, always projects a certain semantic load onto any word that incorporates that root. Linguistically, meaning is not an intrinsic possession of a word; rather, "it is a set of relations for which a verbal symbol is a sign."
> We cannot responsibly assume that etymology is related to meaning. We can only test the point by discovering the meaning of a word inductively. (*Exegetical Fallacies*, pages 28, 32-33.)

In 2 Thessalonians 2:1-3 Paul is making a differentiation of what precedes and what follows. The "gathering together" (Rapture) and then the coming "day of the Lord" follows (for it will not come unless the apostasy comes first and the revealing of the man of lawlessness (Antichrist) is revealed. Even learned, respected men who interpret the word "apostasy" to be a physical "departure" would have Paul essentially saying, "The Rapture cannot happen until the Rapture happens."

But Paul is explicitly warning of certain events as signs; that must take place before Christ's return. Paul is giving a warning about deception. Paul in his writings refers to "deceptions" of all kinds, expressing the need to be very discerning.

In 2 Thessalonians 2:3 the word "apostasy" (*apostasia*) comes from the Greek verb *aphistemi,* which literally means, "to depart," "revolt" or "stand away from a body of truth." Paul spoke of this in (1Timothy 4:1) and used the same Greek word. However, in 1 Timothy Paul added the words "depart from the faith" instead of "depart" by itself, specifically defining the phrase. Paul states the reason for the falling away is because some are listening to demons; deceiving spirits. So some are being deceived by teachings that are in opposition to the Word of God and this is taking place within the Christian church.

Other important point to keep in mind is the order of the passages, the distinct succession of the verses in 2 Thessalonians 2:1-3:
Let no one in any way deceive you by any means, implies that attempts to deceive are at play. Immediately after that verse we read: *For it will not come unless the apostasy comes first,* implying: defection, caused by what is stated in the previous verse: "deceive" (deception). After the deception, comes the *apostasy,* the falling away.

Continuing on, simple logic tells us that out of *the apostasy the son of destruction* (the Antichrist) will emerge—as a result of the falling away, the **apostasy**. His appearing will be preceded by the "great apostasy." He will continue to perpetuate the apostasy and take it to new heights. His rise, his revealing will be in relation to a great falling away from the faith, and it is he who will primarily carry it on and continue to promote false religious doctrines (one-world church) by using deception ("lying wonders") until he finally goes into the temple halfway through the Tribulation declaring himself to be God.

To illustrate further, consider the end-times apostasy in the parable of the leaven showing that the apostasy is going to take place in the last days, and that the infiltration of corrupt doctrines into the church will result in *total* apostasy. In Matthew 13 and 16, the "leaven" is the end-

137

times apostasy (false doctrines) as shown by Jesus in the parable of the leaven.

Jesus warned about false doctrines:

"Another parable He spoke to them: "The kingdom of heaven is like leaven, which a woman took and hid in three measures of meal till it was all leavened" (Matthew 13:33).

"Then Jesus said to them, "Take heed and beware of the leaven of the Pharisees and the Sadducees." How is it that you do not understand that I did not speak to you concerning bread?—*but* to beware of the leaven of the Pharisees and Sadducees."

Then they understood that He did not tell *them* to beware of the leaven of bread but of the doctrine of the Pharisees and Saduccees" (Matthew 16: 6, 11-12).

Jesus' parable of the leaven is concerning apostasy in the last days. It is a warning about false teachings and false doctrines, a "standing away from faith." By the Lord's own account, leaven is false doctrine. In Thessalonians 2:3, Scripture teaches that the explosion of false doctrines in the last days will take hold, making the way for Antichrist. The following verses clearly show that some will teach false doctrines that contradict the true teachings of the Bible.

"Now the spirit expressly says that in latter times some will depart from the faith, giving heed to deceiving spirits and doctrines of demons, speaking lies in hypocrisy, having their own conscience seared with a hot iron" (1 Timothy 4:1-2).

"For many deceivers have gone out into the world who do not confess Jesus Christ *as* coming in the flesh. This is a deceiver and an antichrist. Whoever transgresses and does not abide in the doctrine of Christ does not have God. He who abides in the doctrine of Christ has both the Father and the Son. If anyone comes to you and does not bring this doctrine, do not receive him into your house nor greet him; for he who greets him shares in his evil deeds" (2 John 7, 9-11).

138

The great Bible scholar, the late Dr. David L. Cooper, founder and president of the esteemed Biblical Research Society commented on the interpretation of the Greek word *apostasia*:

"One could not find anywhere that the word *apostasia* had taken on the meaning of *departure* before the Sixth Century A.D."
—*Biblical Research Monthly*, October 1948

Therefore as consistent Bible students we must follow the Golden Rule of Interpretation by following the primary, ordinary, usual literal first century meaning of *apostasia* defined as, "A departure from a body of truth."

One World Rule

The prophet Daniel prophesied that there would be a one-world government in the last days.

"Thus he said, The fourth beast shall be a fourth kingdom upon earth, which shall be diverse from all the kingdoms, and shall devour the whole earth, and shall tread it down, and break it in pieces" (Daniel 7:23).

In the previous verse reference is made to, "the whole earth." This final kingdom will be similar to the first world kingdom under Nebuchadnezzar. Almighty God gave Nebuchadnezzar rule over the entire world (Daniel 2:36-38). Although he did not actually rule over all the kingdoms on earth, he was given the entire earth to rule over. The final world government will not only be given power over all the nations, it will also *rule over* them.

According to Paul's account (2 Thessalonians 2:3) the Antichrist is revealed *before* the Tribulation ("for *that Day will not come* unless the falling away comes first and the man of sin is revealed"). In the following verse Daniel indicated that out of the one-world government, the group of ten ("ten kings") will "arise" and out of that group of ten the Antichrist will "arise."

"And as for the ten horns, out of this kingdom [world government] shall ten kings arise [ten unions]: and another shall arise after them;

[Antichrist] and he shall be diverse from the former, and he shall put down three kings" (Daniel 7:24).

Historically speaking, Rome, as a type of government has continued throughout the Christian dispensation. Today, some Bible expositors are expecting the revival of the old Roman Empire, anticipating a geographical revival of the old Roman Empire. However, Rome as a *type* of government does not need to be revived; therefore it is not necessary to be looking for Rome to reappear in its old geographical location, or to confuse some thing like the European Common Market with the "ten kings" of Daniel 7:24.

The Roman *type* of government portrayed in Daniel has never stopped existing. In his prophecies, the prophet Daniel was speaking of types of governments, not geographical locations of governments. Each of the metals represents a different type of government. The image represents time, consecutively from Nebuchadnezzar's era until the Second Coming of Christ. It also represents the types of kingdoms that will emerge. The legs of iron in the metallic image of Daniel 2 continue all throughout the Christian dispensation until the Second Coming of Christ, which is pictured by the stone smashing the image at its feet.

"You **continued looking until** a stone was cut out without hands, and it struck the statue on its feet of iron and clay and crushed them" (Daniel 2:34).

The "stone" symbolically represents Jesus Christ (Matthew 21:42, 44). He will destroy the dictatorial rule of the Tribulation years, and set up His millennial kingdom over which He will reign and rule.

"And in the days of those kings the God of heaven will set up a kingdom which will never be destroyed, and *that* kingdom will not be left for another people; it will crush and put an end to all the kingdoms, but it will itself endure forever. Inasmuch as you saw the stone was cut out of the mountain without hands and that it crushed the iron, the bronze, the clay, the silver, and the gold, the great God has made known to the king what will take place in the future; so the dream is true, and its interpretation is trustworthy" (Daniel 2:44-45).

The "ten kings" come out of the world government. Therefore, looking for "ten kings" or ten nations that will fulfill the prophecy of

140

Daniel 7:24 before the one-world government is established—is untimely and pointless. Scripture does not teach us how long it will be before the "world government" is divided into ten unions. The world government comes into place *before* the "ten kings." Notice in Daniel 7:24 cited on the previous page, that the Antichrist "shall arise after them" meaning after the ten kings [ten unions] come to power out of the collapsed world government.

The collapse of the one-world government will be a strong clue that Antichrist is close to making his grand center stage entrance onto the world scene. Scripture is unclear how long after the ten unions are created that Antichrist will emerge. But when he does arrive on the prophetic scene, this man will be so charismatic and convincing that most of the world will fall for his lies.

Antichrist will be seen as the answer to the world's pressing economic and social problems, not for the narcissistic monster he will later prove to be. His agenda to subvert God will go forward at supersonic speed. The Tribulation will shift into gear when he convinces Israel to sign the covenant of Daniel 9:27. The Tribulation will then begin and accelerate at greater intensities right up until the Lord returns.

Believers will not see Israel sign the covenant (Daniel 9.27) with Antichrist because they will have been taken up in the Rapture earlier. But they should see preparation for the signing of the impending covenant. When the "overflowing scourge" (Isaiah 28:15) unleashes terror upon the Middle East nations, the signing of the covenant cannot be far off.

When the Lord promised to take all believers up to the glory of heaven in the Rapture, He did not also say believers will be free of problems before that day arrives. In fact Jesus said, "In the world you will have tribulation" (John 16:33b). It would take nothing more than a worldwide economic collapse or the "right type of crisis" to bring about a one-world type government; and it could happen very quickly, hastening the timing of the Rapture/Tribulation.

If we look at the daily news headlines, signs can be identified that a one-world government and a one-world economic system are hovering in the foreseeable future; propagated worldwide by powerful political "players" as the best and only solution to the world's declining economic and social stability.

Apostasy Everywhere

"All Scripture is given by inspiration of God, and is profitable for doctrine, for reproof, for correction, for instruction in righteousness."
—2 Timothy 3:16

Next, I will discuss more about the apostasy—the abandonment of true and accurate teachings of the Bible. This apostasy, this falling away from the truth of God's Word will bring about a universal church (1Timothy 4:1). We can see this falling away taking place all around us today, paving the way for the formation of that church. It is a specific sign, a forerunner of the approaching Rapture and Tribulation.

As the Tribulation draws near, acceptance of false doctrines will increase and take hold in greater degrees. Faithful believers should point out heresies and contradictions in a loving manner even to fellow believers, because without realizing it *some* well-meaning Bible teachers are promoting theories that are contrary to Scripture. When Scripture talks about the importance of having "fellowship" (Hebrews 10:25) with other believers, it does not mean we are to transform the Word of God into something it is not.

It is also obvious that there are also plenty of "spiritual" teachers who know what they are teaching is not biblical, and are proud to do so. They will not take a strong stand for the Word of God, and send out confusing messages that contradict every word that comes out of their mouths, so they don't "offend" anyone or lose any donation money. Apparently offending the God of the universe does not concern them. Such individuals are obviously phony Christians that the Lord warned us about.

Scripture is filled with warnings that as the Tribulation gets closer false teachings will escalate and ultimately result in a one-world religious system. It is astounding yet biblically prophetic how many false teachers and false prophets present themselves to the world through the Internet, books, television, radio, and in the pulpit as Bible "experts," "teachers" or "mentors."

"Always learning and never able to come to the truth."
—2 Timothy 3:7

An epidemic of these self-designated and self-elevated "experts" are bringing forth and parroting one confusing concept after another. Many of their doctrines are tortured interpretations of the Bible, raising the level of biblical apostasy to an all time high. Some biblically related information posted on the Internet is really good, very edifying. But some of the dynamics that go on remind me of a "Wild West" high-stakes gambling showdown where a potpourri of self-styled "spiritual" and Pop Christian "gurus" put down stakes (their websites) vying to win the big pot (adulation, fame, glory, money). This Wild West showdown has prompted many non-Christians to dismiss the authenticity of the Bible. Misinformation on the Internet is widespread.

All too often, deficiently researched "teachings" are offered that contradict the Word of God. I cannot see how displaying confusing information is doing anything to serve the Lord, or to help people to grow and mature in the Lord. This is all the more reason to hold our Bibles close and study the truths of Scripture each day.

Scripture passages carefully interpreted using the Golden Rule of Interpretation (cited on page 218), supported by the direction of the Holy Spirit is a good guide to use to substantiate any presentation. Otherwise, the true meaning of the Scriptures can be easily corrupted and misused. Self-righteousness is a direct insult to the Lord who so selflessly gave His life for each and every one of us.

"But we are like an unclean thing, and all our righteousnesses are like filthy rags" (Isaiah 64:6).

"And whosoever exalts himself will be humbled; and he who humbles himself will be exalted" (Matthew 23:12).

[Jesus said,] "But many *who are* first will be last, and the last first" (Matthew 19:30).

More Concerning the Tribulation Years

The Tribulation will be the most devastating time in all of history. A very mesmerizing leader will become the world ruler. He will emerge promising peace, hope, change, and prosperity for everyone. It will look like he will be able to solve all the world's problems. He will even appear to succeed in making a "peace" deal (a covenant) with Israel and her enemies. He will promise to protect Israel. But this man will be the greatest enemy the nation of Israel has ever had and he will turn against her, breaking his promise.

Halfway through the seven-year Tribulation, this charismatic leader—the Antichrist—will become indwelt by Satan himself (Revelation 13:3-4). The timing of this indwelling coincides with Revelation 12:7-12, when a war breaks out in heaven during the mid-point of the Tribulation and Satan and his angels are cast down to earth, never again to have access to the heavenly realms. It is at this time that Satan literally takes over the body of this charismatic leader.

Antichrist will then enter the rebuilt temple in Jerusalem and declare that he is God. He will demand to be worshiped. Those who refuse to do so will be put to death. From this point on planet Earth will become increasingly deluged with unfathomable demonic activity.

When Antichrist first appears, he will deceive millions into following him because of his beguiling, cult of personality. Instead of bringing peace, he will bring tyranny like never before. Life will become unbearable. It will be hell on earth. When Antichrist signs the false peace covenant with Israel, the Tribulation will begin in full force.

Israel will be deceived by Antichrist and will in fact be signing a covenant with death. The rebuilt temple that will be defiled by Antichrist is not the same temple that will be built by the Lord for the Millennium (Zechariah 6:13).

Shortly *before* the Tribulation begins, Scripture shows that an of demonic beings, the "overflowing scourge" will strike terror in Israel and throughout the Middle East.

The prophet Joel saw and described the following events that take place *before* the Tribulation starts. Keep in mind that in the following verse Joel stated: "for day of the Lord is coming, for it is at hand" (certain). The "day of the Lord" is in reference to the Tribulation.

Joel 2:1-11

"Blow the trumpet in Zion, and sound the alarm in My holy mountain! Let all the inhabitants of the land tremble; **for the day of the LORD is coming, for it is at hand**: A day of darkness and gloominess, a day of clouds and thick darkness, like the morning *clouds* spread over the mountains. A people *come*, great and strong, the like of whom has never been; nor will there ever be any *such* after them, even for many successive generations.

A fire devours before them and behind them a flame burns; the land is like the Garden of Eden before them. And behind them a desolate wilderness; surely nothing shall escape them. Their appearance is like the appearance of horses; and like swift steeds so they run. With a noise like chariots over mountaintops they leap, like the noise of flaming fire that devours the stubble. Like a strong people set in battle array.

Before them the people writhe in pain; all faces are drained of color. They run like mighty men, they climb the wall like men of war; every one marches in formation, and they do not break ranks. They do not push one another; everyone marches in his own column. Though they lunge between the weapons, they are not cut down, they run to and fro in the city, they run on the wall; they climb into the houses, they enter at the windows like a thief.

The earth quakes before them, the heavens tremble; the sun and the moon grow dark, and the stars diminish their brightness. The LORD gives voice before His army. For His camp is very great; for strong *is the One* who executes His word. For the day of the LORD *is* great and very terrible; who can endure it?"

The army of demonic beings described in Joel continues into the Tribulation for an unspecified period of time. This demonic army is not related to the demonic hordes referenced in Revelation chapters nine or sixteen. When Antichrist advances to power he may very likely dominate and take control of the "overflowing scourge" promising to stop the onslaughts of the demonic beings (Isaiah 28:15). It seems that Antichrist will keep the "overflowing scourge" tame, but for only a limited time. When the nation of Israel signs the covenant with the Antichrist, they may be given the impression that he will hold back the "overflowing scourge."

"And he will make a firm covenant with the many for one week [7 years]; but in the middle of the week [3.5 years] he will put a stop to sacrifice and grain offering; and on the wing of abominations *will come* one who makes desolate, even until a complete destruction, one that is decreed, is poured out on the one who makes desolate" (Daniel 9:27).

It is the signing of this covenant that actually begins the Tribulation. Antichrist adheres to the stipulations in the covenant for a time, but then allows the demonic beings once again to take up their crusade of terrifying and brutalizing Israel as well as other nations:

"Because you have said, "We have made a covenant with death, and with Sheol [hell] we are in agreement. When the overflowing scourge passes through, it will not come to us, for we have made lies our refuge, and under falsehood we have hidden ourselves." Your covenant with death will be annulled, and your agreement with Sheol will not stand; when the overflowing scourge passes through you will be trampled down by it" (Isaiah 28:15, 18).

To convey even more details about how serious and frightening the Tribulation will be, I am going to briefly discuss John's vision regarding the Sixth Trumpet Judgment beginning with Scripture from Revelation 9:13-21:

"Then the sixth angel sounded: And I heard a voice from the four horns of the golden altar which is before God, saying to the sixth angel who had the trumpet, "Release the four angels who are bound in the great river Euphrates," So the four angels who had been prepared for the hour and day and month and year were released to kill a third of mankind" (Revelation 9:13-15).

"Now the number of the army of the horseman was two hundred million; I heard the number of them. And thus I saw the horses in the vision: those who sat on the horses in the vision: those who sat on them had breastplates of fiery red, hyacinth blue, and sulfur yellow; and the heads of the horses were like the heads of lions; and out of their mouths came fire, smoke and brimstone. By these plagues a third of mankind was killed—by the fire and the smoke and the brimstone which came out of their mouths "For their power is in their mouth and their tails for their tails are like serpents, having heads; and with them they do harm" (Revelation 9:16-19).

A popular theory which started at least several decades ago claims that Red China can gather into action an army of two million soldiers and fulfill the prophecy given in Revelation 9:16-19.This interpretation is significantly flawed. The previous description in Revelation 9 portrays the heads of the horses to resemble the heads of lions. Fire, smoke and sulfur come out of their mouths. Their tails are like snakes that inflict harm on people. The riders wear breastplates that are fiery red, dark blue and yellow.

It is obvious that the creatures are not horses and men. These are demons riding demonic creatures. It is not difficult to understand from the language used in the verses that these creatures are not symbolic entities. They are exactly what they are described to be and they are not men, certainly not Red Chinese soldiers. No humans could possibly resemble the description given of the demonic beings. Throughout Scripture, the east is consistently in reference to Mesopotamia (Assyria and Babylonia), which also applies to the verses here (Revelation 16). China cannot be part of this equation. China cannot be properly interpreted to represent "the kings of the east."

Moreover, if Scripture is alluding to a human army, which it is not, the nation of India could just as easily fulfill the number requirement. "The kings of the east" of chapter sixteen of Revelation are not the Red Chinese. They are "Mesopotamian" kings. Modern day Mesopotamia would include Iraq, parts of eastern Iran, southwest Iran and southeast Turkey. It should be remembered that any passage in Revelation or any book of the Bible that does not show itself, to be symbolic is to be taken literally, unless the word or words are used symbolically elsewhere. The following examples will clarify this statement. In Revelation 17:1-8 the great whore is described. Then in verses 9-18 the angel explains who the whore is as well as the kings, their kingdoms, the beast, the Lamb and the waters. In Revelation 13:1-8 the beast that comes out of the sea is described. He has seven heads and ten horns, and looks like a leopard, bear and lion. The heads, horns and beasts are not explained in this chapter, but they are explained in chapter 17 and in Daniel 7:17-26.

The demonic army of Revelation nine is not related to the events of Revelation sixteen. The demonic army of two million is part of the Trumpet judgments, and the events of sixteen are part of the Bowl judgments. These two judgments occur at two different (separate) times during the Tribulation years and have no relation to one another. Further study of what you have just read here regarding Revelation nine and sixteen is encouraged. Reasonable Bible scholars including Arnold Fruchtenbaum, are in agreement that the Red Chinese cannot comprise the two hundred million army of Revelation sixteen, and that there is no correlation between the events of Revelation nine and Revelation sixteen (*Footsteps of the Messiah*, 1993, p.310). These shocking revelations, the events just described are very difficult to comprehend. We would certainly like to think they must be symbolic. But Scripture is precise and tells us that there will be heavy demonic involvement during the Tribulation and some inconceivably frightening events will transpire during that time.

The Word of God gives us warnings that we must take very seriously. Satan is a relentless enemy who is gearing up for the final battles of his despicable life. He knows he will be completely destroyed, but he is going to create as much misery as he can during the final years of world history. Please receive Messiah Jesus today as your Savior, and you will be spared from the horrors of the Tribulation. The prophet Joel, and Luke foretold more about specific signs that will take place before the Tribulation begins. These signs continue to get more intense throughout the Tribulation, right up until the Lord returns at His Second Coming.

"And I will show wonders in the heavens and in the earth: blood and fire and pillars of smoke. The sun shall be turned into darkness, and the moon into blood, **before** the coming of the great and awesome day of the LORD" (Joel 2:30-31).

"And there will be signs in the sun, in the moon, and in the stars; and on earth distress of nations, with perplexity, the sea and the waves roaring; men's hearts failing them from fear and the expectation of those things which are coming on the earth, for the powers of the heavens will be shaken" (Luke 21:25-26).

"Watch therefore, and pray always that you may be counted worthy to escape all these things that will come to pass, and to stand before the Son of Man" (Luke 21:36).

When we place our trust and faith in Jesus the Messiah as our Lord Savior, we can count on being taken up to the protection of heaven before the actual Tribulation begins. As believers, we may witness some harrowing events, but it will be much, much worse during the Tribulation years. When you see or hear of the fulfillment of the prophecies quoted in the previous verses, you can be sure the Rapture and the beginning of the Tribulation are very near.

In the DVD, *Return of the Nephilim,* Dr. Chuck Missler makes a convincing argument that it is very possible there could be some type of extraterrestrial (ET) event in the last days. Something very deceptive could happen that is underwritten by Satan. During the Tribulation, Antichrist and his False Prophet will insist that Antichrist must be worshipped. The Scriptures on the next page give a clue that something might happen that will attempt to put an entirely new spin on how life is perceived. Some type of new and extremely convincing, but fake, reality might be offered to the world, very possibly an alien (demonic) invasion of some sort.

Whatever it is, you can be sure it will be a campaign to completely try to discredit Messiah Jesus. Scripture tells us a "False Prophet" will work directly with Antichrist to deceive millions with counterfeit miracles during the Tribulation. This False Prophet will most likely be the leading figure for the prophesied apostate, one-world religious system that will be in place during the Tribulation. There will be those who will come to faith in Christ during those frightening seven years, but it is much better to do that now. Spiritual deception will be at an all-time high at that time and most people will be fooled.

Jesus warned us about spiritual deception in the last days:

"The coming of the lawless one is according to the working of Satan, with all power, signs, and lying wonders, and with all unrighteous deception among those who perish, **because they did not receive the love of the truth, that they might be saved**. And for this reason, God will send them strong delusion, that they should believe the lie" (2 Thessalonians 2:9-10).

"For false christs and false prophets will rise and show great signs and wonders to deceive, if possible, even the elect" (Matthew 24:24).

The Lord's Dramatic Return
The Second Coming of Jesus the Messiah

Christ's promised return takes place at the end of the Tribulation, at the final battle of Armageddon:

> "Behold He is coming with clouds, and every eye will see Him, even they who pierced Him. And all the tribes of the earth will mourn because of Him. Even so, Amen" (Revelation 1:7).

> "And I saw three unclean spirits like frogs *coming* out of the mouth of the dragon [Satan], out of the mouth of the beast [Antichrist], and out of the mouth of the false prophet. For they are spirits of demons, performing signs *which* go out to the kings of the earth and of the whole world, to gather them to the battle of that great day of God Almighty.

> "Behold, I am coming as a thief. Blessed *is* he who watches, and keeps his garments, lest he walk naked and they see his shame." And they gathered them together to the place called in Hebrew, Armageddon" (Revelation 16:13-16).

> "Then the Lord will go forth and fight against those nations, as He fights in the day of battle. And in that day His feet will stand on the Mount of Olives, which faces Jerusalem on the east. And the Mount of Olives shall be split in two, from east to west, making a very large valley; half of the mountain shall move toward the north and half of it toward the south" (Zechariah 14:3-4).

> "Now I saw heaven opened, and behold, a white horse. And He who sat on him was called Faithful and True, and in righteousness He judges and makes war. His eyes were like a flame of fire, and on His head were many crowns. He had a name written that no one knew except Himself. He was clothed with a robe dipped in blood, and His name is called The Word of God.

> And the armies in heaven, clothed in fine linen, white and clean, followed Him on white horses. Now out of His mouth goes a sharp sword, that with it He should strike the nations.

And He Himself will rule them with a rod of iron. He Himself treads the winepress of the fierceness and wrath of Almighty God. And He has on His robe and on His thigh a name written: KING OF KINGS AND LORD OF LORDS" (Revelation 19:11-16).

"And I saw the beast, the kings of the earth, and their armies, gathered together to make war against Him who sat on the horse and against His army. Then the beast [Satan] was captured, and with him the false prophet who worked signs in his presence, by which he deceived those who received the mark of the beast and those who worshipped his image.

These two were cast alive into the lake of fire burning with brimstone. And the rest were killed with the sword which proceeded from the mouth of Him who sat on the horse. And all the birds were filled with their flesh" (Revelation 19:19-21).

Thousands of years ago, Jesus the Christ, Yeshua Ha Mashiach, came into the ancient world as a vulnerable babe, truly like a lamb to the slaughter. He did that for you and me, for our eternal salvation. But now He returns as a triumphant mighty warrior to reclaim planet Earth; that which is His. He puts an end to the long, harrowing battle with Satan and all the misery he has forced upon mankind. He is a loving God, but He is also a just and righteous God.

Scripture reveals when the Lord appears at the final battle, the world leader (the Beast)—who is the Antichrist—his demons, and his cohort, the False Prophet—the world religious leader, along with all the nations will try to physically fight off the Lord, the God of the universe! Jesus will immediately put a stop to the burgeoning siege with His Word alone—with simply a verbal command. He will defeat Antichrist and all the blood thirsty, power-hungry hordes. He will rescue Israel and the entire planet from complete annihilation; then and only then will there be peace on earth.

"And then the lawless one will be revealed, whom the Lord will consume with the breath of His mouth and destroy with the brightness of His coming" (2 Thessalonians 2:8).

"For the word of God is living and powerful, and sharper than any two-edged sword, piercing even to the division of soul and spirit, and of joints and marrow, and is a discerner of the thoughts and intents of the heart" (Hebrews 4:12).

The following passages describe such an event:

"And the winepress was trampled outside the city, and blood came out of the winepress, up to the horses bridles, for one thousand six hundred furlongs [180-200 miles]" (Revelation 14:20).

"He shall strike the earth with the rod of His mouth, and with the breath of his lips He shall slay the wicked" (Isaiah 11:4b).

During the Tribulation, Scripture reveals the False Prophet (the world religious leader) will be Antichrist's accomplice. He will manipulate the lives of those who were not removed by Christ to the safety of heaven in the Rapture. He will have satanic powers and will deceive many into following Antichrist and taking the mark of the beast. Without that mark, there will be no way to carry out commerce or function in the world system (Revelation 13:16-18, 14:20).

I can only imagine how incredibly bereaved many of those who rejected the Lord before the Rapture will be. Many will come to faith in Messiah Jesus during the Tribulation, those who will refuse to worship the one-world leader, Antichrist. But, as I said earlier, it will be extremely difficult for them. There will also be those who have been so deceived that they will robotically follow Antichrist and the False Prophet, doomed to an eternity in hell.

Because we are living in the last days, there has already been an overwhelming outpouring of evil spirits, ruling those who willfully go against God's principles and participate in demonically inspired lifestyles. Depraved, corrupt behavior has become the "norm." False religious practices, the occult, and other ungodly New Age practices have infiltrated nearly every aspect of society.

Even secular humanism, which includes psychology and psychiatry, has become a huge religion in and of itself. These humanly derived practices completely miss the point that it is only through the risen Christ that emotional, psychological and social problems can be totally healed. These lifestyle conditions are signs of the times about which Jesus Himself warned. False teachings and false prophecies are becoming an epidemic throughout the entire world— leading up to the implementation of the coming one-world religious system.

"And I saw thrones, and they sat on them, and judgment was committed to them. Then I saw the souls of those who had been beheaded for their witness to Jesus and for the word of God, who had not worshipped the beast or his image, and had not received his mark in their foreheads or on their hands. And they lived and reigned with Christ for a thousand years" (Revelation 20:4).

We see from the previous Scripture that those who become born-again believers in Christ during the Tribulation will rule and reign with Him and that there will be a literal, one-thousand-year earthly, millennial kingdom. All believers will be part of Christ's earthly millennial kingdom. There will be true peace on the rejuvenated-earth because of the leadership of Jesus Christ. That time is coming soon, most likely in our lifetime. Until then, the struggle for Jerusalem and all of Israel—that tiny sliver of a nation will continue to be an ongoing issue with today's self-serving so-called leaders of the world.

It seems nearly every time there is an incident involving Israel the majority of the nations immediately and unfairly point, their fingers blaming Israel as the cause of whatever the particular incident might be. God said it would be so, and those who come against Israel will experience His righteous anger.

Jerusalem Is the Physical and Spiritual Center of the World

Scripture tells us God's name, His eyes and His heart are forever tied to Jerusalem, His *chosen* city.

> "Thus says the Lord GOD: This is Jerusalem; I have set her in the midst of the nations and the countries all around her" (Ezekiel 5:5).
>
> "Yet I [God] have chosen Jerusalem, that My name might be there...For now I have chosen and sanctified this house [the Temple], that My name may be there forever; and My eyes and My heart will be there perpetually...In this house of God and in Jerusalem, which I have chosen out of all the tribes of Israel, I will put My name forever" (2 Chronicles 6:6, 7:16, 33:7b). Scripture sequencing (partially) taken from: *A Cup of Trembling: Jerusalem and Bible Prophecy* by Dave Hunt.

Zechariah 12:1-3

> "The burden of the word of the LORD concerning Israel, thus declares the LORD who stretches out the heavens, lays the foundation of the earth, and forms the spirit of man within him, 'Behold I am going to make Jerusalem a cup that causes reeling to all the peoples around; and the siege is against Jerusalem, it will be against Judah. **And it will come about in that day that I will make Jerusalem a heavy stone for all the peoples; all who lift it will be severely injured**. And all the nations of the earth will be gathered against it.'"

The previous passages explicitly state that Jerusalem is God's beloved favored, holy city. Jerusalem is the pivotal point in these last days. Anyone who comes against Jerusalem or tries to take it from the Jewish people is guaranteed to experience the Lord's fury. Jerusalem belongs to the God of the Bible—to Israel. Attempts to internationalize this sacred city will result in total mayhem: The final battle of Armageddon.

Will the World Ever End?

**"Heaven and earth will pass away,
but My words will not pass away." —Mark 13:31**

Some analysts try to teach that the world will never end, but the Bible does not say that. The word "world" is not found in the original Greek text. For example, the King James translation of the Bible uses the word "world" in Ephesians 3:21:

"Unto him *be* the glory in the church by Christ Jesus throughout all ages, world without end. Amen."

But that is not an accurate translation. The old English version of the King James Bible stating "world without end" carried a meaning in that day of "endless duration." However, the word "world" should never have been inserted into the King James when indeed it is not found in the original Greek text. The 1901 American Standard Version of the Bible, translated out of the original tongues teaches:

"Unto him *be* the glory in the church and in Christ Jesus unto all generations for ever and ever. Amen" (Ephesians 3:21).

The New American Standard Bible translation states:

"To Him be the glory in the church and in Christ Jesus to all generations forever and ever" (Ephesians 3:21).

The New King James Bible has corrected and clarified the passage:

"To Him be the glory in the church by Christ Jesus to all generations, forever and ever. Amen" (Ephesians 3:21).

This type of misinterpretation of Scripture is a good example of how the intended meaning of a verse can be changed. Without careful study and research that goes into interpreting the meaning of a verse, the accurate and true meaning of the Scripture is changed to take on the meaning of something else, entirely.

At the end the Tribulation the world will be destroyed by fire, then rejuvenated—resurfaced by the Lord. After the one-thousand-year millennial reign of Christ, heaven and earth will pass away and He will create a new heaven and a new earth (Revelation 21:1). Just prior to writing about the creation of the new heaven and the new earth in Revelation 21, in Revelation 20 and 21 John wrote:

"And I saw a great white throne. And him that sat upon it, from whose face **the earth and heaven fled away; and there was found no place for them** [heaven and earth]" (Revelation 20:11).

"And I saw a new heaven and a new earth, for the first heaven and the first earth **are passed away**; and the sea is no more" (Revelation 21:1).

The Millennial Reign of Messiah Jesus and Eternity

The Millennium is a period of time beginning after the Second Coming of Christ, after a short seventy-five day interval (Daniel 12:11-12), and will continue for a period of one thousand years. The Millennium is the *better world* that *is* coming soon!

"And the LORD shall be King over all the earth.
In that day it shall be—"The LORD *is* one,"
And His name one." (Zechariah 14:9)

After the Millennium, the eternal kingdom will begin, as referenced in Revelation 21 and 22. But first, all born-again believers will taken-up to heaven in the Rapture while the Tribulation takes place on earth. In Revelation 20:4-6, John wrote that Messiah Jesus is going to be literally, physically ruling upon the earth during the one-thousand-year millennium. All true believers in their new, immortal glorified bodies will be assisting Him.

Early one morning on a Christian radio station I heard a Bible teacher completely destroy the meaning of the true millennial kingdom. He did a hatchet job on Revelation 20:4-6 and John 14:2-3. He allegorized the Scriptures twisting them so badly that he completely took them out of context and changed the entire meaning of the verses. He actually said:

"The Millennium is the kingdom of God within our hearts, and that is what Jesus meant when He said that there are many mansions in His Father's house. We are the mansions. The Millennium is within our hearts, because God dwells there."

This same Bible "teacher" who so boldly convoluted and changed the meaning of Scripture has a large ministry and offers a hefty supply of "teaching" materials for sale. We cannot be too careful when studying the Word of God because apostasy and false teaching seems to be lurking everywhere in these last days. Once again we must be very careful not assume what is being taught is correct (Acts 17:11).

Some teachings confuse a number of events and characteristics of the Millennium with those of the eternal kingdom described in Revelation 21 and 22. At the end of the Millennium heaven and earth will pass away, as if they simply disappear or cease to exist, then the Lord will make **all things anew**. John describes this as "fled away." But at the end of the

Tribulation, the earth is burned up. These are noticeably two different events. In the book of Revelation, John described what he saw:

"And I saw a great white throne and Him who sat upon it, from whose presence earth and heaven fled away, and no place was found for them" (Revelation 20:11).

By Peter's account (2 Peter 3:10), at the very end of the Tribulation the earth will be destroyed in a different way—by intense heat. It will be burned up. Peter goes on to say in 2 Peter 3:13, "according to His promise, we look for new heavens and a new earth." How did Peter get that idea? It could not have been from the reference to a "new heaven and new earth" declared in Revelation 21 and 22, because Revelation had not been written yet. His reference came from Isaiah 65:16-20. At the very end of the Tribulation the Lord creates "new heavens and a new earth" (Isaiah 65:17), which will last for the entire one-thousand-year millennial reign of Messiah Jesus.

This is what Peter wrote:

"But the day of the Lord will come like a thief; in which the heavens shall pass away with a great noise, and the elements shall be dissolved with fervent heat, and the earth and the works that are therein shall be burned up. Seeing that these things are thus all to be dissolved, what manner of persons ought ye to be in all holy living and godliness, looking for and earnestly desiring the coming of the day of God, by reason of which the heavens being on fire shall be dissolved, and the elements shall melt with fervent heat? But according to his promise, we look for new heavens and a new earth, wherein dwelleth righteousness" (2 Peter 3:10-13).

The prophet Isaiah wrote about God's promise of the new millennial heavens and millennial earth:

"So that he who blesseth himself in the earth shall bless himself in the God of truth; and he that sweareth in the earth shall swear by the God of truth; because the former troubles are forgotten, and because they are hid from mine eyes. For, behold, I create a new heavens and a new earth; and the former things shall not be remembered, nor come into mind. But be ye glad and rejoice for ever in that which I create;

for, behold, I create Jerusalem a rejoicing, and her people a joy. And I will rejoice in Jerusalem, and joy in my people; and there shall be heard in her no more the voice of weeping and the voice of crying" (Isaiah 65:16-19).

In Isaiah 65:18 we see the word "forever."

"But ye be glad and rejoice forever in that which I create; for, behold, I create Jerusalem a rejoicing, and her people a joy."

A person looking at the previous verse not knowing or thinking about the Old Testament Hebrew meaning of the word "forever" would say this verse must be referring to eternity, an indefinite, endless span of time, easily mistaking what the prophet Isaiah wrote in Isaiah 65:18-19 to be referring to eternity because of the word "forever" used in verse 18. And without careful scrutiny, also assume those verses refer to the same "new heaven and a new earth" in Revelation 21.

However, the Hebrew meaning of the word is often determined by its context, but in Greek the meaning of the word determines the *meaning* of its context. In the Old Testament, in the Hebrew language the word "forever" is Ad Olam. Below, we see that it takes three English words to relate or to express the meaning:

1. Continuity;
2. Perpetuity (an indefinite period of time);
3. Duration (which can refer to endlessness).

The Hebrew word "Ad Olam," does not mean "forever" as we know it in English. For example, in 1 Kings 2:11a, we learn, "And the days that David reigned over Israel for *were* forty years" indicating "continuity." In 1 Chronicles 28:4a we read, "Yet the LORD, the God of Israel, chose me from all the house of my father to be king over Israel forever." King David did not rule "forever" as we use the term in every day English. In actuality David ruled for forty years. "Forever" in these passages means that David ruled forty years without a break in his reign: "continuity." "Duration" is the length of time that he actually reigned, and "perpetuity" would be *until* David died.

The application, the use of the Old Testament word "forever," in Hebrew—Ad Olam, is demonstrated in Isaiah 32. The prophet Isaiah spoke of the seven-year Tribulation in verses 9-18 indicating once the

Tribulation begins it will continue without stopping, without any break. However the word "forever" is used in the following passage in reference to the seven-year Tribulation, which is a definitive span of time: "Because the palace has been abandoned, the populated city forsaken. Hill and watch-tower have become caves **forever**, a delight for wild donkeys, a pasture for the flocks" (Isaiah 32:14).

Immediately in the next verse, verse 15, Isaiah referenced the one-thousand-year Millennium using the word "forever," even though one thousand years is a definite span of time, not forever (endless) as we know it in the English language.

"Until the Spirit is poured upon us from on high, and the wilderness becomes a fruitful field, and the fruitful field is counted as a forest, then justice will dwell in the wilderness, and righteousness remain in the fruitful field.

The work of righteousness will be peace, and the effect of righteousness, quietness and assurance **forever**. My people will dwell in a peaceful habitation, in secure dwellings, and in quiet resting places" (Isaiah 32:15-18).

Clearly the word "forever" does not always mean a lengthy or an endless duration of time. We also see by reading Isaiah 32 that the word "forever" in verse 14 is in reference to the seven-year Tribulation, and then following in verse (18) the word "forever" is referring to the subsequent one-thousand-year Millennium. Neither of these events last an endless duration of time, "forever" as we know it in the English language. Therefore, the Hebrew term "forever" has its meaning determined by the context which is evidenced in Isaiah 32.

Another verse from Isaiah 65 that is often misinterpreted is verse 19. Many Bible "teachers" take that verse and try to tie it to Revelation 21:4. In Isaiah 65:19 the Lord is precisely speaking specifically about those in Jerusalem, not the entire millennial population:

"And I will rejoice in Jerusalem, and joy in My people; there will be no more the voice of weeping and the voice of crying."

During the Millennium there will still be some problems with sin. Some tears will be shed and there will be death. In the eternal kingdom spoken of in Revelation 21, there will be no more death, and no one will have tears or pain. Isaiah 65:19 addresses the millennial reign of Christ, and Revelation 21:4 is in relation to the eternal kingdom. Once again, these are two distinctly different events with two different time references. However, many make the mistake of thinking that Isaiah 65:19 is speaking about the same event stated in Revelation 21:4. Isaiah 65 is in reference to the millennial kingdom, and Revelation 21 deals with the eternal kingdom.

"And he shall wipe away every tear from their eyes; and death shall be no more; neither shall there be mourning, nor crying, nor pain, any more" (Revelation 21:4).

The key verse here to understanding the passages in 2 Peter (3:10-13) is found in Isaiah 65:16. The burned up, damaged earth is created anew; resurfaced. Scripture indicates it will not be not totally destroyed. Isaiah wrote: "the former troubles are forgotten, and because they are hidden from My [God's] sight!" "Forgotten and hidden" do not mean destroyed completely and do not mean vanished or "fled away" as will be the case *after* the Millennium when God makes "all things new" for the eternal kingdom (Revelation 21:5).

After the Tribulation God will hide (conceal) the damaged earth and the heavens, and change their condition with newly created acts, newly created material. We must be careful to take every passage according to related passages. Isaiah 16 must be taken into account before interpreting verses 17-19, or else the true meaning of the subsequent passages is lost.

The prophet Jeremiah also wrote about the condition of the heavens and the earth at the end of the Tribulation supporting Isaiah 65:16-17:

"I looked on the earth, and behold, *it was* formless and void; and to the heavens, and they had no light. I looked on the mountains, and behold, they were quaking, and all the hills moved to and fro.

I looked, and behold there was no man, and the birds of the heavens had fled. I looked and behold, the fruitful land was a wilderness; and all its cities were pulled down before the LORD, before His fierce anger.

For thus says the LORD, the whole land shall be a desolation, yet **I will not execute a complete destruction**; for this the earth shall mourn, and the heavens above be dark, because I have spoken, I have purposed, and I have not changed My mind nor will I turn from it" (Jeremiah 4:23-28).

Notice, that the Lord said He "will not execute a complete destruction" of the earth and "the heavens will be dark." This again is not the same "fled away" condition of the heavens and the earth that takes place at the end of the Millennium when God will make "**all things new**." In the 1901 American Standard Version of the Bible, verse 27 reads: "For thus saith Jehovah, the whole land shall be a desolation; **yet will I not make a full end**."

In Zephaniah 1:18 we also read:

> "Neither their silver nor their gold will be able to deliver them in the day of Jehovah's wrath; but the whole land shall be devoured by the fire of his jealousy: for he will make an end, yea, a terrible end, of all them that dwell in the land."

Once again, we see a reference to the land being "devoured" by fire, which does not translate as "fled away" as John described in Revelation 21. The verse states that the Lord will make "a terrible end" of those who "dwell in the **land**." He will end the existence of all those who have corrupted this world. The **land**, which is the surface of the earth will be "devoured," not the entire earth. The prophet Isaiah further wrote that "the inhabitants of the earth are burned" and that *few* men would be left at the end of the Tribulation:

> "Therefore the curse has devoured the earth, and those who dwell therein are found guilty: therefore the inhabitants of the earth are burned, and few men left" (Isaiah 24:6).

Keeping these things in mind, earlier in the second chapter we discussed that Scripture tells us that it will take Israel seven years to clean-up (burn) the implements of war left from the battle of Ezekiel 38 and 39 (Ezekiel 39:9). Since the earth is burned up with fire at the very end of the Tribulation, it is not possible for the weapons left from that war to burn into the Millennium. They would never survive the fire of the earth. We also know that Antichrist will turn against Israel at the midpoint of the Tribulation causing the Jewish inhabitants to flee (Matthew 24:15-16; Revelation 12:6, 14).

Therefore, the Jews will not be able to burn those weapons during the second half of the Tribulation. They will not be there. Again, we can see another reason why those weapons will not be able to be burned into the Millennium. The point I am also making here is that Scripture gives us strong indication that the battle of Ezekiel 38 and 39 discussed in length earlier, may very well occur at least three and one half years *before* the Tribulation begins, in order to fulfill the prophecy of Ezekiel 39:9-11:

"Then those who inhabit the cities of Israel will go out and make fires with the weapons and burn them, both shields and bucklers, and bows and arrows, war clubs and spears and for seven years they will make fires of them.

And they will not take wood from the field or gather firewood from the forests, for they will take the spoil of those who despoiled them, and seize the plunder of those who plundered them, declares the LORD God."

The Lord also tells us Israel will be the preeminent nation during the Millennium (Isaiah 62:1-4), and the curse will be lifted, therefore Israel will not need to burn the "plundered" weapons during the Millennium.

"And He said to me, "Son of man, *this is* the place of My throne and the place of the soles of My feet, where I will dwell in the midst of the children of Israel forever" (Ezekiel 43:7a).

Another distinction between the millennial reign of Christ and the eternal kingdom is the sin factor. In Isaiah 65:20, which references the millennial kingdom, we learn: "and the sinner being a hundred years old shall be accursed." In eternity no sin will abound. Once again we see the millennial kingdom is not the same as the eternal kingdom. During the Millennium those who are in their natural bodies will still have a carnal sin nature, and sin will still exist. But Messiah Jesus will physically, literally be on His throne, in the temple on top of Mt. Zion bringing sinners to salvation, and righteousness will reign.

Scripture is filled with distinct differences between the millennial city and the eternal city (the New Jerusalem, the holy city which will descend from heaven). For example, both cities have flowing rivers. The millennial city where Messiah Jesus will dwell is ten miles by ten miles (Ezekiel 48:30-35). The eternal city is 1200 miles cube (Revelation

21:15-17). The eternal city in Revelation 22:1 has no temple, but there is a river that comes from the throne of God. In the millennial city, there is a river that emanates from the millennial temple (Ezekiel 47:1-12). During the Millennium, the twelve tribes of Israel will have land partitioned for them with the sea as the western boundary (Ezekiel 47:15-20). In the eternal city, there is no sea (Revelation, 21:1b).

The Millennium and then continuing on into the eternal kingdom are the future homes for all those who place their faith and trust in Messiah Jesus. We are given glimpses of these places throughout Scripture.

In reference to the Millennial Kingdom:

Zechariah 6:13a; 8:3:

> "Yes it is He [the Lord Himself] who will build the temple of the LORD, and He who will bear the honor and sit and rule on His throne. Thus says the LORD, I will return to Zion and will dwell in the midst of Jerusalem.

> Then Jerusalem will be called the City of Truth, and the mountain of the LORD of hosts *will be called* the Holy Mountain."

Zechariah 14:10-11:

> "All the land shall be turned into a plain from Geba to Rimmon south of Jerusalem. *Jerusalem* shall be raised up and inhabited in her place from Benjamin's Gate to the place of the First Gate and the Corner Gate, and *from* the Tower of Hananel to the king's winepresses. *The people* shall dwell in it; and no longer shall there be utter destruction, but Jerusalem shall be safely inhabited."

Messiah Jesus will return at the end of the Tribulation, reestablish the earth and the heavens, set-up His millennial kingdom, and sit upon the throne of His glory, the throne of David. His righteous order will be implemented. Israel will be leveled at the beginning of the Millennium (Isaiah 40:4), and Mount Zion will be a high mountain (Isaiah 2:2). The millennial city of Jerusalem will be at the top of Mount Zion. Messiah Jesus will continue to cleanse from sin those who receive Him during the Millennium.

Those who survive the Tribulation, the burning fire of the earth, and do who not take the mark of the beast, and get saved at the end of the Tribulation will enter the Millennium in their natural bodies. Some will not get the gospel in its fullness until they actually see the Lord as Matthew told us:

"But he who endures to the end shall be saved" (Matthew 24:13).

In the following passage, Isaiah gives a description of the fire and horrors of the Tribulation and the small number who will survive:

"The sinners of Zion are afraid; trembling hath seized the godless ones; who among us can dwell with the devouring fire? Who among us can dwell with everlasting burnings? He that walketh righteously, and speaketh uprightly; he that despiseth the gain of oppressions, that shaketh his hands from taking a bribe, that stoppeth his ears from hearing of blood and shutteth his eyes from looking upon evil; he shall dwell on high; his place of defense shall be the munitions of rocks; his bread shall he given *him*; his waters will be sure" (Isaiah 33:14-16).

Out of the ravages and ruins of the Tribulation emerge those who survive. The Lord will separate the saved and the unsaved. The unsaved will go into "everlasting punishment" and the saved into the Millennium, graciously blessed with eternal life with the Lord (Matthew 25:31-46). During the Millennium Messiah Jesus will literally rule the earth and its inhabitants.

All believers in their new glorified bodies, those who were taken-up in the Rapture will be given responsibilities according to their faithful service and devotion to the Lord, as recorded in: Luke 19:11-27; Revelation 20:2-6; Revelation 2:26-28; 3:12, 22; 1 Corinthians 6:2-3.

The overall curse put upon mankind since the fall of Adam and Eve will be removed. An ecologically, biologically superior environment will prevail, including fresh produce filled with complete nutrition and organic perfection, clean healthy air, pure water and every good thing imaginable—and much, much more will be part of the millennial blessings.

It will not be quite the perfection of the eternal order following the Millennium, but the millennial years will be richly blessed and righteousness will prevail because of the rule of Jesus Christ. Social justice (transformation) will prevail without the fear of anyone being robbed or hurt in anyway. A strong and constant sense of the presence of the Lord, and His majesty will cover the entire earth (Isaiah 11:9).

"For *there will be* peace for the seed: the vine will yield its fruit, the land will yield its produce, and the heavens will give their dew; and I will cause the remnant of this people to inherit all *things*" (Zechariah 8:12).

"Then justice will dwell in the wilderness, and righteousness remain in the fruitful field. The work of righteousness will be peace, and the effect of righteousness, quietness and assurance forever. My people will dwell in a peaceful habitation, in secure dwellings, and in quiet resting places" (Isaiah 32:16-19).

"And many peoples will say, "Come, let us go up to the mountain of the LORD, to the House of the God of Jacob; that He may teach us concerning His ways, and that we may walk in His paths."

For the law will go forth from Zion, and the word of the LORD from Jerusalem. And He will judge between the nations, and will render decisions for many peoples; and they will hammer their swords into plowshares, and their spears into pruning hooks. Nation will not lift up sword against nation, and never again will they learn war" (Isaiah 2:3-4).

Every person born during the Millennium will be considered a child until he is one hundred years old. If by the age of one hundred that person has not yet accepted the Lord Jesus as Savior, he will be rejected by Him and suffer the same fate as all those who has rejected Him in this life (Isaiah 65:20).

The children born during the Millennium are the offspring of those who physically survive the Tribulation, those who realize the truth of Messiah Jesus and receive Him as their Savior during that horrible seven-year ordeal. Those individuals will be allowed to enter the Millennium. They and their descendents will populate the millennial earth. During the Millennium predators will no longer hunt down their victims. Animals of all types will live together in perfect harmony.

Isaiah 11:6-9

"The wolf also shall dwell with the lamb, the leopard shall lie down together with the young goat. The calf and the young lion and the fatling together; and a little child will lead them. The cow and the bear shall graze; their young ones shall lie down together; and the lion shall eat straw like the ox.

The nursing child shall play by the cobra's hole, and the weaned child shall put his hand in the viper's den. They shall not hurt nor destroy in all My holy mountain, for the earth shall be full of the knowledge of the LORD as the waters cover the sea."

In Reference to the Eternal Kingdom and the New Jerusalem:

The vast majority of people will be saved up until the last years of the Millennium. At the end of the thousand years, Scripture tells us that Satan—who was bound in the bottomless pit, is then loosed for a short time at the end of the Tribulation (Revelation 20:7). He deceives some of the unsaved and recruits the final millennial youth generation into one last great rebellion against the Lord. The camp of the saints and the beloved city will be surrounded, but fire from heaven will devour the rebellious attackers (Revelation 20:9).

The Great White Throne Judgment

"For it is written, as I live, saith the Lord, to me every knee shall bow, and every tongue shall confess to God. So then each one of us shall give account of himself to God" (Romans 14:11-12).

After the one-thousand-year millennial kingdom, the Great White Throne judgment will take place when everyone who died in their sins is judged—those who never accepted Messiah Jesus as Savior and Lord. It will be too late for salvation in Christ for those who did not want to receive the truth while they were still alive.

"And I saw a great white throne, and him that sat upon it, from whose face the earth and heaven fled away; and there was no place found for them. And I saw the dead, the great and the small, standing before the throne; and books were opened: and another book was opened, which is *the Book of Life*: and the dead were judged out of the things which were in the books, according to their works" (Revelation 20:11-12).

"And the sea gave up the dead that were in it; and death and Hades gave up the dead who were in them: and they were judged every man according to their works. And death and Hades were cast into the lake of fire. This is the second death, *even* the lake of fire. And if any was not found written in the Book of Life, he was cast into the lake of fire" (Revelation 20:13-15).

As we have just read we learn those who die in their sins without accepting Christ's free gift of salvation will actually be judged from a written record found in books and "according to their works" (Revelation 20:12). It will be too late for those who die in their sins to repent and receive Christ. All born-again believers will not be part of this judgment because of Christ's sin pardon.

The Eternal Kingdom

After the Great White Throne judgment, the eternal kingdom will begin. No sin or corruption will exist ever again. Everything passes away (Revelation 21:1), and the entire universe is recreated:

Revelation 21:4-6

"And I saw a new heaven and a new earth: for the first heaven and the first earth are passed away; and the sea is no more. And I saw the holy city, New Jerusalem, coming down out of heaven from God, made ready as a bride adorned for her husband.

And I heard a great voice out of the throne saying, Behold, the tabernacle of God is with men, and he shall dwell with them, and they shall be his peoples, and God himself shall be with them, *and be* their God" (Revelation 21:1-3).

"And He shall wipe away every tear from their eyes; and death shall be no more; neither shall there be mourning, nor crying, nor pain, any more: the first things are passed away. And He that sitteth on the throne said, Behold, I make all things new. And He saith, write: for

168

these words are faithful and true. And He said to me, they are come to pass. I am the Alpha and the Omega, the beginning and the end."

The Lord has a special place throughout eternity for the Jewish people. Scripture teaches that upon walking into the holy city of the New Jerusalem, individuals will have to walk under and over the name of a Jew:

"And he carried me away in the Spirit to a mountain great and high, and showed me the holy city Jerusalem, coming down out of heaven from God, having the glory of God: her light was like unto a stone most precious, as it were jasper stone, clear as crystal; having a wall great and high; having twelve gates, and at the gates twelve angels; and names written theron, which are *the names* of the twelve tribes of the children of Israel" (Revelation 21:10-12).

The eternal city—the New Jerusalem will have streets of pure gold, clear like glass and phenomenal jewel laden gates and walls. The city will not have or need the light of the sun or the moon because the Lamb—the Lord Jesus, will be the light (Revelation 21:23). Revelation 21:24, shows that new nations will be created for the eternal kingdom that will glorify the Lord. Their inhabitants will not be sinful beings:

Revelation 21:22-27

"And I saw no temple in it, for the Lord God, the Almighty, and the Lamb are its temple. And the city has no need of the sun or the moon to shine upon it, for the glory of God has illumed it, and its lamp *is* the Lamb.

And the nations shall walk by its light, and the kings of the earth shall bring their glory into it. And in the daytime (for there shall be no night there) its gates shall never be closed.

And they shall bring the glory and the honor of the nations to it; and nothing unclean and no one who practices abomination and lying, shall ever come to it, but only those whose names are written in the Lamb's Book of Life."

Perfection and exquisite beauty will be found everywhere in the Lord's eternal kingdom. Any dream or imagined thought we might have of a perfect world will seem utterly insignificant when compared to the magnificent glory of the Lord and His eternal provisions.

John describes more as we read on into Revelation 22:1-3:

"And he showed me a river of the water of life, clear as crystal, coming from the throne of God and the Lamb, in the middle of its street. And on either side of the river was the tree of life, bearing twelve *kinds of* fruit, yielding its fruit every month; and the leaves of the tree were for the healing of the nations."

And in conclusion, John leaves us with some final messages:

"And he said unto me, these words are faithful and true: and the Lord, the God of the spirits of the prophets, sent his angel to show unto his servants the things which must shortly come to pass" (Revelation 22:6).

"I, Jesus have sent My angel to testify to you these things for the churches, I am the Root and the Offspring of David, the Bright and Morning Star" (Revelation 22:16).

The eternal glory of the Lord is available to anyone who wholeheartedly accepts His free gift of eternal salvation, as long as it is before we take our last and final breath. Scripture tells us there will be those who will wait until they find themselves living through the inescapable terrors of the Tribulation to accept Christ's free gift of salvation. Please don't wait. Tomorrow is promised to no one. Any one of us could take our last breath today. Then it will be too late. The only way we can embrace righteousness and holiness is to be covered by the atoning blood sacrifice of Jesus.

"For He made Him [Jesus] who knew no sin *to be* sin for us, that we may become the righteousness of God in Him. Behold now *is* the accepted time; behold now *is* the day of salvation" (2 Corinthians 5:21, 6b).

Chapter Four

Is Messiah Enough?

Jesus the Messiah Prays to the Only True God
Shortly Before His Crucifixion

John 17:1-5

"Jesus spoke these words, lifted up His eyes to heaven, and said: 'Father, the hour has come. Glorify Your Son that Your Son may also glorify You, as You have given Him authority over all flesh, that He should give eternal life to as many as You have given Him.

And this is eternal life, that they may know You, the only true God, and Jesus Christ whom you have sent. I have glorified You on the earth. I have finished the work which You have given Me to do. And now, O Father glorify Me together with yourself, with the glory which I had with You before the world was.'"

GRACE—Gift Received at Christ's Expense

It is important to point out that many individuals, including a number of believers misunderstand the true meaning of salvation. Salvation is a gift received totally at Christ's expense. There is absolutely nothing we can do to earn our way into heaven, except make a conscious and genuine decision to receive Christ's free gift of salvation by faith. Some well-meaning believers keep busy, busy doing this and that for one organization after another, but spend little—if any time sincerely seeking the Lord and studying His Word with deep, heartfelt surrender. They seem to miss the point of the cross. It is not by works that we are saved, but by what Christ did for us at Calvary.

It is very important to show Christian love by our outward actions and deeds, but our good works should come from a repentant heart as a true reflection of our love and commitment to Christ. This is often referred to as living truly for the Lord or a "fruit of the spirit." It is one thing to keep busy for various Christian causes, to help others and share the love of Yeshua. But to do so thinking any effort on our part will ensure salvation, is a mistake. Involvement with missions or evangelical projects is very important, but a balance of genuine fellowship and worship unto the Lord should not be overlooked. It is through Christ and Christ alone we are saved. When we do give of ourselves it should be because we love the Lord and want others to come to the saving knowledge of Him, not because we are trying to fulfill some sort of mistaken perception of man-made requirements necessary for salvation.

The Finished Work of Christ Jesus

"For by grace you have been saved through faith, **and that not of yourselves; *it is* the gift of God, not of works**, lest anyone should boast" (Ephesians 2:8-9).

"He saved us, not on the basis of deeds which we have done in righteousness, but according to His mercy, by the washing of regeneration and renewing by the Holy Spirit, whom He poured out upon us richly through Jesus Christ our Savior, that being justified by His grace we might be made heirs according to *the* hope of eternal life" (Titus 3:5-7).

Righteousness Through Christ and Christ Alone

"You believe that there is one God. You do well. Even the demons believe—and tremble!"—James 2:19

It is *only* through the Lord Jesus Christ that we are made righteous, because of His death sacrifice the cross. We cannot be made righteous because of the nice things *we* do. We are only made righteous through Jesus Christ, Yeshua Ha Mashiach—the Redeemer of mankind.

It is through Christ and Christ alone that we have a righteous position. Although most religious practices and cults teach the exact opposite—that by doing good deeds or performing various rituals we can attain righteousness. Such false teachings are leading people away from the truth of Christ and into dangerous realms of spiritual deception.

The Lord commanded us to follow His teachings in the Bible, to love, give and to serve. Good deeds and service are very important. They show our obedience to Him, that we are genuine in our faith and that we care about others. But they do not make us holy or get us into heaven.

172

We can only be made righteous and holy by sincerely accepting Jesus Christ as Savior—being born-again, surrendering our will for His will; loving, and trusting the Lord with all our hearts, minds, souls, and strength (Mark 12:30).

"For all of us have become like one who is unclean, and all our righteous deeds are like a filthy garment" (Isaiah 64:6a).

"But when the kindness and the love of God our Savior toward men appeared, not by works of righteousness which we have done, but according to His mercy He saved us, through the washing of regeneration and renewing of the Holy Spirit, whom He poured out on us abundantly through Jesus Christ our Savior, that having been justified by His grace we should become heirs according to the hope of eternal life" (Titus 3:4-7).

"Therefore having been justified by faith, we have peace with God through our Lord Jesus Christ, through whom we have access by faith into this grace in which we stand and rejoice in hope of the glory of God" (Romans 5:1, 2).

Within various Christian and Messianic groups we find some who are caught-up in complex systems of performance, merit-based faith. We are free in Christ, and should not seek to reinvent the salvation message by becoming entrapped in works-based religious structures.

"You have become estranged from Christ, you who attempt to be justified by law; you have fallen from grace. But if it is by grace, it is **no longer on the basis of works**; otherwise grace is no longer grace" (Galatians 5:4; Romans 11:6a).

"Stand fast therefore in the liberty by which Christ has made us free, and do not be entangled again with a yoke of bondage" (Galatians 5:1).

"For Christ *is* the end of the law for righteousness to everyone who believes" (Romans 10:4).

The Apostle Paul's Reminder—Only One Gospel

"I am amazed that you are so quickly deserting Him who called you by the grace of Christ, for a different gospel; which is really not another; only there are some who are disturbing you, and want to distort the gospel of Christ.

But even if we, or an angel from heaven, should preach to you a gospel contrary to that which we have preached to you, let him be accursed.

For am I now seeking the favor of men, or of God? Or am I striving to please men? If I were still trying to please men, I would not be a bond-servant of Christ."

—Galatians 1:6-8; 10-11

Spiritual Deception—Jesus (Yeshua) Warned Us

"Beware lest anyone cheat you through philosophy and empty deceit, according to the tradition of men, according to the basic principles of the world, and not according to Christ; in whom are hidden all the treasures of wisdom and knowledge.

Now this I say lest anyone deceive you with persuasive words. For in Him [Christ] dwells all the fullness of the Godhead bodily; and you are complete in Him, who is the head of all principality and power" (Colossians 2:8; 2:3-4, 9).

While the nations of the world are becoming unglued economically and socially and constantly threatened with nuclear proliferation, Satan is also busy spreading false religious doctrines to keep the masses from realizing the truth of Christ's salvation. Jesus tells His disciples what some of the signs of His return will be:

"Beware of false prophets who come to you in sheep's clothing, but inwardly they are ravenous wolves. Not everyone who says to me 'Lord, Lord,' shall enter the kingdom of heaven, but he who does the will of my Father in heaven.

Many will say to Me in that day, 'Lord, Lord,' have we not prophesied in Your name, cast out demons in Your name, and done many wonders in Your name?" And then I will declare to them, 'I never knew you; depart from Me, you who practice lawlessness'" (Matthew 7:15, 21-23).

"Take heed that no one deceives you. For many will come in My name saying, 'I am the Christ' and will deceive many. Then many false prophets will rise up and deceive many" (Matthew 24:4b-5, 11).

Please don't be deceived by false religions involved in rituals and beliefs glorifying mankind and his established organizations instead of the living God of the Bible. Christ warned that many false prophets and false teachers would arise and increase during the last days. More often than not, these people have very good intentions presenting themselves as respectable individuals but they are teaching false doctrine and are spiritually deceived. These unsuspecting victims of Satan's diabolical agenda are used as his pawns, assisting him with his dirty work.

Satan is an expert at distorting the truth of God's holy Word. The God of the Bible—the God of Abraham, Isaac, and Jacob—is rejected, and anything but the literal interpretation of the Bible is promoted. The Bible is rewritten and debased. Allegiance is given to impersonal deities and entities that are nothing less than demonic spirits masquerading as "beings of light." You may have heard of encounters from those who claim they have had out-of-body experiences and have supposedly entered the "afterworld" and are greeted by "beings of light."

"Behold the days are coming," says the Lord GOD, "That I will send famine on the land, not a famine of bread, nor a thirst for water, but of hearing the words of the LORD.

They shall wander from sea to sea, and from north to east; they shall run to and fro, seeking the word of the LORD, but shall not find it" (Amos 8:11-12).

Some well-meaning individuals call themselves "white witches" or work with a "white light." But these people are treading on dangerous, satanic territory. Those who take on such identities and teachings are usually truly deceived and genuinely want to do good for others, but are being used by dark forces to dilute the truth of the Bible. Satan uses these individuals to create confusion and draw people away from the Lord. The work of such individuals is not biblically supported, regardless of how much they talk *about* the Bible. Even seemingly innocent spells or rituals to invoke "help" go directly against the teachings of the Bible.

The Word of God is emphatically clear that anything other than appealing for help from God the Father in Jesus' name is opening a door to demonic sources. Chain letters that promise "good fortune" are ritualistic nonsense without any basis of validity. They are diversions that have nothing to do with the King of kings and Lord of lords—who is the true source of all our needs (Philippians 4:19). False teachings can be found in churches and synagogues all around the world, and especially within the New Age movement. Satan is an expert at counterfeiting God's miracles.

Dangerous Liaisons

"Beloved, do not believe every spirit, but test the spirits, whether they are from God; because many false prophets have gone out into the world" (1 John 4:1).

"But there were also false prophets among the people, even as there will be false teachers among you, who will secretly bring in destructive heresies, even denying the Lord who bought them, and bring on themselves swift destruction. By covetousness they will exploit you with deceptive words; for a long time their judgment has not been idle, and their destruction does not slumber" (2 Peter 2:1, 3).

"For we did not follow cleverly devised tales when we made known to you the power and coming of our Lord Jesus Christ, but we were eyewitnesses of His majesty.

And *so* we have the prophetic word *made* more sure, to which you do well to pay attention as to a lamp shining in a dark place, until the day dawns and the morning star, arises in your hearts.

But know this first of all, that no prophecy of Scripture is a *matter* of one's own interpretation, for no prophecy was ever made by an act of human will, but men moved by the Holy Spirit spoke from God" (2 Peter 1:16, 19-20).

The Scripture passages you just read emphatically state that an array of spiritual impostors, an alliance of "bad guys" (are competing for your attention and allegiance). For example, the popular New Age movement, which I have talked about quite a bit, also known as the New Spirituality has some enticing and attractive philosophies. But there is nothing "new" about it. It is based on the same old pagan lies that Lucifer has advanced since God created the world:

Love, Peace, Global Consciousness, Harmony, Mother Earth, New Thought, Cosmic Christ, Karma, Psychic and Holistic Healers, Reincarnation, Ascended Masters, Self-Realization, Kundalini, "Spirit," Mysticism, Meditation Techniques, Hinduism, Buddhism, all Eastern Religions, Yoga, Reiki, Gurus, Esoteric Christianity, Goddesses, Psychics, Astral Travel, Tarot Cards, Ouji Boards, Shamanism, Channelers, Theosophy, the Occult, the witchcraft-based cult: Kabbalah,

Metaphysics, Dowsing, Radionics, Psychic Surgery, Spirit Guides, Astrology, Numerology, UFOs, Apparitions of Saints (really demonic deceptions), Silva Mind Control, Hypnosis, Aura, Avatar, and Divine Alchemy are just some of the headings that fall within the New Age category and go against the God-breathed teachings of the Bible. Reference is frequently made to the "universe" as the god in charge of one's destiny.

Avoid giving the devil an opportunity to draw you into his realm of confusion and underhanded schemes devised to take your soul. Resist, and flee from all forms of "entertainment" dedicated to exploring and promoting anything to do with the occult (Leviticus 19:31). Beware of and stay away from of those who offer psychic predictions (fortune telling). Be careful who you accept counseling from. Let the Word of God be your counselor. Hypnosis, trances of any type, horoscopes, and séances are all areas that open doors to dark forces enabling the devil to get a foothold into our lives. So are *all* the New Age topics I specified in the previous paragraph. They are all windows to demonic influences.

Yes, even "Love" and "Peace" can be used by the forces of darkness to entice us away from the true agape love of the living God of the Bible. A psychic counselor can very readily tell you he or she "prays" to God and comes to us in "peace" to help us with our problems. Don't believe it. Many of these individuals really do think God has given them such gifts, but they are deceived and are being fed information from the powers of darkness.

Even if these psychics have the best of intentions, they are getting their information from dark, evil sources that only *appear* to be friendly. Always remember, Satan and his demons can present themselves as very attractive entities and they use individuals such as psychics and New Age counselors to take people away from the true God of the Bible—working relentlessly to water down and destroy the salvation message. You might even hear them say they love Jesus and that they are "Christians." The Lord implores us not to have anything to do with demonically inspired activities of any kind.

"Give no regard to mediums and familiar spirits [demons]; do not seek after them, to be defiled by them: I am the LORD your God" (Leviticus 19:31).

"There shall not be found among you anyone who makes his son or his daughter pass through the fire, one who uses divination, one who practices witchcraft, or one who interprets omens, or a sorcerer, or one who casts a spell, or a medium, or a spiritist, or one who calls up the dead. For whoever does these things is detestable to the LORD; and because of these detestable things the LORD your God will drive them out before you" (Deuteronomy 18:10-12).

New Agers in general, have the nutritional market cornered and have wonderful awareness when it comes to the importance of eating a healthy diet, especially those who promote a diet of fresh, whole raw fruits and vegetables. My own personal interest in living a healthy lifestyle was my "gateway" to New Age spirituality. I kept meeting individuals who were seriously health "conscious" but most of them also happened to be involved in pagan-related religious practices. Being good stewards of our planet is also very important, but "Mother Earth" is not God, as some of these nice folks tend to believe. Some of the kindest, most thoughtful people are part of the New Age movement. Of course some charlatans use that platform just to rake in money. But that can be said of many others engaged in various organizations, including "Christian" ones.

It grieves me to say that those in the New Age movement are usually very unaware that the Bible truly is the inerrant Word of God. Instead, they involve themselves in pagan ideologies with demonic roots. Prophecy is one major area. They tend to listen to "prophecies" that try to imitate and counterfeit the prophetic Word of God.

One of the cruelest lies I have ever heard is when one of these psychic channelers claim to be communicating with a dead relative. This is a perfect example of one of the devil's ploys to get people to believe all is well on the other side with or without the God of the Bible. Demonic entities victimize grieving families. They pose as dead loved ones and the demonic vessel—the psychic channeler—is conveniently used to tell the lie. Remember, Satan has plenty of power, and his goal is to fool you into believing there is no need for Jesus Christ's free gift of salvation. Dead loved ones cannot speak to you from the "other side." The Bible is very clear on this.

Savvy students of Bible prophecy have been aware that some New Age teachers are promoting Satan's counterfeit to the true, biblical Rapture. Recently, I came across some good information regarding this diabolical scheme. Some New Age writers, channelers and teachers are reporting that "Mother Earth" is going to undergo an intense cleansing. All those who are believers in Yeshua (Jesus) will be removed because they are holding back the "harmony" of the earth. They even claim that they have been given this information by extraterrestrials.

These unsuspecting, naïve souls who are spreading this information, these demonic lies, don't have a clue that they are smack in the middle of the spiritual fight of our lives. The devil knows the Lord is going to remove all believers before all hell breaks loose, begins. Already he is fabricating one lie after another to discredit God's incredible Rapture miracle.

Following is a quote from a well-circulated, popular New Age book. The authors claim that the messages in the book were supposedly channeled by so-called extraterrestrials, the Pleiadians.

The people who leave the time of earth changes do not fit in here any longer, and they are stopping the harmony of the earth. When the time comes that perhaps twenty million people leave this planet at one time there will be a tremendous shift in consciousness for those who are remaining. —*Bringers of the Dawn: Teachings from the Pleiadians*, Barbara Marciniak and Tera L. Thomas

I understand there is a great book by author, Jim Simmons that touches on this coming planetary delusion. He has a profound understanding of New Age teachings that are infiltrating many aspects of our daily lives. You can read more about this satanic subterfuge, this simmering demonically devised plot in his book, *The Last Generation: Current Prophecy, World Events and the End Times*.

I urge anyone involved in New Age practices to take the information presented here and seriously investigate it. This is a matter of spiritual life or death. Eternity is a very, very long time. Please don't let peer pressure, pride or preconceived ideas get in your way and keep you from salvation in Christ. If your livelihood and lifestyle depend on promoting some New Age practices, you will probably strongly resist this message. But you are paying a huge price for short-term monetary gain.

If you die without being saved you will be left with the horror of an eternity without God. All the money in the world won't save you then. If the Rapture and Tribulation take place before you die, you will be faced with the horrifying terror here on earth. Yes, it is possible to get saved during the Tribulation, and great numbers of people will, but life will be very rough and the suffering will be terrible.

Considering that the Rapture is approaching and the Tribulation will erupt almost immediately after within the same 24-hour period, your future finances *will be* negatively affected. So don't let false financial security keep you from receiving the truth of salvation through Messiah Jesus.

"And even if our gospel is veiled to those who are perishing, in whose case **the god of this world has blinded the minds of the unbelieving,** that they might not see the light of the gospel of the glory of Christ, who is the image of God" (2 Corinthians 4:3-4).

You can choose not to believe this message, but at least respect yourself and your life enough by really examining *all* the information presented. If nothing else, at least read some of the books on New Age deception listed in Appendix C.

Inside the New Age Nightmare by Randall Baer is a very important book to start with. I have also included some very good websites on spiritual deception throughout this text and in Appendix B. You can learn more about Randall Baer's experiences with the New Age Movement in Appendix E. Don't allow yourself to become one of the devil's victims. Receive Christ while you still can. I have an excellent link right here to some very insightful information related to many false religions and New Age deception: http://www.crossroad.to/.

I walked away from some very lucrative business opportunities when I became a genuine and committed believer in Messiah Jesus, because those opportunities would have tremendously supported the deceptive New Age philosophies. I did not want to have any part in promoting lifestyles very contrary to my personal beliefs and the teachings of the Bible. I had to walk away. Once I understood the truth I had to let go of anything that would hinder my walk with the Lord. I could not have a divided heart. He has tremendously blessed my life since.

New Age "spiritual" practices fuel the worldly mantra that the accumulation of wealth defines success. It is a trap of enslavement that the ruler of darkness tries to overpower people with. No amount of monetary achievements without the Lord at the helm can compare to the joy and inner peace that comes from having a true, personal relationship with the Lord Jesus. Of course many people know inner beauty, generosity and integrity matter much more than material possessions and wealth. But the glitz and glitter of worldly success is an insidious foe and can seduce the best of us.

It is hard to walk away from great monetary success when we are caught-up in the ways of the world, when we are constantly being told unless we achieve outstanding material success we are not as valuable as those who "have it all." But when we know the Lord and have made peace with ourselves through the Lord's all-encompassing eternal grace, it is very difficult to stay entrapped in the pursuit of fleeting baubles and the so-called pleasures of the world. Only the love and salvation found in Jesus the Messiah can fill the void that so many hurting souls are so desperately trying to satisfy.

If you receive Yeshua (Jesus) as your Savior, He will bless you too, and will open up ways for you to make a living that will honor Him. We cannot be sure how far away the Rapture is, and even if it is farther in the future than most believers hope, the Lord will make the rest of your earthly journey here a blessed one.

Remember, this is a spiritual war and the choice you make concerning whether to accept or reject Jesus Christ, as the true Messiah will determine your destiny forever and ever. There is nothing I want in my life that is not God-supported or God-inspired. I know where my eternal future is. I trust the Lord's promises that say my future will be far better than anything I can possibly dream of.

"Delight yourself also in the LORD, and He shall give you the desires of your heart. Commit your way to the LORD, trust also in Him, and He shall bring *it* to pass" (Psalm 37:4-5).

"For what will it profit a man if he gains the whole world, and loses his own soul?" (Mark 8:36).

For thousands of years now, the Lord has been preparing an eternal home for all His children, for all believers. I can't wait to see my incredible new home!

[Jesus said,] "Let not your heart be troubled; you believe in God, believe also in Me. In my Father's house are many mansions; if it were not so, I would have told you. I go to prepare a place for you. And if I go and prepare a place for you, I will come again and receive you to Myself; that where I am, there you may be also" (John 14:1-3).

A number of dedicated environmentalists and naturalists are involved in building homes in remote places such as Vilcabamba, Ecuador. If you become a believer who understands where we are in prophetic history, you will not have to move to some third world refuge to try to live in harmony with the earth. God has a much better plan for you. He will be in charge of the coming millennial kingdom and that will be the place to settle in and enjoy the Creator's ecological precision. Living in remote locations will not spare you from hell on earth during the Tribulation. Only salvation through Messiah Jesus can save us from that time. Don't think for a minute this earth will be cleaned up by the gang that runs it. It will not happen. All they are going to do is clean out your wallet.

"*I pray that* the eyes of your heart may be enlightened, so that you may know the hope of His calling, what are the riches of the glory greatness of His inheritance in the saints and what is surpassing greatness of His power toward us who believe" (Ephesians 1:18; 19a).

Soon, the entire planet will be humming beautifully with the glory of God's planetary rejuvenation. Don't be left out. Building a personal relationship with the King of the universe is the bridge to realizing the splendor of that pristine world. All believers who are taken up to heaven in the Rapture are promised new "glorified" bodies. We will have a magnificent "glorified," earth too. After the seven-year Tribulation, and after a brief seventy-day interval the millennial kingdom will begin. You can be sure that genetically modified foods and polluted air and water will never again threaten the health of those who are part of God's millennial kingdom.

"For our citizenship is in heaven, from which also we eagerly wait for a Savior, the Lord Jesus Christ; who will transform the body of our humble state into conformity with the body of His glory, by the exertion of the power that He has even to subject all things to Himself " (Philippians 3:20-21).

These are in accordance with the working of the strength of His might which He bought about in Christ, when he raised Him from the dead, and seated Him at His right hand in the heavenly places, far above all rule and authority and power and dominion, and every name that is named, **not only in this age, but also the one to come**" (Ephesians 1:19b-21).

The controversial topic of UFOs has become quite popular. Once again, upon careful examination of Scripture, we find the answers to what the UFO phenomenon is really all about. The true identity of these "extraterrestrials" is most likely tied into the "giants" of old, the Nephilim spoken of in the Old Testament, in the book of Genesis.

"The Nephilim were on the earth in those days, and also afterward, when the sons of God came in to the daughters of men, and they bore *children* to them. Those were the mighty men who *were* of old, men and renown" (Genesis 6:4 NASB).

"Now there was a day when the sons of God came to present themselves before the LORD, and Satan also came among them" (Job 1:6).

"AGAIN there was a day when the sons of God came to present themselves before the LORD, and Satan also came among them to present himself before the LORD" (Job 2:1).

The Nephilim are the offspring of fallen angels and human women. Scripture indicates some of these fallen angels intermingled with women of the earth. Highly regarded experts who analyze this very odd and unusual topic are convinced that demons are most likely disembodied spirits of the Nephilim. These disembodied spirits (demons) need to inhabit something to operate at their full capacity. Fallen angels, however, can apparently manifest without indwelling anything. They can simply appear and do not need to inhabit some thing to carry out their sordid and vile deeds. As far-fetched as it may sound, the unnerving alien abduction reports may very well be connected to demonic entities. In the resource sections I have listed some excellent information on this topic.

No doubt the UFO explosion is all tied into Satan's agenda to deceive and destroy God's redemptive plan for mankind. These ETs are interdimensional beings and part of Satan's demonic army. Dr. Chuck Missler states in his DVD, *Return of the Nephilim*, that two, very respected physicists, Jacques Vallee and J. Allen Heineck, have done extensive research into the UFO question. They both came to the same conclusion: that UFOs are not intergalactic ETs, but are demonic, hyper-dimensional entities that come from another dimension, periodically. Both these physicists came to this conviction through extensive scientific research, without any type of religious involvement or persuasion. The Nephilim seem to be part of this demonic (ET) resurgence. Please look into the very good material I have listed in the resource guides for a thorough study of this relevant, very strange, and peculiar topic.

No one likes to believe he or she is involved in what could be a big "spiritual" lie, especially if there are financial issues involved. New Agers must wake-up soon and realize they are spiritually deceived. The Bible, the Word of God, is available to them if only they would read it, study it, and see that it is the ultimate love letter from God. It tells of the promise of a future, ecologically perfect world, a world without wars, and a pure and healthy planet with the Lord in charge. When Christ returns and sets up His earthly millennial kingdom, the very things these individuals are striving for will become the beginning of an eternal reality for all those who belong to Him. Organic food will be plentiful, and there won't be any "climate change" problems.

"And by the river on its bank, on one side and on the other, will grow all *kinds of* trees for food. Their leaves *will* not wither, and their fruit will not fail.

They will bear every month because their water flows from the sanctuary, and their fruit will be for food and their leaves for healing" (Ezekiel 47:12).

The New Spirituality—the New Age movement is a breeding ground for Satan's masterful lies. Even some nominal Christians are falling prey to these tainted doctrines. The teachings are very seductive, sometimes as a self-aggrandizing alternative to the truth of the Bible. Proponents of New Age philosophies profess a belief in "God," but disregard and trivialize the historical truths of the Bible and the one true God, Yeshua Ha Mashiach, Jesus the Christ. These religions and cults are spiritual death traps designed by Satan himself. He is the prize-winning producer of confusion, depravity and illusionary absurdity.

"And no wonder! For Satan himself transforms himself into an angel of light" (2 Corinthians 11:14).

The one common denominator among these cults and false religions is their denial of Jesus Christ as Lord and Savior. They almost always call Him just a "prophet" or a "teacher." Additionally, some popular religions say Jesus Christ is Lord but create rules and requirements for salvation. They tag on unattainable never-ending requirements that will supposedly result in gaining God's favor to gain entry into heaven based on good deeds and acts of penance. Sadly, the Catholic religion's

185

teachings fall into this category. Essentially this doctrine says Christ's death sacrifice is not enough, that He needs our help; when in fact it is by Christ's sacrifice on the cross alone, and our willingness to fully accept Him by grace through faith that we are made righteous.

Unfortunately, so many trusting people who are locked into the Catholic religious system are deceived and do not understand that they are participating in a church that is based on unscriptural rituals and beliefs. It is a works-based religion. No amount of good works will ever save us. It is Christ and Christ alone who can save us. The Bible also states very clearly and unequivocally that *only* Jesus Christ can be the intercessor for the forgiveness of sins. No human, not even one wearing a shirt with a fancy collar can do the job. And no other "spirit" can save us.

"Who is a liar but he who denies that Jesus is the Christ? He is antichrist who denies the Father and the Son" (1 John 2:22).

"For by grace you have been saved through faith, and that not of yourselves; *it is* the gift of God, not of works, lest any man should boast" (Ephesians 2:8-9).

"For there is one God and one Mediator between God and men, the Man Christ Jesus, who gave Himself a ransom for all, to be testified in due time" (1 Timothy 2:5-6).

Church or synagogue attendance alone, eating special foods to bring you closer to "spirit" (really a demonic entity), and being an exemplary caretaker of the earth will not save you. If you don't think you need a Savior, you will soon find out that only the Lord Jesus Christ can save you. Only He can save this world from impending doom.

"Nor is there salvation in any other, for there is no other name under heaven given among men by which we must be saved" (Acts 4:12).

Two excellent links to explore and find detailed information (articles) on spiritual deception are as follows:

"The Christ of the New Age Movement" at:
http://home.earthlink.net/~ronrhodes/ChristNAM.html.
"The Jesus of the New Age Movement" at:
http://home.earthlink.net/~ronrhodes/JesusNAM.html.

A Biblical Warning About Deceptive
False Teachers and Leaders

"Holding fast the faithful word which is in accordance with the teaching, that he may be able both to exhort in sound doctrine and to refute those who contradict. For there are many rebellious men, empty talkers and deceivers, especially those of the circumcision, who must be silenced because they are upsetting whole families, teaching things they should not *teach*, for the sake of sordid gain."

—Titus 1:9-11

The name of Jesus Christ, and the common titles: "Christian," "Christianity," and "the "Cross" are commonly assumed by those who are not at all representative of genuine Christianity, in the true biblical sense. Because of this it is easy to misidentify Jesus Christ and the true meaning of Christianity with those in our culture who carry Christ's name selfishly, inappropriately, and even diabolically to advance their own agendas. Tremendous misinterpretation and misunderstanding exists as to just *what* authentic Christianity is all about and *who* Jesus Christ really is.

An extreme and devastating example of how the cross has been totally twisted is by examining those who have encouraged and supported anti-Semitism. After all, Hitler was born a Roman Catholic and was never excommunicated from that church despite his horrific crimes against the Jews and humanity. By the world's standards, the Roman Catholic Church most definitely falls directly under the umbrella of "Christianity."

A lack of awareness causes most Jews, as well as the mainstream population to identify true biblical Christianity with the Roman Catholic Church, when in fact there are some very serious, definitive differences. Most Catholics, without realizing it have been taught false doctrines that distort the true gospel message of salvation by grace alone through faith. Instead, the sixty-six books of the Bible are replaced with teachings that are steeped in mysticism, idol worship, rituals, and superstition. God's Word says that we are saved by **grace through faith** in Christ Jesus and not by our own efforts or works (Ephesians 2:8-9).

And then there are the historical problems. Because of the Roman Catholic Church's tragic misapplication of the cross by some greedy evil madmen, the cross now grievously and permanently carries with it indescribable pain to those who have been traumatized by the deplorable, vicious actions of some dangerous, power-hungry men. History reveals that the hierarchy of the Roman Catholic Church has engineered the torture and extermination of hundreds of thousands of innocent Jews as well as Christians. That is tough to hear, isn't it? Nevertheless, within the Roman Catholic Church today there are millions of kind, well-meaning individuals who are unaware of and blind to the darkness that has shaped the religion they hold dear. For the most part, these folks are oblivious to the behind-the-scenes power plays that their "spiritual" leaders, even now continue to engage in.

Most Roman Catholics are wonderful hard-working trustworthy charitable individuals—some of the kindest people I have ever met. But they have not been taught the truth of the Bible. They are deeply involved in a works-oriented religion that fails to take into account the sufficiency of Christ's saving grace. However, over the past thirty-five years or so, more and more Catholics are coming to salvation in Christ (including former nuns and priests) and rejecting the false doctrines of the Roman Catholic Church.

All sincerely deceived Catholics would do well to make it a point to study the Scriptures (not the Catholic "bible") and realize the religion they are involved in essentially rejects the Word of God and replaces it with man-made rules and regulations that are contrary to the Holy Bible. Many similar terms recognized by Christians are used within the Catholic religion. For example: Prayer, Holy Spirit, Jesus, communion. These words are the same words used by true Bible-believing Christians. However, the actual definitions and applications of these words are quite different among Catholics and Bible-believing Christians. Similarities in terminology have caused much confusion for many individuals.

Those without a strong biblical-foundation can easily involve themselves in cultic "spiritual" practices that are leading them away from the true God of the Bible into the spheres of darkness, directly into the deadly grasp of the devil. Each individual is accountable to the Lord for what he or she believes and practices. There is no such place as purgatory. No "priest" can absolve you of your sins, and no one other than Jesus Christ can intercede for us when we pray (1 Timothy 2:15).

Idol worship has long taken a stronghold in the Catholic Church and is in direct defiance and an insult to the Holy God of the Bible. Praying to "Mary" or to "patron saints" or asking such entities to "intercede" for us goes completely against the teaching of the Scriptures. Lighting candles or saying repetitive "prayers" with a rosary will not help us get well if we are ill, or save us and get us into heaven. The Lord is very explicit in admonishing us not to worship idols. **Only prayers to the Father in Jesus' name are to go before the throne of God.** Idolatry is a huge problem within the Catholic Church and within all other man-led religions and cults.

Praying to or idolizing anyone or anything other than Almighty God is a serious affront to the Lord. Calling up dead "saints" by praying to them ("one who calls up the dead") through "prayer" is an abomination to the Lord (Deuteronomy 18:11b-12). An excellent, must-read book on the topic of the Catholic Church: *A Woman Rides the Beast: The Roman Catholic Church and the Last Days* by Dave Hunt. Also, a very important book, especially for those who insist on adhering to the false teachings of the Catholic Church: *The Gospel according to Rome: Comparing Catholic Tradition and the Word of God,* written by James McCarthy.

The following Scriptures give a preview of the fate ahead for those who insist on not accepting the will and Word of God by praying to "saints" or anyone other than Almighty God:

"They shall be turned back and be utterly put to shame, who trust in idols" (Isaiah 42:17a).

"For whoever does these things is detestable to the LORD; and because of these detestable things the LORD your God will drive them out before you" (Deuteronomy 18:12).

"Let all those be ashamed who serve graven images, who boast themselves of idols" (Psalm 97:7a).

An important teaching to view or listen to if you consider yourself a Christian: *Is Your Church New Age, Emergent or Christian?* By Eric Barger. He explores the differences in doctrine and theology of the many different types of so-called Christian churches throughout America today—some of which are Christian in name only. Available in DVD or CD formats. Eric Barger also has some pertinent online teachings available for your viewing from his website as posted in the Resource Guides (Appendix B and Appendix C).

Christ and Christ Alone Can Save Us from the Coming Wrath and from Eternal Suffering

"Jesus said to him, 'I am the way, the truth, and the life. No one comes to the Father except through Me'" (John 14:6).

Regardless of what happens in this world, in this life, if you have truly given your life to Christ and have accepted His free gift of salvation by becoming a born-again believer—your eternal future is safe and secure (John 3:3, 5, 6-7). Our ultimate destiny is eternity. Nothing in this life can compare to the glory the Lord has planned for those who belong to Him.

"But as it is written: Eye has not seen, nor ear heard, nor have entered into the heart of man the things which God has prepared for those who love Him" (1 Corinthians 2:9).

Certainty of God's Witness

"This is He who came by water and blood—Jesus Christ; not only by water, but by water and blood.

And it is the Spirit who bears witness, because the Spirit is truth.

For there are three that bear witness in heaven: the Father, the Word [Jesus], and the Holy Spirit; and these three are one.

And this is the testimony: that God has given us eternal life, and this life is in His Son.

He who has the Son has life; he who does not have the Son of God does not have life" (1 John 5:6, 8, 11-12).

Every Knee Will Bow

"So that at the name of Jesus EVERY KNEE WILL BOW, of those who are in heaven and on earth and under the earth, and that every tongue will confess that Jesus Christ is Lord, to the glory of God the Father."

—Philippians 2:10-11

Demonic forces will not hesitate to stop at absolutely nothing to wrangle and coerce people into believing that the God of the Bible is akin to a mythical giant lording over those who are intellectually and spiritually inferior.

Satan and his devious demonic armies work relentlessly to appeal to one's ego, pride and self-importance, spreading the lie that the God of the Bible and the Bible itself are outdated and irrelevant in comparison to all of today's "sophisticated" philosophies.

Celebrity Chronicles—New Age Celebrities Fulfill Bible Prophecy

There isn't a person alive in this great country who has not heard of some well-known celebrity speak out about a personal involvement in some type of popular New Age practice. It seems to be a pandemic within the entertainment industry. These privileged, ultra-rich icons often have enormous media platforms with huge and faithful followings. Whatever these popular celebrities endorse is more often than not—taken seriously by adoring fans.

Many of these beloved and sought after personalities come from traditional religious backgrounds. Some have emerged from Christian roots, having once embraced Christianity and Jesus Christ, but have strayed and drifted into spiritual heresies. This is part of the great apostasy written about by the apostle Paul. He warned in his First Epistle to Timothy how some will "depart from the faith"—paying attention to "deceiving spirits and doctrines of demons," and how some will not endure sound doctrine. Scripture warns us if we were once believers in Christ—the gospel of Jesus Christ—but walk away from it and do not repent, then the result will be far worse than if we had never known the truth of the Bible:

> "For it is impossible for those who were once enlightened, and have tasted the heavenly gift, and have become partakers of the Holy Spirit and have tasted the good word of God and the powers of the age to come, if they fall away, to renew them again to repentance since they crucify again for themselves the Son of God and put *Him* to an open shame" (Hebrews 6:4-6).

The future is exceedingly grim for those who have fallen into this trap. Not only is this true of rich and famous celebrities, this kind of spiritual deception can happen to any one of us. It happened to me, until the Lord liberated me. In my estimation, anyone who has the power of celebrity carries with him or her tremendous power and influence. A celebrity has the power to affect millions of people positively or negatively. Having been quite involved in New Age teachings, I am deeply concerned about the seemingly boundless pulpits celebrities have to influence the lives of others.

New Age ideology is always presented in a way to appeal to our humanity: to love one another, to help one another, to grow together for the good of everyone. But through that attractive door, heretical sinister teachings are introduced and exploited. Some very public and persuasive celebrities have bought into the lies of the occult. They often promote dangerous spiritual doctrines, and go out of their way to do so.

Encouraging others to be the best they can be is admirable. No doubt some of the philosophies some public figures share are exhilarating and beneficial. However, teaching that Jesus is not the only way to heaven is spiritual suicide. Teaching or recommending teachings of those who water down the truth of the Bible is the blind leading the blind. Tragically, most of these renowned personalities are oblivious to the fact that they are promoting lies birthed right in the pit of hell by the father of lies, the devil (John 8:44).

When I finally realized the absolute truth of the Bible, through the admonition of the Holy Spirit, I understood the Lord is a loving God, but also a righteous and just God with some specific guidelines for living. It was then that I was truly set free. God does not want to send anyone to hell. I have already explained how we cannot enter the holy presence of God in our sin state. We decide to either accept Him or reject Him. God gives us free will to do as we choose.

Despite what some who are household names may promote, and would like you to believe, Jesus the Messiah did die for you and for me, to save us from an eternity of inconceivable misery. We are all engaged in an all-out spiritual war, and some popular celebrities seem to have been taken hostage by the enemy, and could very well be suffering from a type of spiritual "Stockholm syndrome" when the hostage begins to side with and work with the captor.

It is not unusual to witness celebrities using vast media outlets to promote distorted spiritual teachings. These media soapboxes are often used to spin New Age heresies. The Word of God warns us not to accept those who deny the deity, the sovereign power, and incomparable stature of the historical Jesus, the true Messiah. A common teaching in New Age celebrity circles is the promotion of the "oneness" of everything in the universe.

The New Age conviction that "all is one, all is God—you are God, I am God, we are all God" falls apart quickly under scrutiny for many reasons. One fact undermines the entire concept. If what New Agers are saying is right, then that would render the true Holy God of the Bible to be an evil entity, and that is simply not possible. There is without a doubt evil in this world, and that "oneness" cannot exist in this imperfect world. God and evil cannot be "one."

"This is the message which we have heard from Him and declare to you, that God is light and in Him is no darkness at all" (1 John 1:5).

From the moment Lucifer (Satan) rebelled against God trying to usurp Him, and then subsequently cast out of heaven along with his demonic pawns (fallen angels), the conflict between God and Satan has been going full force. There is a distinct difference between the light of God and the powers of darkness. New Age teachers dilute the powers of darkness with their corrupt teachings, offering themselves up to the wiles of the devil. They presume human interaction with what appears to be friendly forces is a trustworthy foundation for truth. The only true light that exists is the living God of the Bible.

The "light" New Agers are promoting is a false, demonic light, one that I addressed earlier in this book. Demons and Satan can appear as beautiful, friendly "light" beings. That is how they get people confused and opened up to false doctrine. And they can be so convincing! These demonic imposters have the ability to make you feel so good about yourself, so good that you can actually call yourself "god." This is done every day by using unsuspecting celebrities who have the power to reach and influence millions.

The New Age movement has the name of Satan written all over it. Some of these famous celebrities who formerly had Christian Baptist roots have chosen to reject the God of the Bible, and embrace spirits of demons. I pray these folks are sincerely deceived, much like I once was. I pray that all good Christians who are praying for the salvation and deliverance of these influential people will continue to pray.

Perhaps when it is all said and done, at least some who are deceived will repent and be freed from the stronghold that the enemies of God have on them. The prophetic Word of God has given us many warnings that this very kind of spiritual deception will flourish shortly before Messiah Jesus returns and takes His rightful place on the throne of David. May the God of Abraham, Isaac, and Jacob awaken these New Age celebrities and their followers from the lies of the devil, and *before* the onset of the coming, prophesied Tribulation years; all the money in the world will not save anyone from that horrific time. Only Jesus Christ can save us from those dark, catastrophic years.

A Course in Miracles—Fraudulent Demonic Teachings

"If we say that we have no sin, we are deceiving ourselves, and the truth is not in us" (1 John 1:8).

Below I have a short quote from: *A Course in Miracles*, an old New Age "classic," a popular book amongst some celebrities. It is chocked full of one blatant outrageous, sacrilegious lie after another. The teachings from this book are a sample of what a great number of celebrities and New Agers subscribe to. The Word of God absolutely refutes such demonic, irreverent false teachings and unequivocally tells us that we "all have sinned and fall short of the glory of God." And that Christ's sacrifice on the cross is the most significant event in all of history, without which we would all be eternally doomed. Whenever you hear the truth of the Lord Jesus Christ deviously twisted and undermined, you can be sure that Satan is behind such a diabolical crusade:

There is no sin.
A slain Christ has no meaning.
The journey to the cross should be the last useless journey.
The name of Jesus Christ as such is but a symbol ... it is a symbol that is safely used as a replacement for the many names of all the gods to which you pray (pages 9-13).

The source of the teachings in *A Course in Miracles* is quite disturbing. The author, atheistic psychologist Helen Schucman, received these teachings by demonic revelations. This study came to her by "mind dictation" and the source identified himself as Jesus Christ (Matthew 24:5). She recalled, "The voice made no sound, but seemed to be giving me a kind of rapid inner diction, which I took down in a shorthand notebook."

Another psychologist, William Thetford agreed to participate in these dictations with Schucman for many years. Thetford was frequently with her as she received the immense collection of spiritually deceptive information—the very foundation of this popular New Age "course in miracles." He naïvely believed she was receiving the original teachings of Jesus Christ to deliver to the world. In other words, lies straight from the pit of hell intended to deceive as many people as possible.

Consequences of Unbelief and Falling Away from the Faith

The following Scriptures make it clear that those who ridicule and deny the truth of Christ—the truth that has been revealed since the beginning of time—face a tragic, fatal future.

"For the wrath of God is revealed from heaven against all ungodliness and unrighteousness of men, who suppress the truth in unrighteousness, because that which is known about God is evident within them; for God made it evident to them.

For since the creation of the world His visible attributes, His eternal power and divine nature, have been clearly seen, being understood through what has been made, so that they are without excuse" (Romans 1:18-20).

"For even though they knew God, they did not honor Him as God, or give thanks; but they became futile in their speculations and their foolish heart was darkened.

Professing to be wise, they became fools, and exchanged the glory of God for an image in the form of corruptible man and birds and four-footed animals and crawling creatures" (Romans 1:21-23).

A Stern Warning for Those Who Reject Almighty God

"And just as they did not see fit to acknowledge God any longer, **God gave them over to a depraved mind** to do things which are not proper, being filled with all unrighteousness, wickedness, greed, evil; full of envy, murder, strife, deceit, malice; *they are* gossips, slanderers, haters of God, insolent, arrogant, boastful, inventors of evil; disobedient to parents, without understanding, untrustworthy, unloving, unmerciful; and although they know the ordinance of God, that those who practice such things are worthy of death [hell], they not only do the same but also give heartily approval to those who practice them" (Romans 1:28-31).

God's Spiritual Armor

"Put on the whole armor of God that you may be able to stand against the wiles [schemes] of the devil. And take on the helmet of salvation, and the sword of the Spirit which is the Word of God.

For though we walk in the flesh, we do not war according to the flesh. For the weapons of our warfare are not carnal but mighty in God for pulling down strongholds."

—Ephesians 6:11, 17; 2 Corinthians 10:3-4

New Spirituality's New Age Angels

What could be the harm in giving our attention to those innocent-looking, adorable little New Age angel statues, books, and home decor that have become so popular in recent years? What is wrong with meditating and asking angels to guide our lives and watch over us? Once again, spiritual deception is the problem. It is one thing to enjoy some attractive and beautiful angelic images, and charming little fairies with delicate wings. But to elevate these creatures to a place of worship is opening oneself up to demonic entities. We have already discussed some of the dangers of delving into areas of demonic strongholds. Satan's primary agenda is to entice us to worship him, and keep us from salvation in Christ.

Remember, Satan is the father of lies and will stop at nothing to convince us he is just a good old boy who means no harm. He can and does appear as an angel of light and his angelic demonic armies are part of his charade. Don't open yourself up to the subterfuge of the devil. Praying to angels, interacting with them through any type of meditative state is spiritually dangerous. Asking angels to guide our lives is asking for serious trouble. Our prayers should always be directed to God the Father, in Jesus' name.

Even with my own history of exploring dangerously deceptive "spiritual" doctrines, I am nevertheless surprised by how many unsuspecting people are falling for another one of Satan's dirty tricks (the angel masquerade). Scripture warns us not to get involved in idolatry in any way. The worship of anything other than the true living God of the Bible is idolatry. Our careers, our homes, our cars, people, our possessions become idols if we worship and love them (idolize them) and we should let go of the "hold" they have on us. We should give that love and adoration to the King of kings—our blessed Savior, the Lord Jesus.

"And we know that the Son of God has come and has given understanding, that we may know Him who is true; and we are in Him who is true, in His Son Jesus Christ.

This is the true God and eternal life. Little children keep yourselves from idols. Amen" (1 John 5:20-21).

"Beware, lest your hearts be deceived and you turn away and serve other gods and worship them" (Deuteronomy 11:16).

Any road that takes us away from the saving grace of Christ should have a giant stop sign at the entrance. Instead, Satan muscles his way in placing enticing welcome signs at the front of those perilous roads. He displays alluring flashing green lights to try to lure us in, using any scheme he can concoct in order to take our attention away from Messiah Jesus. Angels of deceit are everywhere, and you can be sure they are not biblical angels. Angelic beings exist, both good and bad. Remember, Satan was the most beautiful angel who rebelled against God and is still trying to overthrow the kingdom of God.

Attractive paraphernalia found at New Age shops and angel stores are designed to distract us into believing we don't need the Lord, and that nirvana and enlightenment can be achieved by interacting with dubious entities presented as attractive, charming beings. These seemingly innocuous "angel" images are most often promoted within New Age books and trinkets. When New Age authors and teachers suggest we should meditate and ask angels or anyone other than the Holy Spirit to guide us, we should all run away as quickly as possible and seek the true mediator of heaven, Yeshua Ha Mashiach, Jesus the Christ.

We must always remember that Satan and all his demons are supernaturally intelligent beings often disguised as holy angels. They are responsible for the current "angel" obsession in our culture. At the core of this undercover operation is the ultimate deceiver, Satan himself. The world is experiencing an intense outpouring of demonic activity through these fallen angels.

Please be very careful of the books you read, the movies you watch or the counseling you receive. Steer clear of trendy angel reading material that claims to disclose "secret knowledge" about angels. Concealed behind such attractive names such as "angel of divine healing," "angel of light," and "angel of condolence" are most assuredly demonic influences aspiring to have us pay homage to anything or anyone but the true God of the Bible.

The Lord implores us to test the spirits to see if they are from God. A spirit truly from God *always* acknowledges that Jesus is the Christ who came to the world to die for our sins, and rescue us from Satan's bondage as expressed in 1 John 4:1-6. A holy angel of God will not accept worship, but will encourage us to worship Almighty God only. Revelation has several verses instructing us to worship God, never angels: Revelation 2:18; 19:10; 22:8-9. Some New Age teachers tell their followers to pray to angels for health, wealth, power and guidance. Scripture tells us to pray only to the Father in the name of Jesus Christ, His Son. Angels are God's servants and all our attention, worship and praise should go to Him, not to His servants.

"I am the LORD, that is My name; and My glory I will not give to another, nor My praise to carved images" (Isaiah 42:8).

"And have no fellowship with the unfruitful works of darkness, but rather expose them" (Ephesians 5:11).

Ron Rhodes has a great article titled: "Close Encounters of the Celestial Kind: Evaluating Today's Angel Craze." Below are a few important points taken from it. Please read it in its entirety at: http://home.earthlink.net/~ronrhodes/AngelsArticle.html.

The apostle Paul explicitly warned against accepting any "gospel" from an "angel" that goes against the inspired Word of God (Galatians 1:6-8). One would do well to remember that Joseph Smith, the founder of Mormonism, said an angel named Moroni led him to the golden plates containing the Book of Mormon. As well, Muhammad claimed he received the revelations contained in the Qur'an directly from the angel Gabriel (a demonic impostor).

Other religions involving "angelic" messengers include The Church of the New Jerusalem, founded by Emmanuel Swedenborg; Anthroposophy, founded by Rudolf Steiner; the Self Realization Fellowship, founded by Paramahansa Yogananda; and the Unity School of Christianity, founded by Charles and Myrtle Fillmore.

We must not forget that true holy angels of God are not in the business of starting or promoting new religions or giving us revelations that contradict God's Word (see Psalm 103:20; Revelation 22:9). One might also note that the above religious systems radically contradict each other at many key points of doctrine, thereby undermining the reliability of these "angels" as sources of truth.

The Truth About Kabbalah and Other Occult Influences

New Age, occult influences in various forms are being directed at our children and the world in general. Cartoons, books, movies, television programs, and video games are just some of the methods used for disseminating occult messages. These demonic onslaughts are more "signs of the times" forewarned by Messiah Jesus.

These "spiritual" assaults are designed to keep us, and even our youngest children, from the true God of the Bible, and lead them into the occult. Remember, Satan is intensely devious, presenting his lies in attractive, innocent-looking packages. Deceptive public relations skills are his specialty. I have some very good resources listed on the back pages of this book specifically relating to attempts to spiritually, thus morally, corrupt our children. Most promoters of these dark teachings are unaware they are being used by Satan to spread his destructive agenda.

Halloween is a prime example of occult indoctrination. It looks like fun and games, but it is most definitely considered a high holy day amongst witches, occultists, and Satanists. Board games and electronic games lauding the "fun" and allure of magic (magic tricks) are also used to infiltrate and corrupt the vulnerable minds of young children, acting as gateways to other harmful occult practices.

Dabbling with anything from the demonic realm can even lead to destructive lifestyles such as drug and alcohol addiction. The *Harry Potter* craze has been another slap in God's face. A dark, dangerous web of demonic travesties are aimed at our children, offered as innocuous fun, and promoted through highly sophisticated media campaigns. Satan's prime agenda is to ruin lives and keep us from salvation in Christ.

As long as we are on the topic of spiritual deception, I am including the startling and very important testimony of Dr. Stephen M. Yulish. It is part of an article he wrote for L.A. Marzulli's October 2009 newsletter, *Politics, Prophecy and the Supernatural*. In the newsletter, his article is titled: "Kabbalah, Satan, and Me." I will now share some of that article under a new title along with a more detailed testimony provided by him from his personal archives:

Kabbalah Will Kill Your Kid's Soul

By Stephen Yulish PhD

Last winter, as I finished reading David Kinghoffer's L.A. Times article, "Ghosts, Aliens and Us" where he spoke of his experiences with a Rabbi who dabbled in mystical practices at his child's circumcision and how it helped him find meaning in our increasingly secular world. I was immediately saddened by this man's lack of truth, which unfortunately is so prevalent among my Jewish landsmen, i.e. family and friends: "Always learning and never able to come to knowledge of the truth" (2 Timothy 3:7).

They will believe and/or accept almost anything in their quest for truth, anything but Jesus. There are Buddhist Jews and Scientology Jews, and Hare Krishna Jews and Atheist Jews and New Age Jews (Jews often lead various counterculture religious groups and movements as well), but they will not acknowledge or accept Messianic or Christian Jews. They tolerated my Kabbalah and my astrology and my reincarnation, but Jesus was too much.

I once argued with an Orthodox Rabbi from *Aish Ha Torah* in Jerusalem. They try to remove Jews from "cults" like Christianity and bring them back to their Jewish roots. When I told them that I now accepted Christ as my Lord and Savior and I felt that He was the Mashiach prophesied in the *Tanakh* (Old Testament), and therefore I still considered myself a Jew, the rabbi disagreed that I was still a Jew.

He said I would spend eternity in hell boiling in excrement for my belief in Jesus. I was appalled by his distasteful, insulting comment but later found that this is in the Jewish rabbinic commentary, the *Talmud, b.gittin 57a* and also applied to Jesus as well as other so-called apostates.

"While I was a Jew of the Jews, all of those things I now count as rubbish in view of the surpassing value of knowing Christ Jesus the Lord for whom I have suffered the loss of all things in order that I may gain Christ" (Philippians 3:4-8).

As Klinghoffer senselessly pointed out, William James did speak of the 'reality of the unseen' and Cotton Mather did speak of the 'invisible world' in their quest for another level of reality in their search for meaning and Hassidic Jews also do speak of the 'yenne velt,' which is Yiddish for the other world. This quest for godless mysticism has often manifested itself in different ways. Years ago, in my own misguided quest for the truth, I got sucked into this same demonic realm that Klinghoffer now lauded and I am here to tell you what happened.

In September of 2005, a friend sent me an article from *Arutz Sheva* which is, *Israel National News*, titled: "Kabbalist (Rabbi Kaduri) Urges Jews to Israel Ahead of Impending Disaster." I had been very tempted to just delete the article because of my current disdain for anything to do with Jewish mystical lore (i.e. Kabbalah) since I had gotten saved and found real truth. From personal experience, I had found out that Kabbalah was not of God but of Satan, but I decided to read it anyway.

God turned what was meant for evil to good (Genesis 50:20). God had a plan. Let me explain. There has been a resurgence of late in the ancient Jewish mystical practice of Kabbalah as a result of many Hollywood types, some Jewish and some not, falling into this spiritual delusion. Many true devotees of Kabbalah actually believe that this modern Hollywood version is just pop mysticism and they dismiss it. But don't be fooled, even casual dabbling in this type of mystical endeavor, real or hip, can have serious consequences on you and your children's lives. I am not going to give you an intellectual argument for avoiding Kabbalah.

I am going instead to tell you a real story about one person's descent into the spiritual arrogance of Kabbalah and hope that it scares the hell out of you. That person was me!

While I was brought up in a more or less traditional Jewish household and went to an after school Cheder (Hebrew School), from age nine to thirteen to prepare for my Bar Mitzvah, I was always interested in way out things. I loved science fiction novels and as a young teen even wrote a story for *Analog Science Fiction Magazine* about life on Mars. My interests gradually moved into study of philosophy, religion, and mysticism. I became what the Bible speaks of as a Gnostic. I wanted to commune directly with God. Forget the traditional religions and their outdated practices. I was trying to find knowledge (gnosis) of God and become like Him or Her. The apostle Paul dealt with this abomination 2000 years ago: "Turn from godless chatter and opposing ideas of what is falsely called knowledge [gnosis]" (1 Timothy 6:20). "The love of Christ surpasses knowledge [gnosis]" (Ephesians 3:19). "Knowledge [gnosis] puffs up but love builds up" (1 Corinthians 8:1).

I meditated, did lucid dreaming, contemplated my navel, studied astrology, numerology, the paranormal, the supernatural, UFOs, Hinduism, Buddhism, Zoroastrianism, and death and dying research. I studied my dreams, alternate states of consciousness, and gradually found myself studying Jewish mysticism. I was excited to find that the *Zohar* (23 volume so-called Bible of Jewish mysticism) spoke of astrology, reincarnation (gilgul), spirit guides, and many other subjects that I loved. Now I could be so-called New Age and Jewish as well. I had loved it. Sin feels good for a season.

When I was an undergrad student in the sixties, my university was closed for a semester because of the rioting and they offered free classes. I took one on Edgar Cayce, the Sleeping Prophet, which would influence my life for the next twenty years. As a grad student I bought the multi-volume copy of the *Zohar*. One was supposed to be married, forty years old, male, and learned in Torah before one was allowed to study Kabbalah (which means to receive or accept-tradition).

I was male and married but still in my thirties and not that conversant in Torah and Talmud. I was told that it could drive you mad if studied without these restrictions. I laughed at the time, but in a way it did drive me mad. How female, non-Jewish dilatants like Madonna and others can be told that it is all right for them to study Kabbalah is beyond me. It is literally playing with hell fire and they are not even playing by the rules as ominous as they are.

While I was a Professor at the University of Arizona, I wrote a novel, *The Other World*, where I glorified the anti-Eve character Lilith and her cohort Samael (Satan). This book was the most New Age, demonic book that you could imagine. I glorified evil and Satan. I blurred the distinctions between good and evil, reality and dreams, and even male and female. I quoted from the lost gospels found at Nag Hammadi. I read from this at a loft in Greenwich Village in New York. Thank God, my novel was never published. But I had been completely enamored with Kabbalah. I got people to love it.

I even taught adult Bible classes for young Jewish married couples on Kabbalah. I was leading the Jewish masses astray, not to speak of thousands of my college students. I even taught a grad class on "Alternate Conceptions of Reality" where I spoke of reincarnation (Kabbalistic gilgul), karma etc. One of my students committed suicide and everyone he knew wanted me at the funeral because he supposedly loved my class best. I probably helped lead this poor guy to hell with my Kabbalistic notions of reincarnation and the false notion of a second chance.

I left the University in 1983 and became the director of the Jewish National Fund in Phoenix. My interest in Kabbalah continued unabated. I began to do spontaneous drawings (automatic writing) at my desk. These strange detailed bizarre pen and ink pictures would materialize out of the hand of a man who could only draw stick figures. My secretary spotted them and it turned out that she was a witch. I kid you not. Satan was on my trail. She and I would take turns reading each other's minds. She introduced me to an astrologer who said I had the best chart of anyone since Buddha.

I decided to send my drawings to Ruth Montgomery, a leading psychic and author. She wrote me back and told me I had to go see Ann Puryear a leading psychic in Phoenix and follower of Edgar Cayce. I did, and that began a two year-excursion into the darkest side of the New Age movement. Ann's husband, Herb was setting up a metaphysical university and he wanted me to teach Kabbalah-Jewish mysticism. I sent my drawings to a Kabbalistic Journal where they were published for all to see. I showed them to the Rabbis that I knew in Phoenix. At this time I was working for the Jewish Federation and knew them all. They loved the drawings, many of which looked demonic and evil (to me now). They encouraged me to publish them in a book. We talked on gilgul (reincarnation) and how many great rabbis had spirit guides (demons!).

WE talked about anything and everything but Jesus. We were all deceived. At that time my wife took a job in New York and would commute home once a month or so. In 1985, I went to a meeting in LA held by Rabbi Michael Berg, the current guru of Kabbalah, and Madonna's mentor. Hey, he was my mentor twenty years ago. I had read his books and had gone to L.A. to become enlightened. I took my drawings with me. We all immersed in a ritual bath to cleanse ourselves (not naked) and then had meetings, etc. I was into this stuff twenty years before Hollywood ever was. Been there, did that. Rabbi Berg told us how we could become like God.

My marriage disintegrated and I lost my job at the Federation, not because of my Kabbalistic dabbling, which my wife tolerated, but because of other sins. My father died and I was diagnosed with MS. God was trying to get my attention. I found myself working for a Christian company and first met my present wife Paula in 1987. She and others witnessed to me about Jesus. Yeah right! This over educated, know it all, New Age Jew would have nothing of it. Finally, after one year of constant witnessing, and me saying that I would have to see the burning bush for myself, God revealed Himself to me, the worthless sinner of sinners. What Amazing Grace. Paula and I were married in 1990. Ironically during our first week of marriage, Puryear called me, and even though we had not spoken or seen each other in years, asked me to come teach Kabbalah at his new metaphysical university. I told him that we no longer had anything in common and that I had accepted Jesus Christ as my Lord and Savior.

He gasped and hung up the phone. I burned my Zohar, all my New Age books, my earlier novel and all my demonic drawings. Praise God. Thank you Jesus. Beware of any discipline that tells you that it will teach you how to be God. There is only one God and it is not by you or me. Also, be thankful that our God has the mercy and grace to save a worthless sinner like me. There is no sin, not even Kabbalah that cannot be washed away by the blood of Jesus. Now let's go back to September 2005, when I had just finished reading the *Arutzs Sheva* article about Kabbalistic Rabbi Kaduri, the one sent to me by a friend. I knew that it must have been the *Ruach Ha Kodesh*, the Holy Spirit (who had opened my eyes twenty years earlier) who had coaxed me to read what I initially and instinctively did not want to read. What I found strengthened my belief that we are indeed in the last days and that the people of Israel are being setup for the reign of the Antichrist. May God have mercy on their souls.

On Tuesday night, September 13, 2005, Rabbi Yitzchak Kaduri, a rabbi steeped in Jewish Kabbalistic, mystical lore told his Yeshiva class (Jewish school) that Jews all over the world needed to return to Israel due to impending natural disasters, which threatened to strike the world. He had spoken of tsunamis (there was the devastating Indonesian tsunami of 2004 and subsequent ones) and other natural disasters. I asked myself how he could know what was going to happen. Probably because he used gematria (numerology) and other Kabbalistic divinations, witchcraft, and demonic practices that the Lord called detestable to Him in Deuteronomy 18:10-12. Satan knows that his time is short (Revelation 12:12) and he will give people just enough knowledge to condemn them to hell for eternity.

Look what happened to Saul when he went to the witch at Endor to call up the spirit of Samuel (1 Samuel 28:11). He did so against the Word of God in Deuteronomy 18, and died for doing it. "So Saul died for his trespass which he committed against the Lord because of the Word of the Lord which he did not keep and also because he asked counsel of a medium, making inquiry of it and he did not inquire of the Lord therefore He killed him" (1 Chronicles 10:13).

This mysticism; whether it be calling up the dead or Kabbalah divination is serious business and can have dire consequences. Don't play with fire. "God is not mocked, we reap what we sow" (Galatians 6:7). We know from Scripture that the Jews would return to the land of Israel (Ezekiel 36:8) in the end of days. We know that the church is about to be taken up to be with Jesus in the clouds at the Harpazo, the Rapture, and that it will be explained to those left behind as an abduction by UFOs. We know that the man of lawlessness, the Antichrist, will then be revealed and will take his place in the rebuilt Temple and declare himself to be God (2 Thessalonians 2:3-4).

Rabbi Kaduri had said that when the danger comes to Israel, the Temple will be rebuilt and the righteous Messiah will be revealed. Open your eyes Jews and see how Satan used Rabbi Kaduri to call Jews back to Israel to worship the soon to be revealed "unrighteous messiah," the Antichrist, in the soon to be rebuilt Temple. Rabbi

Kaduri had said that many dangers and disasters would come upon the earth. He is correct.

After the Rapture of the saints, the seven-year Tribulation will begin which the prophet Jeremiah called the time of Jacob's Trouble. During that time according to the Prophet Zechariah, two thirds of the Jews will perish (Zechariah 13:8) until the Messiah (Christ) returns and all Israel that is left will look on Him whom they have pierced and wail and their eyes will be opened and they will be saved (Zechariah 12:10; Romans 11:26).

Instead of Jews like Klinghoffer realizing that Yeshua Ha Mashiah, Jesus the Christ, is their Lord and Savior, not only are they going to be left behind at the Rapture but they are going to be misled and deceived once again to accept a false messiah as their Savior and two thirds will die in the Tribulation.

Back in 2005, Rabbi Kaduri said that the supposed Messiah to some, Rabbi Schneerson (he also has since died), told him that Kaduri would live to see the coming of the Messiah. He said the current government of Israel would be the last one of an old era. Sharon would be the last Prime Minister. The new leadership would be that of the messianic era. Wrong, wrong, wrong! Well, Schneerson was obviously incorrect and must therefore have been a false prophet. Rabbi Kaduri died in 2006 before the coming of the Messiah. Sharon was not the last Prime Minister of Israel. Before Rabbi Kadhuri died, he told his followers that the spirit of Messiah had already attached itself to an Israeli and he also had been given the name of the coming Messiah, but it was not to be revealed until one year after his death.

The note when opened said that the coming Messiah will be called: Yehoshua (Joshua) or the Aramaic, Yeshua (salvation). This name, Yeshua Ha Mashiach (literally Jesus the Messiah or the Christ), is unbelievably what some of Rabbi Kaduri's followers called him! The returning Jesus (Yeshua Ha Mashiach) will not be an Israeli man but will come "in just the same way as you have watched Him go into heaven" (Acts 1:11). The Antichrist, however, will be a man. If this "man" is not a false messiah, a false christ, a false yeshua, then call me meshugeh (crazy). If all of this is not a demonic setup for the coming Antichrist, then I don't know what is. The Jews will be deceived to believe that the coming Antichrist is really their Messiah, their Mashiach, but alas they will be wrong. "Look up, those who believe, for your redemption draws near" (Luke 21:28). We are indeed in the end of days.

You can see from reading the very involved testimony of Dr.Yulish that he supports many of the significant points I have already made regarding New Age deception. All the more reason to be spiritually discerning in these last days; carefully dodging the snare of Satan's venomous noose. The material he mentioned (quoted) from the Nag Hammadi is a library of Gnostic books, a collection of "secret" demonic teachings.

Numerology and the Occult

The occult practice of numerology is a teaching using divination to counsel people based on the work of Pythagoris, an early Greek mystic, mathematician and philosopher who also had a strong belief in the immortality and transmigration of souls (reincarnation). Pythagoras himself claimed he had once been Euphorbus, a warrior in the Trojan War, and that he had a memory of all his previous existence; a clear-cut unbiblical demonic concept. The actual origins of numerology predate Pythagoras to the most popular being from the Hindu Vedas (demonic entity). Numerology is loaded with occult leanings building a reliance on numbers rather than Christ's finished work on the cross; popular with Wiccans, witches and others who are fooled by this pagan ritual. This practice extolled highly as a "science" can seem harmless and attractive.

Remember, the devil is very cunning and loves to fool people by using appealing methods that seem to have *some* validity when tested. Always remember, Satan has power and can create ways to try to pull you into his demonic realm. Just because something has the outward appearance of *sometimes* making sense, unless the proposed premise lines up with the Scriptures we can be sure it is a method of pulling us away from biblical truth and into enemy territory. The occult-based "life path number" is touted by numerologists to hold the key to a happy destiny. Stay away from numerology, a dangerous, deceptive practice of divination forbidden by God (Deuteronomy 18:9-12). Make Jesus Christ your Lord and Savior and rely on the Holy Spirit for guidance to you life's path.

Almighty God's Allegiance to Israel

"This is what the Lord says, 'He who appoints the sun to shine by day, Who decrees the moon and stars to shine by night, Who stirs up the sea so that its waves roar -- the Lord Almighty is His Name; Only if these ordinances vanish from My sight,' declares the Lord, 'will the descendants of Israel ever cease to be a nation before Me.'"

—Jeremiah 31:35-36
New International Version of the Bible

Chapter Five

Has the Christian Church Replaced Israel?

A popular movement within the Christian church is Dominion Theology. It is a false theorem misleading many Christians. This ideology has created a clamor of controversy amongst believers for many years. I am going to discuss this especially for anyone who is new to faith in Christ so you will recognize this puzzling, false teaching. Another term for Dominion Theology is "Kingdom Now Theology." It is a corrupt teaching asserting that God has entrusted Man to bring the whole world under the dominion of Christianity. This belief system can sound appealing because of the many social maladies in society. Dominion exponents refuse to accept and acknowledge the obvious fact that until the Lord returns, the conditions of this world will continue to deteriorate. No man will ever be able to bring this world into harmony and unity.

According to the dominion theorists, Christ will not return until the Christian church gains an upper hand and gains control of government and social establishments. However, Scripture simply does not say that. Mankind will never bring peace to this tainted world—that is precisely why the Lord has to come back—to once and for all put a final finish to this age of never-ending escalating chaos, and discord. When the Lord returns it will be at the height of hell on earth. He will come as a warrior, to destroy those who have irreverently taken control of the world. I have already talked about this in some detail in previous sections of this book.

Preterism and Replacement Theology are also two false belief systems that fall within the sphere of Dominion Theology. Preterists teach that "last days" Bible prophecy has already been fulfilled. That claim is preposterous, especially to those who understand biblical Scripture relating to the topic. Preterists deny the Rapture teachings, and convolute all the Bible passages that clearly define the Lord's promised Rapture event.

Replacement Theology promotes the lie that Israel has no further place or standing in God's prophetic plans, and that when Israel underwent judgment for rejecting Messiah Jesus, they were cut-off for eternity. Because of Israel's disobedience, these Bible twisting theorists have come to believe that all the promises that God made to Israel, now belong to the Christian church. These dominionists teach that the Christian church has *replaced* Israel. They consider themselves to be "spiritual Israel." They believe that they and the entire Christian church collectively to be present-day Israel. Their teachings allegorize the literal truths of God's living, holy Word and confound it by saying Israel was cast off forever in 70 A.D., when Jerusalem was captured and the temple was destroyed. And from that point forward all references and prophecies of Scripture regarding Israel allude to what they believe to be spiritual Israel (the Christian church), not the true literal nation of Israel. Nothing could be further from the truth.

This kind of heretical thinking and teaching is dangerously treading on sacrilegious ground and infiltrating many Christian churches. Many of these professing evangelicals are blatantly aligned *against* Israel. This is a tragic-trend gaining momentum in the Christian "church" today. Those involved do not understand their Bibles or are not true Christians and have their own agendas contrary to the God of the Bible.

God's love for Israel has never changed. His blessing for Israel has never been removed. Israel has been under godly discipline, but the Lord has never turned His back on His chosen people. God has never, and will never discard, or abandon His covenant with Israel.

"For you are a holy people to the LORD your God; the LORD your God has chosen you to be a people for Himself, a special treasure above all the peoples on the face of the earth" (Deuteronomy 7:6).

"And yet for all that, when they be in the land of their enemies, I will not cast them [the Jews] *away*, neither will I abhor them, to destroy them utterly, and to break my covenant with them: for I *am* the LORD their God. But I will for their sakes remember the covenant of their ancestors, whom I brought forth out of the land of Egypt in the sight of the heathen, that I might be their God: I *am* the LORD" (Leviticus 26:44-45).

"If his children forsake my law, and walk not in my judgments; if they break my statutes, and keep not my commandments; then I will visit their transgression with the rod, and their iniquity with stripes.

Nevertheless my lovingkindness will I not utterly take from him, nor suffer my faithfulness to fail. **My covenant will I not break**, nor alter the thing that is gone out of my lips. Once I have sworn by my holiness that I will not lie unto David. His seed shall endure forever, and his throne as the sun before me. **It shall be established forever** as the moon, and *as* a faithful witness in heaven. Selah" (Psalm 89:30-37).

A thorough study of the entire chapter of Romans 11, *without spiritualizing* and allegorizing the nation of Israel and its people, will quickly dissolve the false notions purported by those who mistakenly believe themselves to be the remaining remnant of Israel. The following key Scriptures help unravel such false teachings.

"I say then, has God cast away His people? Certainly not! For I also am an Israelite, of the seed of Abraham, of the tribe of Benjamin. God has not cast away His people whom He foreknew. I say then, have they [Israel] stumbled that they should fall? Certainly not! But through their fall, to provoke them to jealousy, salvation *has come* to the Gentiles" (Romans 11:1-2a, 11).

"For I do not desire, brethren, that you should be ignorant of this mystery, lest you should be wise in your own opinion, that blindness in part has happened to Israel until the fullness of the Gentiles has come in. And so all Israel will be saved, as it is written: "The Deliverer will come out of Zion, and He will turn away ungodliness from Jacob; for this is My covenant with them; when I take away their sins" (Romans 11:25-27).

To profess that God has cut-off Israel because of its past disobedience entirely misses the point of God's grace. How often does the Christian church fail today? The Lord put aside Israel for the purpose of evangelism *only*. God has not stopped working in Israel, with the Jews. But He *has stopped* using Israel in proclaiming the doctrine of Christ.

"From the standpoint of the gospel they are enemies for your sake, **but from the standpoint of *God's* choice, they are beloved for the sake of the fathers; for the gifts and the calling of God are irrevocable.** For just as you once were disobedient to God, but now have been shown mercy because of their disobedience, so these also now have been disobedient, in order that because of the mercy shown

213

to you they also may now be shown mercy. For God has shut up all disobedience that He might show mercy to all" (Romans 11:28-32).

> "Because your God has loved Israel, to establish them **forever**, therefore He made you king over them, to do justice and righteousness."
> —Queen Sheba's statement to Solomon
> (2 Chronicles 9:8b)

Israel and the Arab World's Contributions

Israel was dispersed throughout the earth for about two thousand years, but was maintained as a people throughout that worldwide Diaspora, barely surviving unending persecutions, including the Holocaust in which Satan attempted to obstruct the rebirth of modern Israel. Yet miraculously since 1948, the restoration of the nation of Israel has become history. This is tremendous evidence that God has not relinquished His love and blessings on Israel and the Jewish people. Not only does Israel exist, it thrives.

Web searches show one article after another reporting how well Israel is doing and how the Israelis are in the forefront of multiple technologies and businesses excelling tremendously, despite the severely weakened global economy. Israel is considered the Silicon Valley of the Middle East with forty-six per-cent imports from the industrial high tech sector, as reported by World Focus on November 17, 2009 at: http://worldfocus.org/blog/2009/11/17/israel-thrives-as-the-silicon-valley-of-the-middle-east/8458/.

Israel's flourishing agricultural export business has also been a huge economic blessing, an important part of their economy. Against all likelihood, the Israeli's turned a barren desert void of vegetation into an agricultural oasis, as prophesied by Ezekiel. It doesn't sound to me like God has abandoned Israel spiritually or pragmatically.

> "And the desolate land will be cultivated instead of being a desolation in the sight of everyone who passed by, and they will say 'This desolate land has become like the garden of Eden; and the waste, desolate, and ruined cities are fortified *and* inhabited.
>
> Then the nations that are left round about you will know that I, the LORD, have rebuilt the ruined places *and* planted that which was

desolate; I, the LORD, have spoken and will do it" (Ezekiel 36:34-36).

Israel and the Arab World Their Contribution to Mankind is a very informative website all about Israel and the Arab world—their contributions to humanity. Comparison Charts are posted on the site. You will find important information showing the contributions by both Israelis and Arabs. On the website is the following statement:

"All human beings are equal. There are no superior people. The difference is between education and superstition, between reason and fanaticism, between freedom and slavery..."

The research in the Comparison Charts astoundingly shows that the Jewish people are far advanced in all the listed categories:

Part I: The State of Israel and the Arab Countries

Life Quality and Education
Nature and Ecology: Bio-technology
Nature and Ecology: Energy
Science, Health and Technology
Defense and Aerospace Industry
International Solidarity

Part II: The Jewish People and the Arabs

Jewish and Arab Personalities in History
Jewish and Arab Personalities in Modern Times
Personalities in Modern Times
Jewish and Arab Achievements
Nobel Prizes
Miscellaneous

To study the entire website containing detailed, excellent statistics please visit: http://www.imninalu.net/Israel-Arabs.htm .

Israel's water technology business is also booming. You can learn more at: http://www.guardian.co.uk/business/feedarticle/8814836.

Why Prophecy?

The Trustworthy Prophetic Word of God

2 Peter 1:16-21

Eyewitnesses

"For we did not follow cleverly devised tales when we made known to you the power and coming of our Lord Jesus Christ, but we were eyewitnesses of His majesty.

For when He received honor and glory from God the Father, such an utterance as this was made to Him by the Majestic Glory, "This is My beloved Son with whom I am well-pleased"— and we ourselves heard this utterance made from heaven when we were with Him on the holy mountain.

So we have the prophetic word made more sure, to which you do well to pay attention as to a lamp shining in a dark place, until the day dawns and the morning star arises in your hearts.

But know this first of all, that no prophecy of Scripture is *a matter* of one's own interpretation, for no prophecy was ever made by an act of human will, but men moved by the Holy Spirit spoke from God."

Through the Prophet Isaiah, we have two declarations below given by the Lord testifying that it is *He* who is in charge of yesterday, today, and tomorrow. Bible prophecy substantiates that God is who He says He is—the one and only true God. Bible prophecy unveils the future, and fulfilled prophecy authenticates the true identity of Messiah Jesus as "KING OF KINGS and LORD OF LORDS" (Revelation 19:16b).

"Remember the former things long past, **for I am God and there is no other; I *am* God and there *is* no one like Me, declaring the end from the beginning**" (Isaiah 46:9-10a).

"I declared the former things long ago and they went forth from My mouth, and I proclaimed them. Suddenly I acted, and they came to pass. Therefore I declared *them* to you long ago, before they took place I proclaimed *them* to you, lest you should say, 'My idol has done them'" (Isaiah 48:3, 5a).

It is inconceivable to me that anyone could ever disregard the importance of Bible prophecy and that includes a large number of "evangelists" and professing "Christians." Approximately one-third of the Bible is prophecy. The Bible is a unique, precise communication method designed and left to us by the Lord Himself. Fulfilled Bible prophecy distinctly validates the authenticity and precision of Almighty God's holy, unchanging Word.

Prophecy shows God is inseparably engaged in history as it develops and unfolds. The prophetic Word is a dominant factor in determining the heart of the Bible, the heart of God. Prophecy holds a very prominent position in biblical illumination. It is God's way of communicating with us throughout history. Bible prophecy is one hundred percent accurate, one hundred percent of the time.

The role of Bible prophecy is misunderstood and ignored by a vast number of ill-informed, misdirected "believers" (Christians) and the world in general. Once more, we have to look to the nation of Israel. Without a doubt, national Israel plays a vital role in the Word of God and His plan for humanity. Those who ignore or belittle Israel's prominent position in Scripture are living in some sort of warped alternate reality. These individuals are creating their own "bible" by the act of omission. Omitting Israel, God's chosen nation is a precursor to inviting His Almighty wrath.

It is absolutely impossible to accurately decipher Scripture without recognizing Israel as a major player. There is no way to get around this fact without denigrating and reinventing the Bible. Biblical prophecy and the nation of Israel are in a sense, interchangeable. You cannot have one without the other. Israel itself is prophetic in the most profound way: It exists.

The resurrection of the nation of modern Israel is proof positive that prophecy is reliable and true. It is fulfillment of Bible prophecy to the utmost degree. Those who attempt to spiritualize Israel by claiming the Christian church has replaced national Israel in Scripture are contemptuous and spiritually blinded by corrupt interpretations of the Bible. In addition, the erroneous attempt by some to place future prophetic events into some sort of retroactive collection plate of supposed past fulfillments is testament to a glaring attempt to distort

God's perfect Word. The following points made by Bible teacher, John MacArthur, are very true and right in step with the ongoing dynamics in these last days. The Word of God is being wildly bantered about and misinterpreted like never before. Here is an excerpt from his book, *Reckless Faith—When the Church Loses Its Will to Discern* (pages 56, 57, and 58).

A Failure to Interpret Scripture Carefully—Another basic factor leading to the decline of discernment is a widespread failure to interpret Scripture properly. Hermeneutics—Bible interpretation is an exacting science. Good preaching depends on careful hermeneutics. But too much modern preaching ignores the meaning of Scripture altogether. Pulpits are filled with preachers who are unwilling to do the hard work necessary to interpret Scripture properly. They pad their messages with stories, anecdotes, and clever outlines—all of which disguise the weakness or lack of biblical content.

Unfortunately, the standard has sunk so low today that even well known Christian leaders can twist and contort Scripture beyond recognition, and yet no one seems to notice. In this age of existentialism, many people have the impression that Bible interpretation is a subjective exercise. Perhaps you have been to a "bible study" where the method of exploring a text was to go around the room and ask everyone, "What does this verse mean to you?" That is a sure path to confusion and a formula for reckless faith.

To avoid mistaken Bible interpretations it is very important to study:

The Golden Rule of Interpretation

When the plain sense of Scripture makes common sense, seek no other sense; therefore, take every word at its primary, ordinary, usual, literal meaning unless the facts of the immediate context, studied in the light of related passages and axiomatic and fundamental truths, indicates clearly otherwise.

Every Bible student should understand the dynamics taught in the Golden Rule of Interpretation. In addition, please see an excellent more in-depth presentation on the rules of Bible interpretation by the late Dr.

David L. Cooper, titled: "Rules of Interpretation" posted online at: http://www.biblicalresearch.info/page7.html.

In the book of Revelation, John wrote:

> "For I testify to everyone who hears the words of the prophecy of this book: If anyone adds to these things, God will add to him the plagues that are written in this book; and if anyone takes away from the words of the book of this prophecy, God shall take away his part from the Book of Life, from the holy city, and *from* things which are written in this book" (Revelation 22:18).

> "Every word of God *is* pure; He *is* a shield to those who put their trust in Him. Do not add to His words, lest He rebuke you, and you be found a liar" (Proverbs 30:5-6).

A Flawless Integrated Message System from Outside of Time

In this section, we will read more about how the Bible is very different from other "holy" books. Many years ago, at Hal Lindsey's 1995 Prophecy Conference, Bible teacher Chuck Missler delivered a riveting speech to a group of believers in Irvine, California. The points he made then are just as true today. Here are some important, thought-provoking statements from his presentation:

> How many of you believe the Bible is the Word of God? Why? Why do you believe the Bible is the Word of God? Every "holy" book claims to be the "Word of God." The Koran, the Gita, you can make the list. Where do we come off assuming that this collection of sixty-six books is the Word of God? I come from a technical background, information sciences primarily. And the two great discoveries in my life were: number one, it is an integrated message system. Every number, place, name, every detail is there by design. The second thing of course is prophecy.

> I'd like to talk about that a little bit. You and I, because we're into it, may not be sensitive enough to what a preposterous premise we're promoting the idea that history can be written in advance. That's

weird. And I think what we need to look right in the eye is the fact that that is a strange concept, especially to our friends that we are going to share things with. So I'd like to talk a little bit about that, because most of us suffer from a number of misconceptions. Most of us have misconceptions that get in the way of our understanding. We assume that yesterday will be like tomorrow. We feel an hour a thousand years ago is the same as an hour a hundred years from now. In other words, we tend to make an assumption that time is linear and absolute.

When we encounter the concept of eternity, we tend to imagine a line that starts at infinity on the left that goes to infinity on the right. We think of eternity as having lots of time. When we encounter the concept of God, we tend to imagine someone who has lots of time, an infinite amount of time. Well, that turns out to be bad physics for some reasons I am going to come to. If we read Isaiah, Isaiah says it is He (God) that inhabits eternity. Eternity is not having lots of time. It's being outside of the time domain altogether.

Now the one thing I need to point out is that we know today that time is physical property. That's the real impact of Einstein's Theory of Relativity. Time is physical; time changes with mass, acceleration and gravity. Is God subject to gravity? Hardly; He's not subject to the constraints of mass or acceleration or gravity. So, God is not somebody who has lots of time. God is someone who is outside the dimensionality of time altogether. And that's exactly what Isaiah means when he says it is He that inhabits eternity. And that's why God can make the statement, "I alone know the end from the beginning." For you and me, we're in a physical domain right now and time is a physical dimension, so we experience time. But God is outside that.

I am startled as to how many theological paradoxes evaporate once you apply the insights we have from modern physics. Once you recognize that time itself is a physical dimension. If God has the technology to create us in the first place, does He have the technology to get a message to us? Of course He does. The question is: How does He validate the message? How does He let us know it is from Him and not some contrivance or a fraud?

One answer of course is to in fact demonstrate that the source of the message is from outside time by writing history in advance before it happens. And we glibly call that prophecy. Now it's interesting, we have sixty-six books written by forty different guys over thousands of years, and we discover it has two important properties. One, it is an integrated message. As we study carefully we discover that every number, every place, name, every detail is there by supernatural engineering. It has numerical properties that disappear if you remove one letter. Fascinating! Secondly, we also discover that it portrays history before it happens.

Now, we could of course spend our time fruitfully throughout the whole conference just giving examples of how sixty-six books have laid out history in the past precisely, well before it happened. It's worthwhile remembering that the Old Testament was translated from Greek three centuries before Christ was born; the famed Septuagint version of the *Tanakh*—the Old Testament; fascinating. Because many things it describes are described so precisely that the critics have had to try to late date those books. But it is always amusing to have them late date Daniel after the Septuagint version, because he is in the Septuagint version. There it is, and the record he (Daniel) lays out is so precise, it's staggering.

The point is we could spend our time fruitfully talking about prophecies that have been fulfilled. And it's worth doing as a foundation, but I'll leave that to your own diligence at your own time because we're here today for a couple of reasons. The reasons we're together here today, and most of the speakers here today would agree with the statement I'm about to make [is], I believe you and I are being propelled into a period of time about which the Bible says more than it does about any other period of time in history, including the time that Jesus walked the ancient shores of Galilee, or climbed the mountains in Judea. I believe you and I are being plunged into a period of time about which the Bible says more than it does about any other time in human history. And that's staggering.

How Do We Know the Bible Is True?

The "period of time" Chuck Missler made reference to deals with the years just prior to the Second Coming of Christ. This generation is seeing more Bible prophecy fulfilled than any other. The miraculous rebirth of modern Israel is the key to these last days. Much more on the topic of the Bible's validity and incomparable cohesiveness appears on an excellent website: *Is the Bible True?* At http://www.2christ.org/bible /. Please spend some time exploring this entire site and you will find many answers to the questions that further substantiate the truth of the Bible. If you click on the title: "How Do We Know the Bible Is True?" you will see that article offered in thirteen languages.

Another excellent resource, a book by Herbert Lockyer titled: *All the Messianic Prophecies of the Bible,* will help you discover how Yeshua the Messiah fulfilled over three hundred Bible prophecies and how prophecies prove the truth of Christianity.

The Atheist's Nightmare—Fulfilled Bible Prophecies

To read more about fulfilled biblical prophecies, please explore the good information at the following excellent link: "The Atheist's Nightmare" at: http://www.2christ.org/prophecy/.

As already discussed earlier in this chapter, Bible prophecy or God's messages from "outside of time," are always reliable and always one hundred percent accurate. New Age psychics and mystics can never claim one hundred percent accuracy on every prediction they make. But they can tell you *some* things, just enough to keep you "hooked in" to the demonic lies that there is more than one true God, that hell doesn't exist, and that there are many ways to get to heaven or to reach "nirvana."

Chapter Six

Eternal Separation—Why Hell?

We *all* have everlasting existence. What we need is everlasting life. We are going to spend eternity somewhere. Have you thought about *how* and *where* you will spend eternity?

> "For the wages if sin is death, but the gift of God is eternal life in Christ Jesus our Lord" (Romans 6:23).

> "And inasmuch as it is appointed unto men once to die, and after this cometh judgment; so Christ also, having been once offered to bear the sins of many, shall appear a second time, apart from sin, to them that wait for him, unto salvation" (Hebrews 9:27-28).

Hell was made for Satan and his demons (fallen angels). It was not meant for mankind. By choosing to reject Jesus as Lord and Savior, the only other alternative is to follow the devil. You might say, "I am not following the devil; I am a nice person. I don't believe in hell." Guess what? God says we are *all* sinners, we all "fall short"—"for all have sinned and fall short of the glory of God" (Romans 3:23).

I can't remember a day in my life when I did everything just right. Can you? We all fall short, and it is the Lord who stands in on our behalf and declares us righteous. That is precisely why He took it upon Himself to die on the cross to take those sins from us.

> "He has delivered us from the power of darkness and conveyed *us* into the kingdom of the Son of His love, in whom we have redemption through His blood, the forgiveness of sins"(Colossians 1:13-14).

By accepting Christ's free gift of salvation—because of Him—we are purified so we can enter into the presence of a Holy God—the holiness of heaven. I choose to believe Christ when He tells me there is a literal place that is filled with so much torment and anguish that only He can save us from it. Christ holds the key to salvation and eternal life. There is no other way, despite what biblically illiterate people would have you believe. Avoid hell by personally receiving Him as your Lord and Savior. Blind allegiance to man-made philosophies and religions will only hurt you. Here are some Scriptural references to that horrific place called hell:

"And these [who reject Christ] will go away into everlasting punishment, but the righteous [believers] into eternal life" (Matthew 25:46).

"The wicked shall be turned into hell, *and* all the nations that forget God" (Psalm 9:17).

"Then He will also say to those on the left hand, Depart from Me you cursed, into the everlasting fire, prepared for the devil and his angels" (Matthew 25:41). [Jesus is speaking of the people in the final judgment.]

"But for the cowardly and unbelieving and abominable and murderers and immoral persons and sorcerers and idolaters and all liars, their part *will be* in the lake that burns with fire and brimstone, which is the second death" (Revelation 21:8).

Scary stuff. It defies logic. Inconceivable: "Everlasting fire; the lake which burns with fire and brimstone." Surely these statements must be allegorical and mythological. No, that is not what the Lord says. He says this is the real condition of a real place called hell. We mortals are limited in our understanding of the broad scope of this insidious spiritual war. Trust and believe in the One who died for you.

"But God demonstrates His love toward us, in that while we were yet sinners, Christ died for us. Much more then, having been justified by His blood, we shall be saved from the wrath *of God* through Him.

For if while we were enemies, we were reconciled to God through the death of His Son, much more, having been reconciled, we shall be saved by His life" (Romans 5:8-10).

"And this is in the testimony: that God has given us eternal life, and this life is in His Son. He who has the Son has life; he who does not have the Son of God does not have life" (1 John 5:11-12).

"And He delivered us from the domain of darkness, and transferred us to the kingdom of His beloved Son. In which we have redemption, the forgiveness of sins" (Colossians 1:13).

In the following verse Christ speaks of His death sacrifice on the cross, the payment for all of mankind's sins, and His resurrection, as well as the fact that He holds the key to life and death:

"I *am* He who lives, and was dead, and behold, I am alive forever more. Amen. I have the keys of Hades and of Death" (Revelation 1:18).

The Biblical Research Studies Group has an outstanding series of articles on these related topics: Unseen Worlds of God, Angelic Hosts, Satan, Demons, Sheol, Gehenna, Heaven, the Eternal Heavens and the Eternal Earth. Many questions you may have on these subjects will be answered by studying the related articles at:
http://www.biblicalresearch.info/page15.html.

Where Do We Go Immediately After We Die?

The Bible tells us that after believers die their souls and their spirits are taken directly to heaven, because all their sins are forgiven by having received Jesus the Messiah as Savior and Lord of their lives (John 3:16, 18, 36).

"We are confident, yes, well pleased to be absent from the body and to be present with the Lord" (2 Corinthians 5:8).

We discussed the Rapture earlier when all living believers are called to the refuge of heaven just prior to the Tribulation. But since all believers who die before the Tribulation go to be with Messiah Jesus at the moment of death, what is the point of a resurrection at the Rapture for dead believers?

Scripture teaches the *spirits* and *souls* of all believers at death go to be with Christ, but their physical bodies remain in the grave "asleep." It is at the Rapture that *all* believers will receive their glorified, immortal bodies which they will have for all of eternity (1 Thessalonians 4:13-17 and (1 Corinthians 15:50-54). At the Rapture the bodies of those who died, whose spirits and souls are with the Lord will be resurrected, and become newly glorified bodies rejoining their souls and spirits.

Those who do not receive Jesus Christ as Savior, and die in their sins meet a very different fate. It means everlasting, eternal punishment. Unbelievers right away upon death go to a transitory place of detention, to await their final resurrection, judgment, and their ultimate place of everlasting damnation.

Luke described a wealthy man being tormented *immediately after death* (Luke 16:22-24). We have already discussed Revelation 20:11-15 where John wrote about how all the unbelieving dead will be resurrected and judged at the Great White Throne judgment, which takes place after the millennial reign of Christ. It is at that judgment all unbelievers will be released into the lake of fire, their final eternal home.

By studying Scripture we see that after death, a person resides in an interim heaven or hell. After these temporary residences each person will go to their forever, eternal destinations depending on whether they accepted or rejected Christ's free gift of salvation.

The actual "whereabouts" of that eternal destiny is what changes. All believers will enter the one-thousand-year Millennium, and after that the new heavens and new earth of Revelation 21:1. After the white throne judgment all unbelievers will be permanently condemned to the lake of fire spoken of in Revelation 20:11-15.

"Then death and Hades were thrown into the lake of fire. This is the second death, the lake of fire" (Revelation 20:14**).**

"And if anyone's name was not found written in the Book of Life, he was thrown into the lake of fire" (Revelation 20:15).

What Must I Do to Be Saved?

Have you thought about *how* and *where* you will spend eternity? Have you truly made Jesus Christ the top priority of your life? Are you ready to face Him, the King of kings, the Lord of lords, the Creator of the universe? Receive Christ, escape the coming Tribulation and spend eternity with Him.

If you have read these pages and have never made a genuine, from the heart lifelong commitment to Messiah Jesus or if you have been disillusioned by religion including the human failings of Christians, please do not reject the love and forgiveness of Christ. He wants each one of us to have a one-on-one close, growing relationship with Him. It is not about religion. It is about a personal, ongoing relationship with the Lord Jesus Christ.

I implore you to please contemplate carefully and realize the forever consequences of living outside of God's saving grace. No one can enter the kingdom of God (heaven) without accepting Christ's free gift of salvation. Contrary to what the devil would like you to believe, hell is a real place. As you know there is no perfect person inside or outside of Christ's forgiveness.

Eternity beckons. It is quickly approaching. Its visibility looms, closing in on the last images of prophetic radar. The final chapters in this cosmic war are about to be played out. Spaceship earth is fast approaching the harbor of eternity. Hold on to Jesus and you will arrive safely at your destination.

What Does Salvation in Jesus Christ Really Mean?

"For God so loved the world that He gave His only begotten Son, that whoever believes in Him should not perish, but have everlasting life. For God did not send His Son to condemn the world, but that the world through Him might be saved" (John 3:16-17).

"That if you confess with your mouth Jesus *as* Lord, and believe in your heart that God raised Him from the dead, you shall be saved; for with the heart man believes, resulting in righteousness, and with the mouth confesses, resulting in salvation" (Romans 10:9-10).

"For whosoever shall call upon the name of the Lord shall be saved" (Romans 10:13).

We can have a close, personal relationship with the Lord when we are born-again by the Holy Spirit and come to repentance. The spiritual rebirth Jesus spoke of is necessary in order to be saved, in order to have a personal relationship with Him, and to be able to understand the Word of God through the guidance of the Holy Spirit.

"But the natural man [unsaved person] does not receive the things of the Spirit of God, for they are foolishness to him; nor can he know them because they are spiritually discerned" (1 Corinthians 2:14).

"Jesus answered and said to him, "Truly, truly, I say to you, unless one is born-again he cannot see the kingdom of God." Nicodemus said to Him, "How can a man be born when he is old? He cannot enter a second time into his mother's womb and be born, can he?"

Jesus answered, "Truly, truly, I say to you, unless one is born of water and the Spirit, he cannot enter into the kingdom of God. That which is born of the flesh is flesh, and that which is born of the Spirit is spirit. Do not marvel that I said to you, 'You must be born-again'" (John 3:3-7).

"The Lord is not slow about His promise, as some count slowness, but is patient toward you, not wishing for any to perish but for all to come to repentance" (2 Peter 3:9).

When we sincerely accept Christ and receive Him as our Lord and Savior, we are filled with God's Holy Spirit and are spiritually "born-again." Water baptism is a public testimony showing we have placed our faith in Jesus. Being baptized as a child, a ritual performed by some religious groups will not get us into heaven. Neither will church or synagogue attendance.

Each person is personally accountable to God and must make his or her own decision to either accept or reject God's saving grace. God gave us free will. It is up to each of us to choose eternal life with God or eternal torment and separation from God. Choose Jesus Christ and you will be saved forever.

[Jesus said,] "Truly, truly, I say to you, he who hears My word, and believes Him who sent Me, has eternal life, and does not come into judgment, but has passed out of death into life" (John 5:24).

Christ took on the sins of the entire world through his death on the cross to give us *all* the opportunity to be with Him for eternity and keep us from hell and the lake of fire (1 Timothy 4:10). He suffered for us, so *we* won't have to suffer an eternity of inconceivable torment. But each individual must choose either to accept Christ by following His commandment to be "born-again," genuinely repenting and placing Him first. Or face an eternity of horror. If you are uncertain about where you will spend eternity, you can choose to place your trust in Messiah Jesus right now. Tomorrow is not promised to any one of us. Death can be a very imminent event, completely out of our control. Please don't put off the most important decision of your life.

"Behold, now is the accepted time; behold, now *is* the day of salvation" (2 Corinthians 6:2b).

"I say to you that likewise there will be more joy in heaven over one sinner who repents than over ninety-nine just persons who need no repentance" (Luke 15:5).

You can come to faith in Christ, and be "born-again" by praying a personal prayer of repentance and faith. The words you use are not important. Your sincerity and genuine commitment to the Lord is what counts. Saying a prayer, then walking away and forgetting about the Lord does not count for salvation. The sincere intent of your heart is what matters to God. There has to be true *repentance*, a true change of heart; a repentant heart that will seek Him first and leave behind habits and lifestyles that are contrary to His will, His teachings. The following verses express the heart confession necessary in order to be saved.

"That if you confess, with your mouth Jesus as Lord and believe in your heart that God has raised Him from the dead, you will be saved; for with the heart man believes, resulting in righteousness, and with the mouth he confesses, resulting in salvation" (Romans 10:9-10).

If you are not sure what to say, follow this simple heartfelt prayer, but you must mean it with all your heart:

Heavenly Father, I accept your Son, Jesus Christ, as my Lord and Savior. I believe in His death, burial and resurrection. I realize I have made many mistakes in my life. I have been confused and deceived by the lies of this world. Please forgive me. I ask you to come into my life, regenerate me and fill me with your Holy Spirit so I can be born-again and saved by your grace. I want this to be a new beginning and have a close, personal relationship with you. I want to learn more about you through prayer and careful Bible study. Help me to truly repent and live my life in a way that is pleasing to you. Please write my name into the Lamb's Book of Life. I pray this in the name of Jesus the Christ (Yeshua Ha Mashiach), the Messiah of Israel and of the world. Amen.

If you have made a genuine, new commitment to Messiah Jesus by receiving Him as your Lord and Savior, this is the most important day of your life. It is also the most significant event of your life. You have now become an heir of God. It is through Christ's strength in you that you will be able to move forward and overcome obstacles that may come your way. Growing in the Lord is a daily surrender of your will for what God's will is for your life. After all, He is now your heavenly Father, (Abba) in Hebrew, which means daddy. He wants what is best for you. Go to Him with all your concerns and pour your heart out to Him. Everything that is important to you matters to God. Nothing is too small or insignificant.

Deliverance from Bondage

Romans 8:1-4

"Therefore there is now no condemnation for those who are in Christ Jesus. For the law of the Spirit of life in Christ Jesus has set you free from the law of sin and of death.

For what the Law could not do, weak as it was through the flesh, God *did*: sending His own Son in the likeness of sinful flesh and *as an offering* for sin, He condemned sin in the flesh, so that the requirement of the Law might be fulfilled in us, who do not walk according to the flesh but according to the Spirit."

Romans 8:14-18

"For as many who are led by the Spirit of God, these are sons of God. For you did not receive the spirit of bondage again to fear, but you received the Spirit of adoption by whom we cry out, Abba, Father.

The Spirit Himself bears witness with our spirit that we are children of God, and if children, then heirs—heirs of God and joint heirs with Christ, if indeed we suffer with Him that we may also be glorified together.

For I consider that the sufferings of this present time are not worthy to be compared with the glory which shall be revealed in us."

The indwelling of the Holy Spirit occurs the very moment we turn to Christ by faith (1 Corinthians 12:13). At the moment of our spiritual birth, the Spirit of God comes to live within us bringing Christ to our hearts. He then places us (spiritually baptizes us) into what is termed the body of Christ or body of Messiah (His church). The Holy Spirit never takes a vacation or goes away on long walks. Once filled with the Holy Spirit, one is always filled with the Holy Spirit. However, considering the way we can all "fall short" and the carnal manner in which some believers continue to conduct their lives, one wonders if the Holy Spirit truly lives inside some of them, or if they were ever truly saved.

Accepting Christ—being "born-again" one day and subsequently receiving the Spirit of God (the Holy Spirit) at a later time is not Scriptural. However, being "filled" with the Holy Spirit is an ongoing, continuous experience in the sense that it is up to each one of us as believers to allow the Holy Spirit to direct our lives, our behavior, to be continually filled by Him—to yield to Him. In that regard we can and should be "filled" with the Holy Spirit often. We should do our best every day to give ourselves over to the Holy Spirit and avoid quenching His loving guidance.

"And do not grieve the Holy Spirit of God by whom you were sealed for the day of redemption" (Ephesians 4:30).

The Holy Spirit is the abiding presence of Christ's presence within us. Scripture dogmatically reveals if the Spirit of God does not live in us, we do not belong to Him. The indwelling of the Holy Spirit happens to every truly repented believer once and only once at the time of salvation; just as salvation is a one-time gift—a "done deal" so to speak. I have heard some Christian church leaders say, "We are a Spirit-filled church," implying that they have a special move of God or something beyond what other true Christian churches have.

"However, you are not in the flesh but in the Spirit, if indeed the Spirit of God dwells in you. But if anyone does not have the Spirit of Christ, he does not belong to Him" (Roman 8:9).

All genuinely born-again believers are Spirit-filled or they are not truly saved, and there are no special or additional "fillings" of the Holy Spirit given to select individuals. As born-again believers, we are all equal in Christ. However, how each individual treats and relates to the Holy Spirit is a strong determining factor for spiritual growth. In that sense only, some churches are more Spirit filled than others, only because of the way each individual at that church relates to the Holy Spirit. Through prayer and true devotion to the Lord we are continuously filled with the Holy Spirit.

I'm Saved, Now What?

After we are saved we are far from perfect. The Bible teaches that mankind is innately sinful, that sin is part of our nature. Even after we are saved, every believer is going to sin on occasion. I used to wonder about what happens to a believer if he falls into sin. Are we expected to never do anything wrong or never make a mistake again? I knew I was saved by God's grace. My commitment and repentance were sincere, but I questioned what would happen if I did make a mistake. Would my salvation be forfeited? Could I lose my salvation? We find part of the answer to that question in the First Epistle of John:

"If we confess our sins, He is faithful and righteous to forgive us our sins and to cleanse us from all unrighteousness. If we say that we have not sinned, we make Him a liar, and His word is not in us.

My Little Children, I am writing these things to you that you may not sin. **And if anyone sins, we have an Advocate with the Father, Jesus Christ the righteous; and He Himself is the propitiation for**

our sins; and not for ours only, but also for *those of* the whole world" (1 John 1:9-10; 2:1-2).

Once we are saved, we are made righteous through Messiah Jesus. No matter how hard we try, not one of us can be without sin. But through Christ we are forgiven and made righteous. When we do stumble and sin, we should do just as we have read in the previous Scripture, "confess our sins" to the Advocate, "Jesus Christ the righteous." By the renewing of our minds, and through our love for the Lord, we will want to please Him and do our best to shun sinful transgressions.

Our *daily* walk with the Lord should demonstrate a day-to-day, moment-by-moment surrender of our will to the Lord's will—a daily inner house cleaning. When we do fall into sin, we place a wedge between God and ourselves, even to the point of grieving the Holy Spirit. Unless we acknowledge (name) our sins directly to God, repent and reestablish (restore) our right relationship with the Lord, we cannot have a genuine relationship with Him.

"This I say, therefore, and testify in the Lord, that you should no longer walk as the rest of the Gentiles walk, in the futility of their mind, having their understanding darkened, being alienated from the life of God, because of the ignorance that is in them, because of the blindness of their heart; **and be renewed in the spirit of your mind, and that you put on the new man which was created according to God**, in true righteousness and holiness" (Ephesians 4:17-18, 23-24).

"Let no corrupt word proceed out of your mouth, but what is good for edification, that it may impart grace to the hearers. And **do not grieve the Holy Spirit of God**, by whom you were sealed for the day of redemption" (Ephesians 4:29-30).

"Do not quench the Spirit" (1 Thessalonians 5:19).

I have found that it is very important to get into a regular, disciplined daily routine of spending time alone with the Lord through prayer and Bible study. When we give Jesus our first thoughts every morning and go immediately into prayer we get into synch with Him. His will for our lives becomes more evident. If the morning hours don't allow for lengthy prayer and Bible study, at least spend *some* time in prayer and read *some* Scripture before starting the day's activities. Always try to make a good effort to put the Lord first. After all, it is He who we can thank for saving us from an eternity of suffering and providing all believers with a glorious eternal future.

Spending time with Him should always be at the top of our list. Then, later in the evening find a way to make more time to commune with the Lord. What could be better than spending time with the Creator of the universe, with the One who loves and cares for us more than anyone else? As we focus each day more and more on God, and include Him in all that we do we grow and mature as believers. Time devoted to the Lord (devotions) will help us grow in our faith. As we get closer to the Lord many situations in our lives will most likely need to change in order to be true to our commitment to Him. Sometimes those we are closest to will not understand our love and devotion to the Lord if they themselves do not have a strong personal relationship with the living God.

"Abide in Me [Jesus], and I in you. As the branch cannot bear fruit of itself unless it abides in the vine, neither can you unless you abide in Me" (John 15:4).

Always pray for wisdom and understanding before beginning your Bible study—in a quiet place away from any distractions. Many audio versions of the Bible are available to assist with the learning process. Add them to your personal library and listen to them often.

Various DVDs, movies relating to the Bible are easy to find. *Charlton Heston Presents the Bible* is a good choice. Other similar DVDs can be found on the Internet or at your local Christian bookstore. Also, try to get into the practice of memorizing Scripture. Memorizing one Scripture a week is a good goal to set. Let the Holy Spirit lead you and teach you as you explore your Bible.

As you spend time learning more about God's Word, you will grow closer to the Lord. Prayer time and Bible study will become your priority, and the things you once thought were so important to you will no longer be so interesting.

The Word of God and your relationship with the Lord will become an intrinsic part of your life. Getting involved in a good Bible-based church can also be a good way to grow in the Lord and meet other committed believers. It might take time to find the right church. A good way to fellowship with others is through smaller home groups offered by some local churches.

In his first letter to Thessalonica, the apostle Paul wrote:

"Rejoice always; **pray without ceasing**; in everything give thanks; for this is God's will for you in Christ Jesus" (1Thessalonians 5:16-19).

"Pray without ceasing?" How is that possible? We can continually pray by simply having an open heart to the Lord and a joyful reverence toward Him throughout our day—making Him the constant uppermost part of our lives. Even when we are busy with our daily routines, we can surrender our thoughts to the Lord with reflective attitudes and grateful hearts, always making a conscious effort to quietly acknowledge Him in everything we do. It isn't so easy to succumb to the traps and temptations of the world when our hearts and minds are reflecting upon the Lord. We must protect ourselves and stay close to the Lord at all times with our faithful prayers. When we reach what I call, the point of no return, nothing can replace the time spent with the Lord in quiet reverence.

"Therefore take up the whole armor of God, that you may be able to withstand the evil day, and having done all to stand. Stand therefore, having girded your waist with truth, having put on the breastplate of righteousness, and having shod your feet with the preparation of the gospel of peace; above all things taking the shield of faith with which you will be able to quench all the fiery darts of the wicked one.

And take the helmet of salvation, and the sword of the Spirit, which is the word of God: praying always with all prayer and supplication in the Spirit, being watchful to this end with all perseverance and supplication for all the saints" (Ephesians 6:13-18).

Our heavenly Father, the mighty, sovereign, omnipotent, omniscient, omnipresent King of the universe sees the entire picture of our lives (past, present, and future). We must trust in Him completely and He will lead us to where He feels is best. After I received Christ as my Savior, I pondered just what it means to truly "repent." Many books have been written on the subject. The full biblical definition of repentance is a change of mind that results in a change of action. One of the best descriptions and definitions of biblical repentance can be found at the *Got Questions* website. I have part of their description listed on the next page.

Many understand the term repentance to mean "turning from sin." This is not the biblical definition of repentance. In the Bible, the word, repent, means "to change one's mind." The Bible also tells us that true repentance will result in a change of actions (Luke 3:8-14; Acts 3:19). Acts 26:20 declare, "I preached that they should repent and turn to God and prove their repentance by their deeds." The full biblical definition of repentance is a change of mind that results in a change of action.

To read more please visit: http://www.gotquestions.org/repentance.html.

Once Saved, Always Saved?

A common saying among believers is, "Once saved, always saved." What does that mean? It means our salvation is secure—from the very moment we make a sincere conscious decision for Christ, continuing on throughout all of eternity. We are saved forever through a *repentant*, saving faith in Messiah Jesus. Intentional willingness to continue living in sin does not reflect true repentant salvation.

A truly saved individual is a new creation in Christ, indwelt by the Holy Spirit and wants to live for Christ. A person who deliberately and shamelessly continues to live in sin with no regard for pleasing the Lord has not made a repentant change.

2 Corinthians 5:17

"Therefore, if anyone is in Christ, he is a new creation; old things have passed away; behold, all things have become new."

1 John 5:4-5

"For whatever is born of God overcomes the world; and this is the victory that has overcome the world—our faith. Who is the one who overcomes the world, but he who believes that Jesus is the Son of God?"

In the following passages Jesus asserts His deity, and also promises **eternal** salvation. God's forgiveness and salvation through Messiah Jesus is forever binding, covering all our sins—past, present and future.

"And I give eternal life to them, and they shall never perish; and no one shall snatch them out of My hand. My Father who has given *them* to Me, is greater than all; and no one is able to snatch *them* out of the Father's hand. I and My Father are one" (John 10:28-30).

"Now to Him who is able to keep you from stumbling, and to make you stand in the presence of His glory blameless with great joy, to the only God our Savior, through Jesus Christ our Lord, be glory, majesty, dominion and authority, before all time and now and forever. Amen" (Jude 1:24).

Respecting the Lord and His Scriptures

A relevant Scripture regarding the life change one should continuously contemplate after receiving Yeshua (Jesus) as Lord and Savior is found in the book of Romans. This is a very important Scripture. I believe I would have never strayed from the Lord in the early days if I had really understood this principle:

"And do not be conformed to this world, but **be transformed by the renewing of your mind**, that you may prove what *is* that good and acceptable and perfect will of God" (Romans 12:2).

It is not uncommon for some believers after getting saved to disregard the importance of "renewing" our minds. Instead of living for the Lord and reevaluating how we should go about living, some believers continue to live with questionable motives or as if they never really made a true commitment to the Lord. Are we really dedicated to God or are we trying to control everything around us? Are we truly saved or using God as an angle to make money or achieve notoriety? It is always best for us to let the Lord be our agent and promoter in whatever we are working on. If we trust Him, and. get out of His way, He will bring results into our lives that He knows are best for us.

As believers, Scripture teaches we should work on the **disciplined renewing of our minds daily**, growing in the Lord, committed to getting a better understanding of God's true will for our lives. Sometimes we can be so busy doing things we think we are doing for the Lord, but miss His best for us. An example of this would be not studying and comparing teachings in the light of Scripture, but instead one might function in complacency—on autopilot, never delving deeply into some important issues of doctrine. Or attending church on Sunday, but the rest of the week spending more time on social events and the selfish pursuit of personal projects that far outweigh the time given to the Lord, things that have nothing or very little to do with renewing one's mind and growing as a believer.

When I was first saved, in the early years, I really didn't understand what it meant to put the Lord first. I was still trying to fit Him into *my* agenda. I told myself I wanted the Lord's will for my life but it took some time to let go and change my daily priorities; to really begin to surrender to the Holy Spirit and consciously begin the process of transforming and the renewing of my mind. It is a never-ending, ongoing process. Salvation should not be the only goal in knowing God. We are saved by faith and faith alone, but we should want learn how to live our lives to please the Lord and follow His teachings—as expressed in Colossians 1:10 (cited on page 253). The salvation message is a revelation of the Holy Spirit that makes known the mind of Christ.

We can all become vulnerable to falling into personal lifestyle comfort zones, and not regularly reexamining the meaning of the Scriptures. When the Lord commanded us to **not** be conformed to this world, but to be "**transformed by the renewing**" of our minds He was sending us a very important message. Every person is individually accountable to God. Perhaps we won't always be popular when we take a strong stand for biblical truth, but at least we will not become part of the "lukewarm" church. Safety in numbers has been proven to be a myth.

Selective acceptance and application of only *some* of the teachings the Lord left us in His Scriptures is guaranteed to keep us from experiencing a close, personal relationship with Him. Messiah Jesus spoke strongly against continuing to live in a manner that would show little commitment to Him (Revelation 3:15-16). Anyone can make a "profession of faith." But *not* everyone who makes a profession of faith follows through with a repentant heartfelt commitment; lifestyle and attitude change.

It is true that some professing "believers" are simply social "pew sitters" with little or no interest in examining the Scriptures, much less applying the teachings of the Bible to their daily lives. But Christ asks more of us. We are commanded to love the Lord with *all* our hearts, souls and strength (Deuteronomy 6:5). If we are sincere in our professions of faith believing God and accepting His teachings in the Bible, then loving the Lord and serving Him should be at the top of our itinerary *each* day; studying our Bibles, spending time in prayer, communicating with fellow believers, and sharing the salvation message with others. Our love for the Lord will spill over into all areas of our lives and life will be a blessing and a joy. I once heard Bible teacher, David Hocking, say: "Many people *think* they are Christians but have no understanding of the Bible."

The job of a believer is to thoroughly study the teachings in the Bible searching the Scriptures *daily,* as taught in (Acts 17:11) and to tell others about the Light—Jesus Christ and His free gift of salvation (Mark 16:15).

"By this My Father is glorified, that you bear much fruit; so you will be My disciples" (John 15:8).

When talking about the mercy and love of the Lord Jesus, Pastor Charles Stanley has stated this about Him: "I'll always be here with open arms. When you come to the end of yourself, I'll be here waiting." When we give up control, put God first and yield to the Holy Spirit we can move *forward* with Christ and truly *grow* as believers.

"I have been crucified with Christ; it is no longer I who live, but Christ lives in me; and the life which I now live in the flesh I live by faith in the Son of God, who loved me and gave Himself for me" (Galatians 2:20).

"Examine yourselves as to whether you are in the faith. Test yourselves" (2 Corinthians 13:3a).

"But do you want to know, O foolish man, that faith without works is dead?" (James 2:20)

According to Scripture, a weak "commitment" is a tremendous insult to the Lord. Messiah Jesus admonished the Laodiceans, and left the same message for us in His Holy Scriptures:

"I know your deeds, that you are neither cold nor hot; I would that you were cold or hot. So because you are lukewarm, and neither hot nor cold, I will spit you out of my mouth" (Revelation 3:15-16).

Some say as long as all believers agree on the "core" issues of the faith—the virgin birth, the Trinity, the death and Resurrection of Jesus, the one God of the Bible, the return of Messiah Jesus, salvation, eternal life, and eternal punishment, that one can interpret Scripture a number of different ways. To imply that other teachings in the Bible can be treated with less responsibility, with less respect than the "core" issues, and be given multiple meanings is in essence usurping the authority of the Bible, and rewriting the inspired, inerrant Word of God.

We should always keep in mind that every passage in the Bible is empowered by the Holy Spirit and has only one primary meaning. However, there may be many *applications*. Every doctrine found in the Bible is absolute. No doctrine derived from Scripture can have two or more correct meanings. It is always the responsibility of every believer to diligently study the Scriptures so he or she has the correct understanding of every doctrine and passage in the Bible (2 Timothy 2:15).

Just because a teaching is popular does not mean it is right. I have observed what I term as the: "I am well-known so I am right" syndrome. If the flawed teaching is popularly accepted it only means more people are misled. Having a popular "following" may have nothing to do with having a genuine Holy Spirit-led relationship with the Lord—which would bring about a humble approach to learning and teaching the Scriptures. It is tragic because this type of person is the most difficult to call to repentance. No matter what you say to point out the problems with their erroneous beliefs and irrational summations they are closed to hearing the truth. And sadly, they are usually so caught-up in their own agenda they are completely oblivious to the idea that what they are teaching could possibly be wrong.

Some time ago I listened to a "teaching" on Daniel, chapter 11:36-45 aired on a Christian radio station given by a well-known pastor who also has a large church-ministry based in Southern California. He actually made this statement:

"Don't forget something—Ezekiel 38 and 39, when the Antichrist and his armies come against the Jews to destroy them."

What? I thought I might have not heard it right, so I went online to hear the teaching again on the pastor's website. And sure enough, that *is* what he said. Then he told his audience that they should read chapters Ezekiel 38 and 39 in the Bible. Apparently *he* needs to read them too because the battle of Ezekiel 38 and 39 is *not* led by Antichrist. Antichrist and the False Prophet will draw together the nations to the final battle at Armageddon, the final battle when Messiah Jesus intervenes, a separate war which takes place well after the battle of Ezekiel 38 and 39. This is basic knowledge that any believer who studies Bible prophecy should be acutely aware of. But those just beginning to study prophecy are at a disadvantage and will be confused when they hear such faulty teaching—unless they do what we are all supposed to do—search the Scriptures ourselves to see if what is being taught is true (Acts 17:11). This pastor/teacher places the Antichrist at the forefront of *both* wars in his sermon, which simply is not true. I was dismayed to hear this from someone who has been in ministry for a very long time with so many followers.

What is a person to do? Because this preacher is in a position of "authority" and prominence, it is a tough situation. Pointing out the error with the best of intentions may not be appreciated and one could be considered contentious. Various ministries should work together with *all* believers with sincere humility and respect—not with a territorial, unapproachable, know-it-all attitude. The Lord commands us to work *together* and love one another (Ephesians 4:1-3).

These disturbing trends concern me very much because when I was a very young believer I heard so many confusing teachings and saw so much hypocrisy I couldn't stand it. So much so that I finally walked away from all of it, as I shared earlier in the first chapter of this book. It is imperative to teach responsibly and not confuse the teachings of Scripture and ultimately risk leading others astray from the Lord. If we give the devil an opening he will eagerly take it. When Scripture is not clear on something or we don't understand it, it is always better to say, "I don't know." But when the Scriptures are straightforward in meaning but misconstrued in their interpretation—that is when a cycle of faulty teaching erupts, taking on a life of its own—quite contrary to the intended meaning of the passages involved.

Considering the touchy dynamics of such predicaments with other believers, it is best to go directly to the throne of God and pray for these kinds of situations, pray that the Lord will convict such individuals and show them the truth. And also pray and make sure that our own studies and teachings are in order.

"Pay close attention to yourself and to your teaching; persevere in these things, for as you do this you will ensure salvation both for yourself and for those who hear you. For God is not a God of confusion, but of peace" (1 Timothy 4:16; 1 Corinthians 14:33a).

On the bright side, I heard an encouraging sermon not long ago by Bible teacher, Chuck Swindoll, reminding fellow believers not to become such "prima donnas" in their ministries that they neglect those who are having difficult times, those who really need help; wise words from an insightful man. We should never be too busy doing "work" for God that we pay little attention to those who are reaching out to us.

Put on the New Self

"Set your mind on things above, not on the things that are on earth. For you have died and your life is hidden with Christ in God" (Colossians 3:2).

"Do not love the world or the things of the world. If anyone loves the world, the love of the Father is not in him. For all that is in the world, the lust of the flesh and the lust of the eyes, and the boastful pride of life, is not from the Father, but is from the world. And the world is passing away, and also its lusts; but the one who does the will of God abides forever" (1 John 2:15-17).

As believers, we are called to be disciples. A disciple is an individual who believes and follows the teachings and truth of Messiah Jesus—a true born-again believer who is actively involved in some type of ministry work for the Lord. As we grow in Christ we increase our "walk" and our devotion to Him. If we truly put Christ first each day, our desire for activities that take us away from Him will decrease. Our heart attitudes—when filled with love for the Lord will automatically desire us to wholeheartedly seek Him. Prayer is how we communicate with our Creator. The Holy Scriptures and prayer are our anchors—our safety nets in a world gone mad.

As we grow in the Lord, being "still" and communing alone with Him through focused prayer and committed Bible study will become our top priority—not multiple "social" activities that distract us from our spiritual growth. The Lord longs to hear from His children. If you cannot stay on your knees while praying, find a way to communicate with your heavenly Father from a position of comfort. He is not a harsh taskmaster who wants us to go through rigid legalistic rituals. He wants to embrace us with all the love that He has, to carry and guide us to our purposeful destinies.

Taking time to communicate with God is a very important aspect of renewing our minds. If we do not have a strong prayer life and devoted study time, how can we serve the Lord and accurately decipher the messages in the Bible or discern His will for our lives? God is always available to us as we seek to make Him our top priority every day.

"But be doers of the word, and not hearers only, deceiving yourselves. But he who looks into the perfect law of liberty and continues *in it*, **and is not a forgetful hearer but a doer of the work**, this one will be blessed in what he does" (James 1:22, 25).

How seriously we take the Word of God, how we think, what we think, how we behave and live our lives is a reflection of just how devoted we are to the Lord, and how authentic we are as believers. When we don't study and know our Bibles and fail to truly *apply* its teachings to our personal lives we cannot genuinely grow spiritually, reap the blessings of the Lord or be effective witnesses and give our best to Him.

Playing Games with God

"Give no occasion of stumbling, either to Jews or the Greeks [Gentiles], or to the church of God: even as I also please all men in all things, not seeking mine own profit, but the *profit* of the many, that they may be saved." —1 Corinthians 10:32-33

It is very disappointing to realize some Christians and non-Christians alike have had some unpleasant experiences with other believers. This is something that cannot be hidden from the world. One might expect sincerity, trustworthiness and forthrightness in relationships from every person who names the name of Jesus Christ, but that is not the reality of the situation. This is a common reason some people do not wish to know more about the Christian faith. We would like to believe those who consider themselves dedicated to the Lord would be courteous, honest, and treat others with respect. But sadly, that is not always so—causing much damage to the positive image most Christians want to portray to the rest of the world.

"Who among you is wise and understanding? Let him show by his good behavior his deeds in the gentleness of wisdom. But if you have bitter jealousy and selfish ambition in your heart, do not be arrogant

243

and *so* lie against the truth. This wisdom is not that which comes down from above, but is earthly, natural, demonic. For where jealousy and selfish ambition exist, there is disorder and every evil thing. But the wisdom from above is first pure, then peaceable, gentle, reasonable, full of mercy and good fruits, unwavering, without hypocrisy" (James 3:13-17).

Pride, the root of self-destruction and also the cause of conflict in relationships can be a prevalent problem among believers and of course the world in general. Paul warned the Corinthians about the problem of spiritual immaturity and selfish pride. It is a much bigger issue than we might want to acknowledge, at first glance. But it is an ongoing issue within Christian circles. Only the Lord can heal us of this common malady—when we recognize our sin, humble ourselves and truly repent of our hurtful actions and self-centered attitudes.

"And I brethren, could not speak to you as to spiritual *people* but as to carnal, as to babes in Christ. I fed you with milk and not with solid food; for until now you were not able to *receive it*, and even now you are still not able; for you are still carnal. For where *there are* envy, strife, and divisions among you, are you not carnal and behaving like *mere* men?" (1 Corinthians 3:1-3).

It is impossible to deny the fact that some believers may get involved in projects that are not for God's benefit, but obviously for selfish-gain. Please don't let Christians who have self-promoting agendas keep you from faith in Messiah Jesus. God is not mocked, and those who think they can manipulate situations to shine a light upon themselves by using God in the process are missing the point of true, absolute surrender to Him. They might fool some people, but they cannot fool God. People like this probably try to persuade themselves (and really believe) God has given them a special calling above all others, propping themselves up on "spiritual" pedestals. In reality, some people are merely creating an opportunity for themselves where they can transfer their own worldly lust for power and control into a more docile arena such as Christian businesses or ministries. It's the same old worldly power trip, the same old song and dance, camouflaged in spiritual sackcloth. There is no place in true heartfelt Christianity for spiritual smugness. Pride is what initially caused Satan to rebel against Almighty God. Pride is still the root of all conflicts. Many people including non-Christians quickly recognize such self-righteous behavior. This type of smugness greatly damages the cause for Christ. The end result is that many soul-searching individuals run away from the salvation message because of poor examples set by some believers.

Only self-examination of one's motives and prejudices, and genuine repentant hearts can help mend the damage done by such individuals. True Christianity is the *life* of Christ within us. Christ is the essence of life itself. When we are all wrapped up in ourselves we cannot yield to the Holy Spirit and we miss the best the Lord has for us—a genuine one-on-one ongoing relationship with Him.

Pride Brings Destruction

"Everyone who is proud in heart is an abomination to the LORD; assuredly, he will not be unpunished. Pride goes before destruction, and a haughty spirit before a fall" (Proverbs 16:5, 18).

"God resists the proud, but gives grace to the humble. Humble yourselves in the sight of the Lord, and He will lift you up" (James 4: 6b, 10).

Some people might see God only as a means to an end and in effect make declarations of faith, based on getting something from Him; a perfect job or spouse, etc. They say a "prayer" to receive Jesus Christ as their Lord and Savior, but a motive is attached. They go through the motions of attending church for a while, talking about God, reading a few Scriptures. But their sincerity is in question. When the Lord does not answer prayer for those seekers the way they want, He is then conveniently placed aside and suddenly—those prayers to "receive" Christ as Savior are revealed to be nothing more than short-lived pleas made only to attain something.

Instead of giving reverence to Almighty God and trusting Him for His best, these individuals foolishly think they know better (selfish pride) and move on searching for other ways to try to get what *they want,* falling into the hands of the enemy—short-circuiting their opportunity for eternal life with God. As long as we are looking for anything outside of Jesus Christ to "fix" our lives or bring us abiding happiness, we can be sure we will find nothing more than webs of confusion designed to entrap us into demonic strongholds and pull us away from the truth of

Messiah Jesus. Satan is an expert at massaging egos and manipulating his way into the lives of those who are easy prey.

"Be of sober spirit, be on the alert. Your adversary, the devil, prowls about like a roaring lion, seeking someone to devour" (1 Peter 5:8).

"Blessed is the man who walks not in the counsel of the ungodly [the unsaved], nor stands in the path of sinners, nor sits in the seat of the scornful; but his delight is in the LORD, and His law he meditates day and night" (Psalm 1:1-2).

It isn't long before those who make weak declarations of faith lose nearly all interest in the King of the universe, essentially rejecting and belittling Christ's incomparable sacrificial gift of salvation, seriously jeopardizing their eternal fate—a dangerous position to take in the midst of this spiritual war.

"For if, after they have escaped the pollutions of the world through the knowledge of the Lord and Savior Jesus Christ, they are again entangled in them and overcome, the latter end is worse for them than the beginning.

For it would have been better for them not to have known the way of righteousness, than having known it, to turn from the holy commandment delivered to them" (2 Peter 2:20-21).

It is very disheartening and an offense to all good Christians when a believer shows little, if any genuine concern for others during difficult times. I always try to keep my focus on the promises of the Lord and His Word, not the behavior of men and women. People will always let us down, but God will always be there for us if we truly seek Him and take self-responsibility for our own growth as believers. Christians are not perfect people. As believers we can strive for higher standards but when we are disappointed by the behavior of others or when we disappoint others, we should remember we live in a fallen world. Until the Lord takes us out in the Rapture or until the day we die, we will always have problems and disenchantments.

Having integrity, striving toward and adhering to high biblical standards regardless of what others say or do, is a positive attribute. Believers who are cautious not to embrace and promote questionable biblically "related" ideas or teachings can be wrongly and unkindly accused of thinking that they are "better than others" or being "edgy." When in truth those who do not go along with the "crowd" are being careful to follow the Lord's admonition to "rightly divide the word of truth" (2 Timothy 2:15b). Such dynamics to "go along with the crowd" reminds me of the same type of counterproductive peer pressure that goes on in the secular world.

"And who is there to harm you if you prove zealous for what is good? But even if you should suffer for the sake of righteousness, you are blessed. And do not fear their intimidation, and do not be troubled, but sanctify Christ as Lord in your hearts, always being ready to make a defense to everyone who asks you to give an account for the hope that is in you, yet with gentleness and reverence; and keep a good conscience so that in the thing in which you are slandered, those who revile your good behavior in Christ may be put to shame" (1 Peter 3: 13-16).

There are many good, faithful believers who work tirelessly to share the gospel, study the Scriptures and spend time humbly teaching others with an attitude of growing together, giving great reverence to the Lord. Those who actually study the Scriptures daily as we are commanded to are the best teachers, because they more unlikely to fall into the teachings of men that hurt the cause of Christ (Acts 17:11). Faithfully teaching and sharing the Word of God ought to be the center of all Christian teaching ministries. All other materials and methods replace the Scriptural utterances of the Lord with the "rationality" of men. Politics, humor, psychology, philosophy, entertainment, personal advice, and personal opinions can never achieve what the Holy Word of God is able to do. Those who continue to "teach" biblically related ideas by using substitutes for the Bible, and without primarily and consistently studying the Word of God each day can easily become victims of their own aberration of Scripture, and become victims of deception as they "turn away from the truth in favor of myths" (2 Timothy 4:4).

"For though by this time you ought to be teachers, you have need again for someone to teach you the elementary principles of the oracles of God, and you have come to need milk and not solid food. For everyone who partakes only of milk is not accustomed to the word of righteousness, for he is a babe. But solid food is for the mature, who because of practice have their senses trained to discern good and evil" (Hebrews 5:12).

A number of Christian publishers and bookstores have placed the glorification of the Lord—the salvation message—and true biblical principles on the back burner. Shamefully, many of them also do not support Israel and are unwilling to publish Christian books supporting Israel. They are completely out of step with the Scriptures regarding God's commitment and love for Israel. Harper Collins purchased Christian publisher Thomas Nelson (October (2011), giving secular control to about fifty percent of the Christian publishing market.

Personal profits come first for many who are in charge of some of these companies, regardless of flowery public professions of love and allegiance to the Lord. The publishers who are faithful and determined to serve the Lord are exemplary and they should receive the support of all believers. Similar problems exist in the Christian music industry.

The majority of those in charge of that industry are all about profit and very little about placing the Lord first, and very rarely about promoting the salvation message. References are made to the Lord, but it is really more about how the name of Messiah Jesus can be used to make money and more money by publishing and promoting all kinds of questionable "biblical insights" or cranking out so-called Christian music. Sincere Christian artists and authors are often up against a torrent of scrutiny to commercialize their work in order to appeal to the "masses" and increase sales.

Holiness, true faithfulness and reverence toward the Lord certainly cannot be found high on the list of priorities of some individuals who are in charge of these types of businesses. The choices we make tell the truth about who we really are (Matthew 7:16-17). The Word of God tells us this type of hypocrisy, apostasy and self-serving shameful behavior will get much worse as Messiah's return draws closer.

The Apostle John Warned Believers to Test the Spirits

1 John 4:1-6

"Beloved, do not believe every spirit, but test the spirits whether they are of God; because many false prophets have gone out into the world. By this you know the Spirit of God:

Every spirit that confesses that Jesus Christ has come in the flesh is of God, and every spirit that does not confess that Jesus Christ has come in the flesh is not of God.

And this is the *spirit* of the Antichrist, which you heard was coming, and is now already in the world.

You are of God little children, and have overcome them, because He who is in you is greater than he who is in the world.

They are of the world. Therefore they speak *as* of the world, and the world hears them.

We are of God. He who knows God hears us; he who is not of God does not hear us. By this we know the spirit of truth and the spirit of error."

Apostasy Comes in Many Forms

One of the most difficult situations for me as a believer is seeing "Christian" impostors cast shame upon all believers with their money raising scams. I cringe when I see this kind of extortion, which is nothing less than a demonic conspiracy to make all Christians look bad. Some of these con artists can quote Scripture forward and backward. They are really slick. All we have to do is turn on television or the radio and we can hear someone from some so-called Christian ministry trying to convince you that if you give them money God will solve all your problems and bring miracles into your life. Disgraceful.

"Even so you also outwardly appear righteous to men, but inside you are full of hypocrisy and lawlessness" (Matthew 23:28).

"Do not be deceived, God is not mocked; for whatever a man sows, that he will also reap" (Galatians 6:7).

Selfishly using the name of God to further a personal agenda is a disgrace and an insult to the Holy God who sacrificed His Son in order that we can be free of condemnation, and be given the blessings of a glorious eternal destiny. It is an affront to God to turn His Holy Word into a means of getting attention and notoriety as if His Word, the Holy Scriptures were given for entertainment or sport. Nowhere in the Bible can Scriptures be found to support using the Word of God as a means of entertainment, or a means to building gigantic wealth empires. Messiah Jesus did not command us to go out and "entertain" people by bantering about opinions and personal interpretations of His Holy Word, or to have open free-for-alls, a menagerie of various personal opinions haphazardly dissecting Scripture.

It is unsettling to come across teachings based on assumptions instead of the Bible; although, those who make a career out of making "assumptions" can even claim to be diligently studying the Bible. Let the proclamations they make determine their biblical integrity. Those who use the Word of God for their own personal gain do so at their own spiritual peril. It is essential to give to ministries who are truly focused on the Lord and doing His work, but there are plenty of shysters who are just trying to get our money. Apparently these conniving charlatans don't understand or care that they are in for a miserable future when they come face to face with God, and are turned away by Him on judgment day.

These swindlers will surely be left here to endure the Tribulation and the party will be over for them. What a price to pay for such reckless voracity. During the Tribulation years counterfeit miracles will increase deceiving multitudes of people into believing the Antichrist and false prophet have good intentions.

"By covetousness they will exploit you with deceptive words; for a long time their judgment has not been idle, and their destruction does not slumber" (2 Peter 2:3).

"Not everyone who says to Me, 'Lord, Lord,' shall enter the kingdom of heaven, but he who does the will of My Father in heaven. Many will say to Me in that day, 'Lord, Lord, have we not prophesied in Your name, cast out demons in Your name, and done may wonders in your name?' And then I will declare to them, I never knew you, depart from Me, you who practice lawlessness" (Matthew 7:21-23).

Generally speaking, televangelism can be a common Christian media-outlet fraught with multiple problems. However, despite the shortcomings of some of these television preachers, there are situations when a viewer can greatly benefit from hearing a televised salvation message. We serve a mighty God who can turn an ambiguous situation into a blessing. Some very good preachers present sermons on television that are a blessing to those who are housebound. Their messages may just be a lifeline to those who are alone, ill, fraught with grief and suffering; and to those who have never read a Bible or would never think of walking into a church.

Former New Age leader, Randall Baer came to faith when tuning in to the salvation message given by a televangelist. It seems the Lord had been intervening in his life for some time trying to rescue him from very dangerous occult practices that had taken over his life. When Randall heard the television preacher, the timing was right and he was ready to receive the Lord's sin pardon. He dropped to his knees gently sobbing with genuine repentance tremendously relieved that he was finally set free from the chains of darkness.

I suspect there is a long list of people who came to faith by hearing the salvation message through a televangelist. When we are truly doing our best to share the Word of God to bring others to Christ, the Lord will bless us. Excellent Bible teachers who are sincere and truly committed to sharing the Word of God through various public venues have a very tough job. They are often unfairly thrown into the same category as the unscrupulous media misfits who are doing a first-rate job at turning people away from the Lord.

If you have been put off by the hypocrisy that can be found within Christian circles and churches, please do not let that keep you from salvation in Christ. Becoming a believer is about having a personal relationship with the Lord, not a legalistic or strained relationship with insincere individuals who claim to be Christians.

Regardless of the multiple problems within some Christian ministries organizations, the Lord has a way of turning less than ideal situations to His glory. Many sincere and wonderful believers are very true to their faith and their convictions. The Lord Jesus is the One to keep our hearts and eyes fixated upon.

There is a saying, "Put God in the center and everything will come together." I would change it to say, "Put God *first* and everything will come together." As long as we look to people to emulate righteousness we will always be disappointed. But the awesome strength and perfection of the Lord will always carry us through whatever comes our way.

"But seek first the kingdom of God and His righteousness, and all these things shall be added to you" (Matthew 6:33).

Self-Responsibility Goes a Long Way

"Therefore let him who thinks he stands take heed lest he fall."
—1 Corinthians 10:1

Guarding against becoming an easy target for the spiritual attacks and chicanery of the devil is a necessity in this world. Believers strongly caught-up in the cares and ways of the world, those who are lacking spiritual and emotional maturity can especially open themselves up to a surge of demonic spiritual attacks. Any believer can be demonically attacked, especially when doing important work for the Lord or when defending Israel.

But when we arm ourselves with the Word of God and prayer, and have a genuinely strong relationship and commitment to the Lord, the devil will flee (James 4:7). Although trying spiritual battles (tests) can happen even when we are strong believers with hearts faithfully focused on the Lord; especially when we are working to expose the devil and his wicked schemes. God will allow devoted believers to go through some

252

harrowing trials to strengthen our faith, compelling us to place our complete trust in Him (James 1:2, 12).

"As you therefore have received Christ Jesus the Lord, so walk in Him, rooted and built up in Him and established in the faith, as you have been taught, abounding in it with thanksgiving" (Colossians 2:6, 7).

"That you may walk worthy of the Lord, fully pleasing Him, being fruitful in every good work and increasing the knowledge of God" (Colossians 1:10).

Claiming one cannot help a particular behavior is a sad excuse for not taking self-responsibility for personal actions. Have you ever heard a believer say, "I can't help it, I've always been this way?" Self-control is a "fruit of the Spirit" as taught in Galatians 5:23. Spiritual and emotional maturity becomes evident when we are consciously grounded and truly surrendered in Christ. Blaming the devil for everything that goes wrong is another weak-willed excuse when we don't want to look within ourselves and take responsibility to make necessary and positive changes in our lives.

"But also for this very reason, giving all diligence, add to your faith virtue, to virtue knowledge, to knowledge self-control, to self-control perseverance, to perseverance godliness, to godliness brotherly kindness, and to brotherly kindness love. For he who lacks these things is shortsighted, even to blindness, and has forgotten that he was cleansed from his old sins" (2 Peter 1:5-9).

Through salvation in Christ and by submitting ourselves daily to God, we are given the opportunity to renew our minds and be free of old negative, unproductive self-destructive behavior patterns. We need to be grounded in prayer, focused on the Word of God and the wiles of the devil will be crushed. He is always on the prowl looking for an easy victim, someone to pounce on and inflict his misery upon.

"Therefore, take up the full armor of God, that you may be able to resist in the evil day, and having done everything, to stand firm. Stand firm therefore, having girded your loins with truth and having put on the breastplate of righteousness, and having shod your feet with the preparation of the gospel of peace; in addition to all, taking up the shield of faith with which you will be able to extinguish all the flaming missiles of the evil one [the devil]. And take the helmet of salvation, and the sword of the Spirit which is the word of God" (Ephesians 6:13-17).

"**Submit therefore to God.** Resist the devil and he will flee from you. Draw near to God and He will draw near to you. Cleanse your hands you sinners; and purify your hearts, you double-minded" (James 4:7-8).

Jesus promised the indwelling of the Holy Spirit to all believers, immediately upon salvation. It is through prayer, careful Bible study with the ongoing guidance of the Holy Spirit that we grow and mature as believers.

"And I will ask the Father, and He will give you another Helper, that He may be with you forever; that is the Spirit of truth, whom the world cannot receive, because it does not behold Him or know Him, but you know Him because He abides with you, and will be in you.

These things I have spoken to you, while abiding with you. But the Helper, the Holy Spirit, whom the Father will send in My name, He will teach you all things, and bring to your remembrance all that I said to you" (John 14:16, 25).

The apostle John wrote:

"These things I have written to you concerning those who try to deceive you. But the anointing which you have received from Him abides in you, and you do not need that anyone teach you; but as the same anointing teaches you concerning all things, and is true, and is not a lie, and just as it has taught you, you will abide in Him" (1 John 2:26-27).

It is very useful to derive good information from books, lectures, scholars and respected Bible teachers to expand one's horizons, but whatever information is being offered should be very carefully *compared* to Scripture by using a strict rule of interpretation:

Take everything literally unless Scripture says it is symbolic or unless it is physically impossible for it to be literal or take place in a literal manner with the exceptions of miracles.

Reading one person's opinion on a biblical topic followed by another's opinion cannot be considered true Bible Study. All we get by doing that is one person trying to teach another's opinions. Receive Messiah Jesus as your Savior and the Holy Spirit will guide you and teach you the proper understanding of Scripture. You will not go through the Tribulation if you are anchored in Christ's salvation. When we allow the Holy Spirit purify our hearts and minds, He will minister to us. Our heart motives must be pure and surrendered to Christ and not man-centered if we want to have a real relationship with the Lord and understand the Scriptures.

"But you have an anointing from the Holy One, and you know all things" (1 John 2:20).

By sincerely praying for the guidance of the Holy Spirit to teach us and when we choose our study materials carefully always placing the Bible in the forefront of our study time each day, we will not be so easily led astray by information resources that contradict the Word of God. No matter how much some individuals want to say, "God is God, He can do whatever He wants"—and use that kind of statement to try to turn the meaning of Scripture to support their own interpretations—God will not go beyond what His Word says. He cannot go against His righteous attributes. He will never lead us beyond what He has already revealed in His Word.

We should be dependent on the Bible and the Holy Spirit for our spiritual awareness and growth, not outside resources. It is great to read Christian material but we should always search the Scriptures to be sure what we accept as truth is in keeping with the Bible. Only one Person should be residing on the spiritual pedestal of our hearts and minds—Jesus the Messiah.

Believers—Contend for the Faith

Our number one priority as believers should always be to point others to Jesus the Messiah—the Redeemer of all mankind.

"Beloved, while I was making every effort to write you about our common salvation, I felt the necessity to write to you appealing that you contend earnestly for the faith which was once for all delivered to the saints [believers].

For certain persons have crept in unnoticed, those who were long beforehand marked out for this condemnation, ungodly persons who turn the grace of our God into licentiousness and deny our only Master and Lord, Jesus Christ.

But you, beloved, ought to remember the words that were spoken beforehand by the apostles of our Lord Jesus Christ that they were saying to you, "In the last time there will be mockers, following after their own ungodly lusts."

These are the ones who cause divisions, worldly minded, devoid of the Spirit. But you, beloved, building yourselves up on your most holy faith; praying in the Holy Spirit; keep yourselves in the love of God, waiting anxiously for the mercy of our Lord Jesus Christ to eternal life.

Now to Him who is able to keep you from stumbling, and to make you stand in the presence of His glory blameless with great joy, to the only God our Savior, through Jesus Christ our Lord, be glory, majesty, dominion and authority, before all time and now and forever. Amen."

—The Epistle of Jude: 1:3-4, 17-21, 24

Spiritual Wisdom and Discernment

Even long after we come to a saving faith in Christ we must be very much on guard for questionable and unsound teachings found *within* the Christian church. We are living in the last days when "falling away from the faith"—the apostasy is steadily increasing, just as Jesus foretold. For example, some individuals will try to convince others that emotional "experiences" are credible tests of biblical, spiritual authenticity.

Experience alone, apart from adhering to the accuracies of Scripture cannot be a reliable gauge by which to test the spirits (1 John 4:1). This is the same lie that keeps many New Agers bound to false doctrines. Some spiritual experiences or encounters are God-given and some are not. Satan has a counterfeit deceptive action for many of God's teachings (2 Thessalonians 2:9; 2 Corinthians 11:14). The devil's aim is to cause confusion and mayhem and he is doing a superlative job.

Many "sheep in wolves clothing" are deliberately infiltrating the Christian church offering confusing, distorted teachings spanning from the emergent church movement, "contemplative prayer" trends—to "seeker-sensitive" doctrines. They are dangerously compromising the gospel by attacking the very basic, core-truths of Scripture. Substitutes for God's redemptive work are running awry—propelled by those who do not accept the authority, inspiration and inerrancy of the Bible.

Because they do not like or want to accept the truths of the Bible, a deceptive tactic used by some "evangelicals" who compromise the Scriptures is this: They say the true meanings of Scripture are "unclear" in an attempt to appear modest and gain popular favor with their target audience, when in truth they are casting doubt upon God's inerrant Word.

Jesus Christ came to earth to die—to set us free from our sins—to give us eternal life and to save us from hell. Some people do not want to accept hell as a real place. Yet hell is referenced in the Bible repeatedly—dozens of times—in both the Old and New Testaments. Those who want to rewrite the Bible don't want to trust God and accept that He knows what is best for them, so they create new doctrines that they can feel "comfortable" with.

If we are truly born-again, saved by grace—redeemed, regenerated and reconciled through Christ's blood sacrifice, then the truths of the Bible are our anchor—our blessed shield and hope in a sinister world fraught with power-hungry, greedy takers. The Word of God and prayer are lifelines for the genuine believer.

"Your word is a lamp unto my feet and a light to my path" (Psalm 119:105).

"Forever, O LORD, Your word is settled in heaven. Your faithfulness endures to all generations; You established the earth and it abides" (Psalm 119:89).

"As the deer pants for the water brooks, so pants my soul for You O God, for the living God" (Psalm 42:1a).

Gaining Spiritual Wisdom

Praying for spiritual wisdom and discernment is an integral part of one's walk with the Lord, especially in these last days. This is the age of confusion and spiritual recklessness. The promises of the Lord strengthen us as we go through our every day lives. His Word is our guiding light. It is so important to spend time reading and studying the Scriptures.

The Word of God is our powerful ally in a very chaotic, desperate world. A better world is coming soon for all believers. Hold on to that promise and trust the Lord. It won't be long now when the cares and concerns of this world are left behind. The apostle Paul recorded the following encouraging Scriptures:

Philippians 4:8

"Finally, brethren, whatever things are true, whatever things are noble, whatever things are just, whatever things are pure, whatever things are lovely, whatever things are of good report, if there is any virtue and if there is anything praise worthy—meditate on these things."

Ephesians 1:11-21

"In Him also we have obtained an inheritance, being predestined according to the purpose of Him who works all things according to the counsel of His will, that we who first trusted in Christ should be to the praise of His glory.

In Him you also trusted after you heard the word of truth, the gospel of your salvation; in whom also having believed you were sealed with the Holy Spirit of promise, who is **the guarantee of our inheritance** until the redemption of the purchased possession to the praise of His glory.

Therefore, I also, after I heard of your faith in the Lord Jesus and your love for all the saints, do not cease to give thanks for you in my prayers: that the God of our Lord Jesus Christ, the Father of glory, may give to you the spirit of wisdom and revelation in the knowledge of Him, in the eyes of your understanding being enlightened;

That you may know what is the hope of His calling, what are the riches of the glory of His inheritance in the saints, and what is the exceeding greatness of His power toward us who believe, according to the working of His mighty power which He worked in Christ when He raised Him from the dead and seated Him at His right hand in the heavenly places, far above all principality and power and might and dominion, and every name that is named, **not only in this age but also in that which is to come.**"

Joshua 1:8

[Joshua wrote,] "This book of the Law [Bible] shall not depart from your mouth, but you shall meditate on it day and night, that you may observe to do according to all that is written in it. For then you will make your way prosperous, and then you will have good success."

The Name Yeshua Means:

"God is salvation in Hebrew."

Isaiah 52:7

"How beautiful upon the mountains
Are the feet of him who brings good news;
Who proclaims peace,
Who brings glad tidings of good *things,*
Who proclaims salvation [Yeshua]
Who says to Zion,
"Your God [Yeshua] reigns!"

Chapter Seven

Especially for Jewish Readers
Important for Everyone

Christianity Has Jewish Roots

"For I am not ashamed of the gospel of Christ, for it is the power of God to salvation for everyone who believes, **to the Jew first** and also to the Greek [Gentiles]" (Romans 1:16).

If you are Jewish and receive Yeshua as your Savior, you are still Jewish! Your Jewish identity and heritage are sustained. The early Christian church was totally comprised of Jewish believers. Salvation in Christ has come to us through the Jewish people. Through the Jews, mankind was given the Word of God. It is essential to study the Hebraic roots of Christianity to understand that without Israel, without the Jews, there would not be a Christian church. I have listed some good resources throughout this book help you explore and understand more about Hebrew Christianity and Messianic Judaism.

Dr. Thomas S. McCall, ThD, is the senior theologian for Zola Levitt's ministry. During his lectures, he always emphasizes that ALL the writers of the Bible, both Old and New Testaments, were Jewish, including Luke. The entire Bible is a Jewish book. Here is a link to an important article regarding this point: http://www.levitt.com/essays/luke.html.

Also be sure to study the "Question and Answer" section of the website. Zola Levitt died in 2006, but his ministry and website are maintained by some Jewish believers offering some wonderful, important information.

Who Is Yeshua?

Please recognize that Yeshua was a native Israeli. He was born from a virgin, Jewish mother and was conceived by the Ruach Ha Kodesh. The prophet Isaiah prophesied:

"Therefore the Lord Himself will give you a sign: Behold, the virgin shall conceive and bear a Son, and shall call His name Immanuel" (Isaiah 7:14).

If you are Jewish, you are probably aware of the Jewish marriage customs during Old Testament days. The engagement (betrothal) period lasted twelve months, and a marriage covenant was made between the prospective bride and groom. They lived apart for those twelve months in preparation for their wedding ceremony. However, they were already considered husband and wife during those twelve months prior to the actual ceremony. The following Scriptures reveal the events, the love and devotion of Joseph, Mary's betrothed husband, when learning of her pregnancy—especially because they had not engaged in a physical relationship that would cause her to be with child.

Matthew 1:18-25

"Now the birth of Jesus Christ [Yeshua Ha Mashiach] was as follows. When His mother Mary had been betrothed to Joseph, before they came together she was found to be with child by the Holy Spirit.

And Joseph her husband, being a righteous man, and not wanting to disgrace her, desired to put her away secretly. But when he had considered this, behold an angel of the Lord appeared to him in a dream, saying, "Joseph, son of David, do not be afraid to take Mary as your wife; for that which has been conceived in her is of the Holy Spirit.

And she will bear a Son; and you shall call His name Jesus [Yeshua] for it is He who will save His people from their sins. Now all this took place that what was spoken by the Lord through the prophet [Isaiah] might be fulfilled, saying,

"BEHOLD, THE VIRGIN SHALL BE WITH CHILD, AND SHALL BEAR A SON AND THEY SHALL CALL HIS NAME IMMANUEL," which translated, means: "GOD WITH US."

And Joseph arose from his sleep, and did as the angel of the Lord commanded him, and took *her* as his wife, and kept her a virgin until she gave birth to a Son; and he called His name Jesus [Yeshua]."

Matthew 1 and Luke 3:23-38 show that Yeshua was brought up by Jewish parents who were both from the lineage of King David and from the tribe of Judah making Him a legitimate successor to the throne of King David.

"He will be great, and will be called the Son of the Most High; and the Lord God will give Him the throne of His father David; and He will reign over the house of Jacob forever; and His kingdom will have no end" (Luke 1:32-33).

Yeshua's birthplace was in Bethlehem, the town King David was from. In the *Tanakh*, the prophet Micah, prophesied that the Messiah would come from Bethlehem and be the future ruler. Here is the supporting Scripture:

"But you, Bethlehem Ephrathah, *though* you are little among the thousands of Judah, y*et* out of you shall come forth to Me the One to be Ruler in Israel, whose goings forth *are* from of old, from everlasting" (Micah 5:2).

Yeshua was born during the time frame when the prophet Daniel said the Messiah must be present and be killed (cut off). He described a time when the Anointed One—the Messiah would be killed as a ransom for many. His atoning death was a prerequisite to bring future, lasting peace to the world. We are still waiting for that peace to come. It is a future event when Yeshua returns. Messiah rose from the dead and is destined to return, to take the throne of David to rule and reign.

"And He [Yeshua] began to teach them that the Son of Man [Yeshua] must suffer many things, and be rejected by the elders and chief priests and scribes, and must be killed, and after three days rise again" (Mark 8:31).

Isaiah the prophet recorded that Messiah would suffer and die to atone for the sins of His people, the nation of Israel—spoken of in Isaiah 53. This had to happen before the Messiah could return and bring true peace to the world. If Messiah was destined to die, and if "peace" is still a future prophecy yet to be fulfilled, then the Messiah of Israel had to come back from the dead, just as we are told in Scripture: "after three days rise again." His eternal fate is to take the throne of David, to rule and reign over this earth, bringing in true, everlasting peace, fulfilling prophecy. Yeshua was absolutely without sin and fulfilled the law without blemish. He kept the Torah and was totally Jewish. Not even the most prestigious rabbis could say He was with sin. They had to fabricate indictments against Him to pave the way for the Romans to execute Him.

There is an undeniable connection between the promises of David and Abraham, the land of Israel, and the role of Yeshua in the promised future redemption of the world. The prophets of the Bible are consistent in their support for this view.

It is essential for all Gentile and Jewish believers, regardless of cultural differences to understand that because of what Christ did for us on Calvary, in God's eyes there is no distinction between saved Jews and saved Gentiles. Culturally, a "born-again" Jew remains a Jew, just as a saved American Indian culturally remains an American Indian. But because of Christ *all* true born-again believers become members of one (the same) spiritual family.

Beginning from the time of Abraham until Christ's death on the cross, humanity was classified into two branches: the Jews and the Gentiles. Since the cross, there are three definitive categories: Jews, Gentiles and the church (believers). **The Christian church is comprised of both Jews and Gentiles who are saved, those who are "born-again" believers.** Scripture clearly teaches that there is equal spiritual status for all believers: "For there is no partiality with God" (Romans 2:11).

Ephesians 2:12-18

"Remember that you [Gentiles] were at that time separate from Christ, excluded from the commonwealth of Israel, and strangers to the covenants of promise, having no hope and without God in this world. But now in Christ Jesus you who were once far off have been brought near by the blood of Christ.

For He Himself is our peace, who has made both one, and has broken down the middle wall of separation, having abolished in His flesh the enmity, that is, the law of commandments contained in ordinances, so as to create in Himself one new man from two, thus making peace, and that He might reconcile them both to God in one body through the cross, thereby putting to death the enmity.

And He came and preached peace to you who were afar off and to those who were near. For through Him we both have access by one Spirit to the Father."

"For there is no distinction between Jew and Greek [Gentile]; for the same Lord is Lord of all, and is rich unto all that call upon Him: for, whosoever shall call upon the name of the Lord shall be saved" (Romans 10:12-13).

God's Chosen People

Gentiles and Jews together: Gentiles who are committed to Messiah Jesus (born-again believers) are grafted into Abraham's promise of the coming Redeemer, Jesus the Messiah (Romans 11:17-24) and together with Jewish (born-again) believers are co-sharers; partakers in what the Lord has promised Abraham—sharing Israel's spiritual life through her Messiah, Jesus of Nazareth (Ephesians 2:11; 3:11).

Believing Gentiles are recipients of the promise of Abraham (salvation through the Messiah Jesus). In the Old Testament "chosen people" is in reference to Israel—the Jewish people because Messiah would come in through the lineage of David. Because of Christ's sacrifice on the cross, both believing Jews and believing Gentiles have become "one."

But the Jews still remain God's chosen people in a special way. After this dispensation ends, and after the Rapture when the 144,000 Jews take the gospel to the world resulting in the salvation of millions, at that point their chosen uniqueness will become very evident again.

Why Is Israel the "Holy" Land?

The Lord Chose to Establish His Name in the Land of Israel

"I will gather them [the Jews] and will bring them to the place where I have chosen as a dwelling for My name" (Nehemiah 1:9b).

"Also your people shall all be righteous; they shall inherit the land forever, the branch of My planting, the work of My hands, that I might be glorified" (Isaiah 60:21).

265

Yeshua Ha Mashiach—Messiah
Eternal God and King

Scripture tells us again and again *who* Messiah is:

> "For unto us a Child is born, unto us a Child is given; and the government will be upon His shoulder. And His name will be called Wonderful, Counselor, Mighty God, Everlasting Father, Prince of Peace.
>
> Of the increase of *His* government and peace *there will be* no end, upon the throne of David and over His kingdom. To order it and establish it with judgment and justice from that time forward, even forever. The zeal of the LORD of hosts will perform this."
>
> —Isaiah 9:6-7

Notice the text: "and the government will be upon His shoulder," and "Of the increase of His government and peace there will be no end, upon the throne of David and over His Kingdom." **These are direct references to Yeshua when He returns to this earth, to rule and reign for 1000 years.** This is a prophecy of the true Messiah, and the establishment of His permanent kingdom, first on the rejuvenated earth and then in the eternal kingdom. Earlier, I quoted: "And He Himself [Yeshua] will rule them [the nations] with a rod of iron" (Revelation 19:15). Finally, there will be peace and order in the world when the Messiah of Israel sits on the throne of David.

Tanakh/Hebrew/Old Testament Prophecies Fulfilled By Jesus Christ—the Jewish Messiah

HUNDREDS of prophecies from the Old Testament have been literally fulfilled by Jesus. A very extensive list of these fulfilled prophecies is featured at: http://www.jesus-is-lord.com/messiah.htm. Please take some time to look them up. There is no denying that Messiah Jesus is the only One who could fulfill all these prophecies. No other "prophet" or "spiritual" teacher can make a claim like this and back it up historically. You will also find some excellent information on rabbis in history and today who have recognized the truth of Messiah Jesus listed on the *Hope of Israel* website. The site also highlights a list of fulfilled prophecies by

Jesus and much more: http://www.hopeofisrael.net/. Be sure to click on "Testimonies" on the left side of the page for the testimonies of rabbis. The site offers an abundance of information for Jews and all believers; it is a superb resource. This site downloads very slowly, but it is worth the wait. Free Bibles are also available. This site is offered in thirty languages, including Hebrew.

Dr. Ron Rhodes, from *Reasoning from the Scriptures Ministries*, has compiled excellent scriptural evidence about the truth of Yeshua: "Jesus Is the Messiah." Please be sure to study his very profound message at: http://home.earthlink.net/~ronrhodes/Jews.html.

On the following pages I cite Isaiah 53, a very important chapter from the *Tanakh*, the Old Testament. It reveals the true identity of the Messiah, Yeshua Ha Mashiach, Jesus the Christ. Please take some time to carefully read and study it. But first, I have some quotes from rabbis from the Ninth and Tenth Centuries commenting on the passages of Isaiah 53:

Rabbi Eleazer Kalir (9th Century) Musaf Prayer

"Our righteous Messiah has departed from us. Horror has seized us and we have no one to justify us. He has borne our transgressions and the yoke of our iniquities, and is wounded because of our transgressions. He bore our sins upon his shoulders that we may find pardon for our iniquity. We shall be healed by his wounds, at the time when the Eternal will recreate him in a new creature. Oh bring him up from the circle of the earth, raise him up from Seir, that we may hear him the second time."

Rabbi Moses, "The Preacher" (11th Century)

"From the beginning God has made a covenant with the Messiah and told him, 'My righteous Messiah, those who are entrusted to you, their sins will bring you into a heavy yoke.' And he answered, 'I gladly accept all agonies in order that not one of Israel should be lost.' Immediately, the Messiah accepted all agonies with love, as it is written: 'he was oppressed and then he was afflicted.'"

Isaiah 53—The Scripture Most Rabbis Like to Forget

Fulfilled Prophecy—The Messiah of Israel

Rabbis in general gloss over Isaiah 53 because they do not want to reconcile just *who* is being spoken of in the prophetic passages. But it is a very important part of the *Tanakh*. It is a critical Scripture revealing Messiah's true identity. Please read it carefully. Yeshua, the Messiah of Israel, took humanity's sins upon Himself and suffered horrifically so you and I, and anyone else who will accept Him would be saved from an incomprehensible, supernatural evil that is literally and methodically hell bent on destroying us.

Isaiah 53 in its entirety:

"WHO has believed our message? And to whom has the arm of the LORD been revealed? For He grew up before Him like a tender shoot, and like a root out of parched ground; He has no *stately* form or majesty that we should look upon Him, Nor appearance that we should be attracted to Him. He was despised and forsaken of men, a man of sorrows, and acquainted with grief; and like one from whom men hide their face, He was despised, and we did not esteem Him.

Surely our griefs He Himself bore, and our sorrows He carried; yet we ourselves esteemed Him stricken, smitten of God, and afflicted. But He was pierced through for our transgressions, He was crushed for our iniquities; the chastening for our well-being *fell* upon Him, and by His scourging we are healed. All of us like sheep have gone astray, each of us has turned to his own way; but the LORD has caused the iniquity of us all to fall on Him.

He was oppressed and He was afflicted, yet He did not open His mouth; like a lamb that is led to slaughter, and like a sheep that is silent before its shearers, so He did not open His mouth. By oppression and judgment He was taken away; and as for His generation, who considered that He was cut off out of the land of the living, for the transgression of my people to whom the stroke *was due?* His grave was assigned with wicked men, yet He was with a rich man in His death, because He had done no violence, nor was there any deceit in His mouth.

But the LORD was pleased to crush *Him* to grief; if He would render Himself as a guilt offering, He will see *His* offspring, He will prolong *His* days, and the good pleasure of the LORD will prosper in His hand. As a result of the anguish of His soul, He will see *it* and be satisfied; by His knowledge the Righteous One, My Servant, will justify the many, as He will bear their iniquities.

Therefore, I will allot Him a portion with the great, and He will divide the booty with the strong; because He poured out Himself to death, and was numbered with the transgressors; yet He Himself bore the sin of many, and interceded for the transgressors."

New Testament References to Isaiah 53

Isaiah 53:1 - John 12:37-38
Isaiah 53:4 - Matthew 8:16-17
Isaiah 53:5-6 - 1 Peter 2:24-25
Isaiah 53:7-8 - Acts 8:32-35
Isaiah 53:9 - 1 Peter 2:22
Isaiah 53:12 - Luke 22:37
Isaiah 53:12 - Mark 15:27-28

Jesus the Messiah—Despised by the World—Rejected by Israel

"Thus says the LORD,
The Redeemer of Israel, their Holy One,
To Him whom man despises,
To Him whom the nation abhors,
To the Servant of rulers:
"Kings shall see and arise,
Princes also shall worship,
Because of the LORD who is faithful,
The Holy One of Israel;
And He has chosen You"
(Isaiah 49:7).

The Moving Testimony of a Jewish Believer

The following testimony is a letter written by my dear, lifelong friend and ministry associate, Terry. It was written especially for her close unsaved friends and family. I met her when we were children, when I could barely speak English. Her older brother Peter became very ill and died when she was just a young teenager. This was very hard for her. Terry named her firstborn child after him.

After I came back to the Lord from my wasted years searching for "truth" within the New Age enclaves, I felt compelled to contact Terry and tell her about the Lord. I sent her a book: *The Case for Christ* by Lee Strobel. She was very polite and nice about it, but of course at the time she did not feel the book was "for her." I began to pray for her. I prayed for her salvation for over fifteen years, and one day she made the choice to respond to the Lord's salvation message and became a genuine believer. We are ministry partners today. I love her and thank God for her, and I thank God for answered prayer! Here is Terry's letter:

This letter is one of THE HARDEST things in my life I have ever done. As afraid as I am to share this with you, it will show you how very important what I have to say is, and that I am going to take the risk! I know while some of you believe in "a God," you have decided to take ideas from different religions and then make up your own. Some of you don't believe in God at all. You wonder if there is a God and if there is, how He can let horrible things happen to "good people," especially children. I know. I was one of those people myself. When my brother Peter died, I couldn't understand how God could take from us such a wonderful person.

After convincing myself that there must not be a God, I still had the sense that there has to be "something" greater than me out there, and I wanted to discover what it is. I turned to Eastern meditation to try to see myself as one with God and the universe. I remember being told I was in control of my universe by my thoughts. I can't remember now what I learned from the assorted books and lectures from the gurus. But I did go back to knowing there MUST be a God, yet did not delve into finding out anything about Him. I just figured I would be good, go to heaven and if wrong, it would all be okay anyway.

When my son, Pete, died—I KNEW there is a God. I remember that something bizarre happened, lasting only a moment. While I was standing in my living room, it seemed like a voice near my left ear was telling me Pete was okay, and that he was safe with the Lord. It made every hair on my neck stand up. I didn't hear anything out loud, but I still experienced something. I feel that God did not allow me to see Pete when I was searching for him, although He did lead me to him. I thought that it was strange that the spot to look for him had not entered my mind until that very moment. It seems the Lord knew I needed to find him, but He also knew that to see what had happened to him would have destroyed me.

When I realized Pete was missing, I called the police but did not wait for them to come. I went immediately to the area where I thought he might be, but I could not see him in the brush from the sidewalk. I went down to the canal and yelled for him, praying to God that I wouldn't find him face down in the water. When I came up the path and looked over the area again, I saw his skateboard on one of the chairs. How could I have missed it? Then as if I had no control, I could not run to him. I ran back home to get Phil, and at that exact moment I saw the police coming out my house. The officer followed me back to the area where Peter was, but he would not let me near him. I knew he wasn't really there anymore.

In the next few days a conversation I had with Pete several months before kept coming into my thoughts. I knew he had found God when he was in jail, but I had asked him to please explore the Jewish religion too, which he did. One day in the car we were talking and I brought up that subject again. He told me he believed Jesus is God's Son and that He died on the cross for our sins. He may have said more, but when I heard him say that I remember thinking, "WOW, for someone who walked to the beat of his own drum, hated the government and religion, this was BIG!!"

Not knowing anything about Jesus, the only impact this had on me was this thought: "What does Pete know and understand that I haven't got a clue about?" That small seed just sat there inside me.

Phil and I would drop him off at church twice a week and at AA meetings. We never had any desire to go to church with him or ask him what he was learning. He sat next to me one day and watched *The Passion of the Christ* on his laptop while I did something else. He did not share with me anything about the movie except to say that it was pretty close to what the Bible says. I was happy he had found something to help him with his addiction but I am sorry to say, I had little interest in "religion" myself. I remember thinking, "This is good for you, but I don't need it."

Going back to those few days after Peter passed, my heart was telling me to go to his church on Saturday evening, and in that way I would be closer to him. I remember thinking: "How will I last the entire hour or so that he used to go for? What am I getting myself into?" Phil did not want me to go alone so he came along. It did not take long for us to realize how God assures us that "all things work together for good to those who love God, to those who are called according to His purpose" (Romans 8:28).

God does not cause bad things to happen, but he allows people to choose to do wicked things. He gives us all free choice. God loves us in spite of our flawed deeds. The Bible says "There is none righteous, no, not one" (Romans 3:10). The Old Testament teaches when the Jews sinned they brought to the Holy Tabernacle an unblemished Lamb to die for their sins. The Lord sent Jesus, His Son to do the same thing in the New Testament on our behalf. John 3:16 says: "For God so loved the world that he gave his only begotten Son, that whosoever believes in Him, shall not perish but have eternal life."

A lot of evidence exists explaining why the Bible is true, so I won't go into that now, but in my heart I know it is the Word of God. If you are interested you might start with some of the books written by, Lee Strobel, *The Case for Christ* and *The Case for the Creator*. He is an award-winning journalist who set out to prove the Bible is not true. What he did find out was that he could not disprove the Bible. This startling realization halted his atheist beliefs, turning him into a true believer and a Christian.

The Bible says, "All have sinned and come short of the glory of God" (Romans 3:23). John 3:3 says, "Verily, verily, I say unto thee, except a man be born-again, he cannot see the kingdom of God." To be "born-again" you must believe God sent his Son to die for our sins. God's message is clear in Matthew 19:24:

> "And again I say unto you, it is easier for a camel to go through the eye of a needle, than for a rich man to enter into the kingdom of God."

It is impossible for anyone to be saved through good works. Man is saved through God's gift of grace, mercy and faith as written in Ephesians 2:8-9:

> "For by grace are ye saved through faith, and that not of yourselves: it is the gift of God: not of works, lest any man should boast."

When I was around fifteen years old, I remember looking at the Bibles my parents had in the house. Both the Jewish Bible with only the Old Testament, and one with both the Old and New Testaments. I also remember looking at some parts of the last book (Revelation) and being very frightened. I did not understand what I read but I could see that some very horrible things were going to happen. It was like a scary movie that I did not want any part of.

I decided to forget about what I had read and felt better. Now having *read* Revelation, I am still frightened, but not for me anymore. I know I am going to heaven. It scares me and saddens me for those I love that they won't be going with me. Heaven and hell are real and eternal and I cannot understand why anyone wouldn't want to investigate and find this out for themselves.

Let's say I am wrong, and there are lots of different ways to get to God. Or that there is no God, and God takes only good people or people can get into heaven because of one of the many other things they believe. Okay, so I am wrong. No big deal. BUT let's say the Bible is right and you are wrong. A very BIG deal! Check it out yourself. The Bible says we will all some day go before God:

> "But why dost thou judge thy brother? Or why dost thou set at nought [despise] thy brother? For we shall all stand before the judgment seat of Christ. For it is written, as I

live, saith the Lord, every knee shall bow to me, and every tongue shall confess to God. So then every one of us shall give account of himself to God" (Romans 14:10-12).

We won't get the chance to see God and say "Oh you are real, NOW I believe." It will be too late. Once you have died it will be TOO LATE. None of us know when we will pass, so be careful thinking, "Someday I will check into this." God does not force us to love Him. I wouldn't want to force you to love me either. You have to want to on your own.

Sadly, someone who is MOST precious to me once asked me, "What would you say to God if you did believe?" I can't remember the exact words. I knew the answer, but it wouldn't come out. I was afraid I would mess up and say the wrong thing. So I told her I would find out and let her know.

Soon after that incident and before I could say anything more, she said: "I don't want to hear anything about God." Well, NOW I am going to say what I should have said then: If you truly want God in your life, say something like this—it doesn't have to be the exact words. BUT you must mean it:

> God, I realize I have sinned and because of my sin, I know I deserve hell. I believe you sent your Son, Jesus, to die on the cross for me. I believe in the death, burial and resurrection of Jesus and believe He is alive and hears my prayers. Please forgive me for my sins and help me to follow your Word. I ask you Lord to come into my heart to be my Savior. I pray this in Jesus' name. Amen.

Next, start reading the Bible, especially Isaiah 53. Talk to believers but MOSTLY talk to God. He loves us and wants to be in our lives. God is always with me. That doesn't mean I order him around and tell him what I want Him to do for me. It means I want to learn what will please Him and to do what He wants. God really wants us to love Him and realize that there is no other true God.

"Jesus said to him [Thomas, the disciple]: "I am the way, the truth, and the life. No one comes to the Father except through Me" (John 14:6).

God wants us to love others and He wants us to share His Word (the Bible) with everyone. In 2 Peter 3:9, we learn:

"The Lord is not slack [slow] concerning his promise, as some men count slackness; but is longsuffering [patient] to us-ward not willing that any should perish, but that all should come to repentance."

In other words, receive Him as Lord and Savior and live a life that is pleasing to Him, based on the teachings in the Scriptures. God does not want to lose any of us! He does give us a choice though, to accept or deny Him. I will still have trials in my life and I will still sin, but now I have the Lord with me. I will ask for forgiveness and strength and put my faith and trust in God. Will bad things still happen? Most certainly! Will I always understand? Not on this earth, but some day things will become clearer to me.

Selfishly I wanted to go to heaven to be with Peter. But now I have the Lord in my heart and I am saved! When I die, I want Peter at my side, *and* I want to see Jesus! Selfishly I want you to all go with me. I feel like a parent who is warning her children about life-threatening dangers, but no one is listening.

I only hope you will investigate this on your own and that you will still want me in your life. I truly love you! One last thought: Remember, this is NOT about any church or religion. It is about having a real relationship with Jesus. Jesus came into the world as a Jew. So did I. I am still a Jew, but I am a redeemed one!

Terry
May 4, 2010

"My people are destroyed for lack of knowledge."
—Hosea 4:6a

Israel's Only Savior

Isaiah 43:1-2

"But now, thus says the LORD, who created you, O Jacob, And He who formed you, O Israel:

Fear not, for I have redeemed you; I have called *you* by your name; You *are* Mine.

When you pass through the waters, I *will be* with you; And through the rivers, they shall not overflow you.

When you walk through the fire, you shall not be burned, nor shall the flame scorch you."

Chapter Eight

Facts Relating to Israel and the Palestinians

"And I will bring again the captivity of my people of Israel, and they shall build the waste cities, and inhabit them; and they shall plant vineyards, and drink the wine thereof; they shall also make gardens, and eat the fruit of them. And I will plant them upon their land, and they shall no more be pulled up out of their land which I have given them, says the LORD thy God" (Amos 9:14-15).

Everywhere we turn on any given day we hear the term "occupied territory" in relation to Israel. We hear it repeatedly: "Israel is living in occupied territory." This tall tale is perpetuated by all the major news agencies in every corner of the world. Ignorance has surely found many friends. In the early part of January of 2012, the Middle East Quartet met to assert their pressure over Israel (again) to stop building homes in their God-given land. Of course this was done—as it always is—under the guise of promoting: "peace." This time the words used to get Israel to try to acquiesce were: "confidence building."

This "confidence building" request by the Quartet was expressed by using the following rhetoric:

Palestinian officials insist they cannot enter full talks with Israel until it freezes settlement building on occupied Palestinian land, saying this threatens the viability of the Palestinian state they would be negotiating for. There was no indication after Monday's meeting that a settlement freeze was being considered by Israel. Mann news Agency January 11, 2012 to keep Palestinian officials in talks after the end of the month, Israeli media reported on Tuesday.

Palestinian officials insist they cannot enter full talks with Israel until it freezes settlement building on occupied Palestinian land, saying this threatens the viability of the Palestinian state they would be negotiating for. There was no indication after Monday's meeting that a settlement freeze was being considered by Israel.

—Mann News Agency January 11, 2012 (Tel Aviv)

In the same meeting with the Middle East Quartet, the proposals on "border" and "security issues" were delegated to the Jordanian Foreign Minister, Nasser Juda. He said that the PLO gave Israel a proposal on *borders* and *security issues* at the first summit and Israeli representatives promised to respond to the proposals in future meetings. I pray that their response will always be, "No, we are not gong to stop building on our God-given land." But within the Israeli government there are those who are not working in the best interest of the Israeli people and are going against God's biblical admonitions not to divide the Land of Israel.

I received the following correspondence in my email inbox from Israel earlier this week. It disturbs me so much that I am including it in this book. It is an example of the devastation and abuse some Israeli families must face. This is not fiction, I am sorry to say. It is a day (night) in the life of many Jewish families in Israel.

ACTION ALERT

Large Destruction forces have arrived to Mitzpe Avichai in Kiryat Arba to destroy the neighborhood in which 8 families live and more than 20 children.

It is now Thursday January 12th, (2012) 3:40 am. They already destroyed the synagogue. Now they are going from house to house to take out the family and then destroy the house.

If you are up and see this email, please call the PM, ministers, members of Knesset and your local Israeli embassy demanding to stop the upcoming destruction.

Nadia Matar and Yehudit Katsover
Women in Green

The destruction was not stopped:

Jews Out!

Women in Green's reaction to last night's destruction in Mitzpe Avihai-Kiryat Arba:

At 2:30 in the middle of the night, with 0 degrees celcius outside, some 20 children were dragged away from their beds together with their parents and were told: "Jews-OUT!"

Immediately thereafter the tractors ran over and destroyed their homes.

The Mitzpe Avichai neighborhood was built on land that belongs to the municipality of Kiryat Arba Hevron and was already destroyed ten times.

Every destruction brings about construction, especially in Mitzpe Avihai, and thank G-d, the neighborhood has already eight families and public buildings.

Once again the IDF used Arab workers to do the dirty work of expelling Jews from their homes and, by the way, these Arabs stole jewelry and work utensils from the expelled Jews.

Women in Green call upon all to donate funds in order to rebuild the neighborhood. We also call upon the Prime Minister to stop hiding behind Ehud Barak and finally start building the Land of Israel proudly. This is the one and only answer to Yair Lapid and Sheli Yachimovitz.

The government of Israel has to stop the game of jumping once to the right and once to the left. It does not help at all. Only with a clear policy of applying Israeli sovereignty over Judea and Samaria, the building of thousands of homes, and the spreading of the population from the shore to the mountains, will deterrence be built. Only this way, will our country be built.

Yehudit Katsover 050-7161818 Nadia Matar 050-5500834
http://www.womeningreen.org/

This type of forced eviction has been going on for many years throughout Israel. About a week later I received a similar email, but the detailed descriptions of the home evictions and demolitions in neighboring communities were *even worse* than what is described here. The Israelis desperately need their Messiah, especially as overall conditions throughout the nation become increasingly more difficult, as the world moves toward the Tribulation years. Following is the website description for Women in Green:

> Women for Israel's Tomorrow -Women in Green, founded in 1993 by Ruth and Michael Matar, is a grassroots movement of women and men, young and old, secular and religious, all bound together by a shared concern, love, devotion and loyalty to the Land of Israel. We are a registered non-profit organization with friends and supporters in Israel and abroad.
>
> Our movement is dedicated to safeguarding our G-d given biblical Homeland. We are popularly known as "the Women in Green" because of the green hats we sometimes wear to show our opposition to the abandonment of parts of our homeland and to the return of Israel to the "Green Line", the pre-1967 borders.
>
> "Eretz Israel Le'Am Yisrael"- "The Land of Israel belongs to the People of Israel" has been our motto since the beginning of our movement.
>
> We act out of our firm belief in the central role of Eretz Israel for the future of the Jewish People. Today, more than ever, we must actualize our possession of our land. In addition to our usual activities of education and hasbara as to the right of the Jewish people to its biblical Homeland, Women in Green is also behind the struggle for a Jewish Shdema and the Yibaneh fund for building and planting in the hills of Judea. One of the places where Women in Green plant trees to safeguard Israel's Statelands, is Netzer; in the heart of Gush Etzion, between Elazar and Alon Shvut.
>
> Women in Green has a new logo: The Magen David represents the Jewish Zionist ideal; the blue and brown furrows of plowed land represent what we stand for: cultivating and safeguarding the Land of Israel.

Occupied Territories?

The following article is quoted from the website titled: *Palestinian Facts*. It is the first in a number of articles in this chapter pertaining to the truth about the Palestinian people.

Are the West Bank and Gaza "Occupied Territories" As Palestinian Arabs Assert?

As a result of the Six Day War, Israel gained all of Jerusalem, the Golan Heights, Sinai, the Gaza Strip, and the West Bank (historically known as Judea and Samaria). Palestinian Arabs often insist on using the term "occupied territories" to describe these areas, usually connected to the assertion that they fall under the 1949 Fourth Geneva Convention.

Yet, Palestinian spokesmen also speak about Israeli military action in Area A as an invasion, an infringement on Palestinian sovereignty. The use of both forms of terminology is a contradiction. If Israel "invaded Palestinian territories" in the present, then they cannot be regarded as "occupied"; however, if the territories are defined as "occupied," Israel cannot be "invading" them.

Israeli legal experts traditionally resisted efforts to define the West Bank and Gaza Strip as "occupied" or falling under the main international treaties dealing with military occupation. Former Chief Justice of the Supreme Court Meir Shamgar wrote in the 1970s that there is no de jure applicability of the 1949 Fourth Geneva Convention regarding occupied territories to the case of the West Bank and Gaza Strip since the Convention: ...is based on the assumption that there had been a sovereign who was ousted and that he had been a legitimate sovereign.

In fact, prior to 1967, Jordan had occupied the West Bank and Egypt had occupied the Gaza Strip; their presence in those territories was the result of their illegal invasion in 1948. Jordan's 1950 annexation of the West Bank was recognized only by Great Britain and Pakistan and rejected by the vast majority of the international community, including the Arab states.

International jurists generally draw a distinction between situations of "aggressive conquest" and territorial disputes that arise after a war of self-defense. Former U.S. State Department Legal Advisor Stephen Schwebel, who later headed the International Court of Justice in the Hague, wrote in 1970 regarding Israel's case:

Where the prior holder of territory had seized that territory unlawfully, the state which subsequently takes that territory in the lawful exercise of self-defense has, against that prior holder, better title. Israel only entered the West Bank in 1967 after repeated Jordanian artillery fire and ground movements across the previous armistice lines; additionally, Iraqi forces crossed Jordanian territory and were poised to enter the West Bank. Under such circumstances, even the United Nations rejected Soviet efforts to have Israel branded as the aggressor in the Six-Day War.

Regardless of how many times the Palestinian Arabs claim otherwise, Israel cannot be characterized as a "foreign occupier" with respect to the West Bank and Gaza Strip. Fundamental sources of international legality decide the question in Israel's favor.

The last international legal allocation of territory that includes what is today the West Bank and Gaza Strip occurred with the League of Nations Mandate for Palestine which recognized Jewish national rights in the *whole* of the Mandated territory, including the sector east of the Jordan River, almost 80% of the original Mandated territory, that was given to Palestinian Arabs and Emir Abdullah to create the country of Trans-Jordan (later renamed Jordan). Moreover, the rights under the Mandate were preserved under the United Nations as well, according to Article 80 of the UN Charter, after the termination of the League of Nations in 1946.

It is important to observe that, from the time these territories were conquered by Jordan, Syria and Egypt in 1948 to the time they were gained by Israel in 1967, the territories were not referred to as "occupied" by the international community. Furthermore, the people living in those territories before 1967 were not called "Palestinians" as they are today; they were called Jordanians and Egyptians. (In fact, before Israel was founded Jews and Arabs alike who lived in the region were called Palestinians. The newspaper was the "Palestine

Bulletin" and later the "Palestine Post" before becoming today's "Jerusalem Post", the Jewish-founded electric company was "Palestine Electric" and so on.) There was no call for "liberation" or "national rights" for the Arabs living there and no Palestinian nation was discussed.

No UN resolution requires Israel to withdraw unilaterally from the territories, nor do they forbid Israelis from going there to live. In particular, the often-misquoted UN Security Council Resolution 242 (and related Resolution 338) makes no such demand or requirement. The demand that Israel stop creating "illegal settlements" is similarly baseless.

Under the Oslo Accords, the "peace process" started in 1991 at the Madrid Conference, Israel agreed to withdraw from the disputed territories and Yasser Arafat's Palestinian Authority (PA) was given control over land chosen so that more than ninety-nine percent of the Palestinian population lived under the jurisdiction of the PA.

But the commitment to Israel's security that was the backbone of the Oslo agreements was never honored by the PA and Israel was forces to periodically re-enter the ceded territory to quell terrorism.

In 2000, Yasser Arafat rejected sweeping concessions by Israel at Camp David—promoted by US Pres. Clinton in an attempt to reach a final peace agreement—and the Palestinian Arabs turned again to violence with the Al Aqsa Intifada.

That is, after the PA was governing nearly all Palestinian Arabs and a generous peace offer with international backing was on the table, the only response Israel got was increased violence. This is the sole reason Israel continues to have a military presence in the disputed territories. [1]

Palestinian Facts is an excellent, detailed website linked below. Please visit it. On the following pages I am including additional, excellent information regarding Palestinian issues.

Endnotes
[1] http://www.palestinefacts.org/

Andrew Roberts Stands Up for Israel
Before the British House of Commons

"We owe to the Jews," wrote Winston Churchill in 1920!

Unlike Churchill's views, in 57 years, the current Queen of England has visited 14 Arab countries, but never visited Israel.

Andrew Roberts, a 47 year-old British Historian who regularly appears on British television and radio, is also an award winning writer featured in *The Sunday Telegraph*, *The Spectator*, *Literary Review*, and *Mail on Sunday* and *Daily Telegraph*. He is also a founder member of José Maria Aznar's Friends of Israel Committee. Here is an edited version of a speech Andrew Roberts gave to the British Government at the Friends of Israel Initiative in the British House of Commons on July 19, 2010:

From Morocco to Afghanistan, from the Caspian Sea to Aden, the 5.25 million square miles of territory belonging to members of the Arab League is home to over 330 million people, whereas Israel covers only 8,000 square miles, and is home to seven million citizens, one-fifth of who are Arabs.

The Jews of the Holy Land are thus surrounded by hostile states 650 times their size in territory and 60 times their population; yet their last, best hope of ending two millennia of international persecution - the State of Israel—has somehow survived.

When during the Second World War, the island of Malta came through three terrible years of bombardment and destruction it was rightly awarded the George Medal for bravery.

Today Israel should be awarded a similar decoration for defending democracy, tolerance and Western values against a murderous onslaught that has lasted 20 times as long.

Jerusalem is the site of the Temple of Solomon and Herod. The stones of a palace erected by King David himself are even now being unearthed just outside the walls of Jerusalem. Everything that makes a nation state legitimate -- blood shed, soil tilled, international agreements, argues for Israel's right to exist, yet that is still denied by the Arab League.

For many of their [Arab] governments, **which are rich enough to have economically solved the Palestinian refugee problem decades ago,** it is useful to have Israel as a scapegoat to divert attention from the tyranny, failure and corruption of their own regimes.

The tragic truth is that it suits Arab states very well to have the Palestinians endure permanent refugee status; whenever Israel puts forward workable solutions they are stymied by those whose interests put the destruction of Israel before the genuine well-being of the Palestinians.

Both King Abdullah I of Jordan and Anwar Sadat of Egypt were assassinated when they attempted to come to some kind of accommodation with a country that most sane people now accept is not going away.

"We owe to the Jews," wrote Winston Churchill in 1920, "a system of ethics which, even if it were entirely separated from the supernatural, would be incomparably the most precious possession of mankind, worth in fact the fruits of all wisdom and learning put together."

Although they make up less than half of 1% of the world's population, between 1901 and 1950 Jews won 14% of all the Nobel Prizes awarded for literature and science, and between 1951and 2000 Jews won 32% of the Nobel Prizes for medicine, 32% for physics, 39% for economic sand 29% for science.

This, despite so many of their greatest intellects dying in the gas chambers! Yet we tend to treat Israel like a leper on the international scene, threatening her with academic boycotts if she builds a separation wall that has so far reduced suicide bombings by 95% over three years.

Her Majesty the Queen has been on the throne for 57 years and in that time has undertaken 250 official visits to 129 countries, yet has not yet set foot in Israel. **She has visited 14 Arab countries, so it cannot have been that she wasn't in the region.**

After the Holocaust, the Jewish people recognized that they must have their own state, a homeland where they could forever be safe from a repetition of such horrors. **Since then, Israel has had to fight five major wars for her existence.**

Radical Islam is never going to accept the concept of an Israeli State, so the struggle is likely to continue for another 60 years, but the Jews know that that is less dangerous than entrusting their security to anyone else.

I recently visited Auschwitz-Birkenau. Walking along a line of huts and the railway siding, where their forebearers had been worked and starved and beaten and frozen and gassed to death, were a group of Jewish school children, one of whom was carrying over his shoulder the Israeli flag.

It was a moving sight, for it was the sovereign independence represented by that flag which guarantees that the obscenity of genocide will never again befall the Jewish people. No people in history have needed the right to self-defense and legitimacy more than the Jews of Israel and that is: what we in the Friends of Israel Initiative demand here today. [1]

The Friends of Israel Initiative is an international effort to "seek to counter the attempts to delegitimize the State of Israel and its right to live in peace within safe and defensible borders," initiated and led by former Prime minister of Spain and People Party's leader José Maria Aznar in 2010. It was co-founded by nine other international figures: Republican Party former United Stated Ambassador to the United Nations John Bolton, Forza—Italia's former president of the Italian Senate, Marcello Pera, Perus's former president, Alejandro Toledo, and British Conservative Party peer, former first Minister of Northern Ireland and Nobel peace prize winner David Trimble.

Endnotes
[1] Article from: Jerusalem News Network, info@jnnnews.com, emphasis added.

Our World: Gingrich's Fresh Hope
By Caroline Glick, The Jerusalem Post
December 12, 2011

Gingrich's Statement about the Palestinians was entirely accurate. That is, the Palestinian people were invented 91 years ago.

Last Friday, the frontrunner for the Republican presidential nomination, former speaker of the House Newt Gingrich, did something revolutionary. He told the truth about the Palestinians. In an interview with The Jewish Channel, Gingrich said that the Palestinians are an "invented" people, "who are in fact Arabs."

His statement about the Palestinians was entirely accurate. At the end of 1920, the "Palestinian people" was artificially carved out of the Arab population of "Greater Syria." "Greater Syria" included present-day Syria, Lebanon, Israel, the Palestinian Authority and Jordan. That is, the Palestinian people were invented 91 years ago. Moreover, as Gingrich noted, the term "Palestinian people" only became widely accepted after 1977.

As Daniel Pipes chronicled in a 1989 article on the subject in The Middle East Quarterly, the local Arabs in what became Israel opted for a local nationalistic "Palestinian" identity in part due to their sense that their brethren in Syria were not sufficiently committed to the eradication of Zionism [Israel]. Since Gingrich spoke out on Friday, his factually accurate statement has been under assault from three directions. First, it has been attacked by Palestinian apologists in the post-modernist camp.

Speaking to CNN, Hussein Ibish from the American Task Force on Palestine argued that Gingrich's statement was an outrage because while he was right about the Palestinians being an artificial people, in Ibish's view, Israelis were just as artificial. **That is, he equated the Palestinians' 91-year-old nationalism with the Jews' 3,500-year-old nationalism.**

In his words, "To call the Palestinians "an invented people" in an obvious effort to undermine their national identity is outrageous, especially since there was no such thing as an 'Israeli" before 1948."

Ibish's nonsense is easily dispatched by a simple reading of the Hebrew Bible. As anyone semi-literate in Hebrew recognizes, the Israelis were not created in 1948. **Three thousand years ago the Israelis were led by a king named David. The Israelis had an independent commonwealth in the Land of Israel, and their capital city was Jerusalem.**

The fact that 500 years ago King James renamed the Israelis "Israelites" is irrelevant to the basic truth that there is nothing new or artificial about the Israeli people. And Zionism, the Jewish national liberation movement, did not arise in competition with Arab nationalism. Zionism has been a central feature of Jewish identity for 3,500 years.

THE SECOND line of attack against Gingrich denies the veracity of his claim. Palestinian luminaries like the PA's unelected Prime Minister Salam Fayyad told CNN, "The Palestinian people inhabited the land since the dawn of history."

Fayyad's historically unsubstantiated claim was further expounded on by Fatah Revolutionary Council member, Dmitri Diliani in an interview with CNN. "The Palestinian people [are] descended from the Canaanite tribe of the Jebusites that inhabited the ancient site of Jerusalem as early as 3200 BCE," Diliani asserted. The Land of Israel has the greatest density of archeological sites in the world. Judea, Samaria, the Galilee, the Negev, the Golan Heights and other areas of the country are packed with archeological evidence of the Jewish commonwealths.

As for Jerusalem, literally every inch of the city holds physical proof of the Jewish people's historical claims to the city. To date, no archeological or other evidence has been found linking the Palestinians to the city or the Jebusites. From a U.S. domestic political perspective, the third line of attack against Gingrich's factual statement has been the most significant.

The attacks involve conservative Washington insiders, many of whom are outspoken supporters of Gingrich's principal rival for the Republican presidential nomination, former Massachusetts governor

Mitt Romney. To date, the attackers' most outspoken representative has been *Washington Post* blogger Jennifer Rubin. These insiders argue that although Gingrich spoke the truth, it was irresponsible and unstatesmanlike for him to have done so.

As Rubin put it on Monday, "Do conservatives really think it is a good idea for their nominee to reverse decades of U.S. policy and deny there is a Palestinian national identity?" In their view, Gingrich is an irresponsible flamethrower because he is turning his back on a 30-year bipartisan consensus. **That consensus is based on ignoring the fact that the Palestinians are an artificial people whose identity sprang not from any shared historical experience, but from opposition to Jewish nationalism.**

The policy goal of the consensus is to establish an independent Palestinian state west of the Jordan River that will live at peace with Israel. This policy was obsessively advanced throughout the 1990s until it failed completely in 2000, when Palestinian leader Yasser Arafat rejected then-prime minister Ehud Barak's and then US president Bill Clinton's offer of Palestinian statehood and began the Palestinian terror war against Israel.

BUT RATHER than acknowledge that the policy – and the embrace of Palestinian national identity at its heart – had failed, and consider other options, the U.S. policy establishment in Washington clung to it for dear life.

Republicans like Rubin's mentor, former deputy national security adviser Elliott Abrams, went on to support enthusiastically Israel's surrender of Gaza in 2005, and to push for Hamas participation in the 2006 Palestinian elections. That withdrawal and those elections catapulted the jihadist terror group to power. The consensus that Gingrich rejected by telling the truth about the artificial nature of Palestinian nationalism was based an attempt to square popular support for Israel with the elite's penchant for appeasement.

On the one hand, due to overwhelming public support for a strong US alliance with Israel, most U.S. policy-makers have not dared to abandon Israel as a U.S. ally. On the other hand, American policy-makers have been historically uncomfortable having to champion

Israel to their anti-Israel European colleagues and to their Arab interlocutors who share the Palestinians' rejection of Israel's right to exist.

The policy of seeking to meld an anti-Israel Arab appeasement policy with a pro-Israel anti-appeasement policy was embraced by successive US administrations until it was summarily discarded by President Barack Obama three years ago. Obama replaced the two-headed policy with one of pure Arab appeasement. Obama was able to justify his move because the two-pronged policy had failed. There was no peace between Israel and the Palestinians. The price of oil had skyrocketed, and U.S. interests throughout the region were increasingly threatened. For its part, Israel was far more vulnerable to terror and war than it had been in years. And its diplomatic isolation was acute and rising.

Unfortunately for both the U.S. and Israel, Obama's break with the consensus has destabilized the region, endangered Israel and imperiled U.S. interests to a far greater degree than they had been under the failed dual-track policy of his predecessors. Throughout the Arab world, Islamist forces are on the rise. Iran is on the verge of becoming a nuclear power. The U.S. is no longer seen as a credible regional power as it pulls its forces out of Iraq without victory, hamstrings its forces in Afghanistan, dooming them to attrition and defeat, and abandons its allies in country after country.

The stark contrast between Obama's rejection of the failed consensus on the one hand and Gingrich's rejection of the failed consensus on the other hand indicates that Gingrich may well be the perfect foil for Obama. Gingrich's willingness to state and defend the truth about the nature of the Palestinian conflict with Israel is the perfect response to Obama's disastrous speech "to the Muslim world" in Cairo in June 2009. It was in that speech that Obama officially abandoned the bipartisan consensus, abandoned Israel and the truth about Zionism and Jewish national rights, and embraced completely the lie of Palestinian nationalism and national rights.

Both: Rubin and Abrams, as well as Romney, justified their attacks on Gingrich and their defense of the failed consensus by noting that no Israeli leaders were saying what Gingrich said. Rubin went so far as to allege that Gingrich's words of truth about the Palestinians hurt Israel. This is of course absurd. What many Americans fail to recognize is that Israeli leaders are not as free to tell the truth about the nature of the conflict as the U.S. is. Rather than look to Israel for leadership on this issue, American leaders would do well to view Israel as the equivalent of West Germany during the Cold War. With half of Berlin occupied by the Red Army and West Berlin serving as the tripwire for a Soviet invasion of Western Europe, West German leaders were not as free to tell the truth about the Soviet Union as American leaders were.

Today, with Jerusalem under constant political and terror threat, with all of Israel increasingly encircled by Islamist regimes, and with the Obama Administration abandoning traditional U.S. support for Israel, it is becoming less and less reasonable to expect Israel to take the rhetorical lead in telling important and difficult truths about the nature of its neighbors. When Romney criticized Gingrich's statement as unhelpful to Israel, Gingrich replied, "I feel quite confident that an amazing number of Israelis found it nice to have an American tell the truth about the war they are in the middle of, and the casualties they are taking and the people around them who say, 'They do not have a right to exist and we want to destroy them.'" And he is absolutely right. It was more than nice. It was heartening.

Thirty years of pre-Obama American lying about the nature of the conflict in an attempt to balance support for Israel with appeasement of the Arabs did not make the US safer or the Middle East more peaceful. A return to that policy under a new Republican president will not be sufficient to restore stability and security to the region. And the need for such a restoration is acute. Under Obama, the last three years of U.S. abandonment of the truth about Israel for Palestinian lies has made the region less stable, Israel more vulnerable, the U.S. less respected and U.S. interests more threatened. Gingrich's statement of truth was not an act of irresponsible flame throwing. It was the beginning of an antidote to Obama's abandonment of truth and reason in favor of lies and appeasement. And as such, it was not a cause for anger. It was a cause for hope.

Footnote
Emphasis added on pages 287-289.

Jerusalem Is Israel's Capital, Despite the Opposing Voices

Since the previous article you just read was written, Mitt Romney met with Prime Minister Benjamin Netanyahu in Israel on July 29, 2012. Mitt Romney did not hesitate to make a strong declaration that Jerusalem *is* Israel's capital—something that the Obama Administration is not willing to do. He also expressed his support for the Israel's right to defend herself. This caused a political earthquake. President Obama's press team immediately responded to Mitt Romney's stance on Jerusalem with their most explicit statement on the issue saying: "He's wrong." And that the capital of Jerusalem should be decided between the Palestinians and Israel in "negotiations," as reported by the Washington Examiner on July 30 2012. So there you have it.

Once again, the Obama Administration is noticeably not standing behind Israel. Earlier this year, on January 20, 2012 General Patrick Dempsey, Chairman of the Joint Chiefs of Staff speaking for the Obama administration told Israeli leaders that the U.S. would not back Israel in an attack against Iran. This historic desertion by the US of Israel is shameful. Iran has viciously and repeatedly threatened to destroy Israel.

Yet Obama has invited the Israel-hating radical Islamist Egyptian President, Mohammed Morsi to visit the White House this September. Morsi has openly declared his support for Hamas and the priority of battling Israel on some level. Morsi's Muslim Brotherhood is seeking a Sharia state in Egypt and a caliphate over the entire Middle East whose capital will be in a "conquered" Jerusalem." The Salafist—a coalition of many hardline Islamist groups, are in full-support of Morsi.

Contrast this with Obama refusing to meet with Israel's Prime Minister Benjamin Netenyahu in late September 2012 when the PM will be here in the U.S. for the UN conference. Netenyahu's request to meet with Obama to discuss the critical situation with Iran's escalating nuclear threat was firmly declined—using the excuse that President Obama is "too busy" because of the upcoming presidential elections. This unprecedented snub by a sitting U.S. president marks a new low in realtions between the prime minister and Obama and will most likely increase the chances of an Israeli airstrike on Iran at some point.

"And in that day will I make Jerusalem a burdensome stone for all people: all that burden themselves with it shall be cut in pieces, though all the people of the earth be gathered together against it" (Zechariah 12:3).

Who Are the Palestinians?
By Ambassador (retired) Yoram Ettinger
"Second Thought"
Israel Hayom Newsletter, December 14, 2011

Contrary to political correctness, Palestinian Arabs have not been in the area west of the Jordan River from time immemorial; no Palestinian state ever existed, no Palestinian People was ever robbed of its land and there is no basis for the Palestinian "claim of return."

Most Palestinian Arabs are descendants of the 1845-1947 Muslim migrants from the Sudan, Egypt, Lebanon, Syria, as well as from Iraq, Saudi Arabia, Bahrain, Yemen, Libya, Morocco, Bosnia, the Caucasus, Turkmenistan, Kurdistan, India, Afghanistan and Balochistan.

Arab migrant workers were imported by the Ottoman Empire and by the British Mandate (which defeated the Ottomans in 1917) for infrastructure projects: The port of Haifa, the Haifa-Qantara, Haifa-Edrei, Haifa-Nablus and Jerusalem-Jaffa railroads, military installations, roads, quarries, reclamation of wetlands, etc. Illegal Arab laborers were also attracted by the relative economic boom; stimulated by Jewish immigration.

According to a 1937 report by the British Peel Commission (*Palestine Betrayed*, Professor Efraim Karsh, Yale University Press, 2010, p. 12), "The increase in the Arab population is most marked in urban areas, affected by Jewish development. A comparison of the census returns in 1922 and 1931 shows that, six years ago, the increase percent in Haifa was 86, in Jaffa 62, in Jerusalem 37, while in purely Arab towns such as Nablus and Hebron it was only 7, and at Gaza there was a decrease of 2 percent."

As a result of the substantial 1880-1947 Arab immigration and despite Arab emigration caused by domestic chaos and intra-Arab violence–the Arab population of Jaffa, Haifa and Ramla grew 17, 12 and 5 times.

The (1831-1840) conquest, by Egypt's Mohammed Ali, was solidified by a flow of Egyptian migrants settling empty spaces between Gaza and Tul-Karem up to the Hula Valley. They followed in the footsteps of thousands of Egyptian draft dodgers, who fled Egypt before 1831 and settled in Acre.

The British traveler, H.B. Tristram, identified, in his 1865 *The Land of Israel*: a journal of travels in Palestine (p.495), Egyptian migrants in the Beit-Shean Valley, Acre, Hadera, Netanya and Jaffa.

The British Palestine Exploration Fund documented that Egyptian neighborhoods proliferated in the Jaffa area: Saknet el-Mussariya, Abu Kebir, Abu Derwish, Sumeil, Sheikh Muwanis, Salame', Fejja, etc. In1917, the Arabs of Jaffa represented at least 25 nationalities, including Persians, Afghanis, Hindus and Balochis. Hundreds of Egyptian families settled in Ara' Arara', Kafer Qassem, Taiyiba a Q alansawa. Many of the Arabs who fled in 1948, reunited with their families in Egypt and other neighboring countries.

"Thirty thousand to thirty-six thousand Syrian migrants (Huranis) entered Palestine during the last few months alone" reported "La Syrie" daily on August 12, 1934. Az-ed-Din el-Qassam, the role-model of Hamas terrorism, which terrorized Jews in British Mandate Palestine, was Syrian, as were Said el-A'az, a leader of the 1936-38 anti-Jewish pogroms and Kaukji, the commander-in-chief of the Arab mercenaries terrorizing Jews in the1930s and 1940s.

Libyan migrants settled in Gedera, south of Tel Aviv. Algerian refugees (Mugrabis) escaped the French conquest of 1830 and settled in Safed (alongside Syrians and Jordanian Bedouins), Tiberias and other parts of the Galilee. Circassian refugees, fleeing Russian oppression (1878) and Moslems from Bosnia, Turkmenistan, and Yemen (1908) diversified the Arab demography west of the Jordan River. Mark Twain wrote in *Innocents Abroad* (American Publishing Company, 1969):

Of all the lands there are for dismal scenery, Palestine must be the prince...Palestine is desolate and unlovely." Analyzing Mark Twain's book, John Haynes Holmes, the pacifist Unitarian priest, the co-founder of the American Civil Liberties Union and the author of *Palestine Today and Tomorrow a Gentile's Survey of Zionism* (McMillan, 1929) wrote:

This is the country to which the Jews have come to rebuild their ancient homeland.... On all the surface of this earth there is no home for the Jew save in the mountains and the wellsprings of his ancient kingdom.... Everywhere else the Jew is in exile.... But, Palestine is his.... Scratch Palestine anywhere and you'll find Israel.... There is not a spot, which is not stamped with the footprint of some ancient [Jewish] tribesman....

Not a road, a spring, a mountain, a village, which does not awaken the name of some great [Jewish] king, or echo with the voice of some great [Jewish] prophet.... [The Jew] has a higher, nobler motive in Palestine than the economic.... This mission is to restore Zion; and Zion is Palestine."

The Arab attempt to gain the moral high ground and to de-legitimize the Jewish State by employing the immoral reinvention of history and recreation of identity was exposed by Arieh Avneri's, *The Claim of Dispossession* (Herzl Press, 1982) and Joan Peters,' *From Time Immemorial* (Harper & Row).

The following two books are also excellent resources for researching the myth that the Jews stole Arab land:

From Time Immemorial: The Origins of the Arab-Jewish Conflict Over Palestine - John Peters

Myths and Facts: A Guide to the Arab-Israeli Conflict, published by American-Israeli Cooperative Enterprise (AICE).

Additionally, another important book: *Should Israel Exit? A Sovereign Nation under Attack,* written by Dr. Michael Curtis; he exposes the ongoing anti-Israel rhetoric that unjustly condemns Israel and refutes the worldwide propaganda against Israel, dispelling the victim mentality and false claims propagated by the Palestinians and their supporters.

Aiding the Palestinians
By Jim Fletcher – Israel Watch
January 2, 2012

I was sickened to read that the US Congress is releasing "aid" to the Palestinians. According to the Associated Press:

"Lawmakers have freed up a little more than 20 percent of $187 million in US assistance to the Palestinians that had been frozen over the Palestinian bid for U.N. membership. Members of Congress have made available $40 million in economic and humanitarian funding for the Palestinians, the State Department said Wednesday. The money is administered by the U.S. Agency for International Development and 'has been vital to establishing and strengthening the foundations necessary for a future Palestinian state,' the department said."

What a sick joke.

The AP also reported that the PLO's best friend in Washington has their backs, too:

"The administration is pressing Congress to release the remaining $147 million that comes from the last budget cycle in which aid to the Palestinians was to total 545.7 million. New funding for the Palestinians will be subject to additional scrutiny and can be blocked if they win full admission to the United Nations before a peace deal with Israel is agreed. The administration has asked Congress for $513.4 million in aid for the Palestinians in fiscal year 2012."

How sick is our world today? The previous paragraphs answer that question. Hard-working Americans are expected to cough-up a half-billion dollars for a terrorist entity! Remember 9/11? Remember scenes of Palestinians in East Jerusalem shouting for joy and passing out candy in celebration?

It is beyond repulsive that we are funding murderers. Add to this insanity the fact that many even now in the West are demonizing Israel's every move, and it is clear that Isaiah was right when he said the day would come when good would be evil and evil would be good.

What we have here is a classic inversion of the truth. The Palestinian Arabs have hated the Jews for a hundred years, or more. Woven into their terror war has been a broader propaganda war that has proven largely successful. It will get worse.

Very few are aware of the origins of the propaganda war against Israel. Shoot, most aren't even aware there is one. They believe whatever comes out of Brian Williams' mouth. They believe the nonsense written by Joe Klein and the dupes with the International Solidarity Movement.

And as I have been saying for some time, the situation is worst in the American church. From Carl Medearis to the growing emphasis on social justice in the pages of *Relevant Magazine*, we are seeing a tidal wave of change from pro-Israel support to what some are calling, "Christian Palestinianism."

But what have the Palestinians been up to, oh, the last several decades?

Originally, due to the influence of the Muslim Brotherhood, Egypt began training and equipping the Arabs in what had been Mandate Palestine.

Between 1949 and 1956, the Egyptian "fedayeen" (terrorists) infiltrated Israel and launched 9,000 attacks that killed 600 Israelis and wounded thousands. One of the most capable killers was the evil Yasser Arafat.

In 1964, Arafat sent Abu Jihad to North Vietnam to study the propaganda tactics of Ho Chi Minh and they had the writings of General Nguyen Giap, as well as Mao's and Che Guevara, translated into Arabic.

(This partly explains the huge number of Che t-shirts—expressing solidarity with the Palestinians—that I saw in the Muslim Quarter of Jerusalem's Old City this past summer.)

Arafat was interested in Ho Chi Minh's expertise in garnering support from left-wing sympathizers in Europe and the US the North

Vietnamese had successfully transformed their story from one of aggressive attacks on South Vietnam into a struggle for "national liberation."

Giap told the PLO: "Stop talking about annihilating Israel and instead turn your terror war into a struggle for human rights. Then you will have the American people eating out of your hand."

The PLO/PA currently has a growing number of American Christian leaders eating out of its hand, as it continues to spread lies about the Palestinian narrative, the story that says all the ills in the Middle East are Israel's fault.

As the Cold War heated up, the Soviets realized the PLO was perfect for fomenting violence and chaos. The Soviets trained PLO terrorists at the Moscow-based Patrice Lumumba People's Friendship University. Romanian intelligence provided the PLO with logistical support while weapons came from the KGB and East German Stasi.

This was in the years immediately preceding the President of Appeasement, Jimmy Carter, and his policies of weakness, which the PLO capitalized on. Within five years of the Egyptian-Israeli peace treaty (in which Israel gave back the whole of the Sinai), Hamas was formed. Hamas says in its charter that it is "the Palestinian branch of the Muslim Brotherhood."

Hello, is anybody listening?

After Arafat launched another terror war in September 2000, Hamas launched 425 terror attacks against Israel, including 52 homicide bombers. A total of 377 Israelis were killed, and 1,646 were wounded. Since Arafat and the PLO/PA came to power in Gaza and parts of the West Bank in 1994, 28,000 terror attacks were launched against Israelis, with 1,700 murdered and another 7,000 wounded.

Twenty.

Eight.

Thousand.

Still, it is Israel that's condemned. It is wholly unacceptable that we are giving a half-billion dollars to these people. Does anybody care? Is anyone going to protest this outrage?

In all this, leftists in America (and a growing number of evangelicals) condemn Israel for the security fence constructed…to save Jewish lives. It is estimated that 90 percent of the terror attacks have been stopped by the fence. Islamic Jihad leader Ramadan Shalah said on Al-Manar TV (Hezbollah) that if the security fence were not in place, "the situation would be entirely different."

No kidding.

Why is the left obsessed and angry about Israel's security fence? Especially in light of the following examples:

"The fence separating Spain from Morocco at Ceuta, the British fence that ran through Belfast in Northern Ireland, the fence dividing North and South Korea, the fence that China built to keep out starving North Koreans, the fence dividing Greek from Turkish Cyprus, the fences between India and Pakistan and between India and Bangladesh, the fence between Batswana and Zimbabwe, the fence between Kyrgyzstan and Uzbekistan, the fence recently built by Saudi Arabia to stop weapons smuggling from Yemen, and of course the controversial security fence planned to extend hundreds of miles on the US-Mexico border."

(This and other information comes from the book, *History Upside Down*, by David Meir-Levi.)

Why doesn't Jim Wallis write extensively about these fences? Why doesn't Lynne Hybels speak at a Christ at the North Korean Checkpoint? Doesn't Brian McLaren play the bongos and sing at sit-ins near the Indian-Bangladesh fence? Isn't that an apartheid wall?

Between 1967 and 1993, the Arab population in the territories grew from 950,000 to more than 3,000,000. Almost 260 new towns emerged. By 1993, almost 300,000 Palestinians worked in Israeli tourism, agricultural and manufacturing. But according to the propagandists—funded by the American taxpayer—Israel has been responsible for genocide against the Palestinian Arabs. But I want you to think about those numbers. Between the time Israel took territory in a defensive war in '67, until the disastrous Oslo Accords brought the mass-murderer Arafat to power in Gaza, the Arab population grew! They were far more prosperous than their cousins in neighboring, oppressive countries.

A half-billion dollars? At a time when Americans can't even pay their own bills? A half-BILLION dollars for *these* people? We should cut the Palestinians a check that would bounce like a basketball at Madison Square Garden.

Jihad Training of Children Using Television and Schools

It is evident, even with the astounding facts you have just read that there are large numbers of people who brush aside the truth about the Palestinians and radical Islam in general. I have even heard some naïve and misinformed (gullible) individuals say that Americans should use their dish TV networks to watch Iranian television news to learn the *truth* about Israel. They ignorantly condemn Israel and flatter the propaganda of radical extremists. Tragic. Apparently these same people are unaware of the intense brainwashing that goes on in Islam.

Search the Web for Arab, Iran and/or Palestinian TV shows/cartoons for kids and you will find these shocking titles and many more: "Hamas TV Show Teaches Kids to Kill Jews," *Jihad Watch.* "Palestinian" TV to "Kids: Christians and Jews are Inferior, Cowardly and Despised," exposed on *Atlas Shruggs.* "Palestinian Kids Raised for War," published by *World Net Daily.* "Hamas TV Children's Show Teaches Kids to Commit Terrorism," "Micky Mouse Teaches Kids to Commit Terrorism" http://www.youtube.com/watch?v=tzlFPm7bymY.
"Teaching the Next Generation to Hate":
 http://www.youtube.com/watch?v=Bra53uzgPDk.

Teaching the Next Generation to Hate, [is] a very disturbing, heart wrenching video. It depicts babies and toddlers dressed as suicide bombers and a kindergarten graduation ceremony—young boys dressed in military paraphernalia, waving green Hamas flags; some wearing masks, brandishing weapons, crawling on the floor—their weapons held high—as they imitate the Hamas military maneuvers, shouting: "Allah Akbar" (Praise be to Allah). One masked child holds a microphone enthusiastically asking these questions followed by the rest of the boys answering, shouting in unison:

"Who is your role model?" "The Prophet!" "What is your path?" "Jihad!" "What is your most lofty aspiration?" "Death for the sake of Allah!"

I suggest that those who are fast to condemn Israel and the Jewish people should begin to educate themselves. Watching the YouTube videos listed on the previous page would be a good place to start and of course reading this book thoroughly and the recommended resources.

Palestinian Mentors Associated with Willow Creek [Church] Association and Religious Left's War on Israel

Stakelbeck on Terror
By Jim Fletcher – Israel Watch
April 23, 2012

(As they are relevant to today's column, I recommend all readers pick up copies of two friends' books: Alex Grobman's, *License to Murder* and Michael Curtis's, *Should Israel Exist?* Each offers amazing information about the efforts to delegitimize Jews and Israel. Both are also available on Kindle. Highly, highly recommended—Jim).

My friend Erick Stakelbeck, a courageous reporter and TV host (CBN's "Stakelbeck on Terror") is superb at connecting the dots. He is also fearless, a much-needed trait in today's harrowing world.

Today he posted an article about the nefarious work of Media Matters, the left-wing watchdog group that targets Christians and Israel. Not surprisingly, Media Matters is close to the White House.

Part of Erick's research uncovered the following:

"It is common for news and commentary by the press to present viewpoints that tend to overly promote...a conservative, Christian-influenced ideology," the group said in its application for non-profit status with the IRS.

301

This is an absurd statement, and a good example of the brazenness of the left to peddle lies. It's quite obvious to anyone paying even the slightest attention that media don't "promote" conservative Christian worldview.

The opposite is true. David Brog, executive director of Christians United for Israel, thinks Media Matters' targeting of Christians is influenced by its (MM) anti-Israel bias.

Erick makes an important point about Media Matters' former senior foreign policy fellow, M.J. Rosenberg:

"Rosenberg routinely uses the label, 'Israel Firsters,' implying that American supporters put the interests of Israel above the United States. It's a charge commonly made by Neo-Nazis and anti-Semitic groups."

It is interesting to note that Media Matters promotes the same kind of rhetoric as that of the American religious left, particularly those who are calling themselves evangelicals. This is an ongoing story that will get much bigger, as more facts come to light regarding the players and agendas involved

There is plenty of evidence, for example, that Rick Warren has already aligned himself with a whole host of anti-Israel friends, in his purposeful drive toward pluralism. And he's been at it a long time. Readers will simply have to figure out if supporting Israel is reason enough to oppose what Warren is about.

In 2008, Rick Warren's Saddleback Community Church hosted presidential candidates Barack Obama and the Republican ringer, John McCain. Warren of course proposed a balanced set of questions, ranging from the environment to poverty—all softball issues in such a forum.

But the group he selected to help him come up with questions for the candidates was most revealing: Faith in Public Life. Self-described as "a strategy center for the faith community advancing faith in the public square as a powerful force for justice, compassion and the common good," this multi-denominational religious group was founded by, among others, Jim Wallis (Sojourners); and Bob Edgar (former head of the National Council of Churches).

Among the board members and advisers for Faith in Public Life: Elizabeth Letzler, member of the PCUSA's Mission Responsibility Through Investment committee and the Israel-Palestine Network (i.e., an Israel divestment proponent); Jim Winkler, General Secretary of the United Methodist Church's General Board of Church and Society—he also sits on the board (with Communist Party USA leader Judith LeBlanc) of the US Campaign to End the Israeli Occupation; and Dr. Nazir Khaja, chairman of Islamic Information Service.

One would have had to have been aware for some time (as I have been) of the anti-Israel views of people like Winkler—a key mover in United Methodist circles—and Mission Responsibility Through Investment committee and the Israel-Palestine Network (i.e., an Israel divestment proponent); Jim Winkler, General Secretary of the United Methodist Church's General Board of Church and Society—he also sits on the board (with Communist Party USA leader Wallis, in order to fully understand the implications of Warren working with them.

What we now have, you see, is a man who is perhaps the most identifiable evangelical in the world linking arms with avowed opponents of a sovereign Jewish state to administer its own defense against relentless terrorism. Fellow "evangelical" Brian McLaren also referenced recently on his blog: (/span>http://brianmclaren.net/archives/blog/proisraeli-and-propalestinian.html) the efforts of Aaron Niequist to be "Pro Israel and Pro Palestinian."

And who is Niequist?

He is the son-in-law of Bill and Lynne Hybels, founders of the monolithic Willow Creek Church outside Chicago. Willow Creek is a huge association of like-minded churches around the country. At 9,000 member churches—Hybels certainly has the attention of many thousands of evangelical Christians. And he and his wife were mentored by a Palestinian beginning in the 1970's, so their animus toward Israel is not new.

I'm going to make a bold statement, but one I think that is backed with common sense: It is not possible that those 9,000 churches do not share Bill and Lynne Hybels' attitudes about modern Israel.

In August 2011, Lynne Hybels hosted a "Summit Lunch" titled: "Leading toward Peace in Israel and Palestine." The tip-off of course that this was to be a left-wing gathering comes in the now ubiquitous use of the term "Palestine," as if they are describing a sovereign nation.

The main presenter was Dr. Gary Burge, a Wheaton College professor and author, whose anti-Israel bias goes way back. It is almost an afterthought to note that Rick Warren and Bill Hybels are chums. They share the same interests and goals.

In other words, what we now have me back to the beginning of this column, to point out that groups like Media Matters are no longer really New York-based groups (and thus far removed in every way from Middle America); they are ideological bedfellows of the leading Christian speakers and writers today.

Rick Warren's associations are the same in many respects as groups like Media Matters. What I've written is the tip of the iceberg in the new war on Israel from the Religious Left in America.

Watchmen like Erick Stakelbeck are heavily out-numbered by the above-mentioned individuals and groups, and more, but I still believe that personal courage and a passionate commitment to truth will win the day.

The important article you have just read gives a good overview of some of the problems with some who call themselves Evangelicals or Christians. Their anti-Semetic, anti-Israel stance is very disturbing and very anti-biblical. Do these "Christians" never read their Bibles? Israel is God's chosen nation. His Holy Book is filled with references to His beloved Israel—which He demonstrates through His promises and prophetic fulfillments of His Word. In chapter five and on page 257 I have already discussed some of the various **tendencies** and beliefs of "Christians" who convolute the Scriptures to suit their own agendas.

The Lord Gave the Land of Israel to the Jews Forever

Genesis 13:14-15

"And the LORD said to Abram, after Lot had separated from him: 'Lift your eyes now and look from the place where you are—northward, southward, eastward, and westward; for all the land which you see I give to you and your descendants forever.'"

Fatah's Top [Palestinian] Religious Authorty Calls for Genocide of Jews
By Itamar Marcus and Nan Jacques Zilberdik
Gatestone Institute January 16, 2012

Last week, the principal Palestinian Authority religious leader, the Mufti Muhammad Hussein, presented the killing of Jews by Muslims as a religious Islamic goal. At an event celebrating the 47th anniversary of the founding of Fatah, he cited the *Hadith* (Islamic tradition attributed to Muhammad) **saying that the Hour of Resurrection will not come until Muslims fight the Jews and kill them**:

"The Hour [of Resurrection] will not come until you fight the Jews.

The Jew will hide behind stones or trees.

Then the stones or trees will call:

'Oh Muslim, servant of Allah, there is a Jew behind me, come and kill him.'"

Palestinian Media Watch reported regularly during the PA terror campaign (Intifada, 2000-2005) on **the repeated use of this *Hadith* by PA clerics on official PA TV to motivate Palestinians to terror attacks, preaching that Muslims had an Islamic obligation to kill Jews.**

The fact that the Mufti quotes this now indicates that this may have remained part of the PA's religious establishment's teachings, even though it is less frequently promoted on PA TV.

The last time official PA TV broadcast a sermon during which this *Hadith* calling to kill Jews was quoted was in 2010.

The years of PA promotion of killing Jews and PA religious leaders' citing this *Hadith* to justify it, may have contributed to the high acceptance of it in PA society. A poll sponsored by the Israel Project last year found that 73% of Palestinians "believe" this *Hadith*. (July 2011, Greenberg Quinlan Rosner)

The moderator who introduced the Mufti at the Fatah event last week reiterated another Islamic belief; that the Jews are the descendants of apes and pigs:

"Our war with the descendants of the apes and pigs (i.e., Jews) is a war of religion and faith."

The Mufti did not distance himself from this hate statement that Islam is in a religious war with the Jews, but added to it that Islam's goal is to kill Jews.

There are numerous collections of *Hadith*, some of which are not accepted as reliable. However, the Mufti stressed that the Islamic belief that Jews will be killed by Muslims as a precursor to Resurrection, is an authentic Islamic belief because it appears in "the reliable" and trusted *Hadith* collections of Al-Bukhari and Muslim.

This Islamic tradition asserts that as the killing of Jews will progress, Jews will hide behind stones and trees, but even they will expose the Jews and call out: *"Oh Muslim, servant of Allah, there is a Jew behind me, come and kill him."* One tree however, called the *Gharqad*, will hide the Jews from the Muslims.

The Mufti in his talk at the Fatah event claimed that in response to this Islamic belief, Israelis have been planting *Gharqad* trees around their cities and towns, in order to have a place to hide from the Muslims who will be coming to kill them.

This is not the first time the Mufti has incited to hatred against Jews in the name of Islam. In a sermon at the al-Aqsa Mosque in 2010, he preached that the Jews are the "enemies of Allah."

The Mufti is appointed by PA Chairman Mahmoud Abbas. He voiced this latest hate speech that Jews are to be killed by Muslims, at an official Fatah celebration. Abbas is also the Chairman of Fatah.

Footnote
Emphasis added on pages 306 and 307.

Ancient Hatred: Understanding Iran's War on Jews
Erik Stakelbeck - www.cbn.com March 23, 2012

WASHINGTON - Iran's supreme leader recently said his country would help any Muslim nation or group that attacks Israel. He's called the Jewish state a cancerous tumor that will be cut out of the Middle East. With Iran's nuclear weapons program advancing daily, that goal may be in sight.

This view of Jews as sub-human sounds a lot like Adolf Hitler and the Nazis, but it goes back much further.

In author Andrew Bostom's book, *The Legacy of Islamic Antisemitism*, he describes Islam's early conquests of Jewish tribes in Arabia.

"Mohamme's frustrations in spreading his message were frequently recompensed by murderous attacks on the Jews," he told CBN News.

Bostom explained that Mohammed demonized Jews because they rejected him as a prophet.

"Mohammed himself invokes some of these themes," he said. "For example, one of the punishments of the Jews is their transformation into apes, or apes and pigs, the verses that are commonly heard now."

This "apes and pigs" imagery is found in Islam's core texts, like the Koran and hadiths. The most notorious is the following hadith, often quoted by al Qaeda, Hamas, and other Islamic terror groups.

"Judgment Day will come only when the Muslims fight the Jews and kill them, until the Jew hides behind the tree and the stone, and the tree and the stone say, 'Oh Muslim, oh servant of Allah, there is a Jew behind me, come and kill him.'"

In some verses of the Koran, Jews are referred to as "perverse," "evil," "greedy," and the "heirs of hell."

The Iranian regime takes these verses seriously, starting with the man who founded the Islamic Republic, the Ayatollah Khomeini.

"His image of wiping out the Jews was that all of the Muslims of the world should get together with a cup of water and simply wash it away. But again, annihilationism," Bostom said.

Today, Jews play a central role in the end time ideology of Iran's mullahs. They believe the Mahdi, or Islamic messiah, will return to earth, conquer Jerusalem, and massacre the Jewish inhabitants of Israel.

Former Iranian President Hashemi Rafsanjani said that while Israel is a one-bomb country, Iran and the Islamic world could survive a nuclear exchange with the Jewish state.

According to this view, the heavy losses would be worth it for the greater good of wiping Israel off the map.

Muslim Persecution of Christians

Muslim Persecution of Christians
GATESTONE INSTITUTE,
By Raymond Ibrahim March 16, 2012

A Pastor was attacked with acid and blinded in Uganda by Muslims screaming, "Allahu Akbar! ["Allah is Greater!"]

Half of Iraq's indigenous Christians are gone due to the unleashed forces of jihad, many of them fleeing to nearby Syria; yet, as the Assad regime comes under attack by al-Qaeda and others, the jihad now seeps into Syria, where Christians are experiencing a level of persecution unprecedented in the nation's modern history. Likewise, some 100,000 Christian Copts have fled their native Egypt since the overthrow of the Mubarak regime; and in northern regions of Nigeria, where the jihadi group Boko Haram has been slaughtering Christians; up to 95 percent of the Christian population has fled. Meanwhile, the "big news" concerning the Muslim world in the month of February (2012)—the news that flooded the mainstream media and had U.S. politicians, beginning with President Obama, flustered, angry, and full of regret—was that copies of the Koran in Afghanistan were burned by U.S. soldiers because imprisoned Muslim inmates were using them "to facilitate extremist communications."

The Muslim world and the Western news agencies have shown great outrage regarding the burning of the Koran (Quran), but little, if any concern whatsoever that the imprisoned Muslim inmates were methodically those Korans "to facilitate extremist communications!" The enemy was trying to use their Korans as communication tools to plot terror against U.S. troops, yet an apology is issued from the U.S. President!! Moreover, Muslims are free to pour acid on pastors, break crosses and desecrate graves and there is no cry of outrage seemingly from anywhere (see next page).

To read the full article visit:
http://www.gatestoneinstitute.org/2949/muslim-persecution-of-christians-february-2012

Islam's Tradition of Breaking the Cross (Excerpt)
GATESTONE INSTITUTE
By Mark Durie March 9, 2012

In the recent destruction of Commonwealth war graves in Benghazi, Libya (YouTube Video), you can see not just the desecration of graves, but attacks on crosses.

The radical Muslims who are kicking over and smashing headstones marked with crosses (and one with a Star of David), also took pains to demolish a tall "Cross of Sacrifice" standing at the edge of the cemetery.

This was no "furious mob" on a "rampage," as a Daily Mail report put it. Nor was there any evidence in what they were saying that they were angry or reacting to Koran burning by the US military.

The men are methodically, deliberately, and in an organized fashion, going about destroying crosses and objects marked with crosses. Their mood seems happy.

Every now and again the cry *Allahu Akbar* rings out, or a chuckle of joy. They pass comments on the graves as they kick them over:

"Break the cross that belongs to those," "This is the grave of a Christian," and, "This tomb has a cross on it: a *kaffir* [disbeliever]."

Escalating Crack Down on Iranian Christians

IRAN - Raids on house churches and mass arrests of Christians in Ahwaz, Shiraz, Esfahan, and Kermanshah signify that a renewed crackdown on the church may be underway in Iran.

March 8, 2012 Iran (**Mohabat News**) - The Islamic Republic of Iran has intensified its crackdown on Iranian Christians during recent weeks. This has resulted in the arrest of a number of Christians in Ahwaz, Shiraz, Esfahan and Kermanshah. In this regard, a reporter of Hrana (Human Rights activists' news agency) has conducted an interview with the head of Iranian Christian news agency, Mohabat News, Saman Kamvar.

To read full article visit:
http://www.persecution.org/2012/03/12/escalating-crack-down-on-iranian-christians/

Iran Orders Pastors to Serve Prison Terms

Worthy News - **Posted on November 29, 2011**
By Stefan J. Bos, Worthy News Correspondent

TEHRAN, IRAN (Worthy News) -- Iran has ordered three evangelical house church pastors to report to prison within a month and serve lengthy jail terms on charges linked to their Christian activities, a well-informed source told Worthy News late Tuesday, November 29. Pastors Parviz Khalaj, Mohammed William Belyad and Behrouz Sadegh Khandjani, of the church of Iran movement, are due to start serving their sentences in the southwestern city of Shiraz in "30 days" said Jason DeMars, director of advocacy group Present Truth Ministries, which has close contacts with Iranian Christians.

"Parviz has two convictions for crimes against the order and is to serve two years. William Belyad was previously convicted of crimes against the order and sentenced to five years in prison. He will [receive an additional one year] to serve a total of 6 years. Behrouz is expected to serve one year in prison," on related charges he added. To read full article visit: http://www.worthynews.

311

Gaza Christians Protest Forced Conversions
By Tzippe Barrow - CBN News - Tuesday, July 17, 2012

JERUSALEM, Israel - Christians in the Hamas-controlled Gaza Strip are taking a public stand against forced conversion to Islam. In an unusual public demonstration, men and women gathered in front of the Church of Saint Porphyrius Monday to protest the abduction and forced conversion of members of their congregation. *YNet* reported that the newly converted Muslims, al-Amash, a 25-year-old man, and Hiba Abu Dawoud, 31, a mother with three children, are staying with a Muslim official for "protection" from their Christian families, according to Gaza police.

"This is not the first time this has happened. In the past, there were cases involving women, whole families, and younger men," Nabanat said. "But there has never before been such a public protest by Christians, which means they've reach the point of terrible desperation." Generally, the pattern is the same:

"There would be a sudden disappearance of the individual(s) for an extended period of time, with no news or no information about them," Nabanat said. "Then comes a sudden announcement that they've converted to Islam. Afterward, they may reappear with armed people around them as "protection."

To read full article on forced conversion of Arab Christians visit:
http://www.cbn.com/cbnnews/insideisrael/2012/July/Gaza-Christians-Protest-Forced-Conversions/

The Mexican-Islamic Connection

Terrorist Group Setting Up Operations Near Border
Hezbollah Considered to Be More
Advanced Than Al-Qaida - May 4, 2011

SAN DIEGO - A terrorist organization whose home base is in the Middle East has established another home base across the border in Mexico. "They are recognized by many experts as the "A" team of Muslim terrorist organizations," a former U.S. intelligence agent told 10News.

The former agent, referring to Shi'a Muslim terrorist group Hezbollah, added, "They certainly have had successes in big-ticket bombings." Some of the group's bombings include the U.S. embassy in Beirut and Israeli embassy in Argentina. However, the group is now active much closer to San Diego.

"We are looking at 15 or 20 years that Hezbollah has been setting up shop in Mexico," the agent told 10News. Since the Sept. 11, 2001 terrorist attacks, U.S. policy has focused on al-Qaida and its offshoots.

"They are more shooters than thinkers ... it's a lot of muscles, courage, desire but not a lot of training," the agent said, referring to al-Qaida. Hezbollah, he said, is far more advanced. "Their operators are far more skilled ... they are the equals of Russians, Chinese or Cubans," he said. "I consider Hezbollah much more dangerous in that sense because of strategic thinking; they think more long-term."

Hezbolah has operated in South America for decades and then Central America, along with their sometime rival, sometime ally Hamas. Now, the group is blending into Shi'a Muslim communities in Mexico, including Tijuana. Other pockets along the U.S.-Mexico border region remain largely unidentified as U.S. intelligence agencies are focused on the drug trade.

"They have had clandestine training in how to live in foreign hostile territories," the agent said. The agent, who has spent years deep

313

undercover in Mexico, said Hezbollah is partnering with drug organizations, but which ones is not clear at this time. He told 10News the group receives cartel cash and protection in exchange for Hezbollah expertise. "From money laundering to firearms training and explosives training," the agent said.

For example, he tracked, along with Mexican intelligence, two Hezbollah operatives in safe houses in Tijuana and Durango "I confirmed the participation of cartel members as well as other Hezbollah individuals living and operating out of there," he said.

Tunnels the cartels have built that cross from Mexico into the U.S. have grown increasingly sophisticated. It is a learned skill, the agent said, which points to Hezbollah's direct involvement. "Where are the knowledgeable tunnel builders? Certainly in the Middle East," he said.

Why have Americans not heard more about Hezbollah's activities happening so close to the border? "If they really wanted to start blowing stuff up, they could do it," the agent said. According to the agent, the organization sees the U.S. as their "cash cow," with illegal drug and immigration operations.

Many senior Hezbollah leaders are wealthy businessmen, the agent said. "The money they are sending back to Lebanon is too important right now to jeopardize those operations," he said.

The agent said the real concern is the group's long-term goal of radicalizing Muslim communities. "They're focusing on developing … infiltrating communities within North America," the agent told 10News.

Notice on the following page the Mexican people, mostly young children, standing by watching the parade of armed, in-your-face Islamic terrorists marching in a Mexican neighborhood. The radical thug at the head of the group is carrying a Soviet made RPG (rocket propelled grenade). It looks like some of the observers are photographing the alarming incident with their cell phone cameras.

Hezbollah Hooks Up with Mexican Drug Cartels

Business Insider – By Grace Wyler | July 14, 2011

(AP)

Islamic terrorist groups are setting up shop in Mexico and forming alarming ties with the country's brutal drug cartels, according to a 2010 internal memo from the Tucson Police Department. The memo, leaked by the hacker group LulzSec as part of its Arizona Department of Public Safety hack, warns that Hezbollah has established operations—and a large arms stockpile—in Mexico.

As evidence, it points to the 2010 Tijuana arrest of Hezbollah militant Jameel Nasr, who was allegedly tasked with establishing a Hezbollah network in Mexico and South America. The memo also recalls the April 2009 arrest of Jamal Yousef in New York, which exposed a huge cache of assault rifles, hand grenades, explosives and anti-tank munitions.

According to Yousef, the weapons were stored in Mexico after being smuggled from Iraq by members of Hezbollah. The memo warns that consequences of partnerships between Hezbollah and Mexico's drug partnerships could be disastrous for Mexico's drug war, given

Hezbollah's advanced weapons capabilities—specifically their expertise with improvised explosive devices (IEDs). It notes that some Mexican criminal organizations have started using small IEDs and car bombs, a marked change in tactics that indicates a relationship with Islamic militants.

Partnerships between Mexican organized crime and Islamic militants are mutually beneficial—and therefore terrifying. The cartels are able to gain smuggling and weapons expertise, as well as access to cheap heroin from Afghanistan and Iran. The terrorists benefit from Mexico's drug war lawlessness and its porous border with their primary target: The United States.

Read more:
http://articles.businessinsider.com/2011-07-14/politics/30060540_1_islamic-militants-hezbollah-cartels#ixzz1pJiaFFu0.

Islamic Terrorists Plot to Attack U.S. from Mexico

Radical Islamists | December 10, 2011
Law Enforcement Examiner
Jim Kouri

Terrorists from several Middle Eastern groups have infiltrated Latin American countries -- especially Mexico -- in order to plot and carry out attacks against the United States, according to an alarming exposé broadcast this week by the world's largest Spanish news network. While the news media in Latin American countries are covering this ongoing story, the U.S. media is delivering scant coverage -- or no coverage at all -- a U.S. law enforcement commander told the *Law Enforcement Examiner*. Univision, a popular multi-national Spanish-language TV network, this week aired a very disturbing documentary titled: "La Amenaza Irani," (Iranian Threat), the documentary uses undercover, never-before-seen video footage to illustrate how Iran's growing political, economic and military ties to Latin America threaten U.S. security, according to a blog published by the Washington DC-based watchdog group, Judicial Watch. According to the JW blogger the Univision documentary is the result of a seven-month investigative report in which college-aged Mexicans infiltrated diplomatic circles in Mexico to obtain recordings that prove diplomats from Iran, Venezuela and Cuba planned a cybernetic attack against the White House, FBI, Pentagon and US nuclear plants. Continue reading on Examiner: Breaking: Islamic terrorists plot to attack U.S. from Mexico - National Law Enforcement Examiner.com.

Iran Terror Network Inside
U.S. and Western Hemisphere

Congressional report: Iran has expanded its terror network inside the US - Special to WorldTribune.com
Friday, March 23, 2012

WASHINGTON - Iran has established a network that could stage major attacks in the United States, a congressional report said. The House Homeland Security Committee has asserted that Iran built a network throughout the United States. In a report, the committee said the Iranian-sponsored Hezbullah is believed to have been directing hundreds of agents for a range of operations.

There is general consensus among dozens of experts as well as current and former law enforcement and intelligence officials interviewed by the Majority Investigative Staff that Hizbullah is the most capable of flipping a U.S.-based fundraising cell into a lethal terror force," the report said. Former drug enforcement official, Michael Braun, said Hezbollah and members of the Iranian Revolutionary Guard are working with cartels. "They are now operating and working in close proximity and collaborating with Mexican and Colombian drug trafficking cartels, not only in the Western Hemisphere, but other locations such as Guinea Bissau in West Africa," Braun said. To read more visit:
http://www.voanews.com/english/news/usa/143709036.html.

40,000 Iranian Agents in Western Hemisphere
July 10, 2012 World Net Daily - Reza Kahlil - http://w.wnd.com

[Excerpts]: Iran has expanded its terror network and now hidden in Latin

317

America, awaiting 'operations' against the US according to a former Iranian official who has witnessed the regime's crimes against humanity inside Iran and has knowledge of its terror network targeting the West. In interviews with the opposition outside Iran, the official revealed that more than 40,000 of the regime's security, intelligence and propaganda forces successfully have been placed over time in Bolivia, Brazil, Guatemala, Nicaragua, Ecuador and Venezuela These forces consist mostly of former interrogators, torturers and security forces along with the members of the Quds Forces. The Revolutionary Guards' intelligence division runs operations out of mosques, which include recruitment, reconnaissance and transfer of arms and cash.

Introduction to the Resource Guides

The best way to locate suggested material is by searching the Internet by book or DVD title. Your local bookstore will carry a number of these items. Some of these great books are now out of print but copies are still available if you search. At the time of publishing all website links are working. However, we cannot control changes. Links are subject to change and are out of our control. If you cannot access the website by typing in the link, try typing in the predominant title of the link. You will find some excellent information on these websites!

Disclaimer: We cannot be in agreement with every detail and point of view by individuals presented in the recommended material and throughout this text. For example, we may have quoted some information from part of a book, but we may not agree with other chapters in that same book. Or some of the information on some of the recommended websites may be in keeping with our beliefs, yet we may not in agreement with some other information offered on the same website.

—Friends of Yeshua Ministries

Appendix A

Resources Particularly Good for: Our Jewish Friends—Valuable for Everyone.

From Time Immemorial: The Origins of the Arab-Jewish Conflict Over Palestine, John Peters

Myths and Facts: A Guide to the Arab-Israeli Conflict - published by American-Israeli Cooperative Enterprise (AICE).

The Legacy of Islamic Antisemitism - In his book, Andrew Bostom discloses Islam's early conquests of Jewish tribes in Arabia and much more.

Blindsided: The Radical Islamic Conquest, an important book written by Egyptian born, Dr. Michael Youseff, senior pastor of *Leading the Way* television and radio ministries.

Jesus in the Hebrew Scriptures: The Identity of the Messiah, Meno Kalisher - The author is a Jerusalem native and pastor of the Jerusalem Assembly—House of Redemption in Jerusalem, Israel. An informative book filled with great insights.

The Messiah of the Tanach, Targums and the Talmud, F. Kenton Beshore - An excellent presentation (booklet) of important Scriptures and information relating to truth of Yeshua the Messiah. This booklet was written *especially* for Jews, but should be read by everyone to gain a better understanding of these key Scriptures.

All the Messianic Prophecies of the Bible - Herbert Lockyer - An excellent book. Discover how Yeshua the Messiah fulfilled over 300 hundred Bible prophecies. Learn how prophecies prove the truth of Christianity.

A Journey of Faith From Shema and Shadows Unto Shiloh and Shalom - Philip Sawilowsky - The author's testimony; Philip accepted Yeshua the Messiah at the age of 16. He was raised in an orthodox Jewish home.

319

When his parents learned of his new faith, they told him to return to synagogue or leave home. Trusting the Lord to take care of him, Philip bravely left home rather than renounce the truth of Yeshua the Messiah. http://olivetreeministry.org/index.html.

Trapped in Hitler's Hell: A Young Jewish Girl Discovers the Messiah's Faithfulness in the Midst of the Holocaust - Anita Dittman with Jan

Through Hebrew Eyes, A Messianic Journey - DVD with Amir Tsarfati - Great for understanding why the Jewish festivals are celebrated and how the traditional Jewish perspective is transformed into a living hope and promise. Available at Koinonia House: http://khouse.org/ .

The Last War: The Failure of the Peace Process and the Coming Battle for Jerusalem, David Allen Lewis with Jim Fletcher.

Messianic Jews Why Should I Care? - DVD - Excellent documentary filmed mostly in Israel, interviews with Jewish believers on how the Ruach Ha Kodesh (Holy Spirit) is touching their lives in the Holy Land. Available at: http://www.jeremiahfilms.com/.

The Twisted Cross, Joseph J. Carr - Exposé on the occult religion of Hitler and the New Age Nazism of the Third Reich.

Israel: A Nation Is Born - DVD - An excellent five-part series presented by former Israeli Foreign Minister, Abba Eban. It chronicles his recollections of and his part in, the creation of the State of Israel in 1948, the subsequent conflicts, including the 1967 Six Day War and the 1973 Yom Kippur War; the Egyptian--Israeli peace treaty and the events of the last decade. Many other excellent DVDs are available through this website: http://www.jeremiahfilms.com/products/INBDVD

The Search - Lorna Simcox - This book is about how the Jewish author came to receive the Jewish Messiah, Yeshua Ha Mashiach, as her Savior. It is a must-read for settling questions about the true Messiah of Israel, available through Friends of Israel Gospel Ministry.

As America Has Done to Israel - John McTernan

The Case for Jesus the Messiah—Incredible Prophecies that Prove God Exists by Dr. John Ankerberg and Dr. John Weldon. This 25part teaching (PDF) is filled with undeniable evidence for the truth of Yeshua, the Messiah. Be sure to visit:
http://www.jashow.org/wiki/index.php?title=The_Case_for_Jesus_the_ Messiah_-_Incredible_Prophecies_that_Prove_God_Exists

http://www.hopeofisrael.net/ - *Hope of Israel* - Jewish outreach. An important resource if you are a Jew or a Gentile. **Includes a good testimonial section, including rabbis who have come to realize Yeshua Ha Mashiach *is* the prophesied Messiah**. Great articles are provided, up-to-date information about Israel. This site loads very slowly, but it is well worth the wait.

http://contenderministries.org/ - Important website about end times, false religions, New Age deception, prophecy. Enlightening articles and much more; excellent resources all pertaining to important biblical studies; Old Testament Messianic prophecies fulfilled by Jesus are cited.

http://www.jnewswire.com/ - *Jerusalem Newswire* is comprised of Bible-believing Christian journalists committed to reporting important Israel/Middle East news stories. This much needed news service operates out of Jerusalem, Israel.

http://www.jnnnews.com/archives.htm - *Jerusalem News Network* -
A very thorough website with information and news reports especially relating to Israel and the Middle East; featured videos.

http://www.camera.org/ - Committee for Accuracy in Middles East Reporting in America

http://www.honestreporting.com/ - *Honest Reporting*: A very popular, excellent UK-based organization dedicated to reporting the truth and defending Israel. This group monitors the media and exposes cases of bias. News agencies are contacted drawing issues of bias to their attention, and 'request change' is administered. This has been very effective holding accountable those who falsely report issues regarding Israel, the Middle East, and various strategic international matters.

http://www.foi.org/ - *Friends of Israel Gospel Ministry, Inc.* This site offers wonderful, educational material. A *free* one-year trial magazine subscription for their excellent magazine titled: *Israel My Glory* is available.

http://www.emetonline.org/about.htm 1 - *Endowment for Middle East Truth* - Excellent articles and news on pressing topics relating to the Middle East, especially in relation to Israel.

http://www.prophecymatters.com/ Jim Fletcher, director of *Prophecy Matters*, is especially well versed in current issues relating to Israel and the Middle East. Jim writes for a variety of publications including: *The Jerusalem Post, WorldNetDaily, OneNewsNow*, and *Israel Watch* which is part of the *Rapture Ready* website. You just have to love Jim for his very intelligent, sharp-witted articles.

http://www.elshaddaiministries.us/ - Pastor Mark Blitz - *El Shaddai Ministries* is a Hebrew Roots Resource and Teaching Ministry. Pastor Blitz states, "Our congregation is faithful to salvation by grace through faith as revealed in the Torah." Reports from Israel; archives of audio and video messages and special events; a very interesting website.

http://www.jihadwatch.org/ - Robert Spencer - Director of *Jihad Watch*, a program of the David Horowitz Freedom Center. This website offers up-to-date information on radical Islam's activities worldwide.

http://www.jewsforjesus.org/welcome - *Jews for Jesus* is a popular organization dedicated to evangelism; mostly run by Jewish believers. This is an excellent website with great articles and much more.

http://www.cjfm.org/ - *CJF Ministries* - Reaching Jewish people with the Gospel of Messiah - A popular radio ministry, great educational material. This is one of my favorite radio shows and websites.

Appendix B

Additional Websites

See pages 386-387 for some excellent links to assist you in your Bible study.

http://www.probe.org/site/c.fdKEIMNsEoG/b.4213839/k.AF17/Probe Ministries.htm - *Probe Ministries* - An excellent website. Exceptional articles relating to cultural issues for all ages including: Cults and World Religions, Theology and Philosophy, Faith and Science, Faith and Politics, Faith and Culture, important Current Issues. Visit the online store for noteworthy books, DVDs, popular radio program online archives.

http://raptureready.com/ - *Rapture Ready* - Todd Strandberg, founder and computer genius/author; weekly commentaries: "Nearing Midnight," "Dear Esther" and much more. An outstanding site for finding up-to-date daily news reports with a large selection of articles on various topics, especially in relation to end-times prophecy; very popular prophecy website, ranked number one in the world; very pro-Israel.

http://www.oneplace.com/ministries/ - This is an outstanding, excellent website offering 65,000 on demand free broadcasts with great Christian radio and Internet ministries; articles, a great Bible Study Tools section, a top-notch site; downloads. This is most definitely a must-explore website with excellent resources.

http://worldviewweekend.com/ - Brannon Howse, president and founder of *Worldview Weekend Foundation* - Interesting, excellent website packed with very important information: Radio, video, television, commentaries, music, interviews and bookstore. The focus is on spiritual discernment, biblical integrity and world socio-economic issues.

http://www.crossroad.to/ - *Kjos Ministries* - Berit Kjos - An excellent website unmasking false religions and dangerous New Age practices.

http://www.letusreason.org/BookRdir.htm - *Let Us Reason Together Ministries* - Great articles on cults including: L.D.S. Mormonism,

Jehovah's Witnesses and other aberrant teachings within the Christian church.

http://home.earthlink.net/~ronrhodes/Downloadable.html.
Dr. Ron Rhodes, *Reasoning from the Scriptures Ministry*: Excellent, must-read information on important very current, topics very relevant today: Recovering from the Recovery Movement, Is Reincarnation Biblical? Close Encounters of the Celestial Kind, Evaluating Today's Angel Craze, Confusion in Christian Music, The Debate over Feminist Theology and much more. Thoroughly research this entire website. You will also find a list of some exceptional, must-read books by Dr. Rhodes.

http://www.understandthetimes.org/ - Roger Oakland is the founder and president of *Understand the Times*, a great in-depth resource on topics relating to these last days, dedicated to worldwide evangelism. This is an excellent resource for exposing false religious systems including the emergent church movement.

http://www.justforcatholics.org/ - A great website, especially good for Catholics with the focus on salvation and other Catholic-related issues; also good for Protestants.

http://www.religiouscounterfeits.org/nas.htm - A very interesting, very informative site on religious counterfeits and New Age deception, including the Catholic connection to the New Age god of pantheism.

http://www.ericbarger.com/ - Eric Barger's, *Take A Stand Ministries*. Downloads available - An online store with great (DVDs, CDs, and books). An outstanding website loaded with vital information under these titles: Cults, Spiritual Warfare, Halloween, The New Age Movement, The Occult and Witchcraft (including Harry Potter and *The Lord of the Rings*), Islam and World Religions, Today's Music and Entertainment, Biblical Apologetics, Prayer and Christian Living, Troubling Trends in the Church, Environmentalism and Prophecy, Globalism, Roman Catholicism, and more.

The John Ankerberg Show - http://www.jashow.org/. A must visit, outstanding website packed with extensive information ranging from Christian apologetics to current social issues, world issues, cults, politics, prophecy and much more. Include this very important site in your daily/weekly Web surfing routine.

http://www.thebereancall.org/ - *The Berean Call* - Dave Hunt and T.A. McMahon - Excellent, reliable website to visit for spiritual discernment issues, including book reviews and up-to-date issues relating to spiritual discernment and biblical integrity.

Behold Israel - Amir Tsarfati, Jewish believer, inspiring speaker, Bible teacher (Israeli website). Be sure to check both links. The first is primarily for news and current events in and around Israel. The second link: *Behold Israel's* App for iPhone and Android available free of charge.

http://beholdisrael.com/app/index.php/c_main/main,
http://www.beholdisrael.com/

Creation Truth and the Evolution Myth

Hope for Today - Dr. David Hocking - Bible teaching ministry, including daily radio shows. **The best teaching I have ever heard on Creation and the myth of evolution:** *Genesis Volume One* is available through his website at: http://www.davidhocking.org/ or call 1-800-752-4253. Look under the *Old Testament Studies* in the catalog section on the website to locate: *Genesis Volume One,* CD or MP3 Download. Share it with everyone you know. He also has other valuable information from news articles related to Israel and prophecy, and a large selection of Bible based teachings offered in various formats.

Without Form and Void - A Study of the Meaning of Genesis, Arthur Custance; a must-read book to understand Creation. Please visit the excellent website which contains the works of Arthur Custance (1910-1985) who wrote extensively on the links between academic knowledge and the tenets of Christianity. These works have influenced Christians worldwide, and his center continues to promote his vision to bring together the established facts of Science and the revealed truths of Scripture. http://www.custance.org/.

God of Wonders DVD - This amazing DVD takes us through the creation story and the gospel with spectacular photography, and tremendous facts about God's handiwork in creation including the examination of the incredible complexity of DNA. This is an awesome DVD everyone should have in their personal library. You can also download an excellent study guide for the *God of Wonders* DVD to use as a teaching tool: http://www.christiancinema.com/downloads/GodWonders.pdf.

Creation in Symphony the Evidence (3 DVD series), *Creation in Symphony the Model*, the scientific basis for the literal six-day creation (3 hour series) - Dr. Carl Baugh. He also has a Creation evidence museum in Texas and more excellent resources available through his great website: http://www.creationevidence.org/.

Appendix C

More Recommended Books and DVDs

The Strongest Strong's Exhaustive Concordance of the Bible - James Strong LL.D., S.T.D., S.T.D. Fully Revised and Corrected by John R. Kohlenberger III and James A. Swanson.

Recommended Bible Versions: The King James, New King James, and the New American Standard. It is good to use these three Bibles along with the 1901 American Standard Version for cross-reference study.

Holman Illustrated Bible Dictionary, 2003 Edition

Holy Bible Complete King James Version Bible on DVD - Alexander Scourby

Liddell and Scott: *An Intermediate Greek-English Lexicon*

Exegetical Fallacies - D.A. Carson

Bauer, Arndt, Gingrich and Danker: *A Greek Lexicon of the New Testament and Other Early Christian Literature*

Louw and Nida: *Greek-English Lexicon of the New Testament Based on Semantic Domains*

The Interlinear Greek-English New Testament: the Nestle Greek Text with a literal English Translation. London: Samuel Bagster and Sons, 1958. Alfred Marshall.

Evidence the Bible Is True from Archeology, Science and Prophecy - CD Rom - Roger Oakland

God in My Corner - A Spiritual Memoir by George Forman, with Ken Abraham - Inspiring, encouraging and motivational. How God became number one for the former Olympic gold medallist, two-time heavyweight world boxing champion, turned pastor.

Absolute Surrender, Andrew Murray - An important book, a Christian classic taking the reader into a deeper Christian maturity and understanding of God's plan for us; a reminder to become absolutely dependent on Christ and not ourselves.

It's the End of the World as We Know It (and I Feel Fine), by Jim Fletcher - "Despite the mockery of the Bible today, we are in fact living in the last days of world history, as outlined in the Hebrew and Christian Scriptures: God has plainly revealed Himself in the Bible." A great read with clever, innovative reflections from the talented author.

The Last Generation, Current Prophecy, World Events, and the End Times, by Jim Simmons

A Cup of Trembling: Jerusalem and Bible Prophecy - Dave Hunt

Another Gospel, by Ruth A. Tucker - Excellent information on cults and world religions that twist the truth of the Bible: Mormonism Jehovah's Witnesses, Christian Science, New Thought and Unity, Scientology, the New Age movement and much more.

The Kingdom of the Cults, Walter Martin - An outstanding classic on the teachings of the cults in our age. Everyone should own a copy of this book.

Nephilim Stargates: The Year 2012 and the Return of the Watchers - Thomas Horn - This is the book to read to gain an understanding about the Nephilim.

The Great Harpazo Deception: The Real Story of UFOs, Stephen Yulish

Alien Encounters: The Secret behind the UFO Phenomenon, Chuck Missler and Mark Eastman

Politics, Prophecy and the Supernatural: The Coming Great Deception and the Luciferian End Game, L.A. Marzulli

Psycho Babble: The Failure of Modern Psychology—and the Biblical Alternative - Richard Ganz. This excellent book exposes the overrated and failed social strategies of secular psychology. The Bible and a true relationship with Jesus the Messiah, Jesus the Redeemer, is the ultimate answer to psychological and emotional issues. The secular alternative is nothing but a band-aid with very short-term results—if any, while disregarding the truth of Christ and the total sufficiency of His healing grace.

Perilous Pursuits, Joseph M. Stowell - A great book that delves into the obsession with significance, with the **human dilemma—obsession with self.**

Deceptive Diagnosis: When Sin Is Called Sickness - David M. Tyler. Kurt P. Grady and Ed Bulkley. Another great book on problems with psychology and psychiatry, especially addressing moral and spiritual issues enabled by secular professionals; labeling morally bankrupt behavior as illness rather than what it really is: sin. Scripture is very strong on not seeking "counsel" from non-biblical sources, for this very reason (Colossians 2:8).

The Fleecing of Christianity - Jackie Alnor - A good book exposing deception within Christian circles including "Christian" television.

Prince of Darkness Antichrist and the New World Order - Grant R. Jeffrey - One of the best books on the coming Antichrist.

Faith Undone, Roger Oakland - Exposing the dangers of the emergent church movement grounded in age-old mystical approach; a highly deceptive teaching leading to Roman Catholicism and interfaith perspectives -- pointing toward the coming One World ecumenical religious system of Revelation 17.

Know Thine Enemy: A Guide to Intelligent Deception - Connie A. Hunt - Learn about the demonic forces behind all forms of the paranormal, and the author's journey from involvement with the occult to the saving grace of Jesus Christ.

A Twist of Faith, Berit Kjos - Especially good for women involved in the Goddess, feminist myths that have replaced biblical fact.

Beyond Seduction, Dave Hunt - A thorough discussion of the biblical and historical view of Christian teachings within the church. Also addressing meditation, the proper view of the self, faith, divine revelations, prayer, healing, and psychological teachings.

Another Jesus Calling - Warren Smith - The author's examination and warning about a very dangerous and deceptive popular book titled, *Jesus Calling* by Sarah Young, which is steeped in New Age lies and promotes another Jesus, and not the biblical Jesus.

The New Evangelicalism - Paul Smith

Angels of Deceit: The Masterminds behind Religious Deceptions - Richard Lee and Ed Hindson

A Time of Departing: How Ancient Mystical Practices are Uniting Christians with the World's Religions, Ray Yungen - Exposing the truth about the dangerous "Spiritual Formation" movement, also known as Contemplative Spirituality, anchored in mysticism and the occult.

The New Face of Mystical Spirituality: Contemplative Prayer - DVD by Ray Yungen exposes the dangers of "contemplative prayer."

For Many Shall Come in My Name - Important book on spiritual deception infiltrating all aspects of society by Ray Yungen.

Queen of All: The Marian Apparitions' Plan to Unite all Religions under the Roman Catholic Church, Jim Tetlow and Roger Oakland

One Minute After You Die - Erwin Lutzer

The Gospel According to Rome: Comparing Catholic Tradition and the Word of God, by James McCarthy.

A Woman Rides the Beast: The Roman Catholic Church and the Last Days, by Dave Hunt - An excellent exposé.

Entertaining Spirits Unaware: The End Times Occult Invasion - David Benoit and Eric Barger - Book or DVD - Excellent detailed biblical information concerning the Modern Witchcraft Movement, Necromancy, Channelers, Psychics, Magic. Especially important for parents, a must-read for everyone, and why EVERY parent should be concerned about Harry Potter. Included are the dangers of occult themed entertainment promotions (Yu-Gi-Oh, Pokémon, Halloween, UFOs, Harry Potter, and more). Important information on the rise of the: Cult of Relativism.

Disarming the Powers of Darkness: What Every Christian Parent Needs to Know About the Occult - DVD - David Benoit

Fourteen Things Witches Hope Parents Never Find Out, by David Benoit - An important book for everyone.

Under the Spell of Mother Earth, by Berit Kjos - An excellent book.

Hidden Dangers in Harry Potter - DVD - Steve Wohlberg *Halloween: Invitation to the Occult?* - CD or MP3 Download - Chuck Missler

Harry Potter: Witchcraft Repackaged: Making Evil Look Innocent - DVD by Caryl Productions.

Deceived by the New Age - Will Baron, A true story, a shocking and enlightening book.

Deceived on Purpose: The New Age Implications of the Purpose-Driven Church, by Warren Smith.

A Wonderful Deception and the Light that Was Dark, by Warren Smith

Redefining Christianity - Bob De Waay

The Real Jesus vs. the Counterfeits - Eric Barger - An excellent teaching on how religions/cults outside the true teachings of the Bible speak about a "Jesus" that is not the real Jesus of the Bible, but rather *a counterfeit Jesus.* Many, sincere, good people are deceived by the imposters. Those following a "different Jesus" are without a Savior (Jesus Christ) and are headed for an eternal torment.

Hath God Said? - Another great book by Eric Barger. Why the Bible is reliable, inspired and infallible. Anyone in doubt about the truth of God's Word should read this book.

Universalism: Is Everyone Already Saved? - Eric Barger shows why the biblical truths of salvation through Jesus Christ alone, the absolute need for a regenerating, "born-again" experience, and the fact that eternal and unending separation from God awaits all who reject salvation through Jesus Christ's sacrificial death.

Is Your Church New Age, Emergent of Christian? - Eric Barger - Explore the differences in doctrine and theology of the different types of so-called Christian churches in the United States today, some of which are Christian in name only (DVD or CD).

The Death of Discernment: How The Shack Became the #1 Bestseller in Christianity by Eric Barger - An extremely important exposé of how unbiblical doctrines contained in the best seller, *The Shack* has deceived countless numbers of Christians and seekers of truth. *The Shack* marks an unparalleled lack of discernment within Christianity.

Global Warming and the Creator's Plan, by Jay Auxy and Dr. William Curtiss - Excellent information on the myth of "man-induced global warming."

Global Warming: A Scientific and Biblical Exposé *of Climate Change* DVD - Dr. Larry Vardiman, and many other scientists. This is an excellent presentation addressing the distortions behind the Global Warming agenda.

Your Eternal Reward: Triumphs and *Tears at the Judgment Seat of Christ* - Erwin Lutzer.

Appendix D

Earthquakes—Increase in Frequency and Intensity

The following excerpts are from a *World Net Daily* article titled: "Japan Today Jerusalem Tomorrow" by Joel Richardson, posted online on March 14, 2011:

> Elsewhere, Jesus told us that among the signs of his return would be earthquakes. But the primary analogy that Jesus used to describe the last days earthquakes were birth contractions, which we all know are universally characterized by a progressive increase in both frequency and intensity:

> > "There will be famines and earthquakes in various places. All these are the beginning of birth pains" (Matthew 24:7-8).

> With all of this in mind, it is fascinating to take note of some astounding statistics that were brought to my attention last year by my friend, Pastor Cecil Boswell, from Nashville, Tenn. Pastor Boswell has spent a lot of time reviewing and calculating statistics from the U.S. Geological Survey. By analyzing the records of ancient earthquakes as well as every earthquake in modern times that registered a 7.0 or higher on the Richter scale, the picture that emerges is portentous indeed.

> From 1 A.D. to 1800 there were approximately 28 major earthquakes recorded in history. This results in an average of one major earthquake approximately every 60 years.

> From 1801-1900 there were approximately 31 earthquakes 7.0 or higher. This results in one major earthquake approximately every 3.2 years.

> From 1901 to 2000 there were 222 major earthquakes 7.0 or higher. This results in an average of one major earthquake every 6 months.

From 2000 to 2003 there were approximately 59 earthquakes of 7.0 or higher. This results in approximately one major earthquake every 24 days. This brings us to recent times. One of the most notable major earthquakes was in Bam, Iran, on Dec. 26, 2003. Exactly one year later, Dec. 26, 2004, Sumatra, Indonesia, experienced another massive earthquake and a subsequent devastating tsunami. Between these two earthquakes, more than 330,000 lives were lost.

From 2004 to 2007, there were 56 major earthquakes 7.0 or higher. This results in an average of one major earthquake every 25 days.

In 2008, there were 12 major earthquakes 7.0 or higher. This results in an average of one major earthquake every 30 days.

In 2009, there were 17 major earthquakes 7.0 or higher. This results in an average of one major earthquake every 20 days.

In 2010, there were 22 major earthquakes 7.0 or higher. This results in an average of one major earthquake every 15 days.

Expect More Intense Weather/Judgment on America
Obama Administration Abandons Israel Again

Paper Details Obama Admin's Alleged Secret Note Sent to Iran: If Israel Attacks We Won't Get Involved - The Blaze, Posted on September 3, 2012 [excerpt]:
The Israeli newspaper Yediot Ahronot published a startling report Monday detailing a message it says was conveyed by the Obama administration – via two European countries – to Iranian officials. The request: if Israel decides to strike Iranian nuclear facilities, the U.S. will not support it and the Islamic Republic should refrain from retaliating on US military installations in the Persian Gulf.

Wall Street Journal - Israeli's Are Right Not to Trust Obama September 1, 2012 [excerpt]: "Though President Obama likes to say he has Israel's "back," "his administration tries to sell to the public a make-believe world in which Iran's nuclear intentions are potentially peaceful, sanctions are working and diplomacy hasn't failed after three and half years."

Israel and the Japan 2011 Earthquake

"I will bless those who bless you [Israel] and curse those who curse you." —Genesis 12:3

On March 11, 2010 the government of Japan denounced Israel's right to build homes in their own nation—on their own land. To the very day, one year later on March 11, 2011—Japan was hit with a ravaging 9.0 earthquake, and then wracked by treacherous, mammoth tsunamis.

Following are some excerpts from various news reports posted on the Internet regarding Japan's ongoing interference against Israel's right to hold on to their God-given land. At Friends of Yeshua Ministries, we are praying for the dear Japanese people—that through their tragedy many will come to faith in the Messiah of Israel—the Redeemer of the world. Other countries pressuring Israel to give up her territories are not immune to a similar catastrophe, including the United States of America—I am sorry to say, as evidenced earlier in this book.

http://www.mofa.go.jp/announce/announce/2010/3/0311_01.html: Statement by Press Secretary/Director-General for Press and Public Relations, Ministry of Foreign Affairs, on the decision of the Government of Israel regarding the construction of housing units at settlements in West Bank including East Jerusalem, March 11, 2010.

Japanese Statements:

The Government of Japan deplores the decisions of the Government of Israel to give permission for the construction of 1,600 housing units in East Jerusalem in addition to 112 units in West Bank just after the Israeli and Palestinian leadership's acceptance of the start of indirect talks. The Government of Japan does not recognize any act that prejudges the final status of Jerusalem and the territories in the pre-1967 borders. Japan demands that the plans should not be implemented.

The Government of Japan continues to request strongly that both parties will act in a way that enhances mutual confidence. Japan sincerely hopes that the indirect talks in the peace process will swiftly develop into the resumption of direct talks between the two parties.

And then again, this year on 1/11, 2/8, and 2/10 Japan released statements telling Israel not to build in east Jerusalem.

http://www.mofa.go.jp/announce/announce/2011/2/0210_02.html: Statement by the Press Secretary, Ministry for Foreign Affairs of Japan, on the situation in East Jerusalem on February 10, 2011.

Japanese Statements:

The Government of Japan is concerned about the Jerusalem municipal planning committee's approval of a plan to build housing units for Jewish people in the Sheih Jarrah of East Jerusalem. Such act goes against the efforts by the international community to resume the negotiations. The Government of Japan does not recognize any act that prejudges the final status of the territories in the pre-1967 borders nor Israel's annexation of East Jerusalem. Japan urges Israel to refrain from any unilateral act that changes the current situation in East Jerusalem. (*This is a provisional translation. The above date denotes the date of the issue of the original press release in Japanese.)

http://www.mofa.go.jp/announce/announce/2011/2/0208_02.html. Statement by the Press Secretary, Ministry for Foreign Affairs of Japan, on measures by Israel on the West Bank and the Gaza Strip February 8, 2011.

Japanese Statements:

Japan welcomes the new series of economic measures announced by Israeli Prime Minister Benjamin Netanyahu and the Quartet Representative, Tony Blair on the West Bank and the Gaza Strip. Japan hopes that based on this announcement, measures will be fully and promptly implemented for economic growth as well as for the improvement of the social and living conditions in the Palestinian territories, particularly the Gaza Strip. Japan will pay close attention to any developments surrounding this matter.

Japan also hopes that these measures will enhance the mutual trust between the Israeli and Palestinian sides, although they are not a substitute for negotiations for Middle East peace. Japan, for its part, calls upon both parties to exert further efforts for the resumption of peace negotiations. (*This is a provisional translation. The above date denotes the date of the issue of the original press release in Japanese.)

http://www.mofa.go.jp/announce/announce/2011/1/0111_04.html: Statement by Mr. Seiji Maehara, Minister for Foreign Affairs of Japan, on the demolition of the Shepherd's Hotel in East Jerusalem, January 11, 2011.

Japanese Statements:

Japan condemns the demolishing of a part of the Shepherd's Hotel in East Jerusalem with a view to constructing new housing units for Jewish people.

Japan does not recognize any unilateral measures that prejudge the final resolution on pre-1967 borders, nor does Japan recognize the annexation of East Jerusalem by Israel. In this regard, Japan urges Israel to refrain from any unilateral act that could change the existing conditions of East Jerusalem. Ambassador Yutaka Iimura, Special Envoy of the Government of Japan for the Middle East, who was in Israel, has already informed Israeli Government officials of Japanese views.

Japan once again strongly encourages both the Israel and the Palestinian sides to focus on the goal of a two-state solution, which is important not only for the Middle East but also for the international community as a whole; to act in such a way that mutual trust will be developed; and to continue efforts for peace tenaciously.

Endnotes
http://www.israelnewsagency.com/japanearthquakeisraelidfhumanitarian aidvictimstsunamiisraaidzakajnewsewishfederationsnuclearforeigministr ydisasterrescuesearch031111.html

Even *after* Japan made it clear it is not a supporter of Israel, when the March 2011 earthquake and tsunami devastated that nation, Israel was the first to respond with humanitarian aid, as you will read in the next section.

God's Command: Israel Undivided

"And the LORD spoke to Moses on Mount Sinai saying, 'Speak to the children of Israel, and say to them: When you come into the land which I gave you, then the land shall keep a Sabbath to the LORD.

The land shall not be sold permanently, for the land is Mine; for you are strangers and Sojourners with Me.

And I will enter into judgment with them there on account of My people, My heritage Israel, whom they have scattered among the nations; they have also divided up My land.'"

—Leviticus 25:1, 23; Joel 3:2b

Israel Among First to Respond with Humanitarian Aid to Japan Earthquake and Tsunami

Jerusalem, Israel ---- March 11, 2011...Israel's heart and soul is quickly responding to the massive 8.9 magnitude earthquake that slammed Japan and the awaiting disasters of lethal tsunami waves now threatening many nations in the Pacific. Israel Prime Minister Benjamin Netanyahu wasted no time in offering humanitarian aid to the victims of Friday's earthquake in Japan.

The Israel Prime Minister's office and the Israel Ministry for Foreign Affairs have announced that the first group of Israel humanitarian experts is now preparing to leave for Japan. "Israel Prime Minister Netanyahu delivered a message to the Japanese government, saying that the people of Israel express their deep sorrow over the tragedy in Japan, and that he will work to provide any help that will be required. The Japanese ambassador expressed his gratitude and said that he will convey the message to his government."

The Pacific earthquake, which was the largest in Japan in over 100 years, hit about 230 miles northeast of Tokyo early Friday morning. Devastating tsunamis with reported waves of over 30 feet followed, wiping out and submerging entire coastal towns. Resulting tsunamis waves have been tracked across the Pacific, with possible damage feared as far away as Hawaii and the U.S. West Coast.

Shachar Zahavi, founder and coordinator of IsraAID, The Israel Forum for International Humanitarian Aid, said: "IsraAID/FIRST disaster relief teams, consisting of first responders, search and rescue specialists, logisticians, emergency medical personnel and water specialists, are now preparing to travel from Israel to the region within the next 24 hours." IsraAID is a coordinating organization for seventeen Israel and Jewish humanitarian groups, including Israel Flying Aid which worked side by side with the IDF in Haiti, has established a Japan and Pacific Earthquake and Tsunami Emergency Fund to assist victims of this disaster. For more information please be in touch: szahavi@hotmail.com or 972.54.678.5033 or go to: http://www.israaid.org.il.

"Israel officially offered its help an hour after the earthquake struck," Shinomya said. "It is very heart-warming, but at this point we do not know exactly what the extent of the damage is, so it is difficult for us to say what can be done." IsraAID is now checking where the team could fly to a nearby country and then trying to make it to northeast Japan, where the tsunami has killed hundreds and devastated cities and towns. "We're in touch with local groups to check the situation in the area," Zahavi told the Jewish Telegraphic Agency. "We're trying to get to the closest airport and then get to the affected area from there."

Following intensive consultations with the Israel Foreign Ministry and with emissaries from the Chabad organization in Japan, the UN-recognized Israel based ZAKA arranged to send a team headed by the organization's co-directors Mati Goldstein and Dovi Maisel, on Saturday evening (after the conclusion of the Sabbath).

A second ZAKA team based in Hong Kong was to leave for the quake area after the conclusion of the Sabbath in their region. ZAKA's experts have extensive experience assisting at natural disasters around the world, including Haiti, the tsunami in Thailand and the Katrina hurricane in New Orleans. The Japan consul in Israel, Mitoshiko Shinomya, told the Israel news Website Ynet that he was heartened by the Israel government's offer of assistance.

"Israel officially offered its help an hour after the earthquake struck," Shinomya said. "It is very heart-warming, but at this point we do not know exactly what the extent of the damage is, so it is difficult for us to say what can be done." Israel, which has dealt with many disasters through wars and terrorism, has become a nation of experts in emergency medicine and trauma.

Israel also has considerable expertise in clean water management. Israelis were among the first on the scene to help during the earthquake in Haiti and the Jewish tradition of reaching out to those in need dictates that they would also offer help to people in Japan and elsewhere stricken by this devastating event.

—Joel Leyden, Israel News Agency

Increased Destructive Weather
Patterns as the Return of the Lord Draws Near

"And there will be famines, pestilences, and earthquakes in various places. All these are the beginning of sorrows. And there will be signs in the sun, in the moon, and in the stars; and on the earth distress of nations, with perplexity, the sea and the waves roaring; men's hearts failing them from fear and the expectation of those things which are coming on the earth, for the powers of the heavens will be shaken."

—Matthew 24:7b-8; Luke 21:25-26

In the Bible there are numerous prophecies about strange and destructive weather patterns. Jesus warned that in the last days there would be an increase of abrupt, catastrophic events. In April 2012, golf ball and baseball to softball size hailstones pounded some areas of Texas and Oklahoma causing severe damage. Hailstones the size of golf balls or ping-pong balls built up into 4-foot-deep drifts in a sparsely populated region of Potter County, Texas after a slow-moving thunderstorm drifted over the Texas panhandle.The following 2012 headlines describe more hard-hitting weather patterns.

- Drenching Damaging Storms Target Deep South
- Very Unusual Start to Tornado Season
- More than 800 Homes Hit in Dallas Area
- Grandma Saves Boy from Twister Pulling at Him
- Extreme Weather USA: 2012 Kicks Off with Record Heat, Tornadoes and Drought
- Much of UK Gripped by Drought Millions Subject to Water Restrictions

Why Is the Heartland of America Being Ripped to Shreds by Gigantic Tornadoes That Are Becoming More Frequent and More Powerful?

What in the world is going on in the heartland of America? Spring has barely even begun and we are seeing communities all over America being ripped to shreds by gigantic tornadoes. A lot of meteorologists claimed that the nightmarish tornado season of 2011 was an "anomaly," but 2012 is shaping up to be just as bad or even worse. These tornado outbreaks just seem to keep getting more frequent and more powerful.

For example, several "super cell" tornadoes ripped across the Dallas-Fort Worth metro area on Tuesday. People all over America were absolutely horrified as they watched footage of these tornadoes toss around tractor-trailers as if they were toy trucks.

Personally, I have never seen a tractor-trailer tossed 100 feet into the sky before. This is not normal. CBS 11 meteorologist Larry Mowry told his viewers that one of these tornadoes was "as serious of a tornado we've seen in years."

What in the world is going on in the heartland of America?

Spring has barely even begun and we are seeing communities all over America being ripped to shreds by gigantic tornadoes. A lot of meteorologists claimed that the nightmarish tornado season of 2011 was an "anomaly", but 2012 is shaping up to be just as bad or even worse. These tornado outbreaks just seem to keep getting more frequent and more powerful.

For example, several "super cell" tornadoes ripped across the Dallas-Fort Worth metro area on Tuesday. People all over America were absolutely horrified as they watched footage of these tornadoes toss around tractor-trailers as if they were toy trucks. Personally, I have never seen a tractor-trailer tossed 100 feet into the sky before. This is not normal. CBS 11 meteorologist Larry Mowry told his viewers that one of these tornadoes was "as serious of a tornado we've seen in years".

So why is this happening? Why is the heartland of America being ripped to shreds by gigantic tornadoes that are becoming more frequent and more powerful? Up to this point in 2012, at least 57 people have been killed by tornadoes across the country.

Thousands more have been injured and countless homes have been reduced to splinters. In fact, there have been a couple of small towns that have been essentially wiped off the map by giant tornadoes. What we are witnessing is not normal.

Prior to the horrific tornadoes that we saw on Tuesday, there had been 326 tornadoes in the United States so far in 2012. That is about twice as many as usual for this time of the year. Overall, the United States only sees about 1,200 tornadoes for the entire year usually. The busiest time of the year for tornadoes is still a way off, and we are on pace for a truly historic year.

But it is not just the number of tornadoes that is the problem. Many of these tornadoes are immensely powerful. The following is how the local CBS affiliate described the damage done by the recent tornadoes in Texas...

> Multiple tornadoes threw tractor-trailers in the air, ripped the roof off an elementary school, leveled houses and shut down airline traffic out of Dallas-Fort Worth International Airport as one of the worst storms in years hit North Texas Tuesday. Baseball-sized hail punched holes through car roofs, and a Red Cross spokeswoman warned the breadth of the destruction may not be cleared until well into Wednesday. The mayors of Arlington and Lancaster declared a state of disaster following the storm strike.

There were even reports of massive "debris balls" in Dallas, Ellis, Johnson and Tarrant counties. These tornadoes picked up huge amounts of debris into the air that were just carried along by the storms. That must have been an absolutely horrifying sight to behold.

A lot of jaw-dropping footage from these tornadoes has already been posted on the Internet: Tractor-trailers can be seen being tossed about like rag dolls.

Have you ever seen anything like that before in your life? I know that I haven't. Look, one bad year can be dismissed as a coincidence.

But two historically bad years in a row? Many would call that a trend. Last year, America experienced one of the worst tornado seasons of all time.

Many Americans will never, ever forget the devastation caused by the tornadoes of 2011. For example, National Geographic reported that a gigantic F5 tornado that ripped through the Tuscaloosa, Alabama area had winds of up to 260 miles an hour. If you drive through Tuscaloosa today you can see that they are still trying to recover. And Joplin, Missouri may never be the same again after what happened to that city last year.

The gigantic tornado that ripped through Joplin was called by some the deadliest single tornado in more than 60 years.

That mammoth tornado ripped a path of destruction through Joplin that was more than a mile wide and more than 6 miles long. You can see some amazing before and after photographs of Joplin right here. But people don't think about what happened to Joplin much anymore because there have been so many other horrific disasters since then.

Overall, 2011 was the worst year for natural disasters in US history. Many were hoping that there would be a return to normalcy in 2012.

Unfortunately, that simply is not happening. In 2012, we have already seen one of the worst tornado outbreaks ever recorded in the month of March in all of American history. A couple of small towns in Indiana were virtually completely wiped out by that outbreak.

Sadly, what we have already seen in Indiana and Texas may just be the warm up act. The truth is that usually May is the worst month for tornadoes in the United States. So how bad are things going to get this year? How many other communities across the nation are going to be absolutely ripped to shreds before tornado season is over this year?

In 2009, there were **1146 tornadoes** in the United States.
In 2010, there were **1282 tornadoes** in the United States.
In 2011, there were **1691 tornadoes** in the United States.
In 2012, we are on pace to far exceed the total we saw in 2011.

> "For we know that the whole creation groans and labors with birth pangs together until now [until Christ's Second Coming]." —Romans 8:22

Appendix E

Excerpts from: Satan's War Against God

By Dr. Thomas Ice

In order to make sense out of end-times Bible prophecy, one must first understand what happened at the beginning in order to know where we are headed and why. Although mankind is intricately involved in history, one cannot understand the purpose and goal of history without God's revelation of the angelic dimensions. The starting point begins with Satan's declaration of independence from God shortly after the creation.

The Battle for Planet Earth Begins

Ezekiel 28 and Isaiah 14 are the two major biblical passages that reveal the entrance of sin in the universe when Satan fell. Ezekiel 28 begins with a pronouncement of judgment upon the prince of Tyre, who turns out to be a reference to Lucifer or Satan who is behind the human king (28:11-19).

"You were the anointed cherub who covers, and I placed you there, you were on the holy mountain of God; you walked in the midst of the stones of fire. You were blameless in your ways from the day you were created, until unrighteousness was found in you," says verses 14-15. Even though created beautiful and good, Satan, the top angel of God fell into sin and took a third of the other angels with him (Revelation 12:4, 9).

Isaiah 14 is the other major passage that teaches us about the fall of Satan. Verses 13 and 14 record Satan's famous declaration of rebellion when he said, "But you said in your heart, 'I will ascend to heaven; I will raise my throne above the stars of God, and I will sit on the mount of assembly in the recesses of the north. I will ascend above the heights of the clouds; I will make myself like the Most High.'" The Lord's response to this declaration:

"Nevertheless you will be thrust down to Sheol, to the recesses of the pit" (14:15). Satan became God's opponent, His adversary who set out to dethrone God and obstruct His plan for history.

After Satan's fall into sin he now sets out to expand his influence by tempting the newly created Adam and Eve to join his rebellion against God who created them. This he succeeded in doing as he tempted Eve and got Adam to join them in rebellion against God.

As a result of Satan's role of deceiving the woman into joining his revolt against God, the Lord cursed the serpent and the woman as follows: "And I will put enmity between you and the woman, and between your seed and her seed; he shall bruise you on the head, and you shall bruise him on the heel" (Genesis 3:15). The outworking of this great conflict between the serpent's seed and the seed of the woman commences.

In the conversations between the Lord and Satan we see that the devil charges God with not being a good God, Who doesn't know what He is doing, and One who can only gain loyalty from a person if He buys them off. We see that Satan's goal is to obstruct the plan of God from unfolding so that he will be able to demonstrate that God does not know how to run the universe, in fact, Satan believes that he could do a better job.

Therefore, the struggle between the seed of the serpent and the seed of the woman has played out in history and will come to a culmination in the last days, during the seven-year Tribulation.

Satan Attacks Israel

The conflict between the seed of the woman and the seed of the serpent becomes focused upon Israel since the Messiah will come forth from God's elect nation. Therefore, if Satan can obstruct God's plan at any point and prevent it from unfolding in history, then he believes that he will have obstructed God's plan and will have proven his initial claim that the Lord does not deserve to be God, the Most High One.

Revelation 12 is an entire chapter that explains why Satan attacks Israel in the middle of the tribulation and attempts to wipe her out. It is because the devil knows that he only has a short while to finally obstruct God's plan and now his only hope is to prevent the second coming of Christ. How can he do that?

He believes he can accomplish that by destroying the Jews, since the second coming will occur when Israel is converted to Jesus as their Messiah and then calls upon Him to come and rescue them at Armageddon or else Israel will be wiped out. Thus, Revelation 12 provides insight into this age long conflict that has been going on from the beginning of history, throughout history and will be an important issue at the climax of history.

Revelation 12 tells us that a third of the angels fell and followed Satan in his original revolt. We learn this when we realize that the stars in this passage are symbolic of angels (compare Revelation 9:1; 12:7, 9). "This is a war in heaven that resulted in the casting of Satan and his angels to earth before the birth of the woman's child, so it belongs to the past. A second war in 12:7-9 is Satan's final attempt to storm heaven, bringing about the child's overthrow after his birth." [3]

The second half of the verse is a clear reference to Satan (the dragon) who stood before the woman (Israel) in anticipation of the birth of Jesus the Messiah, who is the child that the woman gave birth to in the past. Satan did not know the exact moment of the birth of Messiah and so he waited expectantly for the seed of woman to come forth. His attempt to devour the woman's child is seen in the New Testament as Satan inspires King Herod to develop a plot to find and kill Jesus (Matthew 2).

Because the historical events surrounding the birth of Jesus were part of the angelic conflict, the Lord warns the magi from the east in a dream to avoid Herod, "They departed for their own country by another way" (Matthew 2:12). Since Satan was about to inspire Herod to kill all male babies in the Bethlehem area who were in the age-range of Jesus, "an angel of the Lord appeared to Joseph in a dream, saying 'Arise and take the Child and His mother, and flee to Egypt, and remain there until I tell you; for Herod is going to search for the

Child to destroy Him'" (Matthew 2:13). God is always at least one step ahead of Satan.

These kinds of events down through history are part of the angelic conflict, the war between the seed of the woman and the seed of the serpent. Summaries of some of the key events from history are as follows:

The dragon's evil intentions toward the woman's unborn child evidenced themselves throughout Old Testament history. Instances of his hostility surfaced in Cain's murder of Abel (Genesis 4:8), the corrupting of the line of Seth (Genesis 6:1-12), attempted rapes of Sarah (Genesis 12:10-20; 20:1-18) and Rebekah (Genesis 26:1-18), Rebeka's plan to cheat Esau out of his birthright and the consequent enmity of Esau against Jacob (Genesis 27), the murder of the male children in Egypt (Exodus 1:15-22), attempted murders of David (e.g., 1 Samuel 18:10-11), Queen Athaliah's attempt to destroy the royal seed (2 Chronicles 22:10), Haman's attempt to slaughter the Jews (Esther 3-9), and consistent attempts of the Israelites to murder their own children for sacrificial purposes (cf. Leviticus 18:21; 2 Kings16:3; 2 Chronicles 28:3; Psalm 106:37, 38; Ezekiel 16:20).

The attack of Herod against the children of Bethlehem (Matthew 2:16) and many other incidents during Jesus' earthly life, including His temptation, typify the ongoing attempt of the dragon to "devour" the woman's child once he was born. The most direct attempt was, of course, in the crucifixion of Christ. [4]

Prophecy is needed for God to demonstrate in history that Jesus Christ has the right to rule over planet Earth and Satan is nothing more than a liar concerning anything that he speaks about, especially concerning God. This is why God has designed future prophetic events to demonstrate that Jesus Christ is the hero of history. Maranatha!

Endnotes
[3] Robert L. Thomas, Revelation 8-22: *An Exegetical Commentary* (Chicago: Moody Press, 1995), p.124.
[4] Thomas, Revelation 8-22, p.125.

A Former New Age Icon Accepts Christ
Faces of Darkness Exposed

Any form of hypnosis or mediation outside the Bible is dangerous, creating an opening for demonic influence and control. Randall Baer, a former naturopathic physician, author and an internationally known authority on New Age practices and later ignited the world with his riveting testimony, his conversion to Christianity. His New Age, occult dabbling began in his early teen years in the 1960s. He was full of questions about God, the Bible and life, but had no one grounded in the Word of God to help him make any sense of religion or spiritual matters. In his book, *Inside the New Age Nightmare*, he stated:

> Something snapped in me. I no longer wanted to attend what I perceived as sterile and lifeless church services and study groups. I suddenly knew that what I was searching for wasn't there. In the years ahead, I would hear many New Agers telling a similar story. I started going to various libraries searching for truth on my own. The realm of books, I felt, would open up the doors to new horizons.

Randall indicated in his book that he had had a strong, sincere desire to find the truth about, who he was and who God is. He searched through books on religion, philosophy and the occult. At age fifteen, he began practicing hatha yoga and meditation. He had accepted the "Oneness of the Universe" philosophy heralded by the New Age movement. He began taking Marijuana in an attempt to open up "spiritually." He stated:

> One evening I felt that I had an encounter with what I thought was "God." While slowly inhaling the marijuana, all of a sudden the surrounding room disappeared. I found myself floating in the cosmos beyond all sense of time. The boundaries of my body and sense of identity miraculously expanded as I became the "light" and the "light" became me. Feeling like I was effortlessly soaring through infinity, I believed that I had met "god "and was one with the Universe. This was what the Eastern religious philosophies were talking about—pure oneness and enlightenment.

Randall began to see "Nature" as the answer to his spiritual quest. If he could really become one with it, like the American Indians, he would find answers to his questions. Wordsworth and Thoreau became two of his major inspirational writers. Randall would quote Wordsworth: "Come forth into the light of things, let Nature be your teacher." This became the basis and inspiration of his spiritual search.

Randall Baer went from ingesting marijuana to LSD and other hallucinogenic drugs:

A succession of experiences with LSD, mescaline, peyote buttons, psilocybin mushrooms, and hashish with others in my Asian Studies house "blew my mind." Catapulted into extraordinary dimensions beyond my wildest dreams, I rapturously explored what I felt were the indescribable "heavens" of the supernatural realms. Incredible vistas of dazzling rainbow light, beings of pure energy, and mind expanding transformations unfolded with each new experience.

I felt that the psychedelics afforded me access to the very essence of Nature and the cosmos. Here, I thought, I was privileged to know the innermost secrets of the universe known only to Mystics, Saints and Psychedelic voyagers. When I would read some of the books in the college courses I was taking on Hinduism, Taoism, Buddhism, Yoga and Western mystics, time after time my psychedelic experiences matched precisely with these traditions.

But then Randall had his first frightening drug-induced experience:

A few years later, though, I had an LSD experience that should have warned me of the deceptions I had embraced. Shortly after gliding up a crescendo into the peak of the LSD "high" an overwhelmingly powerful demon-spirit took possession of me. I was no longer in control of myself as this demonic force took over the reins.

While part of me watched helplessly, the demon-sorcerer cast a number of powerful spells and gave me visions of hideous darkness. After several hours of tremendous inner torture on this "bad trip" the demon "blew my circuits" and left me like a rag doll. I could not speak for two entire days, and the psychological damage took six months to heal.

After that terrifying encounter, Randall Baer then rejected all drugs as a fast lane to "endless bliss" and focused his attention on mastering enlightenment through more "natural" techniques. He participated in Buddhist chanting and Silva Mind Control. By practicing Silva Mind Control he hoped to train and develop his psychic ability and mind in the direction that would bring him toward "truth." While involved in these mind-control techniques Randall encountered two unique spirit guides, described by him as American Indians:

> What I didn't realize at the time was that everything in Silva Mind Control was based on occult philosophy. The occult was simply repackaged in a de-religionized, Western format that would be acceptable and even appealing to middle-class America. Inner counseling is a type of biblically forbidden practice of "Acquiring familiar spirits," that is, inviting demons disguised as spirit-friends into one's life.

In his book, Randall recounted that calling out to spirits of American Indian pantheism and following the pattern of the vision quest ritual he had "unknowingly opened" himself up to the "wiles of Satan." He had asked for a "vision" and "powers" and got both. He further stated:

> By crossing over into the biblically forbidden territory of occult practices (Deuteronomy 18:10-12), I had ventured onto Satan's turf. The enemy and his demonic legions masquerade many times as angels of light and servants of righteousness (2 Corinthians 11:13-15). This was a constant thread through all my New Age experiences, happening time and time again. **What I was absolutely convinced was truth, was actually an extended series of counterfeits.** The powerful experiences and elegant philosophies in the New Age can be so utterly convincing to even the most well-intentioned persons. This is what is so sad about so many people involved in the New Age.

Randall wrote that through yoga meditation he experienced:

> "Yet another mystical doorway into the further reaches of Satan's New Age landscapes. I also acquired a "familiar spirit"—a demon masquerading as the spirit-hawk with which I felt a close affinity. In a way similar to the American Indians, I had acquired a "power animal," my "spirit helper."

When Randall was a student he spent time a lot of time in ashrams, and became a disciple of the then popular Yogi, Swami Babaji. He received a degree in Religious Studies and later became a naturopathic doctor. He stated:

> I went about opening up a "Natural Health Center" in a medium-sized city in East Texas. In a small, business-zoned house, I offered personalized health care programs, bodywork treatments, weekly "Awakening Your Potential" classes, iridology analysis, meditation and hatha *yoga* classes, health care products, and a host of other products and services.

> I even had a carefully planned "deep relaxation environment" in one room where a special arrangement of colors, plants, aromas art and subliminal tapes and New Age music was created to induce "therapeutic" deep relaxation."

While involved in his naturopathic business, Randall met his future wife Vicki. She was the director of a "New Age Awareness Center." Vicki gave him information about "crystal power" through her "spirit guides." She also gave him a "power object" stone, which had once belonged to an American Indian, a "medicine man."

Randall spoke of his experiences with this quartz crystal:

> Only minutes after focusing on the crystal in a state of trance-like meditation, my consciousness was catapulted into electrifying domains of extra-natural light, the likes of which I had never before perceived. The upper part of my head felt like it wasn't there, like it had become invisible, as my awareness raced upwards at the speed of light. From a high distance, I could see in my mind's eye that my body was trembling and shaking as the power of the experience rattled through it. This was my "crystal initiation" into an entirely different supernatural realm. Wow! Was this "crystal power" or what?

After Randall and Vicki were married in the 1980s they moved to Santa Fe, New Mexico. It was considered a hot spot for new "mystical energies," a "vortex area"- a location that attracts many types of psychic phenomena. Their encounters with the paranormal took hold quickly.

There was no shortage of deceptive demonic entities that would present themselves. Randall recounted:

The spirit world began to speak to us explicitly and directly. All of a sudden Vicki would go into a trance. Then a spirit would come into her body and animatedly speak. I couldn't believe what was happening. The variety of spirits coming and going was astounding - I talked with spirits identifying themselves as "Moses," "Mozart," "White Eagle," "White Cloud," "Serapis Bey," "Ascended Master Kuthumi," "Mary," "Golden-Helmeted Ones," "Green Ray Master" and a host of powerful others. The emanating from these spirits was overwhelming and entrancingly intoxicating.

While meditating, these spirits instructed Randall and Vicki to seek out a group they referred to as the "Space Brothers" and tried to convince them that these "Space Brothers" were part of the "Intergalactic Space Federation" existing in the solar system. These extraterrestrials were supposedly assisting the earth in its "purification process" to take the planet into the "New Age." The "spirit guides" also said that the "Space Brothers" were allied with the "Great White Brotherhood," a supposed universal hierarchy of Ascended Masters, archangels, angels and various of spirit beings who claim to be in charge of all realms of creation.

These spirit beings convinced Randall that his work was to spread the methods of "Crystal Power Techniques" to enable large numbers of people to be "Activated into a higher consciousness of light." According to the spirit guides, the "Higher Councils of Universal Masters," and "Supreme" spiritual beings were part of the crystal power teachings and Randall would be the vehicle in which their message would be distributed. Randall was thrilled. He enthusiastically exclaimed:

Unbelievable! The cosmic "gods" were speaking directly to me, and saying that Vicki and I were "chosen ones" specially handpicked to lead the world into the New One-World Era.

Randall describes his continued deeper involvement with the deceptive world of the occult:

Approximately three months after moving to the northern New Mexico area, my "spirit guides" gave me instructions to write a book on the subject of crystals ... the spirit guides told me to take 12 quartz crystals and lay them out in a circle, to tape another one to the occult "third eye" and to suspend a large pyramid overhead

I was to sit in the very center of the crystals with my head underneath the pyramid. This was supposed to create a "crystal energy field" having amplified "higher vibrations" for receiving channeled thoughts from the spirit guides.

To my amazement, as I would enter a kind of semi-conscious trance, discernible thoughts, inspirations, and pictures would appear in my mind. All this was not my own doing - the spirit guides were actually transmitting their thoughts and influences to me. My job, effectively, was to take notes and then shape up the material into book form.

Randall's books on crystal power became widely accepted, and brought him to worldwide acclaim. Famous celebrities, health professionals and business executives attended his "Advanced Crystal Energetics Training Program." At home, Randall had created what he had termed "The Ascension Chamber."

This special occult breeding ground brought him much attention. It was a designated room packed with crystals, pyramids and various occult symbols. In this chamber he played New Age music, subliminal tapes and used special trance-inducing paraphernalia and videos to help bring about "out of body" experiences.

But Randall's life was about to change dramatically; a terrifying struggle with more demonic entities:

One night, while in the Ascension Chamber, my spirit was roaming some of the farthest reaches of "heavenly light" that I had ever perceived. That night I had an experience that would change by virtually my life forever. During this experience I was surrounded one night, overwhelming luminosity—it was as if I was looking straight into the sun.

Waves of bliss radiated through my spirit. I was totally captivated by power. Suddenly, another force stepped in. It took me by complete surprise. In the twinkling of an eye, it was like a supernatural hand had taken me behind the scenes of the experience that I was having. I was taken behind the outer covering of the dazzling luminosity and there saw something that left me literally shaking for a full week. What I saw was the face of devouring darkness! Behind the glittering outer facade of beauty lay a massively powerful, wildly churning face of absolute hatred and unspeakable abominations - the face of demons filled with the power of Satan. What I saw was the face of devouring darkness! **Behind the glittering outer facade of beauty lay a massively powerful, wildly churning face of absolute hatred and unspeakable abominations—the face of demons filled with the power of Satan.**

For a moment that seemed like eternity, I realized that I was in major league trouble, for this devouring force was now closing in on me. In absolute stark terror I felt powerless to stop what appeared to be inevitable doom. Horror filled me like a consuming flame. Then, miraculously, the same supernatural hand as before delivered me from the jaws of this consuming darkness, and hours later, I found myself waking up the next morning in the Ascension Chamber.

It felt like I had a peaceful nights sleep but, upon awaking, the horror of the past night's experience had left me terribly shaken. My mind was racing uncontrollably in all directions at what felt like the speed of light. My body was shaking involuntarily, sometimes rather violently. This nightmare continued without respite for a full week. I thought I was going stark raving mad. In a month's time, though, my grave situation gradually settled down to some semblance of sanity and normality.

Randall recounts his experience when God intervened in his life:

What I didn't know at this time was that it was JESUS who had intervened by His greater grace into my life. At this point, though, I only knew that some force greater than that of the devouring darkness had done two things: (1) It had shown me the real face of the New Age "heavens" and "angels" that I was so deeply involved with, and (2) It had delivered me from certain doom.

What I knew at this time was that I had made some serious errors in my New Age involvement. I also knew that if those errors weren't corrected, I might face the same horrific experience again. And quite possibly the next time I wouldn't get away. An openness to reconsider my New Age involvements arose in me out of desperate need.

This openness would help me, over the following months, to find a Way, the Truth, and a Life that I had never known before—Jesus Christ. But this journey would not be an easy one. For Satan does not relinquish those he has in bondage without a struggle, as I was about to find out.

Randall began to read the Bible looking for answers. He compared Scripture with New Age teachings. He realized that New Agers selectively choose what they like from the Bible, and reject what they don't like. By studying the Scriptures he became acutely aware of how he had been involved in spiritual practices that God warns us not to take part it. He began to understand the great love God has for all of His creation shown by sending His Son to die on the cross for us, to take on all our sins, so we can be forgiven and live eternally with Him. Randall found hope through Christ, and understood that God could and would forgive him. He was painfully aware that he had become overpowered by demonic powers and had felt a spirit force overtaking more and more of his life until finally, the day came, when he repented of his sins and accepted Jesus Christ as his Lord and Savior—while watching a Christian television program. The salvation message was the focus of the show, and at the end of the message, the televangelist invited all viewers to call on the name of the Lord for salvation and forgiveness.

Randall experienced God's tremendous mercy and love and was set-free from satanic bondage:

I was in such a state now that I was way past feeling self-conscious or silly ... I gently dropped to the floor. As this happened I felt the conviction of the Holy Spirit pierce my heart and I wept in acute repentance ... I had never prayed like this before ... The Lord had cut through my horrific satanic bondage and set me free as he washed my scarlet sins as white as snow. With an absolute certainty, I knew that this was what I had been looking for all my life and never had found till now. This made even the most powerful mystical New Age experience completely pale in comparison...Satan's seductive glowing counterfeit fineries are as cheap, filthy rags compared to the Truth.

Randall Baer's conversion to Christianity did not sit well with his New Age associates. They were very angry and treated him with disdain. His genuine concern for their spiritual, emotional, mental and physical wellness was scoffed at and ridiculed. Although Randall's marriage with Vicki did not last, by Randall's account, they had remained good friends. She *also* repented and cut-off all her New Age involvements, and came to faith in the Lord Jesus Christ. His New Age "friends" did not like it that he was calling out the New Age movement for what is: satanic deception.

Randall, and a small group of friends who came to saving faith in Christ were treated very badly by other New Agers, but Randall and his small group of converts did not waiver in their strong, newly found faith in Messiah Jesus. Their New Age friends whom they once thought were so nice and so "tolerant" of all things showed them selves to be bigoted and cruel. After Randall's conversion to Christianity he wrote the very book I have been discussing here, *Inside the New Age Nightmare* (1989); highlighting his experiences in the New Age movement and how his conversion to the Lord Jesus Christ came about. As the book was about to be published, Randall died a very mysterious and unexpected death. After completing a lecture tour in New Mexico, wherein he further exposed the New Age Movement's deceptions, his car ran off a mountain pass. A number of investigations took place but none were able to uncover whether the mishap was murder or an "accident." However police reports indicate that he was forced off the road— while he was driving and was killed, indicating foul play. Thanks to a good friend, this important book was published and released to the public.

Because Randall was saved, we can be sure that He is with the Lord, safe in the arms of Jesus. If you or anyone else you know is involved in any type of New Age or New Spirituality teachings, please read Randall Baer's book and share the messages in this book. So many New Agers genuinely and sincerely believe they are tapping into goodness and truth, completely unaware of the enormous danger they are in. Spiritual deception is running rampant and will get much worse as we move toward the seven-year Tribulation.

Endnotes
All excerpts are taken from chapters two and three from: *Inside the New Age Nightmare* by Randall Baer. Emphasis added on pages 351, 355.

Security of the One Who Trusts in the Lord

Psalm 91:1-4

"He who dwells in the secret place of the Most High shall abide under the shadow of the Almighty.

I will say of the LORD, "He is my refuge and my fortress; My God in Him I will trust."

Surely He shall deliver you from the snare of the fowler *and* from the perilous pestilence.

He shall cover you with His feathers, and under His wings you shall take refuge; His truth *shall be your* shield and buckler."

Appendix F

Some Key Biblically Related Words and Expressions

Agnosticism - Agnosticism is the belief that we cannot know for sure whether there is a God, or not. Maybe there is a God. Maybe there is not.

Amillinnialism - A false doctrine that teaches there will be no literal millennial kingdom; and that Jesus Christ will return at some point but without any warning signs.

Angels - Created beings serving God and born-again believers. One third of them (fallen angels) joined Satan when he rebelled against God.

Antichrist - Antichrist is the name given to the man referred to in the Bible as the "Man of Sin" or the "Beast." He is a man, who will be indwelt and empowered by Satan halfway through the Tribulation. He will rise to power in the last days and ruthlessly persecute people, especially the Jews during the Tribulation. When Jesus returns, he will destroy him, casting him into the lake of fire where he will also cast Satan.

Apologetics - Simply defined, it is the defense of the Christian faith.

Apostles - The eleven disciples who were chosen by Jesus to go forth and preach the gospel to the nations. (Matthew 28:19-20, Luke 1:26, Acts 1:8, Ephesians 4:11-13).

Archangel - A chief angel, in the New Testament there is reference to: Michael the archangel.

Atheism - Atheism is the belief that God does not exist. Atheists believe that there is no God.

Atonement - Atonement is the act of bringing man and God together. It means the same as "reconciliation." When Jesus died on the cross, he made the Atonement of men possible with God. Therefore, He is called our "Atonement."

Baptism - The word "baptism" refers to the act of being placed into or "immersed" into something.

New believers are "baptized" into water to symbolize the fact that we are dead and "buried" to an old way of life; that Jesus died and was buried in the tomb before He came back to life. Baptism is a testimony to the world of our commitment to Messiah Jesus and as an act of obedience to our Lord.

Baptist - Baptists believe the Bible is God's Word to mankind, true in every detail and our guide to living. Baptists believe that Jesus died on the cross for our sins, that He was buried, and that He rose again. Baptists believe that we can have eternal life only through trusting Jesus Christ for our salvation.

The name "Baptist" comes from the fact that while other denominations practice baptism by sprinkling or pouring, Baptists emphasize baptism by immersion following a commitment to Jesus Christ.

Believer - (Christian) This term is used by some individuals, instead of the word "Christian." It is a term often used by Jewish followers of Yeshua (Jesus). The term "believer" is in reference to one who genuinely believes in Yeshua Ha Mashiach (Jesus the Christ) and is saved by faith; a "born-again" individual.

Born-again - The Bible teaches that when we receive Jesus Christ into as our Lord and Savior, our lives are changed reflecting God's will for our lives. Because of God's redemptive grace we are made new (we are saved). We are even called "new creatures" (2 Corinthians 5:17). To emphasize this total change in our lives, Messiah Jesus called the transformation "born-again." A true Christian or believer is "born-again" (John 3:7).

> "Jesus answered and said unto him, 'Most assuredly, I say to you, unless one is born-again he cannot see the kingdom of God'" (John 3:3). "Do not marvel that I said to you, you must be born-again" (John 3:7). Having been born-again, not of corruptible seed but of incorruptible, through the word of God, which lives and abides for ever" (1 Peter 1:23).

Cherubim - Cherubim/cherubs are angelic beings involved in the worship and praise of God; winged creatures (Genesis 3:24).

Chag Sameach - A Hebrew expression for "joyous festival." It is suitable greeting for Jewish holidays or festivals.

Christ - His full name and title is the Lord Jesus Christ. The word "Christ" is "Messiah" in Hebrew. He is *the* anointed or specially chosen One of God. He is anointed, or specially chosen, to bring salvation to mankind by His death on the cross.

Communion - Communion is a special name for the "Lord's Supper." The word "communion" emphasizes the personal relationship and fellowship we have with the Lord Jesus Christ and with other Christians/believers.

Conversion - This word refers to the total change that takes place when we receive the Lord Jesus Christ into our lives and genuinely give our selves to Him.

Converted - A person who has received the Messiah Jesus into his or her life is often said to be "converted." It refers to the total and complete change that the Lord makes in our lives.

Conviction - The word conviction is most often used when we have behaved in ways that are wrong, and the Holy Spirit reminds us that we have sinned. We express that by saying that we are "under conviction."

People who have never received the Lord Jesus Christ as their personal Lord and Savior sometimes fight "conviction" for a long time before they finally repent and truly surrender to the Lord and begin to process of renewing their minds. True believers will hopefully learn to repent quickly when the Holy Spirit brings conviction.

The word "conviction" is also used to refer to our strong beliefs upon which we base our lives, our belief in the Bible as the complete inerrant Word of God. As Christians/believers we have many strong convictions that we know to be to be true. An example: We have an absolute conviction that Messiah Jesus rose from the dead, and will return at the end of the Tribulation in the Second Advent.

Cult - A cult is a group of people who claim to believe the Bible and even claim to believe in the Lord Jesus Christ. But their actual teachings are so far off from what the Bible truly teaches that the group members (the cult) are not true Christians or believers, but they think they are.

Some examples would be those who do not believe that Jesus Christ is really God, or those who believe that salvation can be attained in some way besides faith in Messiah Jesus. A cult can also consist of persons who have concocted their own "spiritual" teachings, and the Bible is rendered just another "holy" book.

Denomination - A denomination is a Christian group that believes and practices things slightly differently from other Christian groups. Individual churches are often part of a larger denomination. However, all Christian denominations agree that the Lord Jesus Christ is God who became man in order to die for our sins, and that faith and acceptance of Him is the only way to receive eternal life.

Disciple - An individual believing in and following all the teachings and truth of Messiah Jesus.

Disciples - twelve disciples - The twelve men chosen by Jesus (His inner circle) and taught by Him (Luke 6:13-16) in order that they could build His church after His ascension. These same men became the apostles, excluding Judas Iscariot who betrayed Jesus.

Doctrine - Doctrine is a term referring to the teachings and principles that are taught in the Bible.

Elect - Christians/believers are called "the elect." Not because they are special or better than anyone else, but because they have placed their faith in the saving grace of Messiah Jesus. The word "elect" found in Scripture is also in relation to a specific prophesied events and groups of people:

In Matthew 24:22 the reference to the elect are mostly Jews who flee from the Antichrist when his image is displayed in the newly built temple in Jerusalem halfway through the Tribulation. Some Gentiles will also be in that group. A good number of them will have accepted Jesus Christ as their Savior and will be saved during the first half of the Tribulation (Matthew 24:16-22; Revelation 12).

Also the Tribulation saints of Revelation 20:4 who die during the fifth and sixth seals (Revelation 6:9-11; 12-16) and go to heaven as shown in (Revelation 7:9-17) are another group of "elect." But they are not the elect of Matthew 24:31; 25:31-34. For those Jews and Gentiles are the saints (the elect) who do not die during the Tribulation. They will survive the Tribulation and will be alive when Jesus the Messiah returns to earth (Revelation 19:11), and they are the sheep who enter the millennial kingdom in Matthew 25:34.

Emmanuel /Immanuel - means "God with us" in Hebrew.

Epistle - Epistle simply means a letter (as in written correspondence). The epistles of the New Testament follow the form for letters in the first century. Letters in those days were not placed in envelopes, so they began with the name of the sender, followed by the name of the recipient, and then a greeting. However, the Epistle to the Hebrews did not follow this particular style.

Evangelical - Christians/believers who believe the Bible is God's Word and who believe that the Gospel ("Good News") of Jesus Christ should be shared with others, are often called "evangelicals." Christians from many different denominations are called evangelicals.

Evangelism - Evangelism generally means sharing the good news about Jesus Christ. This can be done one-on-one (person to person). It can also be done in large "evangelistic" meetings. Doing the work of evangelism means telling others about what Jesus has done for them, providing them an opportunity to receive Jesus Christ as their personal Lord and Savior.

Exegesis - Exegesis is a term used to describe an approach to interpreting a verse in the Bible by careful analysis. Correct exegesis includes using the context around the verse, comparing it with other parts of the Bible, and including an understanding of the language and customs of the time of the writing, in an effort to understand clearly what the original writer intended to communicate.

Expiation - Expiation is what Jesus accomplished for our sins when He died on the cross. Messiah Jesus Himself took the just death penalty we deserved for sin instead of that penalty being given to us. Jesus (Yeshua) removed the sin that had caused us to be separated from God and that had kept us from having a relationship with God.

Faith - Faith is more than "head knowledge" about the truth of Jesus Christ. Faith means putting our complete trust in Jesus Christ, and in Him alone, to save us from sin, death, and hell.

Fall of Man - God created Adam and Eve in a perfect, innocent state free of sin. They both had the power to choose to obey or disobey God. When they chose to disobey God, they brought sin into God's perfect creation. It led to an overwhelming, chaotic, and devastating change in the entire scheme of Creation, including the nature of Man. Historically; this is called the "Fall of Man."

Fundamentalist - The word "fundamentalist" has a number of meanings. Most often, individuals use it to refer to people of any denomination that believe that the Bible is the Word of God, completely true in all of its parts and totally without error. Some believers, who do believe the Bible is God's Word and without error, yet prefer not to be called fundamentalists because they are concerned they might be perceived as "legalists."

Glorification - Salvation has three distinct aspects: Justification, Sanctification, and Glorification. At the Rapture, all believers will be given brand new bodies that will be perfected and eternal. These bodies are called "glorified" bodies. It is at that very moment that the long awaited "glorification" takes place.

Gospel - "Gospel" literally means "good news." It refers to the good news that Jesus Christ, God the Son, became a man like us. He lived a perfect and sinless life. He died on the cross to pay the penalty for our sins. He rose again and lives forever. He will forgive our sin and give us eternal life when we truly repent and place our faith in Him.

Grace - God offers us His Grace (unmerited favor) by freely giving us the gifts of forgiveness, righteousness, eternal life, peace, joy, and things that we cannot yet fully understand here in our earthly state. It is up to each one of us to individually accept Him and His death sacrifice. Grace truly is the gift received at Christ's expense when He took all the sins of the world upon Himself at Calvary.

Great Tribulation - The Great Tribulation is in reference to the halfway point of the seven-year Tribulation. Antichrist and his cohorts will be in control, severe persecutions will abound. No one will be able to function in the world system without taking the "Mark of the Beast." This will be the most horrific time in world history.

Harpazo - The *NAS New Testament Greek Lexicon*
Strong's Number: 726
Original Word: arpazo
Translated word: Harpzo (har-pad'-zo)

Definition:
1. to seize, carry off by force
2. to seize on, claim for one's self eagerly
3. to snatch out or away
Greek lexicon based on *Thayer's and Smith's Bible Dictionary*.

Heaven - The Bible teaches that heaven is a phenomenal, perfect place that exists in the spirit world. It is the place where God and His holy angels dwell. It is a place where continual, never-ending worship of God takes place. When all true believers die, their spirits go to heaven.

Hell - God's Word tells us that those who reject God's gift of eternal life through Messiah Jesus will go to a horrific place called hell. Hell was prepared for Satan and his angels. It is a terrifying place of incomprehensible torment. But God has provided a way for mankind to stay out of hell. By receiving Messiah Jesus as our personal Lord and Savior, He gives us the gift of eternal life and victory over Satan's plan to deceive us and keep us from the true God of the Bible.

Heresy - Heresy refers to serious errors in what people believe; so serious individuals who believe those things cannot really be Christians/believers. A good example of heresy is to believe that Jesus Christ or the Holy Spirit is not truly God. It is heresy to believe that there is some other way to be saved from our sins other than faith in the Messiah Jesus. It is absolute heresy to believe that Jesus Christ (Yeshua) did not really die for our sins, or that He did not rise from the dead.

Holy Spirit - The Holy Spirit is God. He is the third person of the Trinity. As God, He is Omniscient, Omnipresent, and Omnipotent. He comes to live inside us when we genuinely repent and receive Messiah Jesus as our personal Lord and Savior. The Holy Spirit gives us direction and wisdom for making life's decisions as we make the Lord the priority of our lives and as we learn to listen to His voice.

Hypocrisy - Hypocrisy means "pretense." People who claim to be living for Christ but who are really not living for Christ are filled with of hypocrisy. They are hypocrites.

Imprecatory Prayer - Imprecate - To invoke evil or calamity on those who are ruthlessly mistreating others, upon one's enemies; in keeping with the principle that vengeance belongs to the Lord (Deuteronomy 32:35, Psalm 94:1, Psalm 83).The first nineteen verses in David's prayer in Psalm 109:9 are imprecatory.

Incarnation - The incarnation is in reference to the time when God (who is Spirit) became a man. This occurred when Jesus (God the Son) was conceived, by God the Father by means of God the Holy Spirit in the womb of the young Jewish woman, Mary.

Indwelling of the Holy Spirit - When we truly repent and receive Messiah Jesus as our Lord and Savior, the Holy Spirit of God comes to live inside us. He never leaves us again. The Holy Spirit lives or dwells within us forever.

Inerrancy - The belief that God purposed His Word, the Bible, to be written perfectly and without any errors at all.

Infallible - Infallible is similar to the word "inerrant." Since the Bible is God's perfect Word, it cannot fail or mislead us in any way. It is perfect and complete.

Intercession - When we pray for others, we are "interceding" for them. Intercession or praying for others should be a daily practice.

Jehovah - Jehovah is the English translation of a Hebrew word for God (Yahweh). The 1901 American Standard Version of the Bible uses this translation.

Jehovah Shammah - Hebrew for: Jehovah (God) is there.

Justification - Justification is the act of all our sins being forgiven and cleansed away from us forever. This takes place at the *very moment* we receive Jesus Christ into our lives as our personal Lord and Savior.

Legalism - Legalism can refer to the belief of some people who are not truly believers (Christians). They have the perception that we can be saved by our own efforts and good works.

It can also refer to believers who cannot enjoy their freedom in Christ, through His grace, but rather feel confined to do numerous things not commanded by God. Or there are some believers who feel confined not do things that God does *not* forbid us to do.

Lost - Before we receive the Lord Jesus Christ as our personal Lord and Savior, we are said to be "lost." After we receive the Lord Jesus Christ we are "saved." Lost people do not have their sins forgiven until they truly repent and receive Christ.

L'Chayim - A Hebrew/Yiddish saying that means "to life."

Maranatha - (1 Corinthians 16:22) consists of two Aramean words, Maran'athah, meaning, "our Lord comes," or is "coming." If the latter interpretation is adopted, the meaning of the phrase is, "Our Lord is coming, and he will judge those who have set him at nought." (Comp. Philippians 4:5; James 5:8, 9.) Easton, Matthew George. M.A., D.D., "Definition for *'Maranatha' Eastons Bible Dictionary*": bible-history.com - Eastons; 1897.

Mark of the Beast - A type of physical mark, backed by a system of control that the Antichrist requires and forces everyone to take during the Great Tribulation. Without it, it will be impossible to do anything. Even the basic purchasing of food or accessing one's monetary assets will be impossible without that mark.

Messiah - The word "Messiah" comes from the Hebrew word that is translated by the Greek word that means " Christ." Jesus Christ is the Messiah spoken of in Scripture. See Isaiah 53. *Messiah* is derived from the Hebrew word *Mashiach* (which means "anointed one").

Millennium - The word "millennium" refers to the 1000 years during which the Lord Jesus Christ reigns over the earth after His return to the earth at His Second Coming.

New Testament - The second part of the Bible, B'rit Hadashah in Hebrew.

Old Testament - The first section of the Bible, the Tanakh.

Olivet Discourse - Shortly before Messiah Jesus was arrested He spoke with His twelve disciples about future developments and circumstances. This is noted in Matthew 24-25, Mark 13 and Luke 21.

Omnipotent - Omnipotent means "all powerful." It is a word that describes God, and God alone. He has perfect and total power in the entire universe. He has the power to do anything He chooses to do.

Omnipresent - Omnipresent means that God can be everywhere, and at the same time. Wherever we go, whatever we do, God is there with us all the time. At the same time He is everywhere else with everyone else. Only God is Omnipresent.

Omniscience - Omniscience means that God knows everything, every detail. He has all knowledge. There is nothing hidden from Him. He knows every bit of information about you and me and everyone else on earth as well as every single aspect of the entire universe. We can't hide from God.

Pantheism - Pantheism is the belief that creation (nature) is God. Pantheists believe that the rocks, mountains, earth, stars, etc. are all part of God. Christians, however, believe that God *made all these things.* Although Christians believe God is omnipresent, they believe God is totally separate from *His creation.*

Passover - Passover is part of the feast of unleavened bread, commemorating the epic Exodus when God's covenant people were delivered from Egyptian bondage. On the 14th day of Nisan the sacrificial lamb (animal) was slain.

The blood of atonement upon the doorpost (in the form of a cross) brought salvation as the death angel passed overhead, on the eve of Passover. This was the Old Covenant fulfillment of Passover for *national protection*, and deliverance from the death angel.

On the 14th day of Nisan in 30 A.D. on the eve of Passover, Messiah Jesus was crucified. The blood of the promised Sacrificial Lamb was shed. This was the redemption God provided. It brings salvation to His covenant people delivering them from the bondage of sin and death.

This is the New Covenant fulfillment of Passover for personal salvation. Salvation comes by the atoning blood of Israel's promised Sacrificial Lamb (Jesus). The apostle Paul called Christ "our Passover" (1 Corinthians 5:7). Also see Isaiah 53 in Chapter Seven of this book.

Pentecost - The beginning of the Christian church (Acts 2:1), and the day the Holy Spirit descended and indwelt the believers who had gathered together to pray (Acts 1:12-15, 2:1-4). The disciples began to go forth and preach the gospel.

Reconciliation - Since God is completely holy and since men are sinners, there is a separation, a gap between men and God. Sin separates us from God. Messiah Jesus paid the death penalty for our sin, making it possible for us to be forgiven and cleansed of sin, bringing man and God together by taking away man's sin.

Rededication - Sometimes Christians realize that they have not been really committed to the Lord, and are living their lives in such a way that they grieve the Holy Spirit. When God convicts them that they have been making poor choices contrary to His teachings, they should and need to "rededicate" or renew their commitment to Him. This is done by asking for forgiveness and starting again with a truly repented heart and attitude.

Redeemed - When Messiah Jesus died on the cross—He paid the price for our sin. He purchased us from Satan. We are "redeemed" when we receive Him as or Lord and Savior.

Resurrection - Resurrection means to come back to life in such a way as to live forever and never die again. After His death and burial, the Lord Jesus Christ experienced resurrection. He literally came back to life and He lives forever and ever.

Ru Ha Kodesh - is Holy Spirit in Hebrew.

Sanctification - Sanctification is a process by which God sets apart all those who have received salvation through Messiah Jesus, and through the prompting and guidance of Holy Spirit brings us to a lifestyle dedicated to His purposes. When we grow as believers, we should strive to be more like Jesus, and in that way we experience sanctification, and are "sanctified."

Satan - Satan was once one of the greatest angels ever created by God; also known as Lucifer, and the devil. He became full of pride and self-adulation and rebelled against God. All believers know that Satan was ultimately defeated when Jesus died on the cross, and will not win His war against God.

Saved - A popular word describing Christians/believers is the word "saved." When we receive the Lord Jesus Christ, He "saves" us from the ravages of sin, death, and hell. We are "saved" and will not suffer the coming Tribulation or hell. We have eternal life through Him.

Second Advent - The Second Coming of Christ at the end of the Tribulation.

Security of the Believer - When we receive the Lord Jesus Christ as our Savior and truly repent, He promises to keep us forever. He promises that nothing can ever separate us from His love or take us out of His hand. We are secure forever in Him. No matter what happens to us in this life, we can be confident that Messiah Jesus will never leave us. We can be confident that when we die, we will be with Him forever, for eternity.

Seraphim - Seraphim are creatures with six wings, particularly focused on continually worshipping God (Isaiah 6:2-4).

Shabbat - This is the Hebrew word for "ceasing" or "stopping." This word is also used for the seventh day, the Shabbat; the day work stops (7th day of the week) to rest and contemplate on the Lord.

"For six days work may be done; but on the seventh day there is a Sabbath of complete rest, a holy convocation. You shall not do any work; it is a Sabbath to the LORD in all your dwelling" (Leviticus 23:3).

Shabbat Shalom - This popular Hebrew phrase means "peaceful Sabbath." This is used as a greeting at any time on Shabbat.

Shalom - The Hebrew word for peace and God's blessing; used as a greeting.

Sin - Sin means, "To miss the mark." The Lord has told us in the Bible how we should live our lives. His holy Word is a guideline for our lives. But without a doubt, we have all gone against His Ten Commandments. We have all sinned; no one is without sin. The more we live according to God's commandments, the more peace we will have. But none of us can "fix" our sin problems by just *trying* to be good. That is why the Lord Jesus Christ died on the cross, to pay the death penalty for our sins in our place.

371

Substitutionary Atonement - Christ died in our place. He endured the torture of death by crucifixion so that we could be set free from death, from hell. On the cross, He was our substitute. We should have been the ones to die, but He died for us, giving us an opportunity to live eternally with Him. The word Atonement refers to the fact that when He died, He made it possible for God and man to come together as one.

Temptation - Temptation is when our minds tell is it is okay to do something that God clearly tells us is sin. We are all tempted, even Jesus was tempted. We can choose to do the right thing and win over temptation by keeping the Word of God close to our hearts, and always praying for strength to overcome temptations.

Trinity - The Bible teaches that God reveals Himself as One God Who exists as three *persons*: God the Father, God the Son, and God the Holy Spirit. The word "Trinity" combines the prefix "tri" meaning "three." with the word "unity" which means "one."

Walking in the flesh - Walking in the flesh means living ones life continually succumbing to temptations leading to a life filled with sin with little if any regard for the Lord.

Walking in the Spirit - living our lives in a way that reflects the inner workings of the Holy Spirit dwelling within all true believers.

Works - Deeds, actions. The Lord encourages us to do good *works* but the Scriptures emphatically teach that no amount of *works* or rituals can ever be enough to merit salvation. Only Christ can save us.

Yahweh - is a Hebrew word for God.

Yeshua - Jesus in the name of the Messiah. Yeshua is a Hebrew word that has the root meaning: salvation (Matthew 1:18-21).

Yeshua Ha Mashiach - Jesus the Christ: in Hebrew.

Biblical References to God's Holy Angels

The Bible gives us some marvelous and heroic accounts regarding God's holy angels. Angels are helpers, guardians, official announcers of news, and emissaries of both the mercy of God and the wrath or judgments of God. Here is just a short list of the many biblical references made to God's holy angels:

Angels Are God's Faithful Assistants Reverently Serving Him

"The LORD has established His throne in the heavens; and His sovereignty rules over all. Bless the LORD, you His angels, mighty in strength, who perform His word, obeying the voice of His word! Bless the LORD, all you His hosts, you who serve Him, doing His will" (Psalm 103:19-22).

"The Son of Man will send forth His angels, and they will gather out of His kingdom all stumbling blocks, and those who commit lawlessness" (Matthew 13:41).

"And then He will send forth the angels, and will gather together His elect from the four winds, from the farthest end of the earth, to the farthest end of heaven" (Mark 13:27).

"And *to give* you who are troubled rest with us when the Lord Jesus, is revealed from heaven with His mighty angels in flaming fire, taking vengeance on those who do not know God, and to those who do not obey the gospel of our Lord Jesus Christ" (2 Thessalonians 1:7-8).

"Then I saw an angel coming down from heaven, having the key to the bottomless pit and a great chain in his hand. He laid hold of the dragon, that serpent of old, who is *the* devil and Satan, and bound him for a thousand years" (Revelation 20:1-2).

"And He will send His angels with a great sound of a trumpet, and they will gather together His elect from the four winds, from one end of heaven to the other" (Matthew 24:31).

Angels Can Visit the Earth from Heaven

"And he [Jacob] had a dream, and behold a ladder was set on the earth with its top reaching to heaven; and behold the angels of God were ascending and descending on it" (Genesis 28:12).

"And He said to him [Nathanael], "Most assuredly, I say to you, hereafter you shall see heaven open up, and the angels of God ascending and descending upon the Son of Man" (John 1:51).

We Have Protective Angels

"The angel of the LORD encamps around those who fear Him, and rescues them" (Psalm 34:7).

"For He will give His angels charge concerning you, to guard you in all your ways" (Psalm 91:11).

Angels Can Suddenly Appear to Help in a Time of Need

Even Jesus, was helped by an angel from heaven. When He was fervently praying in the Garden of Gethsemane, He was in agony knowing what He was ahead of Him; that He was about to be crucified and take upon Himself all the sins of the world.

"Now an angel from heaven appeared to Him, strengthening Him" (Luke 22:43).

After Jesus had fasted in the wilderness for forty days and forty nights, Satan tried to tempt Him. But Jesus rebuked the devil and he fled. Immediately after, angels came to minister to Jesus:

"Then the devil left Him; and behold, angels came and *began* to minister to Him" (Matthew 4:11).

"And he [Elijah] lay down and slept under a juniper tree; and behold, there was an angel touching him, and he said to him, "Arise, eat." Then he looked and behold, there was at his head a bread cake *baked on* hot stones, and a jar of water.

So he ate and drank and lay down again. And the angel of the LORD came again a second time and touched him and said, "Arise and eat, because the journey is too great for you." So he arose and ate and drank, and went in the strength of that food forty days and forty nights to Herob, the mountain of God" (1 Kings 19:5-8).

"And when Peter came to himself, he said, 'Now I know for sure that the Lord has sent forth His angel and rescued me from the hand of Herod and from all that the Jewish people were expecting'" (Acts 12:11).

"But the high priest rose up, along with all his associates (that is the sect of the Sadducees), and they were filled with jealousy; and they laid hands on the apostles, and put them in a public jail.

But an angel of the Lord during the night opened the gates of the prison, and taking them out he said, "Go your way, stand and speak to the people in the temple the whole message of this Life. And upon hearing *this* they entered into the temple about daybreak and *began* to teach" (Acts 5:17-21a).

"For this very night an angel of the God to whom I belong and whom I serve stood before me, saying, 'Do not be afraid, Paul; you must stand before Caesar; and behold God has granted you all those who are sailing with you.

Therefore, keep up your courage, men, for I believe God, that it will turn out exactly as I have been told'" (Acts 27:23-25). [An angel comforted Paul and told him that no lives would be lost in the shipwreck.]

"When the morning dawned, the angels urged Lot to hurry, saying, 'Arise, take your wife and your two daughters, who are here, lest you be consumed in the punishment of the city'" (Genesis 19:15).

"Then Daniel spoke to the king, "O king, live forever! My God, sent His angel and shut the lions' mouths, and they have not harmed me; inasmuch as I was found innocent before Him; and also toward you, 'O king, I have committed no crime'" (Daniel 6:21-22).

"Now an angel of the Lord spoke to Philip, saying, "Arise and go toward the south along the road which goes down from Jerusalem to Gaza." This is desert" (Acts 8:26).

"And an angel of the Lord appeared to him, standing to the right of the altar of incense. And Zacharias was troubled when he saw *him*, and fear gripped him. But the angel said to him, "Do not be afraid, Zacharias, for your petition has been heard, and your wife Elizabeth will bear you a son, and you will give him the name John [John the Baptist's birth foretold]" (Luke 1:11-13).

Angels Continually Exalt God and Have His Attention

"See that you do not despise one of these little ones, for I say to you, that their angels in heaven continually behold the face of my Father who is in heaven" (Matthew 18:10).

"And I looked, and heard the voice of many angels around the throne and the living creatures and the elders; and the number of them was myriads of myriads, and thousands of thousands saying with a loud voice, 'Worthy is the Lamb that was slain to receive power and riches and wisdom and might and honor and glory and blessing'" (Revelation 5:11).

"In the year of King Uzziah's death, I saw the Lord sitting on a throne, lofty and exalted, with the train of His robe filling the temple. Seraphim stood above Him, each having six wings; with two he covered his face, and with two he flew. And one called out to another and said, 'Holy, Holy, Holy, is the LORD of hosts, the whole earth is full of His glory'" (Isaiah 6:1-3).

Joseph received guidance and warnings to protect the baby Jesus from an angel in his dreams (Matthew 1:20, 24; 2:13, 19).

Angels Proclaim Awesome News and Important Events

Angels announced the birth of Messiah Jesus to the shepherds:

"And an Angel of the Lord suddenly stood before them, and the glory of the Lord shone all around them; and they were terribly frightened. And the angel said to them, "Do not be afraid; for behold, I bring you good news of a great joy which will be for all people; for today in the city of David there has been born for you a Savior, who is Christ the Lord. And this will be a sign for you: you will find a baby wrapped in cloths, and lying in a manger.

And suddenly there appeared with the angel a multitude of heavenly host praising God, and saying, "Glory to God in the highest, and on earth peace among men with whom He is pleased." And it came about when the angels had gone away from them into heaven, that the shepherds began saying to one another, 'Let us go straight to Bethlehem then, and see this thing that has happened which the Lord has made know to us'" (Luke 2:9-15).

Angels Are Strong and Powerful

"Bless the LORD, you His angels, who excel in strength, who do His word; heeding the voice of His word" (Psalm 103:20).

"Wheras angels, who are greater in power and might, do not bring a reviling accusation against them before the Lord" (2 Peter 2:11).

An angel was very involved in bringing the revelatory visions to the apostle John during his exile on the island of Patmos.

"The Revelation of Jesus Christ, which God gave Him to show His servants—things which must shortly take place. And he sent and signified it by His angel to His servant John" (Revelation 1:1).

"I saw still another mighty angel coming down from heaven, clothed with a cloud. And a rainbow was on his head; his face was like the sun, and his feet like pillars of fire.

He had a book open in his hand. And he set his right foot on the sea and his left foot on the land, and cried out with a loud voice, as when a lion roars. When he cried out, seven thunders uttered their voices" (Revelation 10:1-3).

"After these things I saw another angel coming down from heaven, having great authority, and the earth was illuminated with his glory" (Revelation 18:1).

"Now I, John, saw and heard these things. And when I heard and saw, I fell down to worship before the feet of the angel who showed me these things. Then he said to me, "See *that you* do not *do that*. For I am your fellow servant, and of your brethren the prophets, and of those who keep the words of this book. Worship God" (Revelation 22:8-9).

Accounts and Passages from the Bible and Bible Quotes

The Creation Account	Genesis 1:1-2:7
The Fall of Man	Genesis 3:6-24
The Flood	Genesis 6:1-9:17
The Call of Abraham	Genesis 12:1-9
The Story of Moses and the Freedom of the Slaves	Exodus
The Passover	Exodus 12:1-50
The Ten Commandments	Exodus 20:1-17
David and Goliath	1 Samuel 17
The Shepherd's Psalm (The Lord is my shepherd...)	Psalm 23
The Protection Psalm	Psalm 91
To Everything There Is a Season	Ecclesiastes 3:1-8
Daniel in the Lion's Den	Daniel 6:10
The Birth of Christ	Matthew 1:18-2:23, Luke 1:26-2:40
Sermon on the Mount (Blessed are...)	Matthew 5-7
The Beatitudes	Matthew 5:3-11
The Lord's Prayer (Our Father...)	Matthew 6:9-15, Luke 11:2-4
The Prodigal Son	Luke 15:11-32
The Good Samaritan	Luke 10:29-37
Jesus Raises Lazarus From Dead	John 11:1-46
Jesus Shows His Glory	Matthew 16-17
Palm Sunday	Luke 19:28-44

The Last Supper	Matthew 26:20-25, Mark
Garden of Gethsemane	Matthew 26:36-46
The Betrayal of Jesus	Matthew 26:47-56
The Death of Christ	Luke 23:26-56, John 19:16-42
Resurrection of Christ	John 20, Luke 24, Matthew 28
Christ Ascending to Heaven	Acts 1:1-12
Pentecost Holy Spirit	Acts 2:1-21
The Conversion of Paul	Acts 9:1-31
The Love Chapter	1 Corinthians 13
The Faith Chapter	Hebrews 11

Endnotes
Text courtesy of: http://encouragingbiblequotes.com.

Bible Study and Discipleship

**"But we will devote ourselves to prayer, and to the
ministry of the word." —Acts 6:4**

The apostasy comes into play when studying the Bible. We can never
assume a popular doctrine or teaching is true. I have learned to always go
back to the Bible, to do a cross-reference study and thoroughly examine
what is being taught. I have been guilty of not really doing my
"homework" many times, even long after I was saved, and accepting
some popular beliefs rallied by believers and Christian "leaders" as truth.
But I am much more careful and discerning than I was years ago,
spending much more time examining and reexamining Scripture.

Some individuals often relegate authority or spiritual superiority over
other well-versed believers, assuming they know more and act as if the
Lord gave them a special anointing to "lead." When, in fact He did no
such thing. One is left wondering whatever happened to glorifying the
Lord, and giving the salvation message top priority. Some teachings are
causing much confusion. Confusion never helps advance the true
teachings of the Bible, and can actually hinder the salvation message. As
these last days unfold, the Lord will soon deal with all those who are
disrespecting and using Him for their own personal gain, those who are
unwilling to admit and repent of their folly. These same individuals are
the very ones deluding themselves and others by saying, "What I am
doing is for the Lord. I love the Lord."

"Brethren, let not many of you become teachers, knowing that we
shall receive a stricter judgment" (James 3:1).

"For God is not the author of confusion but of peace, as in all the
churches of the saints" (1 Corinthians 14:33).

As we have already discussed, many churches and some so-called
Bible teachers are increasingly becoming apostate, exactly as the Lord
forewarned. We need to know the Scriptures so we can identify false
teachings. When something does not line-up with Scripture, we must all
be careful not to embrace such teachings. This is an ongoing challenge. I
never assume because someone has written a lot of articles, sold a lot of
books or has a popular media "following" that everything they are
teaching is biblically sound. I find those who are the most trustworthy

and knowledgeable simply consider themselves "students of the Bible" and are quite humble, unassuming and don't tag the word "expert" next to their name.

Many hard working Bible teachers and preachers make tremendous contributions, and they should be applauded for their diligence and devotion to teaching the Word of God. However, it appears far too many believers are eager to volunteer themselves the title of "mentor" or "teacher" or "expert" and place themselves into positions of authority. Some of these individuals are quick to presume that their role is to critique the work of others when their own work is filled with biblically problematic proclamations. No one has "arrived" spiritually, including those with impressive credentials, and *all* believers must study the entire Bible, not substitutes for the Bible (Psalm 1:2; Joshua 1:8). If you have questions about Scripture it is best to go directly to the source, the Bible. Let the Holy Spirit be your mentor and teacher.

"That just as it is written, LET HIM WHO BOASTS, BOAST IN THE LORD" (1 Corinthians 1:31).

If you walk into a Christian bookstore looking for answers, the best section to shop is the aisle where they sell Bibles. This is not to say that there are not numerous wonderful materials that are good study aids. Many excellent books are available, but we must always go to Scripture first as our best and final voice of authority. Much of what is passed off today as biblical "truth" is based on the opinions of individuals who gather their information from commentaries, articles, chitchat, and not regular careful devoted Bible study. None of us can correctly interpret or understand what has been written in the Bible without the teaching of the Holy Spirit (1 John 2:27). We should always keep the Golden Rule of Interpretation in the forefront of our minds as we study the Bible, and all books relating to biblical matters, including this book. I will quote it again:

When the plain sense of Scripture makes common sense, seek no other sense; therefore, take every word at its primary, ordinary, usual, literal meaning unless the facts of the immediate context, studied in the light of related passages and axiomatic and fundamental truths, indicates clearly otherwise.

We know that a physical dragon cannot cast one-third of the stars in space down to earth (Revelation 12:3-4), but the devil who is called the great dragon (Revelation 12:9) can lead one-third of the angels in heaven (Daniel 8:10) to rebel against God and wreck havoc on earth. Good common sense tells us that when Jesus (Yeshua) is called the "Lamb of God" (John 1:29), it does not mean He is a literal lamb. It is symbolic of the fact that He is the Paschal Lamb sacrifice for the sins of the elect.

Those who try to interpret the Scriptures by not using a strict rule of understanding can make any passage say anything they want. For example, as discussed earlier, flawed methods of interpretation have caused some to claim and teach that the two million army of demons spoken of in Revelation 9:16 is the Red Chinese army.

The greatest teacher is the Holy Spirit. As we let Him have more of us, more of our commitment and time, and as we allow Him to renew our minds and grow as believers with pure hearts, He will guide us and teach us. Studying the Bible cannot be a hobby. It is something all believers are commanded to do (2 Timothy 2:15). The more we read the Word of God under the guidance of the Holy Spirit, the more we will understand it.

We are to be "diligent" in studying our Bibles, not material derived from media campaigns that make references to the Bible (2 Timothy 2:15). To simply say, "We can all disagree as long as we all love the Lord" is a weak position, I would say that is just the kind of "lukewarm" attitude that the Lord abhors (Revelation 3:16). If we really "love the Lord" we should all do what He said: Stop teaching the philosophies of men and wholeheartedly begin to study the Scriptures and teach the truth of the Bible.

"If you instruct the brethren in these things, you will be a good minister of Jesus Christ, nourished in the words of faith and good doctrine which you have carefully followed. But reject profane and old wives' fables, and exercise yourself toward godliness" (1 Timothy 4:6-7).

Interpreting Scripture—Careful Hermeneutics

Some argue that a believer cannot fully understand the Scriptures by studying the Bible alone, relying on the teaching of the Holy Spirit (1 John 2:27). It should be noted that the very first Christians thought differently. The Christians in the city of Berea compared what Paul taught with the Scriptures (Old Testament) to determine whether or not he was teaching was the truth. They studied Scripture so they could identify false teaching. Whenever a believer today studies what a Bible teacher, pastor, theologian or commentator teaches he should compare the teachings with the Scriptures.

But one must know the Scriptures (Genesis 1:1 to Revelation 22:21) thoroughly to be able to determine whether or not what someone teaches is correct. Bible study takes time and effort. People usually do not accept or teach false doctrine deliberately.

Continuous neglect in contemplating and applying what it truly means to "serve the Lord" is most probably at the root of most problematic teachings. Habitual chronic laziness, ineptitude, and thoughtlessness in handling Scripture is a tremendous problem that can only be overcome by making a genuine, deliberate commitment to apply 2 Timothy 2:15 and Acts 17:11 to our daily lives:

"Be diligent to present yourself approved to God as a workman who does not need to be ashamed, handling accurately the word of truth" (2 Timothy 2:15).

"These were more fair-minded than those in Thessalonica, in that they received the word with all readiness and searched the Scriptures daily to *find out* whether these things were so" (Acts 17:11).

If a believer tries to learn what the Bible teaches by studying commentaries, he will be doing just the opposite of what the Bereans and all of the early Christians did. If every Christian would diligently study the Bible every day (Acts 17:11), a false teacher could never gain converts. Instead of being tempted to partake in cults, or get caught-up in the mistakes or lies of biblically weak teachers, false teachers and false prophets, a well-versed believer would have strong discernment.

The key to knowing and understanding Scripture is studying as much as possible every day, relying on the Holy Spirit (1 Corinthians 2:10; 1 John 2:27) and Jesus (1 Corinthians 2:16) to teach us.

Studying commentaries, listening to teachings and sermons can be very beneficial. A Spirit led-believer does so with great care, and makes it a common practice. Yet we do not rely on the teachings of men to know and understand Scripture. We study what others say and write to see if our understanding is correct. And when we see that our understanding differs greatly from the majority of commentators and Bible teachers, we must go back and study the Bible even more.

After we have done that and we are thoroughly convinced that our understanding is correct and the majority understanding is wrong—so be it. There are times when the majority is wrong and the minority is right. The perfect example is Martin Luther. As a Roman Catholic priest he concluded that salvation is by grace through faith alone apart from the Catholic Church. He was the minority and the Catholic Church was the majority yet he was right and the Catholic Church was wrong.

Let the holy infallible, inherent Word of God be our daily bread, and on occasion, may we take just a few nibbles here and there from the works of men.

If we simply say, "I have a difference of opinion on some biblical topics" without undertaking a very serious in-depth Bible study and carefully revisiting the Scriptures in question, we can hinder our spiritual growth and our understanding of the Word of God. And if we are in a position of leadership many people could be led astray.

The truth is in the Word of God. The Word of God is in the Bible. The Word of God does not leave room for speculation and guessing games that contradict its content. Selective analysis derived from passages to create desired interpretations is essentially rewriting the true meaning of the Scriptures. To say, "I believe a particular teaching", is not the same as saying, "This is what Scripture clearly teaches." To simply "believe" or assume something to be true does not make it so. As believers, we must be careful not to become part of the growing apostasy or contribute to the false teachings that are prevalent.

Daily Bible study is very important and necessary in order to grow as a believer (Deuteronomy 17:19; Revelation 3:1). It is a good idea to designate a special place at home for Bible study. Be willing to invest in some good study materials: Bibles, Bible dictionaries. Always go to Scripture to check the validity of information offered in any books or commentaries and focus first and foremost on the Word of God. If you have a computer nearby, you may want to use some of the following resources during your study time:

http://www.blueletterbible.org - An excellent resource for online Bible study.

http://asv1901.com/ - A full online presentation of the excellent and reliable 1901 Standard American Version of the Bible.

http://www.biblegateway.com/ - An exceptional site for looking up Scripture, all popular Bible versions are included as well as passage translations in a number of foreign languages.

http://www.e-sword.net/ - A fast and effective way to study the Bible online.

http://www.bible-history.com/ - Bible Maps, Study Tools, Archeology, Ancient documents and much more.

http://www.biblestudytools.com/concordances/strongs-exhaustive-concordance/ - Strong's Exhaustive Concordance Online.

When I don't use a computer to assist with my Bible studies, I like to use the items listed below when I need to look up something:

The Strongest Strong's Exhaustive Concordance of the Bible - James Strong LL.D., S.T.D., S.T.D. Fully Revised and Corrected by John R. Kohlenberger III and James A. Swanson

Thayer's Greek-English Lexicon of the New Testament - Joseph Thayer

Brown-Driver-Briggs Hebrew and English Lexicon - Francis Brown

An Intermediate Greek-English Lexicon - Liddell and Scott

Exegetical Fallacies - D.A. Carson

A Greek Lexicon of the New Testament and Other Early Christian Literature: Bauer, Arndt, Gingrich and Danker

Greek-English Lexicon of the New Testament Based on Semantic Domains - Louw and Nida

Holman Illustrated Bible Dictionary, 2003 Edition

Lexical Semantics of the Greek New Testament, Louw and Nida

Semantics of New Testament Greek, J.P. Louw

I especially like the 1901 American Standard Version of the Bible. I never do a Bible study anymore without referring to it, and I place that translation at the top of my Bible study list. The King James, New King James, and the New American Standard are also good versions to study. Be sure to cross-reference each of these translations doing careful word studies.

Many good audio Bibles are available today. It is good to read the Scriptures aloud, even speaking along with the narrator saying the verses together. I like to listen to Scripture when I am driving. It is also a good to listen to at home while doing chores or making dinner. Listening to Scripture helps keep our hearts and minds focused on the Lord giving us a strong foundation for knowing and sharing the Word of God. Repeating Scripture out loud as we read our Bibles is very helpful in grasping the meanings of the passages.

We should always pray before studying the Bible that the Holy Spirit will lead us and guide us. Have reference tools available as noted above (Bibles, a good variety of Bible dictionaries, concordances) to look up pertinent information regarding some of the points made under "How to Do the Study" located on the next page.

A basic hermeneutical principle to apply when studying Scripture is this:

Take everything literally unless the Scriptures say it is symbolic, or unless it is physically impossible for it to be literal or be fulfilled in a literal manner, with the exception of miracles.

An example to show how this principle works can be found in Revelation twelve:

"And there appeared another wonder in heaven; and behold a great red dragon, having seven heads and ten horns, and seven crowns upon his heads. And his tail drew the third part of the stars of heaven, and did cast them to the earth" (Revelation 12:3-4a).

There is not and there will never be a literal dragon with seven heads and ten horns. If there were such a creature it could not sweep a third of the stars in space and cast them down to Earth. Therefore, the dragon and the stars are symbolic. In verse 9 it says the devil—who is called a "great dragon," and his angels were cast down to earth. We can determine from this that the devil is the dragon and the angels are the stars.

We also know from Daniel 8:9-11 that the "little horn" (Antichrist) casts some of the stars of heaven down to earth. These stars are fallen angels that followed the devil in his rebellion. We see from Daniel and Revelation that the devil and the Antichrist together cast down angels to earth. We know the "little horn" is the Antichrist because in verse 11 of Daniel 8 he claims to be equal to the "prince of the host" (Jesus Christ). In 2 Thessalonians 2:4 we see the Antichrist will claim to be "God."

In chapter nine of Revelation there is a detailed description of demonic creatures. These demonic creatures are real and not symbolic. It is not impossible for there to be creatures as depicted in Revelation nine; they do not do things that are physically impossible for a creature to do.

Here is a helpful guide to Study the Word of God:
1. Determine who the message is being given to and why.
2. Determine if the message is to be understood as being literal or symbolic; using the Golden Rule of Interpretation.
3. Determine the context (what is the subject).
4. Determine the dispensation and if the message is for us today.
5. Find as many passages dealing with the subject as you can.
6. Put together the message of all the passages to determine what is being said.
7. Give clear statements far more importance than unclear statements.
8. Base the message of an unclear statement on a clear one.

Jumpstart Your Understanding of the Gospel

"Gospel literally means "good news." It refers to the good news that Jesus Christ, God the Son, became a man like us. He lived a perfect and sinless life. He died on the cross to pay the penalty for our sins. He rose again and lives forever. He will forgive our sins and give us eternal life when we truly repent and place our faith in Him. The following passages all pertain specifically to the gospel—the salvation message. These passages are important to learn for effective witnessing.

John 1:12-13; 3:1-18, 36; 4:10-14; 5:24, 38-39;6:29, 35-40, 44-58, 63-71; 7:5, 38-39; 8:24; 10:27-30; 17:3; 20:31.

Acts 37-38, 15:9-11.

Romans 3:19-31, 4:1-11, 5:6-11, 15-21, 9:30-10:4, 10:9-13, 17.

1 Corinthians 15:1-4.

Galatians 2:16, 3:1-14, 23-29.

Ephesians 2:8-10.

Titus 3:5-6.

Hebrews 9:11-15; 22; 10:10.

1 Peter 1:18; 23.

1 John 5:10-13.

The Importance of Discipleship

Every true, born-again believer is a disciple of Jesus the Messiah. We should all strive to live like disciples, but we need to learn and understand what that involves. Jesus commissioned His disciples to be witnesses to His resurrection, and to make "disciples of all nations":

> "But ye shall receive power, when the Holy Spirit is come upon you: and ye shall be my witnesses both in Jerusalem, and in all Judaea and Samaria, and unto the uttermost part of the earth" (Acts 18).

> "Go ye therefore, and make disciples of all the nations, baptizing them into the name of the Father and of the Son and of the Holy Spirit: teaching them to observe all things whatsoever I commanded you: and lo, I am with you always, even unto the end of the world" (Matthew 28:19-20).

When a person is saved, trusting solely in Jesus the Messiah as Lord and Savior he is then considered one of His disciples. Although every believer is technically considered a disciple, one must attempt to live like a disciple: Pray often each day: Ephesians 6:18; Thessalonians 5:17. Read Scripture daily: Deuteronomy 17:19; Revelation 1:3. Listen to Scripture on a daily basis: Proverbs 4:1; 8:34; Luke 8:15, 21; 11:28; James 1:22; Revelation 1:3.

Engage in regular, careful Bible study: John 5:39; Acts 17:11; 2 Timothy 2:15. Cultivate relationships with other believers: Acts 2:42; 46-47; Hebrews 3:13; 10:24-25. Share your testimony with others when you feel led by the Holy Spirit: Acts 2:47; 1 Peter 3:15. Help others become disciples: Matthew 28:18b-20; Mark 16:15; 2 Timothy 2:2.

If a believer concentrates on the practices listed above he will become an effective disciple of Messiah Jesus. This does not happen quickly. It takes many years to grow in the Lord and become a strong disciple. But it starts with the daily discipline of being in prayer, focused study and application of the Word of God and regular fellowship with other believers. Learning and studying the Word of God and having a strong prayer life are closely linked.

Hunger and Thirst for the Word of God

Scripture teaches we should have a daily hunger and thirst for God and His Word (not substitutes such as commentaries or articles, etc.): Job 23:12; Deuteronomy 8:3; Psalm 42:1-2; 63:1 and 143:6. Hungering and thirsting for God and His Word means a person desires to know the Lord and have fellowship with Him. The way we do that is by spiritually feeding on and drinking in His Word.

The first way of drinking in His Word is by hearing Scripture; simply read the passages concerning hearing Scripture. Read them out loud. Then move on to reading Scripture, Bible study and memorization. Always pray first for wisdom and guidance from the Holy Spirit. Learning and studying the Word of God and prayer are closely linked together.

Hearing Scripture: Selective listening to: Sermons/teaching in church, radio, television, CDs, DVDs: Proverbs 8:34; Luke 8:15, 21; 11:28; James 1:22; Revelation 1:3.

Reading Scripture: Deuteronomy 17:19; Psalm 42:1-2; 63:1; 143:6; Revelation 1:3.

Bible study: Deuteronomy 8:3; Matthew 4:4; John 5:39; Acts 17:11 and 2 Timothy 2:15.

Memorization of Scripture: Deuteronomy 6:6; Psalm 37:31; 40:8; 119:11; Proverbs 2:1; 3:1; 3: 4:1; 22:17-18.

Meditation on Scripture: Joshua 1:8; Job 23:12; Psalm 1:2.

Holiness and obedience are two reasons we study the Bible: John 15:3; Romans 12:1-2; Ephesians 5:26; 6:14,17; 2 Timothy 3:16-17; Titus 3:5; Joshua 1:8; 1 John 2:3-4.

Getting closer to and knowing our God and Savior is another reason to study the Bible (Jeremiah 9:24; Hosea 6:3; John 17:3; Philippians 3:10; Colossians 1:10; 2 Timothy 1:12; 1 John 2:3). Most people eat at least three meals a day. Must they be told to eat? Do most believers hear, read, study, memorize and *meditate on Scripture* three times a day? Should we not feed our souls as much or more than we feed our bodies?

What about feeding our minds? Do most believers spend more time watching secular movies and television shows than studying the Bible?

Shouldn't all believers be genuinely eager to read the letters that our God and Savior wrote to us—the Bible? Some believers read the New Testament but many do not read the Old Testament. Events recorded in the Old Testament were written for our benefit (1 Corinthians 10:6). We should carefully study the entire Bible from Genesis to Revelation.

Prayer

It is very important for all believers to pray daily and often to keep our personal communication going with the Lord. The Word of God tells us to pray to the Father in Jesus' name (John 14:13-14). Prayer is one of the many basic daily activities of all believers. Reading, hearing, studying and reflecting upon Scripture are the other basic daily activities. We should pray several times a day.

We are encouraged to pray always (Ephesians 6:18; 1 Thessalonians 5:17). We have the example of Paul (Colossians 1:3; 2 Timothy 1:3). We have the example of Timothy (Colossians 1:3). Praying always means to be in constant communication with the Lord. We can make brief requests and express our gratitude while we are on the go and we should pray privately on our knees as the Lord and the apostles did (Mark 14:32-35; 6:12; 22:41; Ephesians 3:14; Acts 7:60; 9:40; 20:36; 21:5).

We should pray in the Holy Spirit (Ephesians 6:18; Romans 8:26; Jude 20). Pray according to the will of God (1 John 5:14-15). Believers can know God's will by studying the Scriptures. Prayer is our way of speaking to the Lord. He speaks to us by His Word. It is a blessing to hear, read, study, and memorize His Word every day—to listen to Him.

There are three types of prayer: praise, intercession (when we pray on the behalf of others) and personal requests. These three types of prayer can be short prayers or lengthy ones. It is a blessing to be devoted to prayer (Romans 12:12; Colossians 4:2; 1 Peter 4:7); meaning we should spend time every day in private prayer on our knees, and in prayer when on the go. We should also pray with others (Acts 1:3; 16:25).

Our Daily Walk with the Lord Includes Forgiveness

"And be kind to one another, tenderhearted, forgiving one another, even as God in Christ forgave you. For if you forgive men their trespasses, your heavenly Father will also forgive you. But if you do not forgive men their trespasses, neither will your Father forgive your trespasses." —Ephesians 4:32, Matthew 6:14-15

Once we have heard and accepted the truth of the Lord Jesus Christ by faith and make a commitment to the Him, **we need to yield to the transforming power of the Holy Spirit** and not "forget" that commitment. We need to be in compliance *with* the Holy Spirit so He can do the necessary renewing work within us. A genuine conversion experience needs to take place in order to be saved. It is our willingness to work *with* the Holy Spirit and *apply* the Word of God to our every day lives that enables us to mature as believers and be "transformed" by the power of the Holy Spirit. When we don't apply ourselves in this way we cannot achieve true intimacy with the Lord.

In order to achieve true intimacy with the Lord it is also important to apply the biblical teaching of compassion and forgiveness to our lives. It is very important to forgive those who have hurt us. Otherwise we will be carrying an emotional load that will hinder our ability to truly grow. It is spiritually and emotionally debilitating and unscriptural to carry a grudge against someone—especially other believers. Our true character, our motives and our spiritual authenticity are revealed by how we respond to and treat others, particularly when it comes to forgiveness. Sometimes no matter how hard we try to rectify a problem, some individuals may be unwilling to take responsibility for their own behavior and let go of feelings of anger and bitterness regarding a difficult situation. Forgive them anyway, even if they are in the "wrong" and move on! Pray for them with love. Remember what Jesus said: "Father forgive them, for they know not what they do" (Luke 23:34).

And if they *do know* what they are doing and won't repent, then they are hypocrites of the worst kind and God will deal with them. The Lord knows who truly belong to Him. He knows the true motives of everyone. Give it all over to the Lord. Let Him fight your battles for you. If you have wronged someone, apologize with all sincerity. If your apology is rejected, then that person will carry the burden and their shallow, superficial character will be exposed—no matter how many excuses they make for their spiteful behavior.

Biblical Principles Regarding Health for Enhanced Wellness When Studying the Bible and for Living

In chapter four I briefly mention how some New Agers have a strong grasp on nutrition and have a wonderful awareness when it comes to the importance of eating a healthy diet, especially those who promote a diet of fresh, whole raw fruits and vegetables; high water content foods.

The Bible is filled with Scriptures urging us to make careful dietary and lifestyle choices. When our bodies are clogged from refined unnatural foods or substances, our energies are diminished and the mental clarity necessary to study the Word of God is hindered. This type of neglect can also contribute to an environment vulnerable to the ravages of sickness and disease.

As we believe the Lord each day for His best for us, we should also take care of His creation by making careful choices in what we consume and by how we choose to live our lives. One day we will all give an account to the Lord. We will look right into Jesus' all-knowing eyes. How much better we will feel if we can say we tried our best to follow His biblical principles, including respecting the bodies he has blessed us with.

When we are saved, we know we will get into heaven, but we should nevertheless try our best to adhere to the Lord's admonitions of setting good examples to others by being good witnesses, and making strong efforts to *apply* the teachings of the Scriptures to the way we live our daily lives. The teachings of the Bible are not concept, but a way of life.

"Or do you not know that your body is a temple of the Holy Spirit who is in you, whom you have from God, and that you are not your own? For you have been bought with a price" (1 Corinthians 6:19-20).

"Therefore, whether you eat or drink, or whatever you do, do all to the glory of God" (1 Corinthians 10:31)

A Final Message from the Author

Leaving Los Angeles—Goodbye Hollywood

"In humility correcting those who are in opposition, if God perhaps will grant them repentance, so that they may know the truth, and *that* they may come to their senses *and escape* the snare of the devil, having been taken captive by him to *do* his will."

—2 Timothy 2:25-26

I wrote the following letter to a dear friend some time ago about my exit from the Arts and Entertainment industry. I am including it in this book at the urging of my publisher and other friends. I am somewhat reluctant to share it, but I am doing so to perhaps help others come to terms with their own personal dilemmas—decisions that they may be faced with when making very important choices for their lives regardless of what others might say or think. Here is the letter:

> One day I hope I can share in detail all the traps and tricks the devil used to try to push me into the front lines of the entertainment industry. What a roller coaster ride. OH MY GOSH!!! The Lord brought me to my knees in L.A. when everything was about to break loose for me in a big way.

> My talent agent convinced me to stop commuting for jobs, leave Virginia and spend some time in L.A. despite the fact that I had already reached a point of tremendous ambivalence regarding my show business "career." I was concerned *how* I could be genuinely committed to the Lord *and* continue to make a good living working with those who are generally opposed to and even hostile to the teachings of the Bible.

> When I arrived in L.A., I found myself quickly losing all interest in the overly hyped-up world of Arts and Entertainment; ever since I came to the realization that the God of the Bible *is* who He says He is, my interest and involvement in a show business career subsided dramatically (no pun intended). Yet, I was torn, mostly because of the great deal of time and work I had put into my training, education and portfolio.

I also felt a sense of commitment to follow through on what I had started, but God's ways are the best ways and the path I was walking on was taking me down a slippery slope. The phone kept ringing for one job after another. My agent was totally miffed by my slow-to-grab attitude about the good job opportunities coming my way.

My photographer, who has photographed every major Hollywood star for decades, was really perturbed, then downright shocked when I left L.A. When I arrived in L.A. during the holiday season of 1994 he called, welcoming me to town saying, "You are the ultimate Christmas present for L.A." I was taken aback by such an over-the-top compliment.

My thoughts after hearing it were, "I don't think that kind of admiration will bring me closer to the Lord." I was never comfortable with any of the Hollywood hyperbole. I think everyone in Hollywood is told that they are the ultimate talent at one time or another.

A number of times he told me that he was a "fan" and was convinced because of my "look" and overall multiple talents that I would become "very successful." All nice, flattering things to hear, but none of it would strengthen my relationship with the Lord or take me on a road where I could openly share the gospel with others. My ego said, "Go!" My heart and love for Christ said, "No!"

My well intentioned wheeling and dealing photographer had also taken a great interest in a series of heavily New Age-influenced fairy tales I had written. As soon as he read the first one he immediately expressed a desire to act as my agent for my books and place them before his good friend—the powerful Mike Eisner, who was then CEO for the Walt Disney Company.

He was convinced my fairy tales were a marketing dream come true. That is when I knew I had to take my faith *very* seriously and examine my recommitment to the Lord and how my life was going to fit into Hollywood. The day of reckoning had arrived for me and I had to make a choice.

Would it be the ways of the world or God's ways? Would I compromise myself for the success my fairy tales could bring and lead others into spiritual confusion? Would I compromise myself acting as a representative for products I did not believe in? Would I contribute to helping young girls feel even more insecure about themselves by continuing to participate in an industry that perpetuates the lie that good looks and large sums of money are what life is about?

It is a known fact that most professing Christians in Hollywood often hide their Christian beliefs or at the very least, minimize their faith so they can get work. Few acting roles are wholesome and usually contain messages totally opposite of Judeo-Christian values. The majority of available roles are filled with sexual promiscuity, extreme violence and other demoralizing messages.

Many of today's "role models" shamelessly pedal vulgarity while corrupting the minds of their "fans." And to quote the very savvy talk show host, Dr. Michael Savage: "A sewer pipe that runs out of Hollywood into everyone's brain." The music industry has similar problems.

Magazine advertisements (which translate into print work for actors and models) are for the most part loaded with ego-stroking psychobabble and advertisements detrimental to one's psyche—all sold with a smile—and the promise of a happier life.

Not to say that there are not some edifying and interesting productions and scripts, but not enough to make a career out of *and* also stay true to one's conservative Judeo-Christian beliefs.

Shortly before I left Virginia I had shared the first two fairy tales of my series with the late Ray Brubaker. We had become acquainted through his Christian television ministry. At that time, although I had recommitted my life to Christ, I still did not totally "get it."

I was still trying to fit God into *my* agenda. My fairy tales were about God but were loaded with New Age mysticism—although in a most charming way. Just the way the devil likes it. I had written them while I was still searching for spiritual "truth" and my perception of the Bible and the God of the Bible were tainted.

Mr. Brubaker very diplomatically pointed out to me that my storyline was great but filled with too many openings that left the truth of the God of the Bible to be inconclusive. It was then that I began to understand if those fairy tales went out before the public en mass and made into a series of animated films; my testimony for Jesus would be at risk—ruined.

The New Age type of storyline in my fairy tales would be embraced by the world—by those who love to water down the truth of Jesus. As time went on I learned that the Lord simply was not going to let me be devoured by the Hollywood moguls. But I had a tough time coming to grips with all of it.

The Hollywood agents involved were ready to push the project forward to try to make a deal because it had such mass appeal—which could result in great monetary gain for everyone involved. But the Holy Spirit was relentless in His conviction that what I had written was an assault to the Lord. It was an agonizing realization for me.

After Ray Brubaker's critique of my books, the Lord *really started* to work on me. I believed Jesus is Lord but I was confused and still had a lot of New Age influences still lurking in my mind working against me. For quite some time the Lord had been ministering to me—trying to get my attention and there came point where I knew I could not be in His world and the entertainment world at the same time. Not if I *really* wanted to make Him number one in my life.

Very soon after I arrived in L.A. my father died very unexpectedly. I never felt as much pressure as I did at that time in my life. I felt completely displaced and shocked. Was I really going to walk away from everything that I had sacrificed and worked for? I had a very impressive, outstanding portfolio showcasing my talents. If I walked away all my years of preparation, all my hard work would be meaningless and the contents of my portfolio would do nothing more than gather dust in my closet. My music alone had taken a great deal of time and effort. I had recorded enough of my original songs to make an introductory album. How I wished I could talk it over with my dad who was now gone, but gratefully, in heaven with the Lord.

While in L.A., I spent all day and late into the night for months and months praying and reading my Bible and listening to every Christian radio station I could find. All the while my agent and photographer thought I was making a huge mistake throwing away such "great" opportunities. Of course they were not believers. The phone was ringing *all the time*, every day with work opportunities, but I was at a spiritual crossroads in my life and I could not allow any distractions.

I let my answering service take most of my phone calls and I went into a long, deep communion with the Lord. I let one big job after another slip away. Everything I had worked for and had been "groomed for." Right there, in the heart of L.A., at the brink of great worldly success the Lord removed from me any desire to be around anything to do with the Arts and Entertainment industry.

Yet, still, it took many years for me to completely break away emotionally on some levels; the devil does not give up easily. *All my life* I had heard from so many people that I should be an entertainer and so many people would say, "You have charisma, you look like a movie star."

About four months after I had started at Lee Strasberg's acting school (part of my Bachelor of Science Media Communications degree program) I was pulled aside and told, "You have a special quality that comes through in your work," and that I should seriously pursue an acting career because I had the talent and the necessary discipline, to get started right away–that I was "ready."

I believe Satan used my desire to be involved in the entertainment industry *all throughout my life* to try to keep me from realizing the truth about God and derail me into a life of confusion, heartbreak and ultimately an eternity without the Lord. While coming to terms with my life in L.A., I randomly gave away Bibles to people I met and shared the Good News about the great Savior of mankind at every possible opportunity.

I attended John MacArthur's church in Sun Valley. I spoke with few people involved in show business, kept a very low profile and made my "quiet" time with the Lord a way of life. My life was changing and I was trying to hold on and learn to trust the Lord, as the Scriptures teach.

Once I realized I could not go on with my career, I did not want to interact with my talent agent or photographer. I was afraid I would get pulled back into their "glitzy climb to the top" world. But I did, at the last moments, finally tell my agent I was no longer interested in a show business career and that I was leaving L.A. He immediately said, "I'll be right over, you can't leave. We have to talk." I told him it was too late. I was not going to change my mind and that I had already packed up my belongings and I was leaving.

I didn't want to become a celebrity of any kind, not even a Christian one. I only wanted Jesus to shine and get all the glory for Who He is. My portfolio has gathered a lot of dust all these years since I left L.A. and I have moments when I still can't believe I really said "no" to all the opportunities that were right there for me to grab. But they really were not opportunities, only deceptive steppingstones that would have taken me further and further away from the truth of Jesus and threatened my close relationship with Him.

If you are ever in doubt about making a choice between God's ways or the ways of the world, always choose God—no matter what. We are living in a world where too many people have little or no interest in having a relationship with Almighty God. Never accept counsel from anyone who does not have very strong, solid biblical principles, and even then be very careful. Even within the Christian circles there are far too many believers who do not understand the tremendous spiritual warfare going on, intricately designed to take us away from the true living God of the Bible and into an unfathomable eternity with the masterminds of evil.

The last song I ever wrote and recorded is titled: *Lord You Are My Everything*, my personal love letter to the Lord expressed in the form of lyrics and music—my way of letting Him know I was finished with the world of Arts and Entertainment, and exceedingly grateful that He rescued me from a career that was inevitably pushing me deeper into a world of spiritual and moral destruction.

Philippians 3:12-14

"Not that I have already attained, or am already perfected; but I press on, that I may lay hold of that for which Christ Jesus has also laid hold of me. Brethren, I do not count myself to have apprehended; but one thing I do, forgetting those things which are behind and reaching forward to those things which are ahead, press toward the goal for the prize of the upward call of God in Christ Jesus."

LORD YOU ARE MY EVERYTHING

You are my, everything.
Without you nothing exists.
The water, the streams,
You made everything.
Hold me Lord.
Carry me when I'm afraid.
Stay by my side.
Keep me faithful and right.

When the night reveals itself
You're always near,
You guide me everywhere.

I love you Lord.
Thank you for dying for me.
You're faithful to me.
You're my, everything.
Show me your will.
What do you want me to do?
How can I glorify you?
I'll try my best for you.

When I try to turn away
And work things out my own way,
How quickly I find out
I need you Lord,
Please don't leave me Lord.

BRIDGE

When the sun reveals itself
I recognize your smile.
You wrap me in your love.
You carry me.
Oh, you carry me.

I love you Lord.
You are my, everything.
You know what's best for me,
You hold my destiny.
You are my only Lord,
You are the light of the world.
I'm saved by your grace.
I'm healed by your love.

BRIDGE

You are my, everything.
Without you nothing exists.
The sun and the streams,
You made everything.
Hold me Lord,
Carry me when I'm afraid.
Show me the way.
Keep me strong keep me safe.

When the sun reveals itself
I recognize your smile.
You wrap me in your love,
You carry me…
Oh, you set me free.

BRIDGE

Show me your will
Show me the way.
Stay by my side. Don't go away.

♥ ♥ ♥ ♥ ♥ ♥ ♥

Lyrics and music written by Kit Rush ©1995

Trust in the Lord with All Your Heart

Proverbs 3:3-6

"Do not let kindness and truth leave you; bind them around your neck, write them on the tablet of your heart. So you will find favor and good repute in the sight of God and man. Trust in the LORD with all your heart. And do not lean on your own understanding. In all your ways acknowledge Him, and He will make your paths straight."

Notes

29. "Collection of Quotes."
http://www.watchmanbiblestudy.com/Quotes.htm.

41. "Islamic Guide: Beat wife 'by hand or stick," *Ynetnews* (March 25, 2012), http://www.ynetnews.com/articles/0,7340,L-4207770,00.html.
Terry Davidson, "Book tells Muslim men how to beat their wives," *QMI Agency,*
http://www.torontosun.com/2012/03/23/book-tells-muslim-men-how-to-beat-and-control-their-wives.

75. *List of Arab nations by Population* (2012 UN estimate)
http://wikipedia.org/wiki/List_of_Arab_countries_by_population.
Israel and the Arab World,
http://www.imninalu.net/Israel-Arabs.htm.
Ruth Eglash, "Israel population passes 7.8 million mark," *Jerusalem Post* (April7, 2012).

83. James Strong Editor, *The New Strong's Exhaustive Concordance of the Bible,* Thomas Nelson Publishers, Nashville, Tennessee, 1996, Hebrew Appendix page 23.

86. "Just How Big Is Israel?" *Look Israel,*
http://www.lookisrael.com/files/justbig.php.

87. "Egypt deploys US tanks, missiles in demilitarized Sinai, near Israel," World Tribune (August 24, 2012)
http://www.worldnewstribune.com/2012/08/24/egypt-deploys-u-s-tanks-missiles-in-demilitarized-sinai-near-israel/.

89. "The First Settlement Outside the Old City Walls,"
http://jerusalem.wikispaces.com/Sir+Moses+Montefiore+and+Jerusalem#Mishkenot She'ananim,
http://www.jewishvirtuallibrary.org/jsource/Society_&_Culture/kibbutz.html.

94. Jim Hoft, "Russian Troops Enter Syria to Assist Assad Regime," *Christian Science Monitor* (March 29, 2012).
John Metzler, "Kofi Annan's Syria deal spares Assad and is backed by China, Russia and Iran," *World Tribune* (March 29, 2012) http://www.worldnewstribune.com/2012/03/29/kofi-annans-syria-deal-spares-assad-and-is-backed-by-china-russia-and-iran/.
Ariel Zirulnick, "Syria violence raises concerns Assad is only

buying time with UN cease-fire deal," *The Christian Science Monitor* (March 28, 2012).

111. Barry Chamish, "And Here's the CFR," *Personal Thoughts Editorial Section* (July 17, 1998).

209. George Knowles, "Pythagoras," http://www.controverscial.com/Pythagoras.htm.

248. Ted Olsen, "HarperCollins Buys Thomas Nelson, Will Control 50% of Christian Publishing Market - Where will Thomas Nelson fit in Murdoch's empire, which already includes Zondervan?," *Christianity Today* (October 23,2011).

313. "Congressional Report: "Iran has Expanded Its Terror Network Inside the U.S," *World Tribune.com* http://www.worldnewstribune.com/2012/03/23/congressional-report-iran-has-expanded-its-terror-network-inside-u-s/.

341. Jason Samenow, "Huge hail pounds Oklahoma town," *The Washington Post* (April 10, 2012) http://www.washingtonpost.com/blogs/capital-weather-gang/post/huge-hail-pounds-oklahoma-town-photos/2012/04/10/gIQApbv28S_blog.html.
"Four-footdrifts of golf–ball sized hail hit Texas,"*Fox News* (April 11).
Jeremy A. Kaplan, "Gigantic, softball-sized hail could be in store for Midwest, South," *Fox News.com* (April 13, 2012).
Brian Merchant, "Extreme Weather USA: 2012 Kicks Off With Record Heat, Tornadoes & Drought," *Treehugger* (April 4, 2012).
Bill Deger, "Drenching, "Damaging Storms Target Deep South," *Accu Weather.Com* (April 5, 2012). http://www.accuweather.com/en/weather-news/drenching-damaging-storms-targ/636.
Charlie Cooper, "Roll Up Your Hose Pipes for the Big Turn-Off," *The Independent* (April 5, 2012) http://www.independent.co.uk/environment/nature/roll-up-your-hosepipes-for-the-big-turnoff-7619295.html.
"Why Is the Heartland of America Being Ripped to Shreds by Gigantic Tornadoes That Are Becoming More Frequent and More Powerful?" - *The Economic Collapse* (April 3, 2012) http://theeconomiccollapseblog.com/archives/why-is-the-heartland-of-america-being-ripped-to-shreds-by-gigantic-tornadoes-that-are-becoming-more-frequent-and-more-powerful.

342-344. Ibid.

Bibliography

Baer, Randall. *Inside the New Age Nightmare*, Huntington House Inc, 1989.

Beshore, Kenton F. with Keller, William R. *When: When Will the Rapture Take Place?* - World Bible Society.

2010 Brown, Diver, Briggs, Gesenius, *The Old Testament Hebrew Lexicon*, BibleStudyTools.com.

Carson, D.A., *Exegetical Fallacies* 2nd Edition, Grand Rapids: Baker Books, 1996.

Butler Trent C General Editor, *Holman Illustrated Bible Dictionary*, Holman Publishers, Nashville, Tennessee 2003.

Fausset, Andrew Robert M.A., D.D., *Fausset's Bible Dictionary*, Fausetts, 1878.

Fausset, Andrew Robert M.A., D.D., "Definition for 'Brimstone' *Fausset's Bible Dictionary*" - bible-history.com - Fausset's; 1878.

Fruchtenbaum, Arnold G., *Footsteps of the Messiah*, Tustin, California: Ariel Ministries, 1982, (Fourth printing) 1993; Revised Edition June 30, 2003.

Hunt, Dave, *A Cup of Trembling: Jerusalem and Bible Prophecy,* Harvest House Publishers, July 1995.

Hunt, Dave, *How Close Are We?* Eugene, Oregon: Harvest House, 1993.

Jeffrey, Grant, *Prince of Darkness - Antichrist and the New World Order,* 1994.

Jeffrey, Grant, *Armageddon: Appointment with Destiny,* Water Brook Press, January 7, 1997.

Jeffrey, Grant, *The Triumphant Return: The Coming Kingdom of God*, Random House 2001.

Koenig, William R., *Eye to Eye - Facing the Consequences of Dividing Israel*, Unspecified Publisher, 2006 Updated Version

Liddell and Scott, *An Intermediate Greek-English Lexicon.* 7th Edition, Cedar Rapids: Parsons Technologies, Inc.

Lindsey, Hal, *Planet Earth—2000 A.D: Will Mankind Survive*, Western Front Ltd, June 1994.

Louw, J.P., *Semantics of New Testament Greek*, Atlanta Scholars.

Marciniak, Barbara and Thomas, Tera L., *Bringers of the Dawn: Teachings from the Pleiadians*, Bear & Company, Sante Fe, New Mexico, December, 1992.

MacArthur, John F., *Reckless Faith—When the Church Loses Its Will to Discern*, Crossway Books, 1994.

McGee, Vernon J., *Thru the Bible, Volume 5*, Thomas Nelson Inc. 1983.

Schucman, Helen, *A Course in Miracles*, Third Edition, Foundation for Inner Peace, 2007.

Strong, James Editor, *The New Strong's Exhaustive Concordance of the Bible*, Thomas Nelson Publishers, Nashville, Tennessee, 1996.

Webster's New International Dictionary of the English Language, First Edition G. & C. Merriam Co., 1928.

God's Overwhelming Love and Mercy

Ephesians 3:14-19

"For this reason I bow my knees to the Father of our Lord Jesus Christ, from whom the whole family in heaven and earth is named, that He would grant you, according to the riches of His glory, to be strengthened with might through His Spirit in the inner man, that Christ may dwell in your hearts through faith; that you, being rooted and grounded in love, may be able to comprehend with all the saints what *is* the width and length and depth and height—to know the love of Christ which passes knowledge; that you may be filled with all the fullness of God. Now to Him who is able to do exceedingly abundantly above all that we ask or think, according to the power that works in us, to Him *be* glory in the church by Christ Jesus to all generations, forever and ever. Amen."

Almighty God—The Beginning and the End

God's divine declaration of His all-encompassing absolute power and majesty—as Creator and King of the universe yesterday, today and forever:

> "I am the Alpha and the Omega, the Beginning and the End," says the Lord, who is and who was and who is to come, the Almighty."
>
> —Revelation 1:8